THE WORLD OF THE OLD TESTAMENT

To Kristin
From Grandma Perkins

1988

THE BIBLE STORY BOOK

Presented to

_____

_____

The BIBLE

STORY BOOK

by
Bethann Van Ness

Illustrated by Harold Minton

BROADMAN PRESS   NASHVILLE, TENNESSEE

© 1963 BROADMAN PRESS
Nashville, Tennessee
All rights reserved
International copyright secured

424–075

Library of Congress Catalog Card Number 63–9758
Printed in the United States of America
50.D62KSP

Preface

The Bible is the greatest of all Bible storybooks. No retelling can do justice to the excitement and richness of stories in the Book itself. The men who spoke as they were moved by God were masterful storytellers along with their other gifts.

But the enjoyment of Bible stories will be lost to children unless someone does retell them.

For the Bible presents this paradox: A book filled with stories that children can understand and love—stories offering them vigorous heroes, rousing adventure, colorful incidents—is written for the most part in a vocabulary beyond their understanding. This is true of modern translations as well as of the older versions.

If boys and girls are to thrill to the stories of Moses and Joseph, of Gideon and David, of the great heroes of the New Testament, then someone must become their translator. Someone must change the unfamiliar words and terms of a Book written for adults into simple, easy-to-understand speech. Someone must select the incidents that have meaning for children and retell them from the viewpoint of a child.

It is in answer to these needs that THE BIBLE STORY BOOK has been prepared.

Those who planned and wrote the book felt that their responsibility goes beyond that of vocabulary simplification. If Bible stories are to attract and hold the interest of children, they must be real *stories:* enlivened with conversation, enriched with background detail and picture words. Children want to see and feel their stories as well as hear—or read—them.

The writer of these stories has met these requirements while remaining true to the Bible text. Imagination has been used to give the stories focus and depth, but no imaginative incidents have been added to the stories.

The form of the stories in this book should prove an inducement for fathers, mothers, and children to read them together. Reading Bible stories in family groups makes a contribution to a child's appreciation of the Bible far beyond what he learns from the stories themselves. Shared experiences in reading deepen family unity.

Older children reading this book should find new interest in exploring the Bible for themselves.

A Bible storybook is useful only if it helps to increase children's interest in and understanding of the Bible itself. That these stories may lay a foundation on which to build a lifetime of friendship with the Bible is the hope of all those responsible for THE BIBLE STORY BOOK.

Contents

STORIES FROM THE OLD TESTAMENT

In the Beginning	13
The Traveling People	19
God's Family	28
The Story of Joseph	59
The Leader God Chose	81
Wars of General Joshua	121
The Hero Judges	135
The Story of Ruth	153
The Man Who Asked Why	159
Judge Samuel	168
Israel's First King	177
Israel's Greatest King	184
Solomon, the Splendid	222
A Kingdom Divided	233
God's Watchmen	270
Proud Israel's End	286
Lonely Judah	289
Ezekiel's Picture Sermons	321
Stories of Daniel	329
Queen Esther	344
Captives Who Came Home	353
Songs and Sayings	372

STORIES FROM THE NEW TESTAMENT

A Child Is Born	382
When the King Came	390
Friends and Enemies	407
Kingdom Adventures	418
He Went About Doing Good	435
Who Is He?	453
Stories Jesus Told	464
Jesus, Son of God	477
Beginning in Jerusalem	511
Adventures in Judea and Samaria	522
Into All the World	533
The Preaching Prisoner	564
More New Testament Letters	582
New Heaven and Earth	589

SUPPLEMENT

Let's Go Exploring in the Bible	597
Index of Stories	666
Index of Characters	670

Full-Page Paintings

OLD TESTAMENT

The Creation	14
Noah and His Sons Building the Ark	23
Jacob Built an Altar	51
Joseph at Potiphar's House	63
Joseph Introducing His Father to Pharaoh	75
The First Passover	91
Bezaleel	107
The Return of the Spies	111
Gideon Tests His Soldiers	143
Ruth and the Harvesters	155
Samuel Helping in the Temple	170
David and Jonathan	190
David and Mephibosheth	207
Heaps of Treasures	218
Building the Temple	223
Elijah and the Widow of Zarephath	239
Prophet's Room at Shunem	256
Amos and the Cheating Scales	273
Isaiah's Vision	281
Hilkiah Finding the Scroll	302
Jeremiah and the Ethiopian	315
Queen Esther	348
Rebuilding the Wall	364

NEW TESTAMENT

Unto Us a Child Is Born 387
Jesus Was Growing Up 391
Baptism of Jesus 395
At Jacob's Well 403
Bringing the Paralyzed Man to Jesus 411
Jesus with a Mother and Child 439
"Zacchaeus, Come Down" 451
The Lost Son 470
The King Is Coming 479
Judas, the Traitor 496
He Is Risen 504
"They Laid Their Hands Upon Them" 517
Philip and the Traveler from Africa 524
Young Timothy 538
Paul Talking with Lydia 543
Paul, Priscilla, and Aquila 547
Letter to Philemon 575

STORIES FROM THE OLD TESTAMENT

IN THE BEGINNING

How God Made the World

WHEN THE WORLD BEGAN, God was there, for he made everything. Nothing at all was made without his planning.

In the beginning when God began to make the heavens and the earth, the world had no shape. It was empty and dark and wet.

"Let there be light," God said.

So light shone on the world for the first time. God liked light, and he separated the light from darkness. Light was day. Darkness was night. God had made the first day.

Next God separated the wet, shapeless, empty world from the sky. Earth water stayed on earth. Sky water was formed into clouds. And above the earth, by the word of God, the heavens were made.

God spoke again, and all the water that covered the earth began to flow into rivers and oceans. Up in the mountains, down in the valleys, the water flowed in the channels he had marked. And that was how he made the earth by his power.

God looked at the new earth and the new oceans, and he knew that they were good.

No plants or grass were growing yet on the earth. It had never rained on the new land. But foggy mists rose from the ground, and dry earth was getting ready for growing things.

When the ground was just right, God made all the different green things, grass and plants. Each kind had its own seeds so that more would always be growing.

Then God made the sun and the moon and the stars.

"Let there be lights," said God.

So he made the great lights to rule the world, the sun to rule by

© 1961, The Sunday School Board, S.B.C.

The Creation

day, the moon and stars by night. The lights were to mark the days and the nights. They were to be signs of the time when spring changed to summer, summer to fall, fall to winter, and winter to spring.

God knew that the shining sun and moon and stars were good for his plan, and he was pleased. Even the morning stars sang together, and all the angels shouted for joy over the world that God was making.

In the deep rivers and oceans something new was happening. God made great sea animals and fish, little and big. In the air above ground, birds he had just made began to fly. God saw that his work was good, and he planned for the birds and fish to build their homes and have their families. There would be more and more of all the living things he had made.

After the birds and fish God made the earth animals and the crawling creatures. Like everything else he had made, they pleased him, too. *Genesis 1:1–25; 2:4–6; Job 38:7*

The First People

Every time God had made something new for his world, he had said, "Let there be light," or "Let the dry land appear," or had given some other command. And it had happened that way. Now the special time for which he had made the earth ready had come. This time God worked in a different way. He used earth materials to make the first person. He made a man. God gave the man breath, his own breath of life. So the man he made became a living, breathing person.

God made that first person to be a little like himself. He was like God in being able to think and decide for himself what to do. He was like God in being able to love and be loved. He was enough like God to have God choose him for a friend.

God gave the first person a home. It was a beautiful garden called Eden. God himself had planted it. All of earth, with all its living creatures, God gave to the man to name, to care for, and to enjoy: all the sheep and oxen, the animals of the fields, the birds of the air, and the fish of the sea. All the plants that were good for food were given to man to use.

So that the first man would not be lonesome, God made another person, the first woman, and she was to be the man's companion and helper. In the Garden of Eden the first man, Adam, and the first woman, Eve, were the first family. They could enjoy and use all the growing things that God had made. God insisted on just one thing: they must obey him.

And so the world and the sun and the moon and the stars, and people, too, were made. God finished his work of creating, and he was pleased with it all.

After all his work God planned a time to stop, a time to rest from work. He rested for a day and he called that day the sabbath. It was to be in all God's world the time in the week when people, too, would stop their work and spend the day with him.

Genesis 1:26–31; 2:1–3

The Beginning of Trouble

In the Garden of Eden the first people had plenty of things to explore. They had interesting work to do. For God had planned a home where they would be happy.

"Everything is yours except one tree," God told them. "Never go near the tree in the middle of the garden, the Tree of Knowing Right and Wrong. Do not eat its fruit. Do not even touch it. For if you do, you must die."

One day the serpent, more sly than any of the creatures, found Eve by herself and began to talk with her.

"Did God really tell you not to eat the fruit of any of the trees?"

"We can eat all we want. But God told us to stay away from that one tree over there in the middle of the garden. If we disobey him, we will die."

"You won't die," the serpent lied. "You see, God knows that this is what will really happen. You will discover all about right and wrong, and then you will know as much as he does."

Eve walked over and looked at the tree. The fruit did look good to eat, and it was pretty. If taking some made you so wise . . .

She tried some of the fruit. Then she called Adam, and she shared with him. Suddenly they both knew that they had done wrong. And, for the first time, they were frightened and ashamed.

That evening God came to take a walk in the garden. Adam and Eve were afraid to meet him, and they ran and hid among the trees.

"Where are you?" God called to them.

They could not hide from God any longer.

"I—I heard you coming, but I was afraid," Adam told him.

"Who has been talking to you? Have you disobeyed me?"

"Well, the woman you gave to be with me, she gave me some of the fruit from that tree. And I ate it."

So God asked Eve, "What have you done?"

"The serpent tricked me," Eve answered, "and I did eat some of the fruit."

God turned to speak to the serpent.

"You will be hated more than all other creatures. You will crawl forever in the dust, and you and the people will be enemies. Forever you will try to hurt them, but they will crush your life."

Then the two first people listened while God told them of their punishment. Now that they had discovered how to do wrong, they could not live in the garden God had planted for them. They would have to go away, and somewhere outside they would have to work to make themselves another home.

Out there, they would plant gardens, but weeds and thorns and thistles would always crowd out the plants, and they would work and work to raise enough food to eat. Out there, they would have sickness and troubles of all kinds. And just as God had warned them, some day they would have to die.

God sent them out, and he himself closed the garden. At the entrance he stationed angel guardians and a great burning sword which turned round and round, flashing in the light.

> So sin came into the world,
> And death with sin,
> Death for all the people,
> For all have sinned.
> But the gift of God is eternal life
> Through Jesus Christ our Lord.
>
> *Genesis 3:1–24; Romans 5:12; 6:23*

THE TRAVELING PEOPLE

The First Two Brothers

SOMEWHERE OUTSIDE the Garden of Eden Adam and Eve found the place where they could make a home. In that home were born the first children, Cain, and his little brother, Abel. The two boys grew up working hard in the fields just as their father did. Cain was a farmer and planted vegetables for food. Abel was a shepherd, and his sheep could give the family warm skins to wear for coats.

There was a day when Cain and Abel planned to offer gifts to God. Abel carefully chose one of the best and finest of the sheep for his gift. Cain picked up an armful of his vegetables. Something about the way Abel brought his gift pleased God. He knew that Abel trusted him, and so he let the young man know how much he liked his gift. But something about the way Cain brought his gift was not good, and God was not pleased.

Cain was furious. His face was ugly to see.

"What's the matter with my gift?" he thought.

"Why are you angry?" Cain heard God asking, and at first he listened. God went on. "When you do what is right, your gift is good. When you do wrong, watch out! Sin is hiding at your door, trying to get in. But you can be strong enough to drive it away if you want to."

Angry Cain stopped listening. The brothers left their offerings and went into the fields. There Cain struck Abel and killed him. Then he walked away.

"Cain!" he heard God calling. "Cain, where is your brother Abel?"

"I don't know. Must I take care of my brother?"

The quiet Voice went on. "Cain, what have you done? Your brother lies dead on the ground, and his blood cries out to me. Now the earth will fight against you. No garden will grow for you. No home will welcome you. A runaway and a wanderer you will be as long as you live."

Frightened Cain begged for help. "My punishment is too hard. I'll have no place to live. Anyone who sees me will try to kill me. And I will never be able to find you."

Once more God spoke. "No one will harm you."

And then he placed his own mark on Cain's body so that whoever saw him would know that he was under God's protection.

So Cain, the first boy on earth, went away from his home and walked alone all the long, long way to the Land of Wandering.

Genesis 4:1–16

People Good and Bad

As the people of the traveling families became better acquainted with the world God made, they began to discover the treasures he had made for them to use.

The Cain people were the first to discover how to make tent homes of animal skins. They found out that when they kept herds of cattle they could have plenty of milk and butter. They discovered how to play songs on a musical instrument made of a bow and strings, something like a harp, and on another made out of a hollow reed or cane. They invented cutting tools made from bronze and iron.

Back in the first home a new baby boy named Seth had been born. When he grew up and had a family of his own, his people discovered a different kind of treasure. They found out that they could pray to God and that he heard them when they prayed.

But the badness the first two people chose by their disobedience was in the world to stay. Evil was always making trouble. Lamech, one of the Cain people, used to brag about killing a man just to get even with him. There were people, though, who loved God and tried to do what was right. One of them was a man named Enoch. His son Methuselah lived longer than anyone else has ever lived. Enoch loved God so much that people knew he walked with God. One day Enoch disappeared. No one could find him. But he had not died; God had taken his friend home with him.

For many, many years the families of the traveling people became bigger and bigger, but people were growing worse and worse. Then there came a time when God looked at his world and saw that it was rotten with bad-thinking, bad-behaving men and women. And he was sorry that he had ever made it. People were so bad they could not go on living. *Genesis 4:17–26; 5*

The Ship That God Designed

Now in all the wicked world there was a good man named Noah. He loved God, listened when he spoke, and obeyed him. God could talk to Noah, and so he told him about his plans.

First Noah learned that he was to undertake a ship-building project. These were his directions:

"Build a wooden ship, an ark, with three decks. Inside, build cabins on every deck. Calk it inside and out with pitch to make it waterproof.

"Make it 150 feet long, 75 feet wide, and 45 feet high. Up near the roof make a window almost all the way around the ark. In one side build a door."

Next Noah learned about God's covenant promise of blessing for him and all his family.

"I am going to bring a flood of water on the earth," said God. "It will destroy every living creature. But I will make my promise of blessing to you.

"You are to go inside the ark with all your family and your sons' families. Take with you every kind of creature, so that you can keep them alive. Take along some of all the kinds of food that is eaten, so that you and all the creatures will have enough to eat."

Noah followed God's directions exactly. Then God gave him more instructions.

"Now go into the ark, you and all your family. Take with you seven pairs of all the animals and birds you will use for food and one pair of each of the rest."

Noah did exactly as he was told.

The great rains began, and the ocean burst out across the land. But Noah and his sons, Shem and Ham and Japheth, and their wives were safe inside the ark. God himself shut the door.

For forty days it rained and rained and never stopped. Everywhere the flood waters were getting deeper. Gently the great ark began to float across the flooded fields, then across the hills. At last it was drifting along on a sea that covered the mountains.

Months went by. There was nothing anywhere but water and a single ship. The people who were too wicked to live were gone. Only Noah was left, and all who were with him in the ark.

God remembered Noah and all the living things with him. One day he sent a wind to blow over the water. The rain stopped, and slowly the flood began to go down. More months went by while the ark floated along on waters that covered the highest mountains. One day it settled gently down and touched the top of one of the high mountains in the land of Ararat.

Forty days later Noah opened the window and let one of the ravens fly out on its strong wings. Back and forth it flew over the water until the land was dry. Next he let a dove fly out. But she could not find a dry roosting place, and she flew back to Noah's hand. A week later he let her out again. That evening she came back carrying a green leaf in her beak. In some places, the trees were above water at last.

Noah and His Sons Building the Ark

© 1963, Broadman Press

It was New Year's Day when Noah discovered that the ground all about the ark was dry, but he waited to leave the ark until he heard God say that at last it was safe to go outside. A year had gone by since he and his wife and his sons and their wives had moved into the ark. Now they and all the creeping, flying, walking creatures came out of the ark by families, back to God's clean earth.
Genesis 6:5–22; 7; 8:1–17

The Rainbow Promise

The first thing Noah did that first day outside the ark was to hunt some stones to make an altar. Then he and his family brought a gift for God, and they worshiped him together. God was pleased by their prayer, and he gave them his blessing.

"All the earth is yours for your home. The animals are yours to use for food, as well as the plants and the fruits.

"To you and your children I will make my covenant promise of blessing. Never again will I send a flood to destroy the earth.

"This will be the sign of my promise for all the time to come. I put my rainbow in the clouds. When I bring the clouds over the earth and you see the rainbow, I will be looking at it, and I will remember my promise.

> "While the earth remains,
>   Seedtime and harvest, and cold and heat,
>   And summer and winter, and day and night
>   Shall not cease."

Genesis 8:18–22; 9:1–17

A Song of Thanksgiving

Bless the Lord, O my soul.
O Lord my God, thou art very great; . . .
Who maketh the clouds thy chariot:
Who ridest on the wings of the wind: . . .
Who laid the foundations of the earth,
That it should not be removed for ever.

Thou coveredst it with the deep as with a garment:
The waters stood above the mountains.
At thy rebuke they fled;
At the voice of thy thunder they hasted away.
They go up by the mountains; they go down by the valleys
Unto the place which thou hast founded for them.

Thou hast set a bound that they may not pass over;
That they turn not again to cover the earth.
He sendeth his springs into the valleys,
Which run among the hills.
They give drink to every beast of the field. . . .
He causeth the grass to grow for the cattle,

And herb for the service of man:
That he may bring forth food out of the earth. . . .
The trees of the Lord are full of sap;
The cedars of Lebanon, which he hath planted;
Where the birds make their nests:
As for the stork, the fir trees are her house.

The high hills are a refuge for the wild goats . . .
He appointed the moon for seasons:
The sun knoweth his going down.
Thou makest darkness, and it is night:
Wherein all the beasts of the forest do creep forth.
The young lions roar after their prey,
And seek their meat from God.
The sun ariseth, they gather themselves together,
And lay them down in their dens.
Man goeth forth unto his work
And to his labour until the evening. . . .
The earth is full of thy riches.
So is this great and wide sea. . . .
I will sing unto the Lord as long as I live:
I will sing praise to my God while I have my being.

From Psalm 104

The Tower of Pride

After the flood Noah and all his family went to work to make new homes and to find food. Since God had told them that they could use the animals of earth as well as the growing things for food, they learned how to hunt. One of Noah's great-grandsons, whose name was Nimrod, is still famous because he was a good hunter.

At first the families stayed together, though they were getting bigger all the time and their home places were crowded. They spoke the same language, and they did things together.

They were traveling slowly toward the east when they came to a wide, flat country. It looked like a good place to settle, for they found clay there that made good bricks, and pits full of pitch they could use for mortar to hold bricks together.

"Let's build a city," someone suggested. "Let's build a tower."

"Let's build it high, higher than anyone has ever seen. Let's build it so tall it will reach to heaven. Then we will be famous. Everyone will know how wonderful we are."

So the tower was begun, and it rose higher and higher. The proud people were busy every minute working on the project that would make them famous. Still higher and higher it went.

But something stopped them right there, for God was watching. When the overseers gave orders to the workmen, nothing happened. No one could understand the orders. For the first time, each man was speaking in a different language. There was no way for the people to work together.

They left the job and began to travel in different directions to find new homes. No one was left to live in quiet Babel, the half-built city, or to work on the proud tower by which men had dared to think they could climb to heaven.

Genesis 10; 11:1–9

GOD'S FAMILY

Pioneer Abram

IN UR, the city by the beautiful Euphrates River, there lived a family. Terah was the father, and his three sons were Abram, Nahor, and Haran. Haran had a son whose name was Lot. Abram and his wife, Sarai, had no children.

God used to talk with Abram, and Abram knew God's voice and listened when he spoke. One day he told Abram to get ready for a long journey.

"Move away from this country and from your relatives, and go to a land that I will show you.

"I will make you to be the beginning of a great nation. I will bless you and make your name famous, and you will be a blessing to all the families of the earth."

Abram and his family packed their things and made ready to go away from Ur. They set out to go to the land of Canaan, and to the land of Canaan they came, though they did not know the road or the name of the country to which God was taking them.

First the long caravan traveled north on the highway along the river and came to a place called Haran. There the people set up their tents and stayed for a while. In Haran the father, Terah, died. Brother Haran had died in Ur, and now brother Nahor decided to stay where they were.

But Abram and Sarai and Lot and their servants, with all the flocks and herds of animals, the donkeys and camels on which they rode, set out again to travel, for God had told them it was time to move.

This time they went west and south, almost to the shores of the

Great Sea, until they came at last to the land of Canaan. Slowly they traveled through the land, living in their tents and moving from place to place to find food for the animals.

They camped at the mountain pass at Shechem. The Canaanites were living in the land then, but God made Abram a surprising promise.

"I am going to give all this land to your children and to your children's children."

Abram, who had no children, still believed God, and he stopped to build an altar where he prayed.

They traveled on toward the south, stopping for a time on a mountain east of Bethel, and there Abram built another altar for a place to pray to God.

They kept on traveling, always toward the south. Now they began to have trouble, for there was a famine in that part of the country, and they could not find enough food. So they went far, far south to Egypt, where there was plenty to eat.

By the time Abram headed north again with his family, he had become a very rich man. He had many, many cattle and sheep, oxen, and camels. He had treasures of silver and gold. Lot was a rich man, too. His flocks and herds were very large.

They traveled back the same way they came and stopped again at Bethel. There they worshiped God together at the same mountain altar where they had worshiped before.

Genesis 12:1–10; 13:1–5

The Story of a Choice

Abram and Lot needed plenty of pasture land for all their animals, and they soon found that they were too crowded on the land around the mountain near Bethel. Lot's shepherds and Abram's shepherds quarreled over the pasture lands and the water.

So Abram called his nephew Lot to his tent and said kindly,

"Let's not have any fighting between our men or between you and me, for we are like brothers.

"Look, there is the land before you. Choose which section you want, and take your men and your herds and go your way. I'll take mine and go somewhere else. You may have first choice."

Lot looked out over the green valley, green as Egypt, where there had been plenty to eat. He saw the Jordan River—plenty of water there for the flocks. He saw busy cities full of people, cities like Sodom, where the people cared nothing at all about God. Life would be easy, Lot knew, there in that green valley.

"I choose the plain country," Lot decided.

So Abram stayed in the hill country, and Lot pitched his tents toward Sodom.

After Lot and his people moved away, Abram, who still had no children, heard God speaking again.

"Look, Abram, all about you, north and south, east and west. All the land that you see I am going to give to you and to your children forever.

"You are going to have so many children and grandchildren, and they will have so many, that they will be like the dust. If any man could count the specks of dust, then he would be able to count your children's children.

"Now go out and walk through your land."

And Abram believed God's promise, though he had no children.

He moved again, with all his herds and flocks, and pitched his tents near the trees of Mamre. There he built an altar near his home, and he worshiped God.

Genesis 13:6–18

The Battle of the Kings

There was war in the land where Abram and Lot lived. Out of the eastern countries four kings came riding with their armies. They burned houses and they stole, and they kidnapped some of the people and killed others.

At first the frightened people gave up, but after they had had that kind of trouble for twelve years they began to fight back. The king of Sodom and four other kings marched out to fight against the four kings from the east.

They all met in the Salt Valley, which was full of pitch pits, and there was a great battle. The five kings and their armies ran for their lives. Some were killed; some fell into the pits; and the rest escaped to the mountains.

So the four kings captured Sodom and the other towns. Their soldiers stole food and everything else they could find, and they carried mothers, fathers, and little children away as their prisoners.

One man escaped. He ran from his ruined home to Abram's

tent in the hills and told Abram the bad news. Lot and all his family had been taken prisoner.

Abram had 318 strong men working for him, trained men who could fight to take care of the flocks and herds. Now he told them to set out after the four kings and the prisoners.

In the night he divided his army, and they made a raid on the kings from all sides. The plan worked well. Abram and his men chased the kings to the north country. They freed all the prisoners and brought them home, with the food and all the other things the kings had stolen.

The news spread fast, and the kings came out to meet Abram on the way home. There came Melchizedek, king of Salem and priest of God, who brought a gift of food and drink for the tired men, and he gave his blessing to Abram:

> "Blessed be Abram
> By God Most High.
> To whom belongs heaven and earth,
> And blessed be
> The Most High God,
> Who has given your enemies into your hand."

Then Abram gave to King Melchizedek one tenth of all the goods captured from the four kings.

The king of Sodom came out to meet Abram.

"You may keep everything you have captured. Just give me the prisoners," he said.

But Abram told him, "I have promised the Lord, the Most High God, that I will not take anything, not even a thread or a shoelace. I do not want you saying, 'I have made Abram rich.'

"I claim the food my men have eaten and what belongs to them."

After it was all over, God talked with Abram again. Perhaps Abram was worrying. The four kings might come back.

"Abram, do not be afraid. I will protect you. I have promised to reward you," God told him.

Abram was thinking about all the promises God had made him, and he said, "Lord God, what are you going to give me? You know that I have no children."

As if God led him by the hand, Abram walked out of his tent. Brilliant stars were the only light in the quiet night.

"Look up, Abram. Count the stars if you can. You are going to have that many children, counting your grandchildren and all their children's children.

"I am the God who brought you from the city of Ur to this land which will belong to you and to them."

And Abram, though he had no children, believed God.

Genesis 14, 15:1-7

New Names

"Abram!"

The man stopped to listen, for he recognized the Voice.

"Abram, I am the Almighty God. Stay close to me, and be a perfect man."

Abram bowed low before his Friend.

"You are going to be the father of many nations. No longer will your name be Abram, 'high father,' but Abraham, 'father of many.' Kings will be among your children's children. And I will make my covenant promise of blessing with you and all your family.

"This land of Canaan where you are now a stranger will belong to your family.

"Your wife, Sarai, you are to call Sarah. I will bless her, and she will have a son."

Abraham just laughed. "I am ninety-nine years old. Sarah is ninety. How can we have a child?"

"You will have a child, and you are to name him Isaac. And I will keep my promise with him."

Genesis 17:1–19

Guests at Abraham's House

It was hot one day, even under the trees of Mamre where Abraham was resting in the shade of his tent door. Looking up, he saw three strangers walking toward him.

He ran to meet them, and he bowed before one of them.

"My Lord, won't you stop awhile with us? I'll send for water, and you can bathe your feet. While you rest under the tree, let me bring you something to eat."

Then he hurried to Sarah's tent and asked her to bake some cakes just as quickly as she could. He went out to the fields where his herds were grazing. Choosing one of the best young calves, he gave orders to have it cooked for the guests.

When the cakes were baked and the meat was done, Abraham brought butter and milk and carried the lunch to his guests.

While they ate in the shade of the tree, he stood near.

"Where is Sarah, your wife?" one of the men asked.

"She is over there in the tent."

"Sarah is going to have a son." The Stranger (who was God himself) repeated the promise Abraham had heard so many times.

Now Sarah was listening, and when she heard that she was to have a baby, she laughed to herself.

"Why did she laugh?" the guest asked. "Is anything too hard for God?"

After their lunch the visitors started out toward Sodom. Abraham walked a way with them, and God went on talking.

"I have heard the cry of wicked Sodom. The sins of the people are hateful. I am going to see whether it is as bad as I hear."

Two of the strangers walked on. Abraham was alone with the third. He was worrying about Lot and his family in Sodom.

"Shall not the Judge of all the earth do right?" he asked.

"Surely you won't destroy all the city, good folks with the bad. If there are fifty good people in Sodom, will you save the city?"

"If I find fifty righteous people there I will save the people."

After all, maybe fifty were too many to ask for. Abraham was still worried.

"Maybe I should not ask this of God, but just suppose there are only forty-five."

"If I find forty-five I will not destroy the city."

"Or forty?"

"For forty's sake I will not do it."

"Lord, do not be angry with me. Maybe there are only thirty."

"I will not do it if I find thirty."

"But maybe there are only twenty."

"I will not destroy Sodom for twenty's sake."

"Lord, I beg you not to be angry. I won't ask again. If there are only ten good people?"

"I will not destroy Sodom for ten's sake."

The third Stranger followed the other two toward Sodom, and Abraham went home.

Genesis 18

A City in Flames

That evening Lot looked out through the open gate in the wall round Sodom, and he saw two strangers coming toward the city. He went to welcome them, and he invited them to spend the night in his house.

After supper, when the guests were resting and before anyone had gone to bed, there came a loud knocking at Lot's door. Outside, a crowd was shouting, pounding on the house.

"Where are those men who came to see you? Bring them out here."

Lot went to the door. "They are my guests," he said quietly.

"Bring them out here," the mob shouted, and they tried to pull Lot away from the door. But the messengers inside reached for him and slammed the door shut behind him.

"This is the kind of wickedness God will not allow," the guests told Lot. "This is exactly why he is going to destroy Sodom.

"Go quickly and warn all your family so that you can be ready to escape the first thing in the morning."

Lot hurried to give the alarm. But his sons-in-law thought it was all a joke and would not believe him.

Early next morning the angels told Lot to hurry out of the city with his wife and his two daughters. When he was wasting too much time along the way, the angels helped him until they were all safe outside the city.

"Now hurry for your lives. Don't look behind you. Don't stop out there on the plain. Hurry, before the fire of destruction catches you."

Off across the flat plain they ran. No one noticed that Lot's wife stopped just a moment to look back at the burning city.

By the time the sun was up, Lot and his daughters were safe. Out on the plain toward Sodom, fire and smoke swirled everywhere. Sodom with its wickedness was gone, and all that was left of Lot's wife who stopped to look back was just a pillar of salt.

Genesis 19:1–29

Two Boys in Abraham's House

There was a new baby in the tent home of Abraham and Sarah. God had kept his promise, and at last Sarah held her own baby in her arms. They named him Isaac, the name that meant Laughter.

"God has made me laugh," said Sarah. "Everyone who hears will laugh with me. Who would have said to Abraham that Sarah would nurse children? Yet, old as I am, I have a son."

The home was happy because of the baby, Laughter, and when

he was old enough to eat with the grownups his father gave a great feast. All the household celebrated.

But Sarah was worried. In a tent nearby lived Hagar, a maid from Egypt, and her son, Ishmael, who had been the only boy in the household. Sarah watched the older boy playing with small Isaac, and she sent for Abraham.

"I want this maid and her son sent away before Ishmael begins to think he is the son in this house," she told him.

Abraham hated to send them away, for he loved the boy. But God was there to help him.

"I will take care of the lad," God promised. "Go on and do as Sarah says. I will be with him, and I will make him the beginning of a great nation, and he will be the father of twelve princes."

Early the next morning Abraham packed bread and a skin bottle of water for Hagar and put them on her shoulder. Then Hagar and young Ishmael walked away from the tents into the wilderness country.

They walked for days over the hot, dry land where there were no roads. At last they could go no farther. Their water was all gone, and Hagar did not know what to do. She found a shady place under a bush for Ishmael. Not far away she sat down and hid her eyes. She could not bear to sit there and watch the boy die.

Ishmael, left alone, began to cry.

Hagar heard her name called. God's angel was speaking to her.

"Fear not, Hagar. God has heard the boy's cry. Get up now, and take his hand. In God's plan he will live and be the beginning of a great nation."

When Hagar opened her eyes, the first thing she saw was a well full of water. So she filled her bottle and gave the boy a drink.

God took care of Ishmael, just as he promised. The boy grew up in the wilderness country and became a great hunter with the bow and arrow.

Genesis 21:1–21; 17:20

Abraham's Great Discovery

There came a day when God gave Abraham a test of his obedience and faithfulness. He called, as he often did,

"Abraham!"

"Here I am," was his friend's answer.

"Take Isaac, your only son, whom you love. Go over to the land of Moriah and offer him there to me as a burnt offering sacrifice."

In the morning Abraham got up early, saddled his donkey, and called two of his servants and Isaac. He cut wood for the burnt offering. Then they set out for the hill land of Moriah. On the third day the party could see the mountaintop where they were going.

"You stay here with the donkey," Abraham told the young men. "Isaac and I will go up yonder and worship and come back to you."

So he took the wood and tied it on Isaac's back. He carried the knife and some burning charcoal in a pot to light the fire. Then they climbed the hill together.

Isaac was puzzled. He looked around.

"Father, here is the fire and the wood. But where is the lamb you are going to sacrifice?"

"God himself will provide the lamb, son," Abraham told him.

So the two went on together.

They came at last to the place God had chosen on the mountain, and there Abraham built an altar. He laid the wood on it. Then he bound Isaac with ropes and laid him on the wood.

He lifted the knife, as he would to sacrifice an animal.

"Abraham! Abraham!" It was the voice of God's angel messenger.

"Do not touch the lad. Now I know how much you love God."

A sudden noise in the bushes attracted Abraham's attention. He saw a ram caught in the thicket by its horns. There was the animal for the sacrifice offering.

Abraham called that place on the mountain by a new name. He named it "The Lord Will Provide." Now he knew that he could trust God no matter what happened.

He had passed the test, and God told him:

"In blessing I will bless you, in multiplying I will multiply your family
As the stars of the heaven and as the sand on the seashore.
And your family shall possess the cities of their enemies,
And in your family all the nations of the world will be blessed."

Then Abraham and Isaac went back to meet the young men, and they all went home together.

Genesis 22:1–19

A Bride for Isaac

It was lonesome in Abraham's tent home. Sarah had died, and Abraham was growing very old. He wanted to find a wife for Isaac —not one of the Canaanite girls who lived nearby, for they did not worship God as Abraham and his family did.

He decided to send Eliezer, his oldest, most trusted servant, back to Haran where he and Sarah had lived for a while and where his brother Nahor and his family still lived. There, among Abraham's own people, Eliezer was to look for a bride for Isaac.

It was a long journey to the north to Haran, and Eliezer packed carefully for the trip. There were presents to pack and food and water to last for weeks and weeks of traveling. When everything was ready, he loaded the baggage on ten camels. With two of Abraham's young men for company, he was ready to go.

Days and days later the procession stopped outside the city of Nahor to rest by the well. Eliezer prayed for God's help, just as he always did at home.

"Lord God, give me success today, and show kindness to my master. Here I am standing by the well where the women and girls of the city will be coming to get water. Help me to choose the right young woman for my young master. Let her be the one to whom I say, 'May I have a drink?'

"And let her say, 'Of course, and I will give your camels water, too.' Let her be the bride for my master's son."

He was still talking to God when the young women began to come to the well. He saw a beautiful girl with a pitcher on her shoulder. She filled her pitcher and turned away.

"May I have a drink?" he asked.

"Of course, sir." She poured a drink for him. "And I will give your camels water, too."

So she filled her pitcher again and again and poured the water into the trough where the camels could drink.

"Tell me, please, whose daughter are you? Is there room in your father's house for us to spend the night?"

He was unpacking some of the gifts now, and he gave her a golden ring and a pair of golden bracelets.

"I am the daughter of Bethuel. And you are welcome to our home. We have room for you, and straw and food for your camels."

Eliezer bowed his head thankfully. God had answered his prayer.

"Blessed be the Lord, the God of my master who has watched

over his whole life. For the Lord has led me all the way to the home of my master's family."

Rebekah ran ahead to tell her family what had happened, and her brother, Laban, went out to meet the guests.

"Come in! Come in! Why are you staying outside? The house is ready for you, and there is a place for the camels. Come in!"

All the family welcomed them. The camels were unsaddled. Water was brought so the men could bathe their feet, and food was prepared for them to eat.

"First I must tell you why I am here," Eliezer said, and he told them all the strange story of his mission, his prayer, and God's answer.

Laban and Bethuel looked at each other.

"The thing has been planned by God. It is not for us to decide. Here is Rebekah. Take her with you and go back to Isaac."

Eliezer bowed, and once more there was a thanksgiving prayer in his heart. Then he and the young men unpacked the rest of the gifts, jewelry and beautiful dresses for Rebekah and presents for her mother and her brother.

"Will you go with this man?" they asked Rebekah.

"I will go," she answered.

Her old nurse and her maids helped her to get ready. Then they all mounted the camels.

"Good-by, and may God send you many blessings," her family called as the camel caravan moved slowly away from Haran.

Many days' journey to the south and west, Isaac was watching the road. One evening he went walking in the fields, thinking about many things. He looked toward the road. In a cloud of dust he saw one, two, three—ten camels coming down the road.

Rebekah, looking excitedly toward her new home, saw him. She alighted from her camel.

"Who is that?" she asked.

"That is my master," Eliezer told her.

Eliezer told Isaac all that had happened. Isaac took Rebekah's hand and led her to his mother's tent.

And so they were married. And now, for the first time since his mother died, Isaac was not lonely any more.

Genesis 24

The Twins Who Made a Bargain

Isaac was the father of the family now. Abraham had died, and the family had buried him near the place where his wife Sarah was buried. Isaac was a rich man, with all the silver and gold and herds of cattle and flocks of sheep his father left him. Now God guided him and blessed him, as he had led and loved his father, for this was the family God had chosen to bring a blessing to all the earth.

Two small boys played around the tents of Isaac's home, two boys who were different from each other as they could be, though they were twins. They grew up to be even more different.

Esau, the older twin, was sunburned and his skin was rough and hairy. He liked to be outdoors and he learned how to be a clever hunter.

Jacob, the younger twin, was a quiet sort of person who liked to stay at home.

Now Isaac loved Esau, and Esau brought his father presents when he came home from hunting, especially venison which Isaac liked very much. Because he was the older of the two brothers, Esau would receive the family birthright upon the death of his father. This meant being head of the family and receiving twice the amount of property inherited by any other children.

One day Esau came home from hunting tired and hungry. He smelled the most wonderful smell, for Jacob was cooking thick lentil soup.

"Give me some of your soup. I'm starved," Esau begged.

Jacob thought fast. Esau had something he wanted more than anything else.

"I will if you give me your birthright."

"Oh, what's a birthright! If I don't get something to eat, I'm going to die, I'm so hungry. What good would it do me then?"

"Swear you will give me your birthright," Jacob insisted.

"I swear. Now give me some food."

So Jacob gave his brother bread and soup, and Esau went about his business, forgetting all about the birthright. But Jacob never forgot.

Genesis 25:25–34

The Man Who Hated Quarreling

It was not always easy for Isaac and his men to find food and water for the sheep and cattle. There came famine times when the family would have to travel to far places to hunt food. And they always had to be on the lookout for good wells of fresh water to drink.

Wherever they went, Isaac discovered that God was with him, loving the family he had chosen and always ready to help them.

"Stay in this country, and I will be with you and bless you. I will keep the promise I made to your father Abraham. Your children's children will be as many as the stars of heaven, and because of them all the earth will be blessed. For Abraham listened to me, obeyed me, and remembered all that I said."

Abraham's men had been busy digging wells and hunting for water in the land of the Philistines where they lived awhile, and Abraham's friend, the king of the country, let him have all the water he needed for his animals. But after Abraham died, the Philistines filled up the wells and spoiled the water.

When Isaac came that way he needed more water. He found the old wells and had his men dig them again. But the Philistines would not let him stay, and the king sent word to him:

"Go away. There are so many of you and your people are so much stronger than we are."

Isaac did not argue or fight. He just moved on to the next valley, and there his men dug another well. But the shepherds in the valley objected.

"This water is ours," they claimed.

Then there was a fight over the water. But Isaac was a man who did not like fighting. He told his men to move on and dig another well.

There was another fight over that well. Isaac just moved away and dug another well. This time there was no fighting.

"The Lord has made room for all of us," said Isaac thankfully.

That night Isaac heard God say,

"I am the God of Abraham your father. Fear not, for I am with you and will bless you and make your family great for Abraham's sake."

So Isaac built an altar, where he worshiped God. Then he told his men to begin work on another well.

Some time later Isaac had visitors. The king of the Philistines, with one of his friends and the general of his army, came to Isaac.

"What are you doing here? You hate me, and you sent me away," Isaac said to him.

"But now we know that God has given you his blessing. We want to make a peace treaty with you. We really did nothing to hurt you, and we sent you away in peace. Now we want to ask you not to attack us, for we know that you are truly blessed by God," they said again.

Isaac never did want to fight, anyway. Now he gave a feast for his guests. After the celebration they agreed on the treaty of friendship, and the visitors went home.

Then workmen came running to Isaac's tent.

"You know that well we have been digging? We just found water again."

And that was how God took care of Isaac, the son of Abraham.

Genesis 26:1–33

Jacob, the Cheat

Isaac was an old, old man. He could hardly see any more, but he still liked to eat, especially the good venison Esau brought home when he went hunting. One day he sent for his son.

"Esau, it may be that any day now I will die. You go and get me some of that venison meat cooked the way I like it, and then I will give you the family blessing."

Rebekah, the twins' mother, happened to be listening. When Esau picked up his bow and arrows and left to go hunting, she whispered to Jacob,

"I heard your father ask Esau to get him some meat and tell him that he is going to give him the blessing.

"Now, son, listen carefully. You go out to the flock of goats and pick out two good young kids. I'll cook them the way your father likes his meat. Then you take it to him. He won't be able to see whether it is you or Esau, and you can make him give you the blessing."

"But, Mother, Father will know I'm not Esau. My skin feels smooth, not hairy like his. And if Father finds out, he's likely to give me a curse, not a blessing."

"Just do as I tell you. I'll take the blame."

So Jacob brought her the kids. While the meat was cooking, she found some of Esau's clothes that still smelled of animals and hunting, and she told Jacob to put them on. Then she laid the skins of the kids on Jacob, her younger son, and his skin seemed rough as Esau's.

Disguised as his brother, Jacob took a bowl of the good meat stew in his hands and went to his father's tent.

"Father!" he called.

"Here I am. Which son are you?"

"I am Esau, your oldest. I brought you the meat you asked for. Come on. Sit up. Then you can give me your blessing."

"You weren't gone very long. How did you find meat so quickly?"

"Oh, the Lord your God brought it to me."

"Son, come here and let me feel you. I want to be sure you really are Esau. Your voice sounds like Jacob. Are you Esau?"

"Yes, Father, I am."

So the old man ate his meat. Then he said,

"Come near, son, and kiss me.

> "See, the smell of my son
> > is like the smell of a field
> > which the Lord has blessed.
> May God give you
> > water in plenty
> > and food to eat.
> Let people serve you
> > and other nations bow before you.
> Be head of this family,
> > and let the others obey you.
> Whoever curses you shall himself be cursed.
> Whoever blesses you shall himself be blessed."

Jacob had hardly left the tent when Esau came hurrying back from his hunting.

"Father, here is your meat. Won't you sit up and eat, and then give me your blessing?"

"Who are you?"

"I am Esau, your son."

The old man began to tremble.

"Then who was in here just now bringing me meat? And who has my blessing?"

"O my father, bless me, too!" Esau cried out. "This is Jacob's doing. He has tricked me twice. He got the birthright away from me, and now he has your blessing. Haven't you just one blessing left for me?"

"Esau, I have made him head of the family. I have made him

lord over you and the rest of the family. What is there left to promise you?"

"Bless me, too, my father."

The old man said slowly:

> "Away from green fields
> Will you live
> And far from the dew of heaven.
> You will be a soldier and a fighter
> And you will serve your brother.
> But when at last you have the chance,
> You will break his power over you."

Esau listened to the old man's words. In his heart he hated Jacob, and he vowed, "Someday I will kill my brother." *Genesis 27:1–41*

The Runaway's Discovery

Jacob was afraid. Now that he had tricked his brother and stolen the blessing that belonged to the oldest son, he knew it was no longer safe for him at home.

His mother had an idea.

"Jacob, hurry away to my brother's home in Haran till Esau gets over being angry. I'll send you word when it is safe to come home again."

Just to make sure that Isaac would not object, Rebekah said,

"I wish Esau had not married those two heathen girls from around here. They make trouble for me all the time. If Jacob does the same thing, I don't see how I can stand it."

The old man sent for Jacob.

"Son, why don't you go to visit your mother's people in Haran? While you are there, look for a wife.

"And may God Almighty give you and your children the blessing he gave to my father, Abraham."

So Jacob left his home, walking by himself to Haran, the faraway place where Abraham had lived so long ago.

He stopped one night in a lonely, rocky place, and he picked up a stone and used it for his pillow. Then he lay down to sleep.

He must have been very lonesome. All his life he had heard about the God of Grandfather Abraham, who was the God of his father, Isaac. But he was Jacob. How could God be with him, too?

As he was sleeping, he dreamed that he saw shining steps that reached all the way to heaven. Angels were going back and forth from heaven to earth; and high above, at the top of the steps, was God himself, saying to Jacob:

"I am the God of Abraham and of Isaac.
This land where you are lying
Will belong to you and to your children,
And they will be many as the dust of the earth,
And they will travel far, north and south, east and west.
In your family all the families of earth will be blessed.
I am with you.
I will keep you wherever you go.
I will bring you back to this place,
For I will not leave you till I have kept my promise."

Jacob woke up. For the first time he knew that God is everywhere. The God of Abraham and of Isaac was the God of Jacob, too.

He set up the stone that had been his pillow and used it for a pillar of remembrance. He called the place Bethel, "House of God," though its real name was Luz.

"This is really the house of God, the gate of heaven, for God is here." For the first time Jacob knew how close God and his people can be. He remembered hearing his father tell about the covenant promise of blessing God gave to Grandfather Abraham and to

Jacob Built an Altar

Isaac. God promised his love and care, and the people of the family he chose were to obey him in everything they did.

Then Jacob told God what he wanted to do for his part of the covenant.

"If God will be with me,
And will keep me wherever I go,
And will give me food to eat and clothes to wear
So that I come back to my father's house in peace,
Then God will be my God,
And I will give back to him a tenth of everything he gives to me."

Then Jacob went on his way to Haran, and he knew that he was not alone any more.

Genesis 27:42–46; 28

A Bride for Jacob

Many, many days later Jacob came to the country where his mother's people lived. He stopped to rest near a field where flocks of sheep were standing around a well, waiting for water. When he saw the shepherds he went up to them and asked:

"Brothers, where do you live?"

"In Haran."

"Do you know a man named Laban? Is he well?"

"We know him. He is well. Look, here comes his daughter Rachel with her father's sheep."

Jacob went over to the well and rolled away the heavy stone cover that kept the water clean. He helped Rachel water all the sheep. Then he told her that he was the son of her father's sister.

Rachel did not stop to talk. She ran home to tell her father about the stranger. Then Laban himself came out to the field to welcome Jacob.

"Come and stay with us in our home," he invited his nephew.

Jacob stayed a month, working for his Uncle Laban just like one of the shepherds. No one said anything about wages until the end of the month, when Laban told him:

"Even if you are part of our family, it is not right for you to be working for nothing. What should your wages be?"

Jacob had a secret. He loved Rachel, and now he could tell her father.

"If you will let me marry Rachel I will keep on working for you for seven years."

They all agreed, and Jacob did work for seven years. But he loved Rachel so much that all the years seemed like a few days.

The day of the wedding came at last. Rachel's parents gave a big wedding feast. The bride came to Jacob wearing her heavy veil. Jacob would not see her face until after the wedding.

But after they were married, Jacob discovered that Laban had tricked him. The bride was not Rachel whom he loved, but her older sister, Leah.

"Why did you do it? Didn't I work for you without pay for seven years so I could marry Rachel?"

"In our country the oldest daughter always marries first. But if you will work for me another seven years, you may marry Rachel."

There was nothing else for Jacob to do. By the rules of the people in that time a man could have more than one wife. If he wanted to marry Rachel, he would have to work for Laban fourteen years, without pay. And that was just what he did. *Genesis 29:1-30*

When the Runaway Went Home

Laban's home was full of people, with his own family and Jacob and his family, the wives, and all the children. There were the boys, Reuben and Simeon and Levi and Judah, Dan and Naphtali, Gad and Asher, Issachar and Zebulun, and their little sister, Dinah. And there was Joseph, son of Rachel, whom Jacob loved best of all.

Jacob had kept his bargain and worked for his uncle for fourteen years. Now he decided it would be better to take his family back to his father's home where he could begin to work for them, and he asked Laban if he might leave.

Laban had never had a better workman than Jacob. When Jacob came, his flocks were small. Now they were big, and Laban was a rich man. Of course he did not want to let Jacob go. So Jacob made a bargain with him.

"Let me have all the speckled and spotted cattle and sheep and goats for my pay, just those you don't want. I'll begin to build up my own flocks and herds. If you will do that, I'll stay awhile longer and work for you."

Laban agreed quickly. "What a bargain!" he must have thought.

Jacob separated his animals and found pasture land for them some miles away from Laban's fields. And he took such good care of them that soon he had more sheep and cattle and goats, and he was becoming a rich man.

Laban and his sons saw what was happening, and Jacob realized that they were not friendly any more. About that time Jacob knew that God was telling him what to do next.

"Go back to your father's country, and I will be with you."

Jacob waited until sheepshearing time, when Laban would be away from home. Then he got together all his own cattle and goats and sheep. He brought camels for Leah and Rachel and the children to ride. Then they all slipped away from Laban's home.

Three days later someone told Laban what had happened, and he set out after Jacob at once. A week later he caught up with the family.

"Why did you do it?" he shouted. "I would have sent you off with music and celebration. You didn't even let me kiss my daughters good-by. You ought to be punished, and I could do it. But the God of your father, Isaac, spoke to me and told me not to interfere."

Jacob was just as angry as his father-in-law.

"What have I done wrong? I worked for you for twenty years. I took good care of the animals that were mine. You would have let me go away with nothing of my own."

Laban must have been looking at his daughters and the grandchildren whom he loved so much.

"Jacob, these are my family. What can I do to hurt them? Let's make an agreement. I will not go any farther to hurt you. And you will not come back to hurt me. May the God of Abraham, who is the God of my father, Nahor, judge us."

So they made their agreement, and they piled stones together and built a remembering pillar. Neither of them would ever go past that pillar to hurt the other. Then they said together,

"May the Lord watch between you and me
While we are absent one from the other."

Genesis 30:25–43; 31

How the Quarrel Ended

Early the next morning Laban kissed his daughters and the grandchildren and went back home. Jacob and his family traveled on toward Canaan.

Jacob had never forgotten the wrong he had done to Esau. The quarrel between the brothers was twenty years old, but Jacob was still afraid of his brother. He sent messengers ahead to tell Esau:

"This is a message from your brother, who wants to be your friend. I have been living with Laban in our mother's country. I want you to know I am coming, so that we can be brothers again."

Back came the men with a message that made Jacob more afraid.

"Esau is coming, and four hundred men with him."

First Jacob got busy. He divided all his people and the animals into two bands. If Esau attacked one band, he reasoned, the other would have a better chance to escape. Then he prayed:

"God of my grandfather, Abraham, God of my father, Isaac, God who said, 'Go back to your homeland, and I will be with you,' I really don't deserve all you have done for me. I am afraid. Save me from my brother. Remember, you promised that our family will be as many as the grains of sand on the seashore."

Next he made ready a present for his brother. He divided goats and sheep, camels and donkeys into groups, each group driven by one of his servants.

"Now go ahead by groups," he ordered. "Put a space between each two. When my brother asks you, 'Whose are these and where are you going?' you are to say,

" 'They are Jacob's, and he sends them as a present to my lord Esau. He himself is following us.' "

Then Jacob sent his family to a safe place across the brook, and he waited alone.

That night he had a strange visitor. An angel messenger from God wrestled with him. All night they wrestled. Jacob tried every hold he knew, but he could not defeat the stranger. Even when the messenger touched his leg so that Jacob could not take a step without limping, he kept on.

"Let me go. It is almost morning," the stranger said at last.

"Not until you give me your blessing."

"What is your name?"

"Jacob."

"Now it is Prince Israel, for you have fought like a prince and won," the stranger said, and he gave Jacob his blessing.

After that, Jacob gave the place of his adventure a new name. He called it Peniel, which meant, "I have seen God face to face." But always after that he limped just a little.

In spite of being sure now that he was never to be without God's help, Jacob was a frightened man. Esau was coming. He could not turn back now.

He left his family and went on ahead. Far off he saw Esau coming, and he ran to meet him. At that very moment Esau began to run, too, straight toward his brother. Jacob bowed low, but Esau threw his arms around his twin brother. After all the trouble, the two made up and were friends again.

Esau saw all the people coming behind his brother.

"Who are they?" he wanted to know.

"The children God has given me in his goodness."

"And what about all the animals I just passed?"

"They are for you. Take them as my gift," Jacob said.

So the old quarrel was forgotten, and the two brothers said good-by. Esau went back to his family in Edom. Jacob traveled on to Canaan. There he bought land, put up his tents, and settled down. And there he built an altar and worshiped God.

So Jacob came home, a rich man with a big family. God promised to give him even greater blessings as he built his worship places, prayed to God, and came to understand what God expected of him and planned for him.

The family was stopping near Bethlehem when two things happened: one was joyous; one was very sad. Joseph's little brother,

Benjamin, was born. And Rachel, their mother, whom Jacob loved so dearly, died.

As they traveled slowly on they came at last to Mamre, where Jacob's grandfather had met the three strange messengers. There Jacob found his father, Isaac.

Not long afterwards Isaac died. Esau came back from Edom, and the two brothers lovingly buried their father in the family burying place where Abraham and Sarah had been buried.

Genesis 32; 33; 35:16–29

THE STORY OF JOSEPH

How a Brother Was Sold

JACOB REALLY WAS like a king or chieftain. His flocks and herds were so big that sometimes his shepherds would have to travel for days to find enough green pastures and water for them.

The older boys in the family were gone from home most of the time, taking care of the animals. Sometimes seventeen-year-old Joseph stayed with them a few days, but his father liked to keep him at home with his brother Benjamin.

The truth is that Jacob loved Joseph more than all the rest of the boys. Naturally the brothers did not like that. And Joseph did not help matters.

He was the only one who wore a fine coat with sleeves which his father had made for him. He carried tales about his brothers back to his father. To make it worse, he used to talk too much about his strange dreams in which he was always the leader.

"Listen to this one: It was harvest time. We were all out in the field together binding up the grain in sheaves. And my sheaf stood straight up, but yours all bowed down before mine."

"Is that so! Do you think you are going to be a king or something?"

"I had another dream." This time his father was listening, too.

"There I was, and the sun and the moon and eleven stars bowed down to me."

That was too much for his father.

"That will do. Do you really think that your mother and I and all your brothers will ever be your subjects?"

The brothers just grumbled as usual.

Many miles from home in Hebron, the older brothers were away hunting pasture land in Shechem. Jacob had had no news of his older sons for a long time.

"Joseph, go and visit your brothers. Find out whether they are all right, and come back and tell me," he said.

So Joseph set out for Shechem. But when he came at last to the pasture lands he saw no sheep and no shepherds.

"You are looking for someone?" a stranger asked him.

"Yes, for my brothers. Can you tell me where they are?"

"They have gone on to Dothan. I heard them talking."

So Joseph traveled fifteen miles farther to Dothan.

When he was still a long way off, the brothers saw him coming.

"Look! Here comes the dreamer!"

"We could get rid of him easily. We could kill him and hide his body in a pit. We could always say some wild animal got him. Then we'd see about this dream business."

Reuben, the oldest brother, said quickly,

"Let's not kill him. Let's just put him down in a pit but not really hurt him."

He had a plan to rescue Joseph later and help him escape.

So the brothers snatched Joseph's beautiful coat away from him, and they dropped him down into a deep pit where he could not possibly climb out. Then they ate their lunch—all but Reuben, who went back to work far across the fields.

The sound of voices and caravan bells and thudding hoofs made the brothers look up. They saw, coming toward them on the highway, a camel caravan of traders on their way from Gilead to Egypt with huge bundles of spices and perfumes to take to market.

Judah had another idea about Joseph.

"After all, it won't help to kill our brother. Let's sell him to those traders. Then we won't be to blame for hurting him."

So they agreed, and it was done. They hauled Joseph up out of the pit, sold him for twenty silver coins, and watched the camel caravan move slowly on south toward Egypt.

The traders were out of sight when Reuben came back and stooped to look down into the pit.

Joseph was not there.

"The boy is gone! Where can I go?" he cried.

There was no answer.

The brothers dipped the fine coat in goat's blood until it was stained and shabby. Then they carried it back to show to their father.

"We found this. Could it be your son's coat?"

Of course he knew that coat.

"It is my son's. Some awful animal has attacked him. Joseph is dead."

The heartbroken father mourned for the son he loved, and nothing comforted him, though all the family did their best.

"I will mourn for him as long as I live," he told them.

Genesis 37

Honor and Shame in the Palace

Joseph, the country boy, was in Egypt, living in a big house full of servants in a city of big houses.

Captain Potiphar, head of the palace guard, had found the boy in the slave market. He liked Joseph the minute he saw him, and so he paid the price the traders asked for him and took him home to be his servant.

Something about the way Joseph went to work made his master watch him. Joseph was careful and faithful and thorough. When he finished a job it was well done. Captain Potiphar began to give him more important tasks, and every time he was pleased with Joseph's work. When he made Joseph head of all the servants in the house, everyone was pleased, and all Joseph's work was well done.

Then Captain Potiphar made Joseph head of the work that was done outside the house in the fields. At last he promoted him to be superintendent of all his business. Only Joseph knew how much money and land and crops and food Potiphar had. The captain enjoyed the pleasant life Joseph's work made possible for him.

Trouble came one day when Potiphar's wife told a lie about Joseph, and Captain Potiphar believed the story. Angrily he had Joseph arrested and locked up in Pharaoh's prison.

Genesis 39:1–20

Governor Joseph

Prisoner Joseph was the same faithful, hard-working young man he had been in Potiphar's house. It was not long before the keeper of the prison discovered that he had a good workman whom he could trust. So he began to give Joseph jobs to do. The jobs became more and more important, until at last Joseph was a trusty in charge of all the prisoners.

Among the prisoners were two of Pharaoh's servants, the head butler and the head baker. Both of them were in prison because they had made their royal master angry.

One morning Joseph found them looking most unhappy. It was all about some dreams. Egyptians believed dreams were sent to tell

© 1960, The Sunday School Board, S.B.C.

Joseph at Potiphar's House

people what was going to happen. But the men could not figure out what their dreams could mean.

"God, whom I worship, would know. Tell me about them," said Joseph.

The butler told his dream first.

"I saw a vine that had three branches. While I was watching, it was covered with blossoms that shot out and turned into ripe grapes. I was holding Pharaoh's cup in my hand, and I reached out and pressed the grapes until the juice filled the cup. Then I handed it to Pharaoh."

"This is what your dream means," Joseph explained.

"Three branches stand for three days. In three days from now, Pharaoh will send for you, and you will be his butler again.

"And when all is well with you, think of me. Just tell Pharaoh about me, and see if you can get my pardon. For I was kidnapped out of the land of the Hebrews, and as long as I have been here I have done nothing to deserve being put in jail."

Next the baker told about his dream.

"There were three baskets of bread piled on my head, and the top basket was filled with all kinds of bread and cake for Pharaoh. But the birds flew down and ate it."

"This is what your dream means:

"Three baskets stand for three days. In three days from now Pharaoh will send for you and will have you put to death."

Three days later it all came true. The day was Pharaoh's birthday, and to celebrate he gave a big party for all his servants. He sent for his head butler and gave him back his old position. But he gave orders for the baker to be hanged.

In prison, Joseph waited and waited to hear from his friend the butler. But no news came. The butler had forgotten.

Two years went by. Now it was Pharaoh's turn to be puzzled about dreams. He sent for his magicians and his wise men, and he told them about his two dreams. They shook their heads.

The news spread through the palace. Then the butler hurried to his master.

"I just remembered something I have done that was very wrong. When Pharaoh was angry with me and had me put in prison with the baker, we had strange dreams, too.

"Right now in Pharaoh's prison there is a young man who used to be the servant of the captain of the guard. He told us what our dreams meant. And it all turned out just the way he said. I came back to the palace and the baker was hanged. I promised to tell Pharaoh about him, but I forgot."

Straight to the prison went Pharaoh's messenger.

"Hurry! Pharaoh has sent for you."

Joseph got ready as fast as he could. He shaved and put on clean clothes and walked up out of the dark dungeon into the sunlight and on to Pharaoh's palace.

"I have dreamed a dream that no one can explain. I have heard about you and your cleverness in understanding dreams. They say there is no one like you," said Pharaoh.

"It is God who gives me understanding. I speak as he tells me," Joseph answered.

"This is my first dream," Pharaoh began.

"I was standing on the river bank when I saw seven cows coming up out of the water. They were fat and well-fed, and they walked over into the meadow and began to graze.

"While I was watching, seven more cows came up out of the river, and they were the poorest, sickest, scrawniest cows I ever saw in all the land. They ate up the good fat cows, and they were still just as scrawny as they were before.

"Then I woke up.

"Next I dreamed that I saw a stalk of corn that had seven good, full ears. And I saw another stalk with seven ears that had been parched dry by the hot wind from the desert. Those burnt, withered ears of corn ate up the good ears."

"God is showing Pharaoh what he is going to do," Joseph told him.

"Both dreams mean the same thing. The seven fat cows and the seven good ears stand for seven years when the crops are going to be good, and everyone will have plenty to eat.

"The seven thin, sick cows and the seven dried-up ears of corn stand for the next seven years, when nothing is going to grow and people will starve.

"Pharaoh dreamed the same thing twice, because it is important for him to know what is going to happen.

"Now this is what Pharaoh should do. Find a man who is wise and careful and make him governor of Egypt. This man should appoint officers in every part of the country to see that food is saved during the seven good years. Have the officers build storehouses near the cities, where food can be kept safe. Then there will be enough for everyone during the famine years that are coming."

Pharaoh nodded his head, much pleased by Joseph's good advice.

"Can such a man be found?" he asked. Then he looked straight at Joseph.

"God has shown you what is going to happen. No one else is as wise and as careful as you are. I, Pharaoh, appoint you to be my governor. In all the land of Egypt you are to be obeyed, and no one will act without your permission."

Quickly the Hebrew prisoner-slave found his whole life changed. On his finger he wore Pharaoh's royal ring with the seal he used to sign his letters. Around his neck was the heavy golden chain worn only by rulers. His clothes were made of the finest linen. He had his own chariot, and when he rode through the city streets all the people bowed to show their respect.

Genesis 39:21–23; 40; 41:1–46

The Hungry Brothers

Governor Joseph went right to work. He traveled over Egypt to find out how the crops were growing. Everywhere he went he discovered that people were harvesting more grain than ever before.

He ordered the people to build huge warehouses near every city, and he organized men to collect the grain for storage.

This went on all the seven years, until so much grain was stored in the warehouses that the officers gave up trying to measure it.

The good years ended, and the hungry years began. The young plants withered and dried up in the fields. Harvest time came, but there was no food to take home or to the market. People ate the last bit of food stored in their own homes.

"What shall we do? Where shall we find food? Give us bread to eat," they begged Pharaoh.

"Go to Joseph. He will tell you what to do."

Now Joseph ordered the doors of the great warehouses opened. Carefully and wisely he organized the work of giving out grain. There was enough food for everyone, but none was wasted.

There were hard times in other countries, too, and the news traveled quickly along the highways:

"Go to Egypt. The Egyptians have plenty of food to sell."

Joseph had his own family now. He had married an Egyptian girl, and the names he gave to his two little boys showed how happy he was. One he called Manasseh, which means Causing to Forget. (God helped Joseph to forget all the years when he was a homesick slave.) The other he called Ephraim, or Having Plenty. (God helped Joseph to be successful in his adopted country.)

But far away in Canaan, Joseph's father and brothers were hungrier and thinner every day. There was no food left.

Jacob called the brothers together.

"It is time to do something instead of sitting around looking hungry. Go down to Egypt and buy food to save our lives. But leave Benjamin here. I do not want anything to happen to him."

So the brothers set out on the long journey south along the highway to Egypt.

Governor Joseph was at headquarters directing the sale of grain. All day long people came to him to ask for help. Many were Egyptians. More and more people were coming from foreign countries. They spoke strange languages.

And so it happened one day that ten shepherds from the country of the Hebrew people stood before the governor and bowed respectfully.

Speaking in the Hebrew language, they asked for grain. The interpreter who stood beside Joseph repeated their words in Egyptian. But Joseph knew exactly what they were saying. Now to test them!

"Where do you come from?"

"From Canaan, my lord, to buy food."

"No. You are spies, and you are trying to find out how poor this country is."

"No, no, my lord! Truly we came here to buy food. We are honest men, all sons of one father. Truly we are not spies."

"I do not believe you."

"Sir, your servants are twelve brothers, all sons of one man in Canaan. The youngest brother is at home with our father. And one—well, one is no longer living."

"I still think you are spies. But you can prove that you are telling the truth. Send one of your party back to get your brother. The rest of you will wait here in prison until those two come back."

Joseph ordered them arrested and held in prison for three days. Then he sent for them and said:

"I worship and serve God, so I will give you another chance. If you are honest men, one of you will stay here as my prisoner. The others are free to go. But bring your youngest brother back to me, and then you will all go free."

The brothers began to talk among themselves.

"This is just what we deserve for the way we treated our brother."

"I told you not to hurt him," Reuben said. "But would you listen? Now we are all being punished."

Joseph, hearing and understanding every word they said, turned his back on them. He could not let them see that there were tears in his eyes.

He chose Simeon to stay in Egypt. Then he gave his men orders to fill every brother's sack with grain, to slip inside the sack the money each had paid, and to give them extra food to eat on the way home.

That night the brothers stopped their long pack train of heavily loaded donkeys at an inn. One of them opened his sack to get grain for his animal. Quickly he called the others.

"My money! Look! It's all there."

"What is happening? What is God doing to us?" wondered the frightened brothers.

They came home at last with plenty of food for everyone and with a strange story to tell their father.

"We told him again and again that we are not spies. But he insisted we must take Benjamin back to prove it," they finished the account of their adventure.

They opened their sacks of grain for Jacob to see how much they had brought. Then they discovered that all their money had been returned to them.

Now Jacob, too, was frightened.

"It is too much," he grieved. "You have taken my children away. Joseph is gone. Simeon is gone. Now you want to take Benjamin."

"My father, I will be responsible for him," Reuben offered. "If I don't bring him back to you safe, you may order my own two sons to be killed."

Jacob shook his head.

"My son shall not go. His brother is dead. If anything happens to him, it will kill me."

Genesis 41:47–57; 42

"I Am Joseph"

So the brothers stayed at home. They divided the grain from Egypt and made it last as long as possible. Then it was gone. And still nothing would grow in their fields.

They were so hungry. At last Jacob told his sons they must go back for more food.

"It's no use, Father. That man said we would not even see his face unless we take Benjamin, too," Judah told him.

"Oh, why did you have to tell him you have a brother!"

"But he asked us all kinds of questions: 'Is your father still living?' 'Have you another brother?' We had to tell him. How did we know he would ask for Benjamin?"

"Father, let me take Benjamin," Judah offered. "I promise you I will take care of him. And if anything does happen, I'll take the blame. If we don't go, we are all going to starve."

Jacob gave up at last.

"If you must go, do this. Take the man a present. Take the best we have—some ointment and honey and spices and nuts. And take back twice as much money as before and all the money you found in the grain sacks.

"Now go, and may God give you mercy when you meet that man."

Governor Joseph was at headquarters directing the sale of grain, and he saw them coming, all nine brothers and Benjamin. He sent for his head servant.

"Take these men to my house. Make ready a feast, for at noon they will have dinner with me."

The frightened brothers did not know what to think.

"It must have something to do with the money that was returned to us," they decided. So they stopped the servant at the door of Joseph's house and tried to give him back all the money.

"Don't worry about that. You did pay me. Your God, who is your father's God, gave you treasure in your sacks," said the servant. Then he brought Simeon to them, and they all went indoors to wash up for dinner while the servant fed their pack animals.

When Joseph came home, they bowed respectfully and offered him the presents they had brought from home.

"Are you well?" he asked. "Tell me, is your father well? Is he still alive?"

"My lord, he is in good health."

Just then Joseph recognized Benjamin.

"Is this the youngest brother you told me about? May God be gracious to you, son."

Then he hurried away to his room. No one must see that he was crying. He washed his face, went back to his guests, and ordered dinner to be served.

It was not considered proper for Egyptians and Hebrews to eat together. So Joseph sat at a table alone where he could see all the brothers. Now and then he sent them special food from his table, and always there was five times as much for Benjamin as for the others. So they ate and talked and laughed together.

Later Joseph gave orders: "Fill everyone's sack, just as much as each can carry with him. Put all the money back in the sacks. And put my silver cup in the sack of the youngest."

Early next morning the brothers saddled their animals, loaded them with the heavy sacks, and headed north toward Canaan.

They had not gone far when Joseph sent after them.

"Up! Follow those men, and when you find them, say,

" 'Why have you returned evil for good? Why did you steal from my master?' "

"We could not steal from him," insisted the terrified brothers when the servant caught up with them. "We brought back all the money we found in our sacks the last time. How could we steal from your master's house?

"Just search us. If one has stolen anything, let the punishment be death. And all the rest of us will be your master's servants."

"It shall be as you say," the servant agreed. "Only the thief shall be my servant. The rest of you may go free."

They began to search every man's sack, starting with the oldest brother. When they came to Benjamin's grain sack, there inside lay Joseph's silver cup.

Eleven miserable men loaded their pack animals again and headed back to the city. They were brought before Joseph, and they bowed to the ground before him.

"What have you done?" Joseph demanded. "Did you think that you could get away with this kind of thing?"

Judah spoke for them all.

"My lord, what shall we say? We only know that God is punishing us for something that we did. Now we are willing to be your slaves, all of us."

"But that would not be just," said Joseph. "I will punish only the guilty person. The one who stole my cup shall stay as my slave. The rest of you go home in peace to your father."

Judah stepped closer to Joseph.

"My lord, let me speak with you. I beg that you will not be angry.

"You asked if we have a father or a brother. And we told you that our father is old, that he has one son, a young lad whom he loves, and another son who is dead.

"You told us you wanted to see our youngest brother, and we told you what our father would say. But you told us we could never see you again unless we brought him to you.

"When our father sent us back to you for more food, we told him what you said. And he told us,

" 'Two sons I loved above all others. One is dead. If you take the other, too, it will end my life.'

"And so I promised him, 'If I do not bring Benjamin back, I will take the blame forever.'

"Now, my lord, let me stay as your slave in his place, and let him go home with the others to our father. How could I go to our father and the lad be not with me?"

That was the happiest, proudest moment Joseph had ever known. He sent everyone but his brothers out of the room, and when they were alone, he said,

"I am Joseph. Is my father really still alive?"

The brothers were too terrified to answer.

"Come nearer." Joseph reached out his arms to them. "I really am your brother whom you sold into slavery in Egypt.

"Now, don't grieve. Don't be angry with yourselves. There have been two years of famine. There will be five more. God sent me here to save people's lives.

"So it was not really you who sent me here, but God. He has given me so much power that I am like a father to the whole country, even to Pharaoh himself.

"Now, hurry back home to our father and tell him to come to Egypt as quickly as he can. You shall live in your own land, in

Goshen, all the family and all the flocks and herds. You will be safe there, and I will see that you have plenty to eat during the next five years of famine.

"Hurry and tell my father all that you have seen."

Then he kissed Benjamin and all the brothers, and though they were grown men, they cried for joy.

The news spread fast, for the servants had been listening outside the door, and they could not help hearing the men's loud voices. Someone went straight to Pharaoh to tell him the good news, for everybody liked Joseph. Pharaoh sent for Joseph at once.

"Send your brothers to bring your father and all your family here," he said. "I will give them land, and they will have plenty to eat. Send wagons for the women and children to travel in. But tell them not to worry about packing their goods and furniture. They can have anything in Egypt for their own."

So the long caravan set out for Canaan, wagons full of gifts, pack animals loaded with grain and bread and provisions.

"Go in peace!" called Joseph as he waved good-by.

Genesis 43; 44; 45:1–24

A New Home in Egypt

The brothers came home—all the brothers, and Benjamin, too—with the good news.

"Joseph is living! He is governor of all the land of Egypt."

That was too much for the old man to understand.

"It is true," they insisted. Then they told him the story.

Jacob looked again at his beloved Benjamin. He counted the wagons in the long caravan. At last he believed them. Slowly his face broke into a smile.

"This is all I ever asked for," he said. "My son Joseph is alive. I will go and see him before I die."

The long journey began. Before they had gone very far, Jacob

© 1963, Broadman Press

Joseph Introducing His Father to Pharaoh

sent out word for everyone to stop when they came to Beersheba.

At the altar in Beersheba where his father Isaac once had worshiped God, Jacob wanted to worship again before they left the land.

That night God spoke to Jacob:

> "I am God, the God of your father.
> Fear not to go down into Egypt,
> For I will make of you a great nation.
> I will go down with you into Egypt,
> And I will surely bring you back again."

So, knowing that this journey was one more step in God's plan, Jacob and all the family traveled far, far south to Egypt.

When they were near the border, Judah went on ahead to ask Joseph for directions to the land where they were to live. So Joseph called for his chariot and rode out to meet his father in Goshen. And he hugged his father, and both men cried for joy.

"Now I am ready to die, for I have seen your face, and I know you are alive," said Jacob.

There were not many people living in the land of Goshen where they stopped. It was a fine land for raising cattle and sheep, big enough for many people, and separated just a little from the Egyptians. Joseph had a plan.

"Father, you and my brothers and I will go to Pharaoh and tell him that you are all here. And when he asks,

" 'What do you men do?'

"You must say, 'Your servants have been shepherds and herdsmen all our lives.'

"Then he will let you have Goshen, for the Egyptians do not like shepherds, and they will be glad to keep you as far away as possible."

Everything happened just as Joseph planned. He took five of

his brothers and introduced them to Pharaoh, and the great ruler welcomed them.

"What is your occupation?"

"Your servants are shepherds, like all our family. We have come to live in your land, for there is no pasture for the flocks at home. Now if it is pleasing to Pharaoh, we would like to live in Goshen."

"The land is yours," Pharaoh told Joseph. "Your father and brothers are to have the best of everything. They are to live in Goshen, and if any of the men are well skilled in caring for cattle, I would like to have them among my herdsmen."

Then Joseph introduced his father, and Jacob gave Pharaoh his blessing.

So the Hebrews settled in the land of Goshen.

Genesis 45:25–28; 46; 47:1–12

The Grandfather Blessing

The bad years went on, each year a little worse. But there was still plenty of food in the warehouses. The people spent all their money for food. Then they came to Joseph.

"What shall we do now? We are starving."

"Bring me your cattle and your horses and your sheep, and use them for money," he told them.

So he added to Pharaoh's herds and flocks, and they became very, very great.

When the people had sold all their animals to buy food, they came back to Joseph.

"What shall we do now? We are starving."

"Sell me your land."

So he added to Pharaoh's land, and Pharaoh had great riches: money, herds and flocks, and land.

"Now, sow this seed which I give you," Joseph directed the people. "You shall have the use of the land which you sold. Only you must bring to Pharaoh one fifth of all the crops you raise."

For seventeen years Jacob lived with his family in Goshen. He lived through all the famine years, and when good years came again, he saw his big family, with all the herds and flocks, grow bigger and stronger each year.

One day the brothers sent for Joseph.

"Our father is sick," they said.

Joseph hurried to him with both his sons, Manasseh and Ephraim.

The old man pulled himself up and sat on the side of his bed.

"Long ago at Luz, God came to me and promised me a great family, and he promised that the land would belong to us.

"Now here in Egypt you have two sons. I want to adopt them as my own sons, and they will share in the family inheritance."

The old man was nearly blind. He peered at the two boys.

"Bring them here, and I will give them my blessing."

Joseph showed them where to kneel by their grandfather's bed, Ephraim on the left and Manasseh, the older, on his right.

Jacob stretched out his hands, but he placed his right hand on the younger boy's head, his left hand on the older boy's.

> "May the God whom Abraham and Isaac served,
> God who fed me all my life,
> God who saved me from all evil,
> Bless the lads.
> May they remember my name
> And the name of Abraham and Isaac.
> May their family become very great on earth."

"Father, wait!" Joseph tried to lift his father's hand from Ephraim's head and place it on his older brother.

"This one is the older. Put your right hand on his head."

"I know, son. He will be the father of a great and important family, too, but his brother will be the father of a great nation."

So the grandfather gave his blessing to all the family, and he said to Joseph just before he died,

"Promise that you will not bury me here in Egypt but back home in the family burying place with Abraham and Isaac."

So they carried his body back, and a great funeral procession went along in his honor. Only the women and children and flocks stayed behind in Goshen. It was such an impressive funeral that the Canaanites who watched them far off wondered about it and said,

"The Egyptians are really mourning very greatly."

After their father was dead, Joseph's brothers began to worry again.

"Now Joseph has a chance to get even with us for what we did to him."

So they hurried to him to talk it over.

"Before our father died he asked us to tell you for him,

" 'I ask that you forgive your brothers for their sin against you.' So now we are asking you to forgive us. We are your servants," they said.

Once again there were tears in Joseph's eyes.

"Don't be afraid. Am I in God's place to judge? You did plan evil against me, but God planned it for good, so that many people might be kept alive. Now don't be afraid. I will look out for you and your children."

And so they lived together. Joseph grew to be an old, old man, and his grandchildren used to come to see him and climb up on his lap.

He gave his big family his blessing and asked them to make him a promise.

"God will surely stay with you and take you back to the land he promised to Abraham, to Isaac, and to Jacob.

"Promise me that when you go back you will carry me with you and bury me in our land."

Years later his people kept their promise, and Joseph was buried with respect and honor in the land God promised to give to his people.

Genesis 47:13–31; 48; 49; 50; Joshua 24:32

THE LEADER GOD CHOSE

The Adopted Baby

IT HAD BEEN A LONG, long time since Joseph brought his father and his brothers and the rest of the family to live in the land of Goshen. When they came with all their sheep and cattle and oxen, they were just a big, big family. Now there were so many of them that the Egyptians began to think of them as people of another country. There were so many that the new Pharaoh, who did not know about Joseph and the way he had saved Egypt, began to be afraid of them.

Just suppose there should be a war, he reasoned. Suppose the children of Israel joined one of the enemy countries and fought against the Egyptians. Something must be done to keep them from getting too strong before that could happen.

He sent out orders that the Hebrew people would have to leave their flocks and herds and go to work building big storehouses in his two new treasure cities.

First they had to make the bricks they used. Then they had to build the high walls of the buildings. And all the time they worked guards stood by with whips in their hands to keep them working. The proud people of the family God chose had become slaves.

But in spite of all the hard work, the Hebrew families just went on growing bigger all the time, and there were more and more Hebrew people. Pharaoh sent out another order:

"Every baby boy who is born in a Hebrew family is to be thrown into the Nile River. The girls may live."

And so there was a secret in one of the Hebrew homes. Three-year-old Aaron and his big sister Miriam never talked about it. Father Amram and Mother Jochebed never mentioned it. There was a new baby boy in the family.

They could hide him for a while, but by the time he was three months old he was too big to hide. But his mother had a plan. She made a small boat-shaped basket out of reeds that grew in the shallow water at the edge of the river. Carefully she plastered it inside and out with sticky pitch to make it waterproof. Then she laid her baby inside.

She placed the little boat just at the water's edge among the flags that were growing there. She showed Miriam where to hide close by to watch. Then she went home.

It was the time when Pharaoh's daughter came with her maids to the river to bathe. And she was the one who discovered the little basket rocking gently in the water.

Quickly she sent one of her maids to bring it to her. When she opened it, the baby began to cry.

"Look! This must be one of the Hebrew babies." The princess' voice sounded very gentle, for the small girl who was watching and listening ran up to her and asked,

"Would you like to have me get one of the Hebrew women to take care of the baby for you?"

So with the princess' permission Miriam ran to get her mother.

"I want you to take this child and be his nurse. I will pay you your wages. Take care of him for me." The princess laid the baby in his own mother's arms.

And so he went back home. But now he was not hidden.

Just as soon as he was old enough the princess sent for him. His mother took him to the palace, and there he grew up as the princess' adopted son. Moses was to be his name, she said, because it meant "drawn out," and she had drawn him out of the water.

Exodus 1; 2:1–10

Runaway from the Palace

Moses grew up in the palace, learning how to be a prince. But he never forgot that he was really one of the Hebrew slave people. Every day he could see them working on the buildings. No matter how hot the sun was shining or how tired the men were, there was never a chance for them to rest. The guards stood right beside them watching, shouting orders, punishing, beating them to make them work faster.

One day Moses lost his temper. He saw one of the Egyptian guards beating a Hebrew workman. Before he stopped to think, Moses struck the guard and killed him.

No one was looking. Moses dragged the man's body away and buried it in the sand.

Next day he was out walking, and he saw two of his own people in a fight. Before he stopped to think, he was mixed up in that fight, too, doing his best to separate the men.

"Who made you a prince and a judge over us? Are you going to kill us the way you killed that Egyptian?" one of them snapped.

Moses was frightened. How had the news leaked out? If Pharaoh heard, it would not be safe for him to stay in Egypt.

That was just what happened. But by the time Pharaoh sent the guard to arrest Moses, he was far down the road.

One day he sat down to rest beside a well in Midian. Seven sisters, all daughters of Jethro, the priest of Midian, came to the well to get water for their father's sheep.

No sooner had they filled the watering troughs, so the sheep could drink, than some shepherds drove them away to make room for their own flocks. Moses jumped up to help the girls.

When the sisters came home their father asked,

"How is it that you are back so early today?"

"An Egyptian drove off the shepherds and helped us water the sheep," they told him.

"Where is he? Why didn't you invite him home with you? Call him so that he can eat supper with us."

And that was how Moses found a home far away from Egypt. He married one of the sisters and became a shepherd, working for Jethro.

Exodus 2:11–22

How God Called His Leader

Back in Egypt one Pharaoh had died and another Pharaoh had taken his place. It was harder now than ever before for the Hebrew people to live with their cruel masters, and many a time they cried out for someone to help them.

God, listening to the people he had chosen, remembered his

promise to bless the family of Abraham and Isaac and Jacob. Now he began to carry out his plan to take his people back to the land he had promised to give them.

Moses was far away from home one day. He had taken the sheep over near the mountain country to find fresh green grass. And as he walked slowly along with them he saw a blazing light. He went closer to see what was wrong, and he discovered that a bush was afire, yet it was not burning up.

While he was watching he heard someone call his name.

"Here I am," he answered.

The voice was coming straight from the fire where God was speaking.

"Moses, come no farther. Stop and take off your sandals, for you are standing on holy ground.

"I am God, the God of your father, God of Abraham, God of Isaac, and God of Jacob."

Moses hid his face, for he was afraid to look now.

"I know the troubles of my people in Egypt, and I am ready to rescue them. I am going to take them away to their own land where there is room for everyone and plenty for all to eat.

"Moses, I want you to go to Pharaoh, get my people away from him, and take them out of Egypt."

"But," said Moses, "I'm not an important person. Who am I to go to the great Pharaoh?"

"I will be with you. And I will tell you how you can be sure that I am sending you. When you have brought the people out of Egypt, you will all worship God here at this mountain."

"But," said Moses, "when I go to the children of Israel and tell them, 'The God of your fathers sent me to you,' and they say, 'What is his name?' what am I to say?"

"Tell them the God WHO IS THE LIVING GOD sent you to them. I AM GOD, the God of your fathers, and this will be my name forever.

"Now go to Egypt. Call the leaders together and tell them what I am going to do. Then go with them to Pharaoh and say to him,

" 'The Lord God of the Hebrews has met with us. Now we ask your permission to go on a three days' journey into the wilderness country to sacrifice to our God and to worship him.'

"He will not let you go. But I am going to do wonderful things in Egypt, and after that he will let you go."

"But," said Moses, "they are not going to believe me or even listen to me. 'God never spoke to you,' they will say."

"Moses, what is that in your hand?"

"My rod." Moses looked at the tall shepherd's rod he used to guide and protect his sheep.

"Throw it on the ground."

When Moses did that, it turned into a snake. Moses ran.

"Now reach out and take it by the tail."

When Moses obeyed, he held his old, trusted rod in his hand.

"This will be a sign to them that God has appeared to you."

"But," said Moses, "I'm not a good speaker. I talk too slowly, and I don't know the right words."

"Moses, who made man's mouth? Now go, and I will teach you what to say."

"But—" Moses began. He could think of no more excuses. "Send whom you want to send," he said unwillingly.

"There is Aaron, your brother. He can speak well. Even now

he is coming to meet you. I will tell you what to say. You will tell him, and he will speak the words for you. Now take your rod and go."

So Moses said good-by to Jethro, and with his wife and his sons he set out for Egypt. Along the way Aaron came to meet him, just as God had promised, and they all went on together.

Exodus 2:23–25; 3; 4:1–17

The Fight for Freedom

The first thing Moses and Aaron did in Egypt was to call together the leaders of their people, and Aaron told them the news. The thankful people did believe him, and they bowed their heads and worshiped God.

The next thing was to speak to Pharaoh.

"This is a message from the Lord God of Israel. Let my people go out into the wilderness to worship me."

"Who is this God?" Pharaoh shouted. "I don't obey him. I do not know him, and I will not let your people go. What are you trying to do? Take my slaves away from their work? You want me to give all those people a holiday? Get to work yourselves."

Then he sent an order to the overseers of the workmen.

"These Hebrew people are getting lazy. 'Let us go away to worship,' they say, and they want to stop their work.

"Now do this. Instead of giving them the straw they need to make their bricks, send them out to get their own straw. But see to it that they make just as many bricks as they do now."

So the tired men had to hunt in the fields for leftover stubble for straw, and they had no time to make bricks. Finally a group of Hebrew men went to Pharaoh to beg for help. Pharaoh just laughed.

"You are lazy. Make bricks. Make bricks, and make as many as you always did."

The unhappy men met Moses and Aaron on the way back from the palace, and they complained,

"Now Pharaoh hates us, and everything is worse than ever."

By this time Moses was ready to give up.

"Why did you ever send me?" he asked God. "It is worse than ever, and you haven't rescued these people yet."

But God had not finished. Now he sent Moses and Aaron back to Pharaoh.

"When he asks you to show him a sign, Aaron is to throw the rod at Pharaoh's feet, and it will turn into a snake."

And it happened just that way.

Then Pharaoh called for his best magicians, and they did the same trick. Only Aaron's rod-snake swallowed up all the magicians' rod-snakes.

Still Pharaoh was hardhearted and said he would not let the people go.

God told Moses what to do next.

In the morning he and Aaron met Pharaoh by the river.

"The Lord God of the Hebrews has sent me to tell you, 'Let my people go.' But you would not listen," Moses said to him.

Aaron stretched out the rod and struck the river. All the water turned to blood. Dead fish came floating to the top. The water smelled so bad that no one could drink it.

"My magicians do the same trick." Pharaoh was hardhearted, and would not let the people go.

A week later God sent Moses and Aaron back to the palace.

"Let my people go so they can worship me." But Pharaoh said no.

Aaron stretched out the rod, and up from the river came frogs, dozens of frogs, hundreds of frogs. They swarmed into Pharaoh's house, into his bedroom, over his bed, into the kitchen, into the ovens, over the people—everywhere.

"My magicians do the same trick." Pharaoh was not impressed.

Just the same, he begged Moses and Aaron to get rid of the frogs.

"Take them away. You may go out to worship your God."

But when the frogs were dead he changed his mind.

The next sign came when Aaron's rod touched the dust on the ground, and lice—millions of lice—crawled over animals and people. Pharaoh called for his best magicians to see whether they could do that trick. They just shook their heads.

"This thing has been done by God," they told Pharaoh.

But Pharaoh was hardhearted and would not let the people go.

The next sign came when swarms of flies covered everything in the land. But God protected the land of Goshen where the Hebrew people lived.

Then Pharaoh sent for Moses and Aaron.

"Go on and worship God here in Egypt. Make your sacrifices here at home."

"But the Egyptians do not believe in making sacrifices the way we do. Won't they try to kill us when we offer our animal sacrifices to God? Let us travel for three days into the country and worship God."

At last Pharaoh agreed, but he quickly changed his mind.

The next sign was a sickness that killed the cattle, the horses, and the sheep in Egypt. God protected the animals in Goshen where the Hebrews lived.

But Pharaoh was hardhearted and would not let the people go.

This was the next sign. Moses and Aaron threw handfuls of ashes into the air, and sore boils broke out on the bodies of the Egyptians. The best magicians could not even come when Pharaoh sent for them. They had so many boils they could not stand up.

But Pharaoh was hardhearted and would not let the people go.

Next came a terrible hailstorm, with lightning that killed the crops and the trees of the Egyptians. The fields and trees in Goshen were not damaged.

This was the next sign. Swarms of locusts crawled over fields and streets and houses. They ate every blade of grass, every green thing the hailstorm had left.

Now Pharaoh began to beg. "Help me. I have sinned. Ask your God to take them away."

So God sent a strong wind that carried every locust into the Red Sea. Then when Pharaoh was safe again, he was hardhearted and would not let the people go.

Next it was dark, day and night, so that no one could see to walk for three days. Over in Goshen the sun shone clear and bright every day.

But Pharaoh was hardhearted and would not let the people go. Only this time he said to Moses,

"Get out of here, and never come back. If you ever see my face again you will die."

"You are right," Moses told him. "I will never see your face again. About midnight the angel of the Lord will visit every home in Egypt, and the oldest child in every family will die, from Pharaoh's oldest child to the oldest child of every servant. And it will be the same with the animals. There will be such a cry of mourning from every home as was never heard before.

"Then your people will come to me and beg me to leave and to take the Hebrews with me. And I will go."

In great anger Moses left the palace for the last time.

Exodus 4:29–31; 5 to 11

A New Holiday

Suddenly everything was going to be new and different for the people God had chosen.

"Get ready!"

Moses listened to the directions as God gave them.

"Get ready!"

© 1963, Broadman Press

The First Passover

The leaders of the people heard the directions as Moses gave them.

The time had come to escape from Egypt, the time to start on the long, long journey to the land of Canaan. But first there was a new holiday to celebrate, a holiday that would be kept each year in the new homeland.

First the Hebrews were to ask the Egyptians to give them gold and silver and jewelry and clothing to take with them on their journey.

Then each family was to kill a fine young lamb. Over and on both sides of the door of the house the father would make marks with the blood of the lamb. That would show the angel of the Lord, when he came in the night to take every oldest child of the Egyptians, that this was a Hebrew house. Then the angel would pass over, and the family would be safe.

The lambs were to be roasted for the holiday supper. If a family was so small that a whole lamb would be too much to eat, the members would share with a neighbor family, for no meat was to be left over. With the roast they ate bread made without yeast, and green herbs.

They were all to be dressed and ready for traveling when they ate the supper, and they would eat standing up, for at any minute they would be leaving forever the land of Egypt where they had been slaves.

This would be the way they would keep the holiday of the Passover when they came to their homeland. And when the children would ask, "Why do we do this?" the fathers would say, "This is the feast of the Lord's Passover, when he defeated the Egyptians and saved our families."

That night the angel of the Lord went through Egypt, and someone died in every Egyptian family. The sound of crying was heard all over the land. In the night Pharaoh sent for Moses and Aaron.

"Take your people and go. Take your flocks and herds and go at once to worship God."

And all the other Egyptians were saying, "Go!" Gladly they gave the Hebrew people all the silver and gold and jewelry they could carry away with them.

So the Hebrews, fathers and mothers and children, dressed and ready to go, picked up their things and walked away. The long, long journey had begun.

On their shoulders they carried their kneading bowls full of bread dough, wrapped in clothes. They would stop along the way and bake it, for that was the only food they carried. They carried with them the body of Joseph; for long before, his sons had promised him that when his people went home they would bury him in his own country.

Six hundred thousand men, with women and children, and hundreds and hundreds of sheep and cattle, made a long, long line walking down the road to Succoth, miles away. They were not to go to Canaan by the highway, though it was the shortest road. That way led through the land of the Philistines, who were fighting people. The children of Israel were not yet ready to fight to get into their own country.

There was no road to follow through the wilderness land where they went, but God was leading. At night he gave them a pillar of fire for light, and in the daytime a cloud pillar just ahead showed them the way to go.

Exodus 12; 13

Across the Sea to Freedom

All the Hebrews, men and women and children, with their cattle and sheep were camping near the shore of the Red Sea. Back in Egypt Pharaoh heard that all his slaves were gone.

"Get out the chariots, all of them! Call the captains! After the children of Israel! Why did you let them get away?" he shouted.

So six hundred chariots full of soldiers thundered away toward the sea. On the seashore the Hebrew people heard them coming. There they were, caught between Pharaoh's army and the water.

"Moses, Moses, weren't there enough graves for all of us in Egypt? Why did you bring us out here to die?" they complained.

"This is no time to be afraid. Just wait, and you will see how the Lord will save you. He himself will fight for you," Moses promised.

"Speak to the children of Israel. Tell them to go on." That was God giving the orders. "Stretch out your rod over the sea."

The cloud that was standing ahead of the line moved around until it was between the soldiers and the people. Night came.

Out beyond Moses' rod the wind began to blow strong and steady from the east. All night the wind blew. The Red Sea waters divided this way and that way. The road through the middle of the sea was dry between the walls of the water.

The long line of people began to move slowly on again, steadily on and on. Not a single foot was wet.

Behind them the chariots thundered down to the shore and rolled on the dry sea road. A wheel pulled loose in the sand, then another. The soldiers were losing speed.

The long line went on. The last Hebrew stepped on the shore. "Stretch out your hand, Moses."

As Moses obeyed, the sea water came rushing together. The Egyptian army was caught, and not one soldier escaped.

Now it was thanksgiving time for Moses and all the people. They made up a thanksgiving hymn. Miriam, Moses' sister, with her tambourine in her hand, led the singing, and all the women sang with her.

> I will sing to the Lord, for he has won gloriously.
> Horse and rider he has thrown into the sea.
> The Lord is my strength, my song.
> He is my God, my father's God,
> I will give him my praise.
> The enemy said, "After them! Capture them!"
> He blew with his wind, and the sea covered them,
> And they sank like lead in the waters.
> Oh, who is like you, God of glory?
> You saved your people. You will guide them
> To the place you made for them.
> Sing to the Lord, all of you, for he has won gloriously.
> Horse and rider he has thrown into the sea.   *Exodus 14; 15:1–21*

Thirsty Travelers

One day, two days, three days the children of Israel traveled on into the hot, dry desert country.

"Where is water for us to drink?" they complained to Moses.

They discovered a spring, and they hurried to get some water. But when they tasted it they complained again. That water was bitter. But while they stood there complaining, Moses was asking God for help, and God was telling him what to do. Nearby there was a tree that could be used to sweeten the water. Moses threw it into the spring, and when the people tasted again the water was sweet and good.

Once more God was showing his people that he was right there beside them, taking care of them. And he taught them that they must do their part.

"Listen carefully every time God speaks. Remember his rules and keep them, and you will stay well. I am the Lord who protects you and heals you when you are sick," he told them. Then he led them to a shady camping place by twelve water holes where there was plenty of cool, good water.

They forgot so quickly. There was another time when they made camp in a place without water.

"We are thirsty," they stormed at Moses. "Did you bring us all the way out here just to have us and all our animals die in this terrible country? Is God really on our side or not?"

"What must I do? These people are ready to kill me." Moses went to God for help.

"Take up your rod and go on ahead with some of the leaders. When I show you a rock, strike it with the rod."

Out from that rock water came pouring, rushing in a stream. There was plenty for all. *Exodus 15:22–27; 17:1–7*

Nothing to Eat

One of the real troubles in the desert was finding food. The people complained about that, too. The last bit of dough they had brought from Egypt had been baked and the last crumb eaten.

They were hungry. They were sure they were going to starve.

"Oh, why didn't we die in Egypt? At least we had plenty to eat there. Now we are just going to die out here in this desert."

While they were still complaining, God was talking to Moses. "I have heard my people. Tell them they will have meat to eat tonight, and from now on I will send them bread like rain from heaven, all they need every day."

That evening great flocks of quail flew over the camp, and the people ran out to catch them. They had all they could eat.

In the morning as soon as the dew was off the ground they discovered small white flakes all around as far as anyone could see.

"What is it?" they asked. "*Manna? Manna?*"

And that was how it got its name. As long as they were traveling to the Promised Land they had "What is it?" to eat.

"This is the bread God sent to you," Moses explained. "Pick up what you need for each day, no more, for it will spoil when you keep more than your share."

Every day manna was ready for them—every day but one. God had planned his sabbath day for rest and worship. So on the day before the sabbath everyone picked up enough for two days. They could make cakes out of the manna or boil it, or eat it as it was.

And so for a long time they were satisfied. But at last they were tired of manna.

"Why can't we have meat again? Or some of that good fish we had in Egypt? And remember the good green things! Cucumbers and melons and little green onions! Now there's nothing but this old manna, always manna." Grown men and women began to cry like children.

And God, who was listening, told Moses,

"They are going to have meat, not just for one or two days, but for a month, until they are sick of it."

But how? Moses wondered whether he was to have all the sheep and cattle killed. Would all the fish in the sea be brought to feed those hungry people?

That night the wind blew in from the sea, blowing flocks and flocks of quail on every side of camp. Never had anyone seen so many. Never had people eaten so many birds so fast. But while they were still eating, they became sick, so sick that many of them died.

After that the people went on eating manna.

Exodus 16; Numbers 11:4–35

A Tired Leader

More trouble came when the people who lived in the wilderness tried to chase the Hebrews away. It was plain to see that the Hebrews had to get ready to fight. So Moses organized an army, and he made a young man named Joshua captain of the troops.

"Take the men you want for your soldiers and go out tomorrow and fight the Amalekites. I will be up there on the hilltop where you can see me, praying for you, and I will hold up the rod I have carried all the way from Egypt."

That was the way the battle began. But Moses' arm would get tired, and when he rested it, the enemy would advance. As long as he held the rod high, Joshua and his army were winning.

Up on the hilltop with Moses were his brother Aaron and a man named Hur. When they saw how tired he was, they brought a stone for him to sit on. Then they stood beside him, steadying his arm until, just as the sun was going down, Captain Joshua won the battle. And there on the hilltop Moses built an altar for a monument to the battle and a place where they worshiped God.

Messengers went running to the far side of the wilderness to tell Moses' family the good news about the children of Israel and their leader. Jethro, Moses' father-in-law, took Moses' wife and the two boys, who had been staying with him, and went to the camp.

Moses went out to meet them and show them the way to his

tent. There the whole family listened to the story of the Hebrews' adventures since Moses led them out of Egypt. Aaron and the leaders came to call, and the family all worshiped God together. It was a time of great happiness.

Next day Jethro watched Moses at work. It was a long, busy day. Moses had to be the judge when people had quarrels. He had to tell them what to do about their troubles. He listened to their problems. All day long they kept coming to his tent. When it was evening he was tired out.

Jethro was worried. "This is too much for you," he warned. "You ought to have help. The people need you to explain God's rules and laws. But why don't you choose assistants to help you? They must be men who trust God as you do. They must be honest men who always tell the truth.

"Let these assistants take care of the small problems. Let them bring the important problems to you. That way you will have strength enough to lead these people all the way."

It sounded like good advice to Moses. So he chose his assistant judges and put them in charge of all but the hard problems. Then Jethro said good-by and went back to his home across the wilderness country.

Exodus 17:8-16; 18

God's Ten Laws

For months the children of Israel had been traveling, learning step by step a little about God's love and care. Now they were ready for God to teach them his rules for living together.

They were camping near the foot of Mount Sinai. From the clouds drifting round its peaks Moses heard God calling him. He climbed the steep slopes until the camp was far away. As far as he could see across the bare brown plains were rows of tents, herds of cattle, flocks of sheep, busy people.

"You have seen what I did to the Egyptians," the Voice Moses knew so well was saying now. "You know how I protected you, the way an eagle keeps her fledglings from falling, flying just beneath them when they learn to fly, to catch them on her wings if they should fall.

"If you will listen to me and keep your part of our covenant promise, you will be my own people whom I love out of all the world. You will be my special treasure."

Back in camp at the foot of the mountain Moses gave God's message to the people.

"We will do everything the Lord has told us," they promised.

"Then get ready to listen when the Lord God speaks to you from the mountain," Moses said.

The people cleaned the tents. They scrubbed their clothes. They bathed. When all the camp was clean they waited.

Early in the morning, two days later, they heard thunder far off on top of the mountain. Lightning was flashing. Then a fiery, smoking cloud covered all the mountaintop. The people could hear the sound of trumpets coming louder all the time. Moses took the people as far as the foot of the mountain.

"Stay here! Don't go one step farther," he warned. "You must not touch the mountain where God is. Listen, and hear his voice."

Moses left them then, and he climbed the mountain until he disappeared in the smoking cloud. While lightning blazed round the mountaintop, the people waited, more frightened every minute; and that was how Moses found them when he came back.

The Voice that spoke beyond the clouds was saying,

"I am the Lord your God who rescued you when you were slaves in Egypt.
Worship me only, nothing and no one else.
Make yourselves no images to worship.
Speak my name reverently and respectfully.
Keep the sabbath day for God, and do your work on the other six days of the week.
Respect and love your father and mother so that you may live long in the land that will be yours.
Do not murder.
Do not break your wedding promises.
Do not steal.
Do not lie about your neighbor.
Do not be greedy about the things that belong to your neighbor."

"You talk to us, Moses," said the people. "We're afraid. You tell us what God wants."

"Don't be afraid," he told them quietly. "He has come to teach you how to live."

"Come back to the mountain." Again God sent for Moses. There was so much to tell him, so much he would be teaching the people. Joshua went part of the way with him. *Exodus 19; 20:1–20; 24:12–13*

Forgotten Promises

In camp the people waited and waited and waited. A week went by, another week, and then a month and more.

"Aaron! Aaron, where's Moses?"

"He's gone. What will happen to us now?"

"Who's going to take care of us?"

"We have to have a god to take care of us. Let's make one we can see—quickly, before something happens."

Aaron listened to their shouts.

"Very well. Bring me your golden jewelry."

So they did. And Aaron melted the gold and made a small golden image of a calf.

That day there was music and shouting and celebration in camp as God's people prayed before the golden image.

Up on the mountain Moses heard God's stern voice.

"Go back at once. My people have disgraced themselves."

Moses hurried down the mountain. In his hands he carried a treasure, two panels of rock on which were written in God's own handwriting the ten great laws.

By the time Moses met Joshua they could hear the sounds of voices coming from camp.

"That sounds like war," said Joshua.

"I don't hear fighting voices. Those people are singing," Moses decided as they hurried on. He was worried. What was the cause of all the celebrating?

Then he saw the whole awful scene. Round the golden image the people God loved were bowing and singing and dancing.

Moses was angrier than he had ever been in all his life. He hurled the rock panels to the ground, and they broke into pieces. He burned the image and ground it to powder, then threw the powder into the brook from which the people drank.

"What could these people have done to make you do this shameful thing?" he accused Aaron.

"Now, Moses, don't be angry. You know how they are. They were worried because you were gone so long. And so—"

Moses charged out to the gate of the camp and shouted:

"Who is on the Lord's side? Come here. I want to see you."

The loyal men stood by him.

"These other disgraceful men are to be punished by death. See to it."

There was more that must be done. Next day Moses went back to talk to God. This was his prayer:

"These people have been wicked. But, Lord, if only you will, I beg you to forgive them. If you cannot forgive them, then take my name out of your book of remembering."

"I will surely punish those who do wrong. But you are their leader. Take them on to the place where they are to go.

"I will be with you to help you. But if only it were in my people's hearts to keep my commandments!" God told him.

Exodus 31:18; 32; Deuteronomy 5:29

Rules for Living

Though Moses could not see God, he could feel the shining goodness and love of God, and he said,

"If I have been able to please you, I ask you to go on with us. Forgive our sins. And take us back to be your people."

In the dazzling light he heard God say:

"This is my promise. I will do marvelous things for my people. But they are not to worship other gods. I will not have it."

Then he gave Moses the rules for living, and once again the Ten Commandments were written on rock panels for all the people to see. There were rules about worshiping God with sacrifices, and rules about the sabbath day offerings, all kinds of rules to help people live safely in a new land.

"When you harvest the crops, leave a little grain in the corners of the fields, some grapes on your vines, some olives on the trees so that poor people can have a share.

Do not cheat. Do not lie.

Pay a man the wages he has earned by working for you.
Be patient with deaf and blind people.
Do not be a talebearer.
Do not hate your brother in your heart.
Do not try to get even.
Love your neighbor.
Be friendly with strangers, for you were strangers in Egypt."

"If you remember my laws and obey them," God promised, "then I will live with you and walk among you and be your God, and you will be my people.

"There will be plenty of rain in the land, and the crops will grow so that you will have plenty to eat.

"At night you will go to bed, and nothing will make you afraid, for there will be peace in the land."

This time Moses came back to quiet, waiting people. He did not know it, but his face was shining with a special glory that came from spending so much time with God.

Now they listened to every word he said.

"Hear and remember, Israel:

"The Lord our Lord is the only God, and you are to love him with all your heart, all your soul, all your strength.

"All these things you have heard you are to remember.

"Teach them to your children and talk about them when you are sitting together at home, when you are walking along the road, when you get up in the morning, and when you go to bed at night.

"For this is what God expects of you:

"Worship him, obey him, and love and serve him with everything you have, everything you are. And remember, when you hunt for him with all your heart you will always find him."

"All that the Lord has told us we will do. We will be obedient," the people promised.

So then they worshiped God, all together.

Moses was remembering the time he was there alone with God.

"Who am I to go to Pharaoh and tell him to free my people?" he was asking the Voice that spoke from beyond the flames of the bush that did not burn up.

"Surely I will be with you. And when you have brought the people out of Egypt, you will worship God in this very place."

Now it had all come true.

Exodus 3:11–12; 34; Leviticus 19; 26:1–13; Deuteronomy 4:29; 6:4–7; 10:12

A House for God

Outside the camp, far away from the tents where people were living, Moses pitched the meeting tent. That was the place where the people could go to meet God, where he could come to them.

Moses used to go out to the meeting tent to talk things over with God, and when the people saw him walk that way, every man went and stood by his own tent door and watched. When Moses went inside, the cloudy pillar rested by the meeting tent, and all the people worshiped from their tents.

That was how it was at the beginning. On the mountain, when God gave Moses the laws, he gave him a pattern for making a beautiful tent house where the people could have their worship services and bring their sacrifice offerings.

No house of worship has ever been built quite like that tent house. It was made to be part of the camp, to be taken down and packed and carried wherever the people moved.

All the people had a part in building the meeting tent, for it was made from their gifts.

Whoever among the men was a good workman with wood or with gold and silver was to have part in the great project.

Whoever among the women could weave beautiful linen cloth and embroidered tapestries was to have a part.

These were the things they needed:

Gold and silver and bronze from the treasures they had brought from Egypt.

Fine linen cloth and dyes to make the cloth blue and purple and red.

Wood from the acacia trees that grew in the wilderness country.

Red leather made from goats' skins and heavy tent cloth woven from goats' hair.

Olive oil for the lamps, spices and incense, beautiful robes for the priests who would lead the services.

Moses appointed two men to be superintendents. Bezaleel, who was an artist craftsman and knew how to use silver and carve wood was one. Aholiab was his assistant.

They were to receive the gifts, decide how each gift was to be used and how much was needed of everything.

Every morning the people would bring their offerings, first the things they had already, then the wood they cut, the cloth they wove, whatever was completed. The gifts piled up.

At last the superintendents counted and measured carefully, and they sent word to Moses:

"Tell the people to stop. There is more than enough."

And so they worked together.

Round about the court of worship they hung linen curtains so that there was a kind of wall, but no roof.

Just inside was the altar where the priests offered to God the gifts the people brought and the bronze bowls that were used for washing. This was the place where the people worshiped together.

Beyond was the tent house or tabernacle. It was built on a wooden framework with four kinds of curtains for a roof. First there were fine linen curtains beautifully embroidered with angel figures. Next came a heavier kind of tent cloth made of goats' hair. Over that was red leather, and on top of all was a covering of animal skins.

© 1963, Broadman Press *Bezaleel*

Inside were two rooms divided by a curtain. First there was the holy place where the priests went to worship.

In the holy place there were just three things: the beautiful golden lampstand with six branches which were always burning, the incense altar where sweet-smelling spices were burned, and the table where twelve loaves of bread, one for each of the twelve tribes of the children of Israel, were offered to God. Every sabbath, new loaves were laid on the table. Not even the priests were to eat that bread, for it was a thank offering to God for his gift of food to his people.

Beyond the curtain was the most holy place where only the chief priest could go. And he went only one day in the year. Here was the people's greatest treasure, the ark of God's promise.

This was a chest made of wood, almost four feet long, a little more than two feet wide and high. It was covered with gold. Over the top, like a cover, was a beautiful golden statue of two cherubim facing each other, their wings spread out.

But that was not all the treasure. Inside were the rock panels on which were written the Ten Commandments.

No one was ever to touch the ark, so it was made with rings at each corner through which long poles could be slipped when it was time to travel.

So the tabernacle tent house was finished, and the cloud came and covered it over, and God's glory filled all the house.

Exodus 31:1–11; 33:7–11; 35; 36 to 40

When It Was Time to Travel

Because moving day might come at any time, each person had his own job. The families pitched their tents together, and they were responsible for taking care of their own things. But all the men of the Levi family were God's ministers, and it was their duty to take down the tent meeting house and see that the treasures were carried to the next stopping place.

The cloud of God's presence would move away from the tabernacle. That was the first sign that moving time had come. Then two trumpeters would blow their silver trumpets. That was the next sign. Moses would say:

> "O Lord, rise up, and may all your enemies be scattered,
> And may those who hate you flee before you."

Then Aaron would lift the first curtain and lead the work of covering the furnishings and getting the big tent ready for the move.

Just ahead in the daytime went the cloud and at night, the pillar of fire.

Wherever the cloud or the fire pillar stopped, the people set up their tents. First of all the tent house of meeting went up in the center of the big square camp. This reminded the travelers that God was always in the midst of them. In straight rows north and south and east and west the twelve tribe-families set up their tents, and each family's tents marked by its own family banner.

That night the lights in the golden lampstand would be lighted for the first time in the new home. Moses would say,

"Return, O Lord, to the many thousands of Israel."

So day after day the Hebrews lived in the new home, gathering their manna for food, learning God's way, growing stronger together. And when they had worshiped together and brought their offering gifts, they heard Aaron give them God's blessing:

> "The Lord bless you and keep you:
> The Lord smile on you, and be gracious to you:
> The Lord God give you peace."

Numbers 1:51–54; 2; 6:24–26; 10:35

Giants and Grasshoppers

How far away was the Promised Land where the Hebrews would all have homes? Would they travel six months? A year? Six weeks?

God told Moses that it was time to send out an exploring party of twelve men, one from each tribe. These were their orders:

"Find out what the land is like. Is it good for growing crops? Is there wood for building houses?

"Find out about the people who live there. Are they strong or weak? Are there many of them or just a few? Do they live in tents or in houses that are well guarded?

"Bring back some of the fruit that is growing there."

Forty days later the men came back. Their arms were full of ripe figs and rose-red pomegranates. Two of the men bore a bunch of grapes so huge that it had to be slung over a pole and carried on their shoulders.

While the people crowded to see, the men made their report.

"That land is really good. It is full of brooks and fountains and springs. Wheat and barley, grapevines, fig trees and olive trees grow there. Milk is there, and honey, and plenty of bread.

"But the cities are guarded by strong walls. The people are strong. Some of them are giants. We saw them. We felt like grasshoppers beside them."

That was not the way Caleb wanted to make his report.

"Let's go on at once," he said to Moses. "We are strong enough to take the land."

"We can't do it. We'll all be killed," all the camp was whispering, and grown men and women were crying as if they were frightened children.

The Return of the Spies

"God should have left us in Egypt so we could have died there. Or out in the wilderness country. We'll never get to the Promised Land. We'll all be killed."

"Let's get us another leader to take us back to Egypt."

Moses and Aaron, horrified at what the people were saying, knelt on the ground to pray.

But Joshua had not made his report yet. Now he stood by Caleb, and they both begged the people to listen.

"It is truly a wonderful land. If God is pleased with us, of course he will take us there. Only don't rebel against him. The Lord is on our side. Don't be afraid of the people in that land. They won't be able to keep us out."

"Stone the men! Stone Caleb! Stone Joshua!"

All the camp was full of noisy voices. Suddenly they were quiet. The glory of the Lord was shining over the tent house of meeting, and God was speaking to Moses.

"How long will it be until these people believe me?"

"Lord, you are patient and merciful. Forgive them, as you have forgiven them all the way from Egypt," Moses begged.

"I have already forgiven them," God answered. "But they do not trust me, and they must be punished. Only Caleb and Joshua will ever live to go into that land. Tomorrow turn around and go back into the wilderness country. It will be forty more years before my people are ready to go into the land I promised them."

How quickly the people changed their minds!

"After all, here we are so close to the border. Let's just go on and see what will happen."

"Don't do it," Moses warned. "You turned away from God, and he will not go with you now. If you try it, you will all be killed."

But they would not listen. When they tried to make their own small war, Canaanite people came rushing out after them like bees and drove them off.

Slowly, sadly the whole camp began to travel back into the

wilderness country following the cloud that led them.

The Promised Land was forty years away. *Numbers 13 and 14*

Troubles in the Desert

Out in the wilderness country there came another time when the water supply gave out.

"Why did you let it happen?" The old complaints came again, and Moses listened sadly.

"Why did you bring us all the way out here where nothing grows? We'll all die without water."

Moses and Aaron did just what they had done so many times—they prayed. And as quickly as they asked for help God told them what to do.

Carrying his rod, Moses took the people to a great dry rock. But he was angry. He had had enough of whining and complaining.

"Now, you rebels, must we bring you water out of this rock?" he shouted. Then instead of speaking to the rock—as God had told him to do—he struck it in his anger.

Water came pouring out, plenty for people and animals, too. But the great leader and his brother had acted as if they were giving the water to the people. Now they heard their punishment. God would not allow either of them to go into the Promised Land. Someone else would be leading God's people into Canaan, but Moses would go every step with them to the very border of their new homeland.

Another time they wanted food, different food from manna which they ate every day.

"Give us real bread. We're tired of this food, and we're tired of this country where there's no water," they complained.

But the discontented whining suddenly turned into shrieks of fear. Snakes that bit like fire were in every tent, along the paths, under the rocks.

"Moses, help us," the frightened people begged. "We have been wrong. We complained against God. Ask him to take away these snakes."

And God, who forgave as quickly as he punished, gave Moses directions for making a snake out of brass.

"Set it up high on a pole. Tell the men bitten by snakes to look at the brass snake and they will be well."

There were so many times when the people complained. But once there was serious trouble when a group of men decided that they were just as good as Moses and Aaron. They could not see why the men of the Levi family were the only ones who could be God's ministers. And after all, Moses had been their leader all these years and they were not in the Promised Land yet.

The way the trouble was finally settled was something the people always remembered.

The head of each family carried a wooden rod, just as Moses did. God told Moses to have them bring all their rods to the tent house of meeting. Each man's rod had his name on it. Moses laid them all in the tabernacle one night.

In the morning when he went back there were eleven wooden poles all just alike. But one was blooming like a fruit tree in spring time. The name written on that pole was Aaron, who was head of God's ministers.

There was no more argument. God's sign pointed straight to the man whose family he wanted for his ministers.

Numbers 17:1–11; 20:1–13; 21:4–9; 16:3

Victory March

All the years of the wanderings in the wilderness country were over. Of the leaders only Moses and Caleb and Joshua were left. Miriam had died and so had Aaron, and his son Eleazar was the leader of the priests in his place.

The children, who had been too young to be afraid of going into the country where giants lived, were strong men and women now. They knew how to live outdoors, how to take care of themselves, how to obey their leader.

"Now the land is before you," said God. "Go ahead and take possession of it."

Just ahead was the land of Edom, home of the Esau people. But they were kinfolk of the Israel people, and there must be no fighting between them. Moses sent a messenger to ask their king:

"Let us come through your country. We will not go through your fields but straight down the King's Highway. And whatever water we use we will be glad to pay for."

But the king of Edom sent an armed guard to keep them away.

They went on by the kingdom of the Ammonites, for they were the Lot people, and there must be no fighting there.

But when they asked King Sihon of the Amorites for permission to go through his country, and he refused, the new army of the Israelites made ready to fight.

Did not God say, "Today I will begin to put the fear of you in the nations round about"? Did he not say, "I have given the land to you. Now go, and take possession of it"?

And so they did. They captured towns. They added great flocks of cattle to their own. They conquered King Og, the last of the giants, who was so big he had a special iron bed made to fit him. Not one city was too strong for them.

Now they made their camp at last in the plain country of Moab.

*Numbers 20:14–21; 21:21–35; 22:1;
Deuteronomy 2:19–37*

The Talking Donkey

Now King Balak of Moab heard about the people who were marching toward his land, and he called for help. Instead of ordering out his army, he sent messengers to his friend Balaam, the magician.

"There is an army of people from Egypt, and they cover the whole earth. Now come and curse them so I can drive them out. For I know that whoever is blessed by you is blessed indeed, and whoever is cursed is cursed indeed."

Balaam invited the messengers to spend the night while he asked God's advice. Next morning he sent them back.

"I cannot go with you. The Lord has blessed these people, and I cannot curse them."

Back came more messengers, princes this time, to impress Balaam, and they promised him all kinds of rewards if he would only go with them to Balak.

"If Balak were to give me his house full of silver, I could only do as God tells me, no more and no less."

But in the morning Balaam had his own donkey saddled and set out with the princes for King Balak's court.

Suddenly without any warning his donkey turned out of the highway into the field, for the animal could see what no one else saw. Standing right in front, with a sword in his hand, stood the angel of the Lord.

Balaam whipped the donkey and tried to turn her back.

There again, and just ahead, was the angel. But no one could see. And the donkey was caught in a path between two walls. When she tried to get away, she crushed Balaam's foot against the wall.

Balaam whipped the animal again. And now there was no way to get away, for there stood the angel. The patient little donkey simply fell down, and Balaam tumbled to the ground.

Now he was really angry, and he struck her with his staff. Then the donkey began to speak.

"What have I done that you have struck me these three times? Don't I belong to you? And haven't you ridden me as long as you have had me? And have I ever done this before?"

"No, but I should have killed you," Balaam shouted.

Then he saw it, too. There stood the angel, sword in hand.

"Why have you beaten your donkey? If she had not turned aside with you, I would have killed you, for God is not pleased with you."

"I was wrong," said Balaam. "Now I will go back home."

"No. Go with the men, but say only what God tells you to say."

King Balak was waiting impatiently. "So you finally came."

"But I will say only what God tells me to say."

King Balak took Balaam to the top of a high hill where they could see the Hebrew camp stretching out in every direction.

"Build me seven altars, and we will worship God," said Balaam. Then he said,

"From the top of the rocks and from the hills I see them. Who can count them, there are so many!"

"I thought I told you to curse them," stormed the king. "Come, we'll go to another place and try again."

So on the mountaintop King Balak built seven altars.

"Now," he said to Balaam.

"God does not lie the way men do. He keeps his word. Now he has told me to bless, for he has blessed. I cannot undo what has been done.

"God brought these people out of Egypt, and they are strong. No magic can hurt them."

"Well, if you can't curse them, at least don't bless them. Just don't say anything at all," grumbled King Balak.

So they went to another high place and built seven more altars. There Balaam said:

"How beautiful are all your tents, you people of Jacob. From you will come the greatest king, and his kingdom will be great. Blessed is he who blesses you, and cursed is he who curses you."

King Balak was so angry that he could hardly talk.

"I was going to give you a rich reward if you would curse my enemies. I was going to make you rich, and now the Lord has spoiled it all. Now go! Run for your life."

"I am going," Balaam said quietly. "Remember that I told your messengers that I could only say what God told me to say. I am going, but first I will tell you what will become of these people.

"I shall see him, but not now.
I shall see him, not near but far off.
There shall come a Star from the people of Jacob,
A king's scepter from the people of Israel,
And though your house is strong and built upon a rock,
No one will be able to keep these people away."

So Balaam went back home. He had lost the reward, but he had told the truth.

Numbers 22 to 24

It Happened on the Mountain

The Lord said to Moses, "Come up to me on the mountain."

God used to talk with Moses as a man talks with his friend, and Moses asked for special help.

"Lord, you told me to be the leader of these people, but who will go with me? You have told me that I am pleasing you. If I am, Lord, teach me your way of working, for these people are your people, and I must lead them in your way."

"I myself will go with you and help you to finish your work," was God's promise.

"Lord, if you will not go with us, then just let us stay here. But if you are with us and all the people of the earth see that you are with us, they will know that we are special and different. And just so I can be sure where you are, let me see you."

"I will let you understand my goodness and my power. I will give you my love and my mercy. But you cannot see my face. No one can look at God and live.

"But here beside me is a split place in the rocks. Stand there, and while my glory passes by you, I will shelter you with my hand. My face you cannot see, but you will see the afterglow of the place where I have been."

After many, many years Moses led the people to the Promised Land, just across the Jordan River from the place that was to be home.

Then God said to Moses, "Come up to me on the mountain. Once you forgot to honor me, and so you may not go into the land. But you shall see it for yourself."

Then Moses said his good-by to the people he loved.

"Remember this commandment. It is not hard to find or to keep. You do not need to send someone to heaven or across the sea to find it for you. Keep it in your hearts and in your words.

"Love the Lord your God. Keep his laws. This is life for you. Anything else will be death.

"Go the way he sends you. Always remember that God is forever, and his strong, everlasting arms will hold you safe, keeping you from danger."

Then he walked away across the plains, and he climbed to the highest peak of Mount Nebo. From there he looked down on green fields and rushing rivers and trees, houses and towns and gardens, with room enough for all the people and more beside.

"This is the land which I promised to give to Abraham and to Isaac and to Jacob and to their children," Moses heard his Friend's voice again.

There on the mountain Moses died, and God buried him. No one has ever found his grave.

So at last Moses did see God face to face.

Exodus 33:12–23; Deuteronomy 30:11–14; 33:27; 34:1–7

WARS OF GENERAL JOSHUA

Adventure of the Spies

"BE STRONG AND FEARLESS. You are to lead the Israelites to the land I promised to give them. I will be right beside you."

Joshua, the new captain of the Israelites, remembered when he had heard those words. It was the day God gave him his commission, when he met Moses for the last time in the tabernacle. Moses was the leader then, but he was an old, old man. His work was finished. God's marching orders had been for the new captain.

Now Moses was dead. Out of respect for their great leader the people had waited, keeping a time of mourning for a whole month. But it was time now to go on to the new homeland.

"Be strong and fearless," God told Joshua again. "Listen to me. Obey me, and you will win every war.

"Be strong and fearless. Whatever happens, you will know that I am right beside you."

The first thing Joshua did was to call a meeting of his officers.

"Tell the people to get food ready and pack up to travel. We are going to cross the Jordan River and move into the country God has promised to give us." Those were the captain's orders.

Across the river was Jericho, a city with a king, an army, and high, strong walls to protect it. Captain Joshua needed to find out just how strong it really was. So, while the people were packing, he ordered two spies out to see what they could discover.

The two men slipped through the city gates that stood wide open in the daytime. They came to a house built right on the city wall, where they met a friendly woman named Rahab. They asked her to give them a place to stay for the night, and they thought they were safe. But somebody went to the king and told him that there were two strange men in the city. That night soldiers came to arrest them.

Rahab hid the men on the roof under stacks of drying flax she was making ready to weave into cloth. The soldiers hunted for them through all the house and across the fields to the river, but found no one. As soon as the soldiers were gone, Rahab hurried up to the roof.

"I know all about you," she whispered. "I know that God has given you this land of ours. I heard how God helped you to cross the Red Sea when you escaped from Egypt. I know how strong you are. I know your God is the true God of all the heaven and earth. We all do, and we are afraid. The whole city is afraid. No one here is really going to fight you.

"You are safe now. Don't forget who kept you safe. When you come back to capture the city, take care of me and my family."

"Promise not to tell anyone you saw us, and we will help you. Get all your family together here in your house. Mark your window with a red cord so that when we come back we will know where you are, and we will see that everyone in this house is safe," the spies promised.

Then Rahab showed them how to escape from the city, even though the gates were locked for the night. She let them down by a rope through the window, straight down the outside of the city wall.

"Run to the hills and hide there while the guards are searching for you. And remember your promise," she called.

"I will remember," each man said as his feet touched the ground.

Rahab tied a red cord to her window as the two shadowy figures disappeared across the fields toward the hills. Two days later they made their report to Captain Joshua. "God has already given us the land. The people have heard about us, and they are afraid. They will not even try to fight us."

Deuteronomy 31; 34:8–12; Joshua 1 and 2

Dry Path Through the River

Early next morning Captain Joshua gave orders to break camp. With tents rolled up and baggage packed, mothers and children, soldiers and priests, and all the flocks of sheep and herds of cattle marched on until they could go no farther.

Just ahead of them was the rushing, flooded Jordan River, deeper than ever now because snow was melting in the hills, and it had rained all spring. There was no way to go on.

Captain Joshua gave his orders.

"God has a plan for us. Tomorrow you will know about it. Get ready now, everyone. Wash your clothes and bathe. Tomorrow will be a special day when God will show you something you will never forget."

They had a sign to watch for. When they saw the priests lift the covered golden ark of God's promise to their shoulders by the long poles that slipped through rings in its corners, they were all to be ready to follow. But not too close. No one knew the road, but that did not matter. God would show them the way.

"From this day, Joshua, I will be making you a greater leader of these people. They will know that I am with you, just as I was always with Moses," God told young Captain Joshua.

The next day Joshua said, "Forward!"

The priests picked up the ark and walked straight ahead. Straight toward the river they walked, then down into the water.

The minute their feet were wet it happened. Upstream the rushing water of the river piled up and stopped. Downstream the water flowed away. The road across became dry.

"Forward!"

The long line of people began to march across the dry river path while the priests stood guarding the ark. Hurrying, marching lines trudged all day long. Finally everyone was safe on the other side.

Before the priests followed them, Joshua gave another order. He chose twelve men, one from each of the tribes, and he said:

"Bring twelve stones from the river bed for us to carry with us. Someday when your children ask you, 'What do those stones mean?' you will say, 'They remind us of the time God took us safely across the river.'

"And pile another twelve stones there in the middle of the dry river bed for another memorial."

The twelve men obeyed the captain's orders.

"Forward!" The priests walked on safely. Behind them the deep flooded river roared and splashed again on its way.

Eight miles ahead were the high walls of Jericho. But the Israelites did not worry. They stopped along the way to celebrate.

First they piled the stones they had brought from the bottom of the river into a monument.

Those stones were to say for all the time to come:

"God's care for us
Our love for God."

Joshua 3 and 4

When the Trumpets Sounded

There was plenty of food to eat on this side of the river. It was not like the hot, dry desert country where the Israelites had lived for so long. Now it was harvest time, and the grain was ripe. From the grain the people could make bread, so they did not need God's manna any more. The new land was going to be a good place to live.

Captain Joshua stood outside Jericho looking up at the high walls. He was alone, for the frightened people inside had locked the gates of the city. No one went out, and no one could go in.

Suddenly he saw someone else—an armed stranger whose sword flashed in the sunlight.

"Whose side are you on?" Joshua asked.

"I am here as the commander of God's army." Once more God was showing that he was always near.

"Jericho is yours. But keep none of the treasure you find for yourselves," God told him. "This is what you must do."

Joshua listened carefully to the plan for capturing the strong, walled city. And then he obeyed without asking a single question.

Early in the morning the strange attack began. First the soldiers lined up. Then came the priests carrying trumpets made of sheep's horns. Behind them other priests carried the golden ark of God's promise. The rear guard of soldiers was last of all.

"Forward, march!"

Once around the city wall the people marched. The only sounds were the music of the trumpets and the tread of marching feet.

Next day they marched round the city again. There was no sound but the trumpets and the marching feet.

Six days they marched round the city, just once around. There was no sound but trumpets and marching, marching feet.

Just as it began to be light on the seventh morning the army and the priests formed in line again.

"March round the city," the captain ordered. "Forward, march!"

There was no sound but the trumpets and the marching feet. Again, "Forward, march!"

Six times they marched round Jericho.

"Ready, march! And shout!" the order went out to the soldiers and all the people.

The noise of shouting and trumpets and marching feet boomed outside the high-walled city as the Israelites marched round for the seventh time that morning.

From the city walls a low rumble grew to a loud roar. The air was filled with clouds of dust. Cracking, crumbling, crashing, the walls were falling. When the noise died away there was no wall. The great, strong city of Jericho was wide open to Joshua's army.

In a section of the ruined wall where a house was still standing, a red cord hung from a window. As Joshua led his army down the city streets he called for his two spies.

"Guard that house. Protect the family," said the captain.

From that day Captain Joshua was famous in all the land. From that day Joshua knew that God would give him strength and courage.

Joshua 5:10–15; 6

Stolen Treasure

After the battle of Jericho, General Joshua made plans for his army to invade the hill country. About thirty miles away, up on a rocky slope, was the town of Ai. Its walls looked high and strong, but Joshua sent out a scouting party to find out how strong the town really was. The men brought back this report:

"Ai is just a little town. Don't bother to send out the whole army. A small force can easily take the whole place."

So a small army—about three thousand men—marched up the hill to capture Ai. But out from behind the high gray walls the men of Ai came swarming down the hill, and they chased Joshua's soldiers far into the valley. Some were killed as they tried to escape. The rest ran back to camp.

The general heard the bad news, and he was afraid. He went straight to talk it over with God, and in front of the ark he bowed so low that he lay face downward on the ground.

"What has happened, Lord God? How am I going to explain this to all the people? Why did our men run away like cowards?"

"Get up, Joshua. You never will be able to win your wars as long as you disobey me. You have kept for yourselves treasure from Jericho I told you to let alone. Find out who did it and punish him, for you lost the battle because of him."

Next morning Joshua questioned the families. Who in all of Israel had stolen jewels or gold or silver from Jericho instead of giving all the treasures of the captured city to God?

"I did," Achan confessed. "I found a beautiful coat and a great heap of silver coins and a bar of gold, and I hid them in the ground under my tent."

Joshua sent men to dig for the buried treasure. They came back reporting that Achan's story was true. So the given-to-God things were all returned, but Achan's punishment was death, and they buried him in the Valley of Trouble.

"Now go back to Ai, for I have given you the town," God told Joshua. And so, with God to help him, Joshua made plans for the second attack. This time he wanted a big army.

"Go quietly round by the west and north of the hill and hide—" Joshua gave that order to all but five thousand of the men. He told the others: "We will march up the valley road. When the enemy comes out after us, we will turn and run away again. Then you are to advance from the other side, slip into the town, and set fire to every house."

Next morning the king of Ai saw that his enemies were back again. This was going to be easy. His army went charging out the gate in the high wall, down the road, every man of them, to chase away the Israelites.

Joshua raised his spear. From behind rocks and bushes men sprang up by the hundreds, and they swarmed into the undefended town.

The proud, shouting men of Ai looked back to see clouds of smoke rising over Ai. They tried to run back, but the army of Joshua was in front, behind, all around, and there was no way to escape.

And so General Joshua captured Ai. *Joshua 7; 8:1–29*

A Roadside Dedication

There came a day for worship instead of war. The people had come to a green valley between rocky, bare Mount Ebal and tree-covered Mount Gerizim, and each so near the other that a man could stand in the valley and be heard speaking on all the hills. General Joshua gave orders to stop.

Up on Mount Ebal he had his men build an altar where they could worship God with their sacrifice gifts. Of heavy, new, unused stone they made it, and they covered it with white plaster. On the smooth sides Joshua wrote God's laws for his people, the very same laws that God had given to Moses long ago when they were living in the wilderness country.

The men and the women and the children, and the neighbors who chose to live with the Israelites, stood on the mountain slope, and they listened as Joshua read from Moses' message to the people he loved.

> The Lord your God brings you to a good land,
> A land of brooks of water,
> Of fountains and springs from valleys and hills,
> A land full of grain and fruit, olive trees and honey.

> Forget not the Lord your God,
> Forget not to keep his commandments.

For when you listen to him, keep his laws,
Blessed shall you be in the city, and
Blessed shall you be in the field.
Blessed shall you be when you come in, and
Blessed shall you be when you go out.
For you the Lord God opens his treasures.

> Remember, listen to his commandments;
> Remember, listen, and obey.

So the people worshiped together. And now they understood that the laws of God, which had been their laws while they were traveling, were the laws of the land where they would live.

Joshua 8:30–35; Deuteronomy 8:7; 27:3–8; 28:3–6, 12

Tricky Travelers from Gibeon

Now the news of General Joshua and his fine brave army spread quickly through the land, so that even the kings from the faraway places by the sea were afraid. They all made an agreement among themselves to fight together against him. But the people from Gibeon made peace by a trick.

One day some strange-looking men came riding into Joshua's camp. Their clothes were ragged. Their shoes were shabby and dusty. The food they carried with them was old, dry, moldy bread in worn-out sacks. This was their story:

"Away off in our land, a long, long way from here, we heard about you and your God who is so powerful. Our people told us we must come to you to ask for a truce."

"But how do we know you are not really from some strong place nearby?" Joshua's men asked. "We cannot make a truce with any of the people living among us."

"Oh, no, we don't live anywhere near. Look. When we left home long ago these shoes were new. These clothes were clean and bright-colored. This old, dry bread was still warm from the oven. Look at these clothes. Look at this bread. You can see how far we have traveled."

So Joshua and his leaders made a truce with the strangers and promised that there would never be war between them. Then the men rode away.

But three days later, as Joshua and his men were traveling through the new homeland, they came to the strong, rich towns of Gibeon. There they discovered all their friends from the "faraway" land. But Joshua had promised not to fight them, and he must keep his promise. So it was decided this way.

"We will not fight you, but you cannot go free. You and all your people are to be woodcutters and water-bearers for the altar sacrifices to our God."

"We are your prisoners. We will do whatever you say," they gladly agreed.

And so it was from that time on.

Joshua 9

The Battle of the Longest Day

The king of Jerusalem heard how General Joshua won the battle of Ai and how the Gibeon people made a truce, and he was afraid. So he set out with four other kings of the mountain people to punish the people of Gibeon.

"Come quickly! We need your help," they sent word to General Joshua.

"Do not be afraid to go, Joshua," the general heard God say. "There is not a man who is strong enough to fight against you."

So the rescue party set out at once. Up the hills, over the passes, down the steep slopes, all night they chased the armies of the mountain kings. There came a terrible hailstorm, and more of the fleeing soldiers were killed by the huge hailstones than by Joshua's men.

Yet the day was not long enough for all that Joshua must do, and so he prayed. He asked:

> "Sun, be still upon the mountain,
> And moon, over the valley below."

And the sun was still, and the moon waited while the people fought and the battle was won.

There was no day like that day before or afterward.

Joshua 10:1–14

Homesteaders in a New Land

For seven years General Joshua led the fighting in the new homeland. The time had come to divide up the land among the tribes. It was time for the families to settle down on their own land, to build their houses, and to plant their crops.

Thirty-one kings had been conquered. There were still some enemy people living on the boundaries of their land. But when each tribe of families moved to its own place, the men of the tribe could defend their own homes.

"Your work is done, so divide the land among the tribes." General Joshua received his last orders from God, and so for the last time he called his people together.

At Shiloh, midway between north and south, they set up the tent of meeting, and there it was to stay for many years. Inside the tent they placed the ark of God's promise safely behind the inner curtain.

Then Joshua began to tell the families of each tribe where they were going to live. And so at last the people came home: Reuben, Simeon, Judah, Issachar, Zebulun, Benjamin, Dan and Naphtali, Gad and Asher—all the tribes but Levi's. The men of the Levite people were the priests, just as Moses had chosen them. They were not to live in any one place, but they were to be God's ministers, to help and teach the people throughout the country. Joshua sent Levite families to live in forty-eight towns, and near each town he gave them land for their gardens.

While Joshua was dividing the land, Caleb came to ask for land of his own. As Joshua listened he thought of the day years and years ago when the two of them reported on their spying mission over the border of the Promised Land.

"Remember what Moses said when you and I were not afraid to tell the truth?" Caleb began. "He promised me then that I was to have some land. Look at me. The Lord God has let me live till I am eighty-five, but I'm just as good a fighter as I ever was. Remember where we found the giants of Anak? Let me have the mountain where the giants live. This will be my home, and if God will help me, I will drive them all out."

So Joshua gave Caleb the mountain where the giants lived. It was the land he chose. *Joshua 13 to 21*

The General's Good-by

General Joshua was very, very old, and he knew that he was going away, as all men must go. So he called the people of Israel together, for he had a message to give them, a message he had heard from God himself.

"Long ago your great-great-grandfathers lived across the great river, and they worshiped idols as the people around them did. Then I brought Abraham out from that country and led him here to Canaan. Here I gave him his son Isaac. And to Isaac I gave his sons, Jacob and Esau. Esau I sent to Edom to live, but Jacob and his family traveled to Egypt. When you were slaves I sent Moses and Aaron to rescue you, and I punished Egypt.

"You came as far as the sea, with the Egyptians close behind you, and when you prayed for help I sent the darkness to hide you until you escaped. Then you lived in the wilderness a long, long time, and I brought you here where I drove out the people, but not with your swords or your bows and arrows.

"I have given you a land you did not work for, and towns you did not build, and orchards and fields you did not plant."

Joshua went on speaking.

"You have seen all that God has done for you. Now be brave enough to keep on following him. When the Lord God fights for you, one man of you will be strong enough to chase a thousand.

"In your hearts you know that God has kept his word to you. Of all the blessings he promised, not one has failed to come to you.

"Now honor God by serving him truly and honestly. If this seems wrong to you, then decide whom you are going to serve—either those idols of the people across the great river or the idols of the people who used to live here.

"As for me and all my family, we will serve the Lord God only."

All the people answered,

> "We will serve the Lord, for he is our God,
> And when he speaks we will obey."

So Joshua wrote down a record of their promise, and he had a great stone set up there for a monument to mark the place.

Then they all traveled to their own land to work to build their homes. But Joshua died that day, and was buried on a hillside on his own land.

Joshua 23 and 24; Judges 2:6–9

THE HERO JUDGES

Judge Ehud's Victory

YEARS WENT BY in the new homeland, and now the people who had been children when General Joshua died were men and women, and their children were growing up. People were forgetting their promises to love God and worship him only. They were building altars where they prayed to the gods of the heathen people of the land. And always when they forgot God there was trouble.

In those days there were no kings or generals to lead the people. Each one said, "I do what I think is right." And, with no leaders to tell them what to do, the people were too weak to fight their enemies.

Those were the times of the judges or champions. When the people remembered to ask God for help, he would send them a leader to be their judge in peace time and their general when there was trouble.

This is the story of left-handed Judge Ehud, who saved his people from big King Eglon.

The people had forgotten God's ways, and when big King Eglon captured Jericho they were too weak to defend themselves. For eighteen long years they had to work for King Eglon. But when they remembered, when they asked God to rescue them, he sent them a leader named Ehud.

Greedy, cruel King Eglon must somehow be removed, Ehud knew. This was his plan: He would go to visit King Eglon, and he would say that he was bringing a present from the people of Israel. But, hidden under his coat, he would also be carrying a two-edged dagger.

When he arrived, Ehud gave his present to the king. Then he said,

"I have a secret message for you, O king."

King Eglon sent away all his people, and he invited Ehud to meet him in his private summer room on the roof of the palace.

With the two-edged dagger Ehud stabbed the king. Then he slipped out of the room, locking the door behind him; and he escaped from the palace.

The guards thought their king was resting and did not want to be disturbed. So it was a long time before anyone discovered what had happened. Judge Ehud had time to get safely away to the hill country.

With his trumpet he sounded the call to arms, and he led the Israelites in a great battle against their enemies. After that there was peace for eighty years. *Judges 2:10–18; 3:12–30; 17:6*

Captain Lightning's Muddy Battle

After left-handed Judge Ehud died, the people began to forget God again. First they built some altars where they worshiped the gods of their neighbors. Then they let God's altars tumble down. And then trouble came.

King Jabin lived in the north country near the sea. Once, long before, Captain Joshua and his army had fought King Jabin and four other kings from the north. There had been a great battle, and the kings had run for their lives.

Down from the north country King Jabin's army came riding in iron chariots drawn by galloping horses. Captain Sisera and his soldiers stole whatever they wanted from the Israelites, and they made the people pay huge taxes to King Jabin.

Soon there was no Israelite army left to fight, no shields or spears to fight with. No one traveled on the highways any more.

They hurried along on their journeys by back roads and lanes.

For twenty years everyone did just what King Jabin ordered. And then at last the people remembered God. Sorry and ashamed, they asked him to help them.

In a house shaded by a palm tree there lived a family who obeyed God and kept his laws. The mother was Deborah—Judge Deborah, the people called her, for they used to go to see her to ask for advice and help. She listened to their troubles, and as she listened she became sure that God wanted her to help them.

She sent for the man she chose for her people's leader. Barak, or Lightning, was his name.

"This is God's commission," she told him. "You are to enlist an army of ten thousand men and take them to camp on Mount Tabor. Captain Sisera is going to take his army down the valley by the Kishon Brook, and you can attack him there."

"I can't do it by myself. You go with me."

"If I do, the honor of winning will go to a woman, not to you," she warned him.

A new brave army of volunteers followed Captain Barak to the mountain camp. Down in the valley the tent people were watching. When Captain Sisera came riding that way, one of them showed him the way the new army had gone.

So Sisera led out his army, all his soldiers, his nine hundred iron chariots, and his galloping horses.

"Up, Barak! Up, Lightning! This is the day of your victory. God is out there waiting for us," Deborah shouted.

Ten thousand soldiers charged down the mountain. As they advanced on the enemy, storm clouds darkened the sky. The mountain shook in the noise of the wind and the thunder. The rain poured down in torrents, and the brook turned into a rushing river. Out over the flat plain poured the flood waters, and mud held the chariot wheels fast.

King Jabin's soldiers leaped from their chariots. They struggled to get away, but they slipped and fell under their own horses' trampling feet. Captain Barak's army was everywhere, like the storm. Not a soldier escaped.

Captain Sisera ran for his life, away from the plain, away from the battle, and he came to the homes of the tent people.

"Come in and rest, sir. Lie down. Lie down and rest," he heard the woman Jael saying. He did not stop to find out whether she was a fighter like all the rest of the Israelites.

"I'm so thirsty. Give me a drink," he begged as he lay down, and she covered him with a blanket.

She brought him fresh milk, and he told her, "You stand there in the tent door, and if anyone comes by asking whether a man is here, you say no." Then he went to sleep.

Jael was a fighter. She had no spear, but she picked up a tent stake for a sword, and with a hammer in the other hand, she drove it through his head as he lay sleeping.

So Captain Sisera died, and the Israelites were free from King Jabin. But the songs they sang about the victory gave the honor to a woman.

>Praise to the Lord who fought for Israel
>When the people had a mind to fight.
>Hear, all you kings, and listen, you princes,
>For God himself fought from the heavens.
>Earth shook, and the skies poured down rain;
>The stars in their courses fought against Sisera,
>And the flood swept his army away.
>Honor to Jael, of all women!
>At her feet he bowed, he fell, he lay down;
>Where he bowed, there he fell dead.
>May all of God's enemies die as he died,
>And all who love God be strong,
>Like the shining glory of the sun.

Judges 4 and 5

How Gideon Was Drafted

The people of Israel were in trouble again. The farmers sowed their seed and prayed to the god Baal to send them good crops. But before they could harvest their grain, the camel riders from the south country came trampling over their fields. Midianite raiders swarmed over the country thick as clouds of grasshoppers, stealing and burning and destroying. When they went away there was no food left for people or animals.

For seven years it went on. Miserable and poor and hungry, the people were hiding in caves in the hills. Then at last they remembered their broken promises, and they begged God to forgive them and to help them.

In a secret place a little below the ground, where the farmers used to press out the juice from their grapes, a man named Gideon was threshing his father's wheat. He hoped the Midianites would not find him. Looking up from his work, he saw the Lord's angel sitting in the shade of an oak tree.

"God is with you, man of great strength."

Gideon stood up straight.

"If he is, why do we have so much trouble? Why has he turned us over to the Midianites?"

"Go and rescue your people from them."

"Oh, my Lord, you can't mean me. Why, my family is poor, and I'm the youngest, least important person in the family."

"You can be sure that I will be with you," insisted the angel messenger.

Gideon was thinking it over.

"My Lord, if you really want me, show me a sign to help me believe this is all true. Let me go and get you something to eat; and wait, I beg you, till I come back."

In a few minutes he returned with a lunch of roasted meat, fresh bread, and soup. The angel messenger was waiting.

"Take the meat and bread and lay them on this rock. Now pour out the soup on the ground," Gideon heard the strange order.

But he obeyed without a question. The angel touched the food with the end of his traveler's staff. The offering burst into flames, and the whole feast was burned just as the sacrifice offerings to God were burned. But the angel guest had disappeared. Gideon built an altar of the rocks that were lying on the ground.

That night in his father's house, where the Baal altar smoked with burning sacrifice gifts to the heathen idol and the wooden worship pole stood high beside it, Gideon could not sleep.

"Gideon, tear down the Baal altar. Cut down the pole. Build instead an altar for God. Split the worship pole into firewood for God's altar, and offer a sacrifice gift there to him."

While it was still dark, Gideon went out to find ten of his most trusted servants to help him. And when the sun came up, the old altar was gone. Smoke was rising from God's altar.

"Who did it? Who dared?" people were asking.

"Gideon, son of Joash, did it. Bring him out! Punish him!" They were pounding on the door.

Gideon's father stood quietly beside the new altar.

"If Baal is a real god, let him fight for himself and prove it," he said. No one said a word.

Judges 6:1–32

How the Captain Chose His Army

Bad news came to Gideon's house. Over in the valley the camel riders from Midian and all the Amalekite people were camping, getting ready for a big raid.

Gideon picked up his trumpet and sounded a warning that would bring every fighting man who could hear it. He sent messengers to the faraway towns and called for volunteers. But Gideon himself was not yet sure that he was the right man to lead them.

"Lord God, if I am really the man you want, show me a sign," he asked. "Tonight I'll lay a fleece of wool on the ground. Let the dew fall only on the wool, and all the ground around be dry. Then I'll know."

Early the next morning Gideon picked up a sopping wet fleece and squeezed a bowlful of water from it. All the ground around was dry.

But he wanted to be very, very sure.

"Lord, my God, don't be angry with me. Just one more time, let me lay the fleece on the ground. If all the ground is wet and the wool alone is dry, I will be sure."

Next morning he picked up the dry fleece, and he saw that only it was dry.

Thousands of men were answering his call to fight. By every road the volunteers came marching, and their big camp was set up just to the south of the Midianite camp. Gideon was sure now that he could win with his big army. But God's plans were different.

"Gideon, the army is too big. When you win, the people will claim they won the victory. They must learn that they can win only with God's help. Tell those who are afraid to go home."

The captain watched them go. Twenty-two thousand men went back home. But he still had an army of ten thousand soldiers.

"Gideon, the army is too big. Take the men to the river, and tell them to drink. Put in one group those who stop just long enough to scoop up the water in their hands and lap it the way a dog drinks. Put in another group those who kneel to drink."

Gideon obeyed. God told him to send home those men who knelt to drink and to keep those who drank from their hands. Just three hundred men were left.

"By the three hundred men I will save you, Gideon."

Judges 6:33–40; 7:1–7

The Battle of Lights and Noise

Over in the hills the great, strong army from Midian was waiting.

"Gideon, are you afraid?" In the night Gideon heard his Lord speaking. "Take your orderly with you, and slip over to the enemy camp. Listen to their talk."

So the two men crept out in the darkness. From the other camp they heard voices.

"Friend, I just had the strangest dream. I thought I saw a little piece of barley bread fall down on one of our tents, and the tent came down." (Hebrews were so poor that they ate barley bread.)

"Bad news, soldier! That could be nothing else but the sword of Captain Gideon. Their God has already won the battle for him."

Listening, Captain Gideon bowed his head. Quickly the men went back to camp.

"Up, men! God has given us the victory," he sent out the word. He divided his three hundred soldiers into three groups of one hundred each, and he told them to surround the camp. He gave to every man a lighted torch, a trumpet, and an empty pitcher.

"Watch me. Do as I do," he said as he hid the light of his torch inside his pitcher.

"When I blow my trumpet, shout:

Gideon Tests His Soldiers

" 'For the Lord! For Gideon!'

"Then smash your pitchers."

There was not a sound as the three companies crept around the Midianite camp. Suddenly Gideon's trumpet blared out in the stillness.

"For the Lord! For Gideon!" three hundred voices shouted.

Trumpets! Smashing pitchers! Three hundred blazing torches lighting the whole camp!

"For the Lord! For Gideon!"

The men stayed where they were, but the frightened Midianite soldiers woke from a sound sleep and began to fight one another.

The trumpets sounded again, and the great army of Midian and the Amalekite neighbors began to run. Gideon and his men were close behind them. Soldiers from neighbors' lands joined them. Across fields and hills and valleys they chased the invaders, all the way to the Jordan River and far on the other side.

And so at last the Lord won the victory for Gideon, and for a long, long time there was no more fighting in the land.

Judges 7:8–25

Story of the Talking Trees

As soon as Gideon's war was won, the grateful people wanted to make him their king, and his son king after him. But Gideon would not listen to them.

"God is your king. I will not rule over you. Nor shall any of my sons be king," he told them.

After Gideon died, people again began to forget about God. But the sons of Gideon did not forget that the Israelites had wanted their father to be king.

"All of us brothers cannot be your leader. It's much better for you to have one of us. So I shall be your king," Abimelech announced. Then he ordered that all the other brothers should be killed. But Jotham, the youngest brother, escaped, and he fled to the mountains. He told his friends this story.

"The trees went out to find a king who would rule over them. They asked the olive tree, " 'Come and be our king.'

" 'Should I give up my good olive oil and go to be head of the trees?' the olive tree answered.

"So they asked the fig tree to be their king.

" 'Should I give up my good, sweet fruit and go to be head of the trees?'

"So they asked the grapevine, 'Come and be our king.'

" 'Should I give up my sweet juice and go to be head of the trees?'

"So they went to the briar bush.

" 'If you want me to be your king, then come here and stay in my shade,' answered the briar bush that made no shade at all. 'But if you don't, I'll set fire to the woods and burn down the forest.'

"Now," said Jotham when he had finished his story, "if you have really honored my father by letting my brother be king, all is well. But if not, he will destroy you as the forest is destroyed by the briar bush fire."

After that he had to run for his life and hide. And there was fighting and trouble among the people, like fire in the forest, all the days that his brother was king. *Judges 8:22–23; 9:1–21, 57*

"Say the Password"

Other judges there were in Israel—Ibzan, who had thirty sons and thirty daughters; and Abdon, whose forty sons and thirty grandsons rode on seventy donkey colts. And there was the judge named Jephthah, who used a clever speech test to trap escaping soldiers.

Before Jephthah became a judge his jealous stepbrothers had run him out of the country. But when soldiers from Ammon attacked Israel, the wise old men sent for him.

"Come and be our captain," they begged. And when they promised he could be their chief when the fighting was over, he went home with them.

This was the way he used the speech test: His men were trying to capture soldiers of Ephraim who were slipping across the river. Now everyone knew that the people of Ephraim could not make the sound of "sh." So when a soldier came asking to be allowed to cross the river, orders were:

"Make him say 'shibboleth.'" (The word meant either a river or an ear of grain.)

"Sibboleth," a man would say.

"Arrest him!"

"Shibboleth."

"Pass, soldier."

So it went on as long as there was a single escaping soldier left, and not one got away. *Judges 12:8–9,13–15; 11:1–11; 12:4–6*

Strong Fighter for Israel

Who in all the land had not heard about Samson the strong man, who fought his people's enemies and was so powerful that no one could capture him?

Before he was born, his mother knew he was to be a great hero. That was in the days when the Philistines, who came of the pirate people from the sea, used to raid the farms and towns of Israel.

"You will have a son," an angel told her when she had no children at all. "You must see that he never drinks any wine. He must not eat any of the forbidden meats. He is to be a Nazirite in God's service, and as a sign, he is to let his hair grow long.

"When he is grown to be a man, he will fight for his country and drive out the Philistines."

Who in all the land had not heard of Samson's cleverness?

One day as he was traveling through the country a lion attacked him. With his bare hands Samson the strong tore the animal in pieces and left the body lying on the ground.

Not long afterward he came that way again. He discovered that a swarm of bees had settled in the lion's body, and that it was full of honey. With both hands he tore off pieces of honeycomb and ate it as he walked along.

Then he made up a riddle.

> Out of the eater came something to eat,
> And out of the strong came something sweet.
> What is it?

No one could guess the answer until he gave a hint, and then they knew.

> What is sweeter than honey,
> and what is stronger than a lion?

Who in all the land had not heard how he fought against the Philistines, though he had been bound with strong ropes? With his great strength he burst the ropes, and, having no weapon to fight with, he picked up from the road a dried-out piece of bone from a donkey's jaw.

No one was strong enough to fight against him, and the Philistines were beaten off that day.

Who in all the land had not heard his victory song?

> With a donkey's jawbone I have slain them,
> Heaps upon heaps,

> With a donkey's jawbone
> I have slain a thousand men.

Who in all the land had not heard how he escaped in the middle of the night, though the city gates were locked, and the Philistines were only waiting until it was daylight to capture him?

At midnight Samson slipped quietly down to the heavy locked gate in the city wall. He pulled up gate, post and all, put them on his shoulders, and carried them all the way to the top of the hill by Hebron. But when the Philistines went to look for him he was gone.

Who in all the land had not heard how Samson loved a woman named Delilah and how the Philistines tried to make her find out why he was so strong?

"If they do one thing," said Samson, "I'll be like any other man. Tell them to bind me with seven strong new bowstrings that have never been used."

So Delilah let him be bound tight with the seven new bowstrings, and the Philistines hid in the room to see what would happen.

"Samson! Look out! The Philistines are here!" Delilah shouted.

Samson's strong arms burst the seven new bowstrings like threads, and he was free.

"You played a trick on me. Now tell me what really is the secret," Delilah begged.

"Tell them to bind me with new ropes," said Samson. "Then I will be as weak as any other man."

So Delilah let him be bound with new ropes.

But when she shouted, "Samson! The Philistines are here!" he burst the ropes like threads, and he was free.

"You made fun of me. Now tell me what really will hold you," Delilah insisted.

"You weave my hair into the cloth that is being woven on the loom," said Samson.

Samson went to sleep and she did.

"Samson! Wake up! The Philistines are here!"

Samson tossed his head, and away he went, cloth, loom, and all.

After that Delilah pouted and complained and begged and worried him until at last he told the secret.

"I am strong because I am a Nazirite in God's service. My long hair is the sign of my promises to God. If it should ever be cut, my strength would be gone."

He fell asleep, and Delilah sent for a man to cut off his long hair.

"Samson! Wake up! The Philistines are here!"

But Samson was weak, too weak to escape.

They made him their prisoner, and they put out his eyes. Then they carried him to town, and there they chained him in the mill house, and they made him walk round and round, turning the heavy millstone that crushed grain into meal.

People came to watch him, and they laughed and joked to see the strong man working like an animal.

But Samson's hair was growing again.

"It's time for a celebration," said the people. "Dagon our god gave Samson to us. Let's have a feast for him, and we'll bring Samson to amuse us."

So they crowded into the great court of pillars at the temple of Dagon, thousands of them, for the celebration.

"Bring Samson here! Bring him out to make us laugh!" they shouted.

A boy was sent to lead blind Samson out, and he stood by the middle pillars of the great building. People were crowding inside. They were even standing on the roof.

"Put my hands on the pillars," Samson whispered to the boy.

Then he prayed to God just as he used to pray to him long ago.

"Lord God, remember me. Make me strong only this one time. Let me fight the Philistines once more, and I am ready to die with them."

His right hand grasped one pillar. His left hand grasped the other. He bowed his strong back with all his old, fierce strength. The great columns began to crack and to split.

He tore the pillars loose. The roof, already overloaded with the crowds of people, came crashing down on the throng below. Thousands of the Philistines were killed. And Samson, too, died in the ruined building.

Then his sorrowing brothers came to get Samson's body, and they buried him beside the grave of his father, Manoah, the Quiet One.

Who in all the land has not heard how in his death Samson did more to help his people against the Philistines than in all the twenty years he was their leader?

Judges 13 to 16

Stolen Silver, Stolen Priest

It was in the time when the people of Israel had no king to be their leader, and each man decided for himself what he should do. Up in the hill country near Mount Ephraim a man named Micah said to his mother,

"Remember the money that was stolen from you? I took it, and I have it now."

And he gave her back all the money he had stolen.

"May God give you his blessing, Son. I wanted you to have that money all the time. I promised I would give it to you to make a silver image so we could worship God."

So she took some of the silver to the silver maker, who melted it and made an image. Then Micah ordered a priest's coat to be made. He chose one of his sons to be the priest and lead them in their family worship.

Down near Bethlehem there lived a young man who was one of the Levite people, a real priest. As he set out to find a place to live, he came to Mount Ephraim to Micah's house. Micah said,

"Stay with us. Be like my father. Be our family priest, and I will pay you with money and a suit of new clothes every year, a place to live, and food to eat."

So the Levite stayed at Micah's house, and Micah was proud.

"Now the Lord God will be good to me, because I have a real Levite for my own priest," he said.

Of all the people of Israel the families of the tribe of Dan had not yet settled down on their own land in the new homeland. About this time they sent out five strong, wise men of the tribe to explore the country and find the best place to settle.

The five men came to Mount Ephraim to Micah's house, and

there they spent the night. When they heard the Levite talking, they recognized his voice.

"How did you get here? What are you doing?" they asked.

"Micah hired me for his priest."

"Then ask God's advice. Shall we go on this way? Will we find the place we are hunting?"

"Go in peace. God sees the way you are going."

So the men traveled on, and they found just the land they wanted. They returned home, and they came back with the rest of the tribe. On the way they stopped at Micah's house, and they picked up the image and the priest's coat.

"What are you doing?" demanded the Levite.

"Sh! Come with us and be our priest. Isn't it better to be priest for a whole tribe than for just one family?"

So the Levite decided to go along with them.

But Micah was angry, and he and his friends set out after the strangers and shouted for them to come back.

"Why, Micah, what is wrong? Why have you come out with all these people?" the men of Dan shouted over their shoulders.

"You've taken the gods I made, and my priest, and what have I left for my own?"

"Micah, don't make so much noise. Some of us might get angry, and you might be killed." The people of Dan kept right on their way.

Micah turned around and went home. They were too strong for him to fight. And in their own land the Dan families built their worship place, and there the Levite priest led them when they worshiped God.

That is the way it was in the time when the people had no leader, and every man decided for himself what he should do.

Judges 17; 18:1–26

THE STORY OF RUTH

It was in the time of the judges, and there was famine in the land, even in Bethlehem, called the "House of Bread." But in Moab beyond the Salt Sea there was plenty to eat.

So Elimelech and his wife Naomi and their sons, Mahlon and Chilion, moved to Moab.

There the boys grew up and married. There the father died, and later the sons died, too. So Naomi was alone, far away from home, with her Moabite daughters-in-law.

By this time travelers were reporting that there was food for all in the country round Bethlehem. So Naomi decided to go home. She and the girls started out to travel together, but they had gone only a little way when Naomi stopped. Gently she said to Ruth and Orpah,

"You need not come with me. Go back to your own mothers. May the Lord God be as kind to you as you have been to me, and may he help you to find homes of your own."

"No, we will go with you," they insisted.

She would not listen. Instead, she told them good-by. Finally Orpah kissed her and walked away.

"You go with her," Naomi urged Ruth.

But Ruth's arms were round Naomi, and her words were full of love.

"Ask me not to leave you. Let me follow you. For where you go I will go, too. Where you stay I will stay. Your people shall be my people. Your God shall be my God. Where you die I will die, and there will I be buried."

So the two traveled on together, and at last they came home to Bethlehem. At first Naomi's old friends hardly knew her.

"Can this be Naomi, the Happy One?" they wondered.

"Not Naomi, not Happy. Call me Mara, the Sad One," the lonely woman told them.

She had no money. But there was a way even Ruth the stranger might earn their food.

It was in the early summer, and all the farmers and their workers were busy out in the fields harvesting the barley crop. There was an old, old law in the land about the harvest. When there was food, all must share, even the poor who had no land. This was the law of the gleaners.

"When you harvest your grain, leave a little in the fence corners and at the end of the rows. If you drop an armful, let it stay where it is. This shall be for strangers."

"Let me go out and see who will let me glean in his fields," Ruth offered.

"Go, my daughter."

So the girl from Moab went to work with the girls of Bethlehem, and she happened to go to the fields of the farmer named Boaz. And the neighbors, seeing how the stranger went out to work for Naomi, nodded their heads and smiled.

Work in the fields was going well when Boaz went out to check on his harvesters.

"The Lord be with you," he greeted them.

"The Lord bless you," they answered.

He noticed the stranger at work with his own people.

"Who is she?" he wanted to know.

"Why, she is that Moabite who came home with Naomi. She asked permission to glean, and she hasn't stopped working since morning."

"You are welcome here, my daughter. Stay here with us. Whenever you are thirsty, go get a drink from our water jars. And at lunch time go over and get something to eat with my harvesters," Boaz said to Ruth.

© 1963, Broadman Press

Ruth and the Harvesters

"Why are you doing this for me? I don't belong here. I'm a stranger, different from all of you."

Boaz smiled. "I've heard how you left your father and mother and your own people to come home with Naomi. May the Lord God whom you have learned to trust reward you for what you have done."

Ruth went back to her work, and Boaz said quietly to his harvesters, "Be sure to drop extra grain as you go. When you have stacked the sheaves, pull out some and leave it for her."

So Ruth gleaned her barley, and in the evening when she beat the chaff away from the grain she had nearly a bushel to take home. She gave it to Naomi, along with a handful of roasted barley she had saved from her lunch with the harvesters.

"Where have you gleaned today?" Naomi wanted to know. "Whoever took care of you, may the Lord God bless him for his goodness."

"The man is called Boaz," Ruth told her.

"Now the Lord is truly good to us. Boaz is our cousin, one of our nearest kin."

"He told me to stay with his harvesters till the work is over."

"That is well, my daughter."

So Ruth worked straight through the barley harvest, then on through the wheat harvest.

Naomi was making plans. If they worked out, Ruth would have a home of her own and a husband. But it must be done according to the custom of the people.

Since Boaz was their cousin he could buy their land. When he bought it he bought the right to marry Ruth, so that a family might stay with its land. Somehow Ruth must tell him. Naomi made careful plans.

The harvesting was nearly over. In the evening when the breeze blew in from the sea, the men would all go to the wide, flat threshing floor and beat the wheat until the chaff blew off with the wind and the good grain was left. They would work late and sleep there by the grain to guard it.

"My daughter, dress carefully, and wear your best. Go with the others, but don't let Boaz see you till everyone has gone to sleep. Then slip in and lie down at his feet."

"I will," said Ruth.

It was very dark. Quietly she slipped past the heaps of grain and lay down on the ground at Boaz' feet.

"Who's there?" he whispered.

"I'm Ruth, and you are my cousin. You have the right to buy our land."

Boaz could guess the rest. She might have married any one of the young men of Bethlehem, but she had come to him.

"May the Lord God bless you, for you are even kinder to me than you have been to Naomi.

"Don't worry, Ruth. I'll do all you are asking. But there is another man who is even closer kin to you than I, and in the morning I must see whether he wants to claim his right to the land."

Long before it was light Ruth slipped away, carrying her mantle filled almost to bursting with Boaz' gift of grain.

Naomi was waiting.

"What happened, my daughter?"

Ruth told her the whole story, and Naomi nodded, smiling.

"Just wait a little while. The man won't rest till he attends to this business today."

The first thing in the morning Boaz went to the gate in the wall round Bethlehem where all the town went in or out. Before long the man he wanted to see would come by.

He saw the man coming, and he called to him, and he asked ten of the wise old men of the town to stop and be his witnesses.

"The land I would gladly buy, but I cannot marry Ruth," the cousin said when he heard Boaz' story.

So Boaz turned to the people standing round, and he said,

"You are all witnesses that this day I am buying all that belonged to Elimelech and to Chilion and to Mahlon, and I am buying the right to marry Ruth."

"We are witnesses, and may the Lord bless your home," said all the people.

So Ruth and Boaz were married. Then the sad and lonely days were forgotten. And the day a son was born in the home of Boaz and Ruth, all the neighbors came to celebrate with Naomi.

"Blessed is the Lord God who gave you back a family," they said. Naomi held her grandson close in her arms.

The Book of Ruth; Leviticus 19:9; Deuteronomy 24:19

THE MAN WHO ASKED WHY

~~~~~~

Testing Time for Job

LONG AGO in the land of Uz there lived a man whose name was Job, a good man who loved and obeyed God. And he was one of the richest people in all the country round. On his pasture land there were seven thousand sheep, three thousand camels, a thousand oxen, and five hundred donkeys.

In Job's family there were seven sons and three fair daughters. Now each day one of the brothers gave a feast and invited all the others to come. When seven days had gone by, Job would send for them all to come to his house, and the family would worship God together, and Job would ask God to forgive his children for whatever wrongs they had done. After that the feasts began all over again.

One day in the court of heaven the angels and Satan came to give their reports to God.

"Where have you been?" God asked Satan.

"Oh, I've been going here and there on earth, walking up and down."

"Did you ever notice my friend Job? Did you see that there is no one like him on earth, worshiping God and doing no wrong?"

"Why shouldn't he be good? He knows it pays, for you take good care of him and give him everything," answered Satan. "Job is rich and he is getting richer all the time. But just take away the things he has. You'll see how soon he will forget to pray and begin to curse."

"Test him. But do not hurt his body." God was just that sure about his friend Job.

So Satan left the court of heaven.

One day in the home of Job's oldest son, all the sons and daughters were celebrating. A messenger came running to Job.

"The oxen were plowing. The donkeys were grazing right beside them. A band of Arabians attacked us, and they stole the stock and killed the servants. I am the only one left."

Before he finished speaking, another messenger came running to Job.

"We were out in the field, and there was a storm. Lightning struck us, and all the sheep and the shepherds were killed. I'm the only one left."

Before he finished speaking, another messenger came running to Job.

"A storm wind from the desert blew down your son's house, and everyone was killed. I am the only one left."

Poor Job's face showed how deeply he was hurt. But he bowed his head, and this was his prayer:

"I came to earth with nothing, and with nothing I will leave it. The Lord gave. The Lord has taken away. He is good, and I will thank him forever."

There came a day in the court of heaven when the angels and Satan came to give their reports to God.

"Where have you been, Satan?"

"Oh, I've been here and there on earth, walking up and down."

"Did you see my friend Job? Did you see that there is no one like him, worshiping God and doing no wrong?"

"But a man would really fight back for his life. Just let Job get sick, and you'll see how soon he forgets to pray and begins to curse."

"Test him. But you must not take his life." God was just that sure about his friend Job.

So Satan left the court of heaven.

Now Job was miserable. He broke out with sore boils that itched and burned and dried out, only to break open again. His skin turned black and fell off in patches. His eyes burned from crying with the pain. No one wanted to look at him for his ugliness. So he went outdoors and sat down on the ash pile. He picked up a broken piece of a clay pot to scratch his itching skin. And there he sat.

"I wouldn't even try to bear it." That was his wife's advice. "All you have to do is curse God. Then you will die, and it will all be over."

"Foolish talk!" Job said quickly. "The gifts God sends—must they always be what we call good?" *Job 1; 2:1–10*

The Friends Who Came to Help

Three of Job's friends heard about the sick man's troubles, and they came to visit him. But when they saw him they scarcely knew him, so much had the sickness changed him. At first they could not speak. They just sat down beside him. For seven days they stayed there, saying nothing at all.

"Oh, why? I want to know!" Job sobbed at last. "Why didn't God let me die the day I was born? Why does he give life to men, then treat them this way?

"I cannot sleep for the pain when I go to bed. I cannot eat. No one wants me. All the others have gone away. Not one of the servants comes when I call.

"Why must it be? Why doesn't God let me die? I want to know."

"Now, Job, don't get your feelings hurt if we give you some good advice," said friend Eliphaz. "After all, we are older than you—older than your father. Remember how you were always telling other people what they should do? Now you need to listen. Just be patient.

"Remember, God never punishes good people. But the wicked ones—they are always punished. So you must have done something very, very wrong. If I were you, I would pray to God, and I would go on believing everything he does for us is good.

"He sends the rain on earth. He takes care of unhappy people and keeps them safe. Why, you should be glad when God punishes you, for all this must be for your own good. You'll see. Everything will turn out all right."

"But I want to know," Job insisted. "What have I done that was wrong? God, why don't you forgive me? I want to know."

"Now, Job, you can't talk this way," said friend Bildad. "God is a true judge of men. If you do right and pray, then he will reward you. He does not forget a good man. But he will not help the wicked."

"I know," Job agreed. "But I can't find him. Where is he? How does a man talk to God and know he will hear? Where is he?

"Oh, I know he is around when he moves the mountains and turns them upside down. By his power he stretches out the heavens, and he tramples smooth the ocean waves. He made the stars—the Bear, Orion, and the Pleiades. But he passes me by. I cannot find him.

"He gives. He takes away, and I cannot stop him. I cannot even ask him, 'What are you doing?' He is too great for me.

"If he were like a judge on earth, I could go to him and ask for a fair trial. I would say to him, 'You made me, and you gave me my life. You have always taken care of me. Why don't you forgive me and let me alone? God, I want to know!'"

"Now, Job, you probably have not been punished as much as you deserve," said friend Zophar. "What makes you think just hunting for God gives you the right to find him?

"You can't expect to understand God. You are talking like a stupid man, and a stupid man won't be wise till the day a wild donkey's colt is born a man—which is never, of course. Just be good, and everything will be all right."

By that time Job was angry.

"You think you are the only people who know!" he shouted at his friends. "You no-good doctors! Oh, I know—if I were you and you were sick like me, I'd be talking like you. But I have just as much sense as you. I want to talk to God!"

Job 2:11–13; 5:8–27; 8:1–7; 9; 10:1–14; 11

Job's Discoveries

Then Job made his first great discovery. Somehow he began to think more about God, less about himself. He was still sick and grieving over his troubles, still lonely in spite of friends who tried to help. Somehow he knew. He said:

"Everything that lives is in God's hands. All my life I have heard it. Now I know it is true. I am sure. And I know that even if he takes my life, I will still be trusting him.

"Call to me, Lord, and I will answer. Or let me speak, and answer me," he said quietly.

"All I want is to talk with God as a man talks with his neighbor. But he does not answer when I call. It is dark, and I cannot find my way. I do not know where to go.

"But someday surely God will find out about me. Maybe, if my troubles were all written down in a book that would last forever maybe then he would find out."

Then Job made his next discovery, although nothing had changed but his own thinking. Somehow he knew. He said to his friends:

"Someday *I* shall see *God!*

"I know that my Redeemer lives! Someday he will be standing here on earth, and though my body dies, I shall live again. I shall see God. I shall see him for myself."

Job 13:15; 16:21; 17:7,12–13; 19:23–27

"I Want to Understand"

"I cannot find him anywhere. I go ahead, but he is not there. I go back, but I cannot find him. But he knows where I am, and when he has finished testing me, I shall be as he wants me.

"But why did it all happen to me? I want to know. I want to understand.

"Just how do men find understanding? They have discovered all about the earth. They know where to look for silver and gold and iron. But where can they find the answers to their questions?

Where do they find understanding? Can they discover it in the mines? Can they buy it with gold?

"Only God knows the answers. For he weighed out the winds. He measured the waters of the rivers and the oceans. He charted the road for the thunder and the lightning to travel.

"And he told man, 'Obeying God, that is understanding. Keeping away from all that is wrong, that is understanding.'

"I know all that is true. Just the same, I wish everything were just the way it used to be. God was watching over me, and I was sure he was my friend. I walked in the dark unafraid, for his candle lighted my way. My children were with me. When I went walking in the city, people were respectful. Now they laugh when they see me. Those days I was always doing things for others. I helped the orphans and the widows. I found ways to help lame people and blind people.

"Now this pain never lets me rest. It chokes me like a tight collar. I never hurt anyone. I was never proud or selfish. Why has all this happened to me? I want to know."

Would the man never stop talking about how good he was? His friends were angry with him again, and no one spoke. A younger man named Elihu came walking by the trash pile. He listened politely.

"May I speak?" he asked at last. "Job, everyone knows God speaks to us in our dreams or in the punishments he sends us. All this time he has been talking to you.

"You have been wasting your time complaining, saying words that have no meaning. You ought to be asking,

" 'Where is God, my maker, who teaches me songs to sing in the night?' Stand still, Job, and look for God in his thunder, his rainstorms, his clouds, and his shining light spread wide on the ocean. You will not understand him, but you will learn to respect him."

Job 23:8–10; 28; 29; 30; 32; 33

When Job Stopped to Listen

Suddenly the wind came blowing, whirling round the men, and in the sound of the wind Job heard God talking to him.

"Who is this man who talks about things
    he does not know?
Stand up now, Job, like a man.

Where were you when I built the earth?
Where are its foundations?
Who laid the cornerstone
When all the morning stars sang together,
And all the angels shouted for joy?

Who told the ocean to come no farther on the land?
Where is the road to the place where light lives?
Where does the darkness stay, Job?
Have you discovered where the snow is stored?
Can you lead the stars across the sky?
Can you send out the lightning?

Or can you help the wild things to find their food,
The hungry lion cubs, ravens that cry for hunger?
Do you know the secret places where wild goats are born?
Did you teach the eagles how to build their nests
    on the highest rocks?

Are you like God, Job, to argue with him?
If you are, then you are strong enough to save yourself."

Very quietly Job began to answer questions instead of asking.
"Lord, now I know you can do everything. I have been talking without thinking, about things that are too wonderful for me.

"Hear me now, and let me speak, Lord. All this time I have only heard about you. Now I see who you really are."

Job 38; 39:1–2; 42:1–5

And So Job Passed the Test

And now it was friend Eliphaz' turn to listen instead of talking, while God spoke.

Job was not being punished. Trouble is not God's sign that people have done wrong.

"Now take seven bulls and seven rams, and give them to Job for a present, and he will pray for you," God told the men.

So Job prayed for his friends, and when he prayed for them, this is what happened.

His brothers and his sisters and all his friends came to his house to eat dinner with him and sympathize with him, and each one brought him a gift.

Now God gave Job twice as much as he ever had before. Well again, he went back to work. And before long, he had twice as many animals as before—fourteen thousand sheep, and six thousand camels, two thousand oxen, and a thousand donkeys. Seven sons and three daughters were born in his family. And in all the land none were so fair as the daughters of Job.

Job 42

JUDGE SAMUEL

God Sent a Baby

HANNAH and her husband, Elkanah, lived at Ramah, up in the hill country near Mount Ephraim. From Ramah it was only eleven miles to the house of God at Shiloh, the place where the ark of God's promise was always carefully guarded. Eli, the kindly old minister, was the one who kept the house of God, and he and his sons were in charge of the sacrifice offerings the people brought to God.

One year the family from Ramah came bringing their gifts. It was a time of celebration, but Hannah did not feel like being gay with the others. So she slipped away, and just inside the house of God she began to pray. Her eyes were red from crying. Her lips were moving. But only God could hear the words she was whispering.

"Lord God, remember me," she was pleading. "Give me a son. Let me have a baby, and I promise that I will lend him to you as long as he lives."

She acted so strangely that Eli, who was sitting nearby, noticed her, and he was worried.

"How long will you go on like this?" he scolded gently.

"My lord, I have been doing nothing wrong. I have just been telling God all my troubles."

"Then go your way in peace. And may God give you all that you asked in your prayer."

Hannah smiled, and then she went back to meet the others, and they all feasted together.

A year went by. Once again Elkanah and the people of his

house went to Shiloh to take their gifts and worship. But this time Hannah stayed at home in Ramah taking care of their very new baby, the boy they named Samuel, which meant, "I asked God for him."

When Samuel was old enough they all went to Shiloh together. Hannah and Elkanah carried gifts for Eli, and Hannah told him,

"Sir, I am the woman you saw standing here praying for this child. Now God has given me all that I asked. So now I give my son to him. As long as he lives he will belong to God."

And the family prayed there together. *1 Samuel 1*

God Spoke to a Boy

The boy Samuel moved into the house of God to live there with Eli and help him tend the lamps and guard the ark of God's promise and meet the people when they brought their gifts to God.

Every year his father and mother came back to Shiloh for a visit. Every year his mother brought him a new coat she had made from linen cloth she spun out of flax that grew in the fields at Ramah.

Eli would give them his blessing:

"May the Lord send you other children to take the place of the boy you have lent to him."

A little girl, then another, and three small boys were born in the home at Ramah. But the oldest brother never left Eli.

Now Eli was gentle and good. But his sons were selfish and evil. Up to the house of God the people brought their gifts of meat which were to be boiled in huge kettles and then shared by all together. But Eli's sons would run out with long forks and spear the best meat for themselves. When someone would bring meat to be roasted on the altar as a gift to God, the sons would send a servant out to beg,

© 1957, The Sunday School Board, S.B.C.

Samuel Helping in the Temple

"Meat for God's ministers!"

Then he would take away the best part of the roast before it could be offered to God.

It was dark one night in the house of God, and very still. The old man, Eli, who was almost blind now, was sound asleep. The lamps were burning dimly. Young Samuel, too, was asleep.

"Samuel!"

Samuel called sleepily,

"Here I am," And he ran to see what Eli wanted.

"I did not call. Go back to sleep."

So Samuel went back to bed.

"Samuel!"

"Here I am."

Samuel stood beside Eli's bed.

"I did not call, son. Go back to sleep."

The third time Samuel ran to Eli the old man said,

"Go back, and if you hear the call again, say,

" 'Speak to me, Lord. Your servant is listening.' "

And the voice called again:

"Samuel! Samuel!"

"Speak to me, Lord. Your servant is listening."

Then God talked to Samuel.

"I am going to punish the sons of Eli for their wickedness. Because he has never tried to stop their evil ways the whole family must be punished."

Samuel did not sleep any more that night. Early in the morning he slipped quietly out and opened the doors of the house of God, but he said nothing at all to Eli.

"Samuel, my son," he heard the old man call.

"Here I am."

"Tell me what happened. You must not keep anything back."

So Samuel told him the sorry story.

"The Lord God does what he knows is right," Eli said quietly.

From that time on Samuel was growing up, with God to teach him and guide him. And he remembered all that God taught him, so that soon the people learned that they could trust him and take his advice, for they knew that he was wise and good. The whole country knew that he was their next leader. *1 Samuel 2:11–36; 3*

No Magic in the Ark

There was more and more fighting going on now, for the Philistines, who long ago traveled across the sea and settled along the coast, were stealing land from the people of Israel.

One day there was a great battle. The men of Israel went out to fight, but four thousand of them never came home. The rest dragged themselves back to camp where the wise old men were waiting.

"Why did God punish us today?" they were asking.

"Let's send to Shiloh and get the ark of God's promise. If we had it here with us, the Philistines would not be able to hurt us."

So they sent a messenger to Shiloh where Eli's two sons were guarding the ark in the house of God, and they brought the ark back with them to army headquarters.

Over in the camp of the Philistines the soldiers were startled to hear shouting and cheering.

"What's that?"

"Their gods must have come into their camp."

At first they were afraid. Then they began to fight harder.

"Act like men! These are the same gods who made so much trouble for the Egyptians, and we know what happened to them.

"Up and fight! Are you going to let those Israelites make slaves out of you?"

So the battle began again, and it was worse than before. One after another Israelite soldier fell dead, and the wounded lay on the ground. When the Philistines slipped over to steal the ark of God's promise there was no one left to guard it.

Back at Shiloh an old, old man sat waiting by the roadside for news of the battle. His eyes were blind, but he could hear running footsteps. He could not see the messenger's torn coat or his dusty face, but he heard the heartbreaking message:

"We have run away from the enemy. Thousands of men have been killed. Your sons are dead, too. And the ark is gone."

The old, old man heard the bad news quietly. When he knew the ark was gone he fell from his seat. Eli was dead.

Never again would the ark of God's promise come to Shiloh. Never again would people live there, for the whole town was destroyed. Everywhere there was sadness and mourning.

1 Samuel 4

How the Ark Came Home

In Ashdod, city of the Philistines, there was a house that belonged to Dagon, huge and ugly idol with a man's body and the tail of a fish. To Dagon's house the soldiers proudly brought the captured ark, and there they set it down.

Early next morning the people came to see their stolen treasure. Dagon was lying on his face, flat on the ground before the ark. Quickly they set him up again.

Next morning they came back. But Dagon was lying on his face, and his head and his hands were cut clean off from his body. That was just the beginning of their trouble. Sickness broke out. Hordes of mice ate up their food.

"God is angry at us and at Dagon. What shall we do with his ark?"

"Let's send it to our neighbors over in Gath."

So they did. And trouble followed along with the ark.

Then the people of Gath sent the ark to Ekron, the next town, and so it went on for seven long months. Nobody wanted the ark.

At last the Philistines asked their magicians how to get rid of the ark.

"Send it back. But be sure to send gifts with it, golden gifts in a treasure chest. Perhaps if you offer a proper gift to the God of Israel he will stop punishing you.

"You must build a new wagon to carry the ark. Place it carefully in the wagon, with the golden gifts beside it. Bring two cows with their calves, but tie up the calves in the barn. Hitch the cows to the wagon. If they leave their calves here and head straight toward the land of the people of Israel, we will know that all this trouble has been God's punishment. If not, we'll know it was just bad luck."

So that was what they did. And without a driver the cows left their calves behind and headed down the road, lowing as they went.

In the wheat fields near Bethshemesh the Israelite harvesters were at work. Suddenly they looked up, and they saw the wagon with the covered ark coming toward them. With shouts of joy they ran to meet it, and there in the field beside the road they knelt and gave thanks to God.

But some of them were curious, and they looked inside the ark, lifting the cover that was never to be opened. And disobeying the law, they died there in the field.

Then all the people were afraid. They looked at one another and they asked, "Is anyone here able to take care of the ark?"

They sent a message up to their friends in the hills.

"The Philistines have brought the ark back to us. Now you come and get it."

So the men from the hills came for the ark, and they carried it up to the house of Abinadab and his son, Eleazar. For twenty years it stayed there, and Eleazar, who became a priest, guarded it all those years.

1 Samuel 5; 6; 7:1–2

They Wanted a King

Those were hard times in the land of Israel. The Philistines kept raiding the border towns, stealing crops and herds and burning homes. People were forgetting God. They were making heathen idols to worship, just the way the Philistines did.

The old house of God at Shiloh was gone, and there was no place where they could meet to worship. Sadly they prayed that God would help them. Sadly they remembered all the evil things they had done.

"If you mean what you say, with all your hearts, throw out those idols," Samuel told them.

So they listened, and they smashed their foolish idols, and they all went to Mizpah, where Samuel met them. There they humbly bowed their heads and said, "We have sinned," and they worshiped God together.

But while they were all away from home, the Philistines came marching.

"Pray for us! Keep praying for us! Pray that God will save us!" the Israelites begged Samuel.

The Philistines came marching on. But God was listening to his people. From the hilltops thunder rolled and crashed. Confused, the enemy stopped. The men of Israel burst out of the meeting place, and they chased the invaders far, far to the south.

Samuel set up a marker near Mizpah where they fought. "All the way God has helped us," this Stone of Help would tell people long, long after the battle was over.

So there was peace for a time, for the Philistines stayed at home, and they even gave back the towns they had stolen. It was safe for Samuel to travel round the country, and once a year he went to Bethel, then to Gilgal, then to Mizpah, then home to Ramah, teaching the people and serving as their judge.

All his life long, Samuel worked for his people, and when he was an old man he made his sons judges, too. But the sons were selfish men, interested only in making money.

"We will not have your sons to be our judges," warned the wise old men who spoke for the people.

"We want a king so we can be like other nations. Choose us a king."

"A king will draft your sons to drive his chariots and to be soldiers in his army," Samuel warned them.

"A king will take your daughters to be his cooks and bakers.

"He will take your farms away and give them to his servants.

"He will tax your crops and your sheep, and you will be working for him instead of for yourselves.

"Then you will cry out for help because of your king," Samuel warned them.

"Just the same, we want a king like other nations."

"Listen to them, and choose a king for them, Samuel."

That was God speaking.

1 Samuel 7:3–17; 8

ISRAEL'S FIRST KING

How Samuel Chose the King

DOWN THE HILL ROAD from Mount Ephraim, through one town and then the next, two men walked slowly, searching as they went. One was Saul, son of Kish the farmer, and he was a young man, handsome, head and shoulders taller than anyone else. With him was one of the family servants.

For the donkeys had strayed away from the farm, and the two men had traveled three days without finding anyone who had seen them.

"Let's go back. My father will be worrying about us instead of the donkeys," Saul said at last.

"There is a wise man in this town who knows many things. Let's go to him first. Maybe he can tell us where to look," the servant suggested.

"But we have nothing to give him," Saul objected. "Even our bread is gone."

"I have one silver coin," the servant offered.

So Saul borrowed his money, and they set out for the house of Samuel, the wise one.

And it happened that Samuel was looking for them. For only the day before, Samuel had received an important message from God.

"Tomorrow about this time I will send a man to you. Anoint him captain over my people, for he will rescue them from the Philistines and lead them in their battles."

The strangers came into town just as Samuel was going out to the place of worship on the hill.

"Samuel! Look! There is the man." Samuel heard the Voice that speaks to a man's heart.

"Can you tell me where the prophet lives?" Saul asked as he greeted Samuel.

"I am the prophet. Come and worship with me now. Then be my guest tonight. And about the donkeys, don't worry. They have been found. The important thing now is you and your family."

"But I'm only Saul, and my family is smallest and least important in all the land," the young farmer told him.

But that evening Saul and his servant were Samuel's guests at supper. Late into the night, up on the rooftop terrace, Samuel and Saul talked together. Early next morning Samuel walked with the travelers to the edge of town.

"Send your servant on ahead. I want to speak with you alone," Samuel whispered.

In the gray dawn light the old man took a small bottle from a pocket in his robe, and he poured some oil on the young man's head. It was the sign that a man was chosen to be king.

"So God has appointed you to be his prince," Samuel told him. "This is what will happen next. When you come to the place where Rachel was buried, two men will meet you, and they will say,

" 'The lost donkeys are safe at home. Now your father is worried about you.'

"When you come to the wide plain, you will meet three men on the way to Bethel. They will be carrying three small goats, three loaves of bread, and a bottle of wine. They will share their bread with you.

"When you come to the hill of God where the Philistines have a fort, you will meet a group of prophets, and they will be making music with their harps and tambourines and flutes and lyres. You will join them, and for a while you will be a prophet, too.

"When all this comes true, remember that God is right there with you. You will be a different man from this day on."

It all happened just as Samuel said. But when Saul joined the band of prophets, the people could hardly believe their eyes.

"What has come over Saul? Is he one of the prophets, too?" they wondered.

From the moment Saul said good-by to Samuel he really was a different person. When he went home his uncle asked him, "Where have you been?" Saul only said, "To hunt the donkeys. When we couldn't find them we went to Samuel, and he told us they had been found."

And he said not a word about being king. *1 Samuel 9; 10:1–16*

The King's First Victory

Samuel called a meeting of the Israelite people at Mizpah, and there he told them the news.

"You asked for a king. Come, take your places as families before God."

So they lined up, and Samuel chose the Benjamin tribe, Saul's family group. From the Benjamins he pointed out Saul's family. But when he looked for Saul the young man was not to be seen.

They found him where he had slipped away, hiding behind the

baggage. When he stood up no one could miss him, for he was taller than all the rest.

"This is the man God has chosen to be your king," Samuel announced.

"God save the king!" the people shouted.

Then Saul went home to Gibeah, and with him went a band of loyal soldiers.

But some worthless ones laughed and said,

"How can this man do anything for us?"

They brought him no presents, gave him no greeting. Saul said nothing at all.

No sooner had Saul and the others gone home than there was trouble again. The old enemy was ready to fight, and the bad news came to Gibeah where Saul's family lived.

"What's the matter? Why is everyone crying?" he asked when he came in from working in the fields.

When they told him, he was angry enough to fight at once. So he called in his army from all the country round. Next day he had three companies of fighting men, and with them he led the attack against the Ammonites. By noon the battle was won. It was a great victory for Saul.

"Now where are the men who said, 'How can this man help us?' Let's kill them all," the people shouted.

"Not one man shall be killed," Saul told them. "It is God who saved us." Instead, Samuel led them all to Gilgal, and there they worshiped God together, and they promised to be true to Saul. It was a day of gladness, for the king was brave, and his people loved him.

This is what Samuel told them:

"If you will love God and serve him and obey his voice, then all will be well with you.

"But if you disobey, if you rebel against his laws, he will punish you as he punished your fathers and your grandfathers. Remember all the things the Lord God has done for you. Serve him with all your hearts.

"He will not forsake you, for you are his own people."

1 Samuel 10:17–27; 11; 12

How Saul Lost His Kingdom

After Saul became king, he made up his mind to drive the enemy Philistines out of the land. He had an army of two thousand men. Prince Jonathan, his son, had an army of a thousand. Jonathan led the first attack against a small Philistine fort, and then there was trouble. King Saul sent out the alarm through all the land.

The Philistines—thirty thousand chariots and six thousand riders on six thousand horses—came to the attack. The Israelites had no chariots at all, no heavy weapons for fighting.

The people were afraid. Some of them hid in caves and bushes, in pits and among rocks. Some escaped across the Jordan River.

But Saul stayed on duty. He had to wait to attack until Samuel could come and lead the sacrifice offerings, for they must ask God's help first. But Samuel was late, and the frightened people were scattering.

"Bring the things for the offering to me. I will make the sacrifice to God instead of Samuel," King Saul ordered.

No sooner had they finished than Samuel arrived.

"What have you done?" the old man wanted to know.

"The people were getting away, and you were late. There were the Philistines. So I decided I had better make the sacrifice myself."

"Foolish Saul! A king is not a priest. You have disobeyed God. He was going to make you and your family rulers of Israel forever. Now you have lost the kingdom. God has found a man after his own heart, and he will be king of the people instead."

That was one way Saul lost the kingdom.

The wars went on, little and big, and King Saul never gave up fighting to make his people free. He won a great battle over the Amalekites, and Samuel warned:

"Don't take any prisoners. These are God's orders. Don't even capture any of the animals or food or treasure. That all belongs to God."

But Saul thought, "It seems a shame for a great king not to spare the lives of a few of the enemy." And he thought, "It seems a shame to destroy all those good sheep and oxen."

But he reported to Samuel:

"Everything has been done just as God ordered."

Samuel kept listening to far-off sounds.

"Then why do I hear sheep bleating and oxen lowing?"

"Well, the people did rescue some of the sheep and oxen for a present. They wanted to make a sacrifice to God."

"Wait, and I will tell you what God has said to me this very night," Samuel said sternly.

"When you were nobody at all, didn't he choose you to be captain of all the people of Israel? Didn't he send you out to destroy the Amalekites and everything that belongs to them?"

"Yes, and I obeyed. It was the people who took the animals for a gift to God."

"Would God rather have gifts or obedience?" Samuel asked.

"To obey is better than to offer sacrifices.
To listen is better than to bring gifts.

"Because you have turned away from God, he has turned away from King Saul."

The great king began to plead.

"I have sinned, for I have broken God's law. But I was afraid of the people. Now forgive me, I beg you, and come with me so I may worship God."

Samuel turned away, but Saul tried to catch his coat to hold him. The cloth split, and the old man walked away.

"God has torn the kingdom from you. Now he is giving it to someone who will make a better king," was his good-by.

Samuel went home, and so did King Saul, and the two men never met again. But Samuel grieved for Saul as long as he lived.

And that was the second way Saul lost his kingdom. He would be king as long as he lived. But none of his sons would be king after him.

1 Samuel 13:1–14; 15

ISRAEL'S GREATEST KING

Youngest Son, the Shepherd

The Lord is my shepherd; I shall not want.
    He makes me to lie down in green pastures.
He leads me beside still waters;
    He restores my soul.
He leads me in paths of righteousness
    For his name's sake.
Even though I walk through the valley
      of the shadow of death,
    I will fear no evil;
For thou art with me;
    Thy rod and thy staff
They comfort me.
    Thou layest a table before me in the presence
      of my enemies.
Thou anointest my head with oil; my cup overflows.
    Surely goodness and mercy shall follow me
All the days of my life;
    And I shall dwell in the house of the Lord forever.

The boy who took care of his father's sheep in the fields and on the hills outside Bethlehem was the youngest of eight brothers. His family never worried about the sheep as long as he was with them. He would find them the greenest grass to eat, and clear, clean water to drink. With his rod he would guide a straggler away from danger. With his strong hands he would fight off a prowling lion or bear. With his slingshot, loaded with one of the smooth round stones from the brook, he could fire a straight shot at a hungry animal hiding in the shadows. When the sheep were quiet, he liked to make up songs, and he would sing the words to music he played on his harp.

One day while the boy was out with the sheep an important guest came to his father's house.

"The prophet Samuel is here, and he has come to worship with you and all the family." Jesse came hurrying to welcome Samuel as soon as he heard the message. But Samuel did not tell his real reason for coming. That was his secret. He could still hear God telling him,

"It is time to forget your grief because Saul is no longer a good king. I have already chosen the next king. Go to Bethlehem, and there in Jesse's home you will find him."

Samuel watched carefully as the brothers came together to worship. First came tall, good-looking Eliab.

"Surely God has chosen him," thought Samuel.

But in his heart he heard,

"Do not judge by the way he looks. The Lord sees a man's heart, and he knows what he really is like."

Next came Abinadab. The Lord had not chosen him, either.

Seven tall sons of Jesse came by to greet Samuel. Still he had not found the right one.

"Are all your sons here?" he asked Jesse.

"Well, there is one more, the youngest. He's out with the sheep."

"Send for him," said Samuel.

In came young David, red-cheeked, handsome, standing straight and tall.

This is the one, Samuel knew.

And then before all the family he made the sign that David was chosen to be king. He lifted a flask of oil over David's head and let drops of oil fall on his hair.

From that time on David knew that God was with him and guiding him in some special way because he had special work for him to do.

He went back to his sheep, wondering and dreaming about the plans God had for him. *Psalm 23; 1 Samuel 16:1–13; 17:34–36*

Music-Maker in the King's House

There was trouble in the king's house, for Saul was sick in his mind. He was worried and unhappy, and he lost his temper easily. He no longer trusted any of his friends. His servants and friends tried to think of ways to help him.

"Music might help the king," they suggested.

King Saul liked the idea.

"Find me a man who plays well, and bring him here," he ordered.

Someone remembered Jesse's son who tended the sheep and played wonderful music on his harp. And so David came to the king's house, bringing gifts from his father for the king.

The minute King Saul saw the young man he loved him, and he sent word back to Jesse.

"I beg that you will let David stay here with me."

So David would play for the king, and whenever he played, all the ugly, worried, hateful ideas left Saul's mind, and he was quite, quite well again.

1 Samuel 16:14–23

The Boy Who Fought a Giant

There was war in the land. The Philistine army had invaded Judah and was camping in the hills just across the valley from King Saul and his men. Between the camps, down in the valley, both sides were getting ready for a battle.

Out from the enemy camp strode Goliath, the giant nearly ten feet tall. Before him marched a soldier carrying his shield.

"You men of Israel, why do you want to fight?" he roared. "Choose one man and let him fight for you. If he can kill me, we will be your servants. But if I kill him, you shall work for us.

"I dare you, soldiers of Israel! Give me a man, and we will fight!"

Every morning and every evening for forty days he shouted his challenge across the valley. The men of Israel were terrified, king and soldiers and all.

Now David had gone back home to Bethlehem, and he was taking care of the sheep just as usual. The three oldest brothers had gone to war, and Jesse began to worry about them.

"David, go and see how your brothers are. Find out if they need anything. And take some food to them," he told the boy.

So early next morning David left a keeper in charge of the sheep, and he took ten loaves of bread and a basket of parched grain for his brothers, and ten cheeses for their captain, and he set out for the camp.

He found his brothers easily enough. While they were all talking together they heard the giant roaring, "Give me a man!"

"Who is that fellow?" David wanted to know. But the soldiers were hurrying to get out of the way and did not stop to answer.

David went straight to King Saul.

"The men don't need to be so frightened. I will go and fight that Philistine," he offered.

Saul looked straight at his young friend.

"You're just a boy. You can't fight that fellow who has been a soldier for years."

"I have killed a lion, and I have killed a bear when they attacked my father's sheep. Besides, God took care of me then, and he will take care of me now."

"Go, then, and may God be with you," said Saul.

So Saul sent for his own armor, and he had his guards dress David in all the shining metal coat and the arm and leg protectors and the helmet, and they fastened the sword belt round him.

David took one step. He reached down and touched the sword at his side. Then he turned back to the king.

"Sir, I can't use this. I never learned to fight in armor."

So he took off every piece of the king's armor. He picked up his shepherd's staff. He chose five smooth stones from the brook, and he put them in the shepherd's bag he wore at his waist. He took his slingshot in his hand, and out he went to meet Goliath.

The giant came strutting toward him, stamping the ground. He looked all around, and he stared at David. Who was this boy?

"Do you think I am a dog you can chase away with that stick? Come here. I'll give your body to the birds in the air and the animals in the field," he growled.

David said quietly,

"You came out here armed with a sword and a spear and a shield. But I come to you as a soldier of God. I will fight you. I will win. The world will know that God rules in Israel."

The giant came a step closer. David ran up to meet him. He reached in his bag, and he took out one round stone. He slipped it in his slingshot. He took aim. Then he let go.

The giant fell face down on the ground. David ran up to him, and, picking up Goliath's own sword, he cut off his head.

The Philistines turned and ran for their lives. After them went the soldiers of Israel, and they chased the Philistines all the way to the far valley.

1 Samuel 17

When David Joined the Outlaws

Home from the battle they came at last, King Saul and his son, Prince Jonathan, and Abner, captain of the king's army.

But David was not allowed to go home, for King Saul brought him back to his own house, and he made him an officer in the army. David was a hero now to all his people. But the one who loved him best was the king's son, Prince Jonathan. The two young men became the best of friends.

Then the old sickness came back to King Saul. It began when he grew jealous of David. Everywhere the people were making up songs about the great victory over Goliath and the Philistines. They were singing:

> Saul has killed his thousands,
> And David his ten thousands.

"So, this David has his ten thousands, and I have only thousands," Saul grumbled. "What more could he have but the kingdom? Will they take that away from me?"

And from that day on King Saul watched David suspiciously. But all the other people of Israel loved their hero-soldier. He became the most popular person in the land.

David still played his harp for the king. But the music did not help any more. Instead, Saul became angry. One day he sat listening, twisting his spear in his hand. Suddenly he lifted it high and hurled it at David. He meant to pin him to the wall, but David jumped aside and slipped out of the room.

David and Jonathan

So Saul gave orders that David was to be arrested and killed.

When Prince Jonathan heard the bad news, he hurried straight to his father. David was like his own brother. Already he had shared everything he had with him, and David was wearing Jonathan's own robe, carrying his own sword and his own bow. He must find some way of saving David's life.

"My father, the king must not sin against David. He has done nothing wrong. He risked his life to fight Goliath."

Listening, the king began to change his mind. So once again they could be together, Jonathan and David and Saul.

But the sickness came back, and Saul threw his spear at David again. This time David escaped and fled to another town.

He was hiding there when he heard that the king's soldiers were on their way to capture him. David went to find Jonathan.

"What have I done? Why does the king want to kill me?" he asked.

"You must be wrong. He wouldn't kill you. Wouldn't I be the first to know if he really meant it?" his friend asked.

"But it is true. Your father knows how much you love me, and he does not want you to worry. I tell you the truth—there is just a step between me and death."

"What can I do?" Jonathan wanted to know.

"Tomorrow is the first day of the celebration of the new moon, and I am supposed to sit at the king's table. But I am going to hide. If he misses me, you tell him I asked permission to go home to Bethlehem and be with my family.

"If he says it is all right, I will know I am safe. But if he is angry, then I'll know he means to kill me."

"How am I going to know what your father says?" David asked.

"I'll get word to you. Remember the field with the rocks where you hid? You wait there. I will come out to shoot, and I will shoot three arrows as if I aimed at a target. Then I will send my arrow bearer after them.

"If you are safe I will tell him, 'The arrows are here on this side of you.'

"But if the king is still angry I will say, 'There they are out there beyond you.' Then you must go. But no matter what happens, you and I are friends forever."

In the king's house they all sat down to dinner, King Saul with Prince Jonathan opposite him. Captain Abner sat beside the king. But David's place was empty. The first day King Saul did not mention it. But the second day he wanted to know,

"Where is David? Why isn't he here?"

Jonathan answered just as he and David had planned. The king was furious.

"Why do you see so much of that David? Don't you know that as long as he lives you will never be king? Go bring him here to me, for he must die."

"But why? What has he done?"

With that, the king threw his spear at his own son. Jonathan ran from the table, just as angry as his father.

Early the next morning when no one was around, two people went out to the field. One was a tall soldier. The other was a boy. The soldier stopped and shot a few arrows.

"Run now and get them for me," he told the boy. He shot one more, far beyond.

"See whether that one isn't way out there beyond you," he called. "Hurry!"

Back the boy came with the arrows.

"Now take my bow and arrows back to town," said the soldier.

As soon as the boy was gone, David came out from behind the rocks.

"Go in peace. Between you and me and your family and my family may there be peace forever," Jonathan told his friend. Then the two men said good-by. Jonathan went back to town. But David was to be an outlaw for many a year. *1 Samuel 18:1–16; 19:1–10; 20*

Four Hundred Mighty Men

In the Country of the Caves, not far from Bethlehem, Adullam's Cave was big enough to hold a small army, and safe as a fort. That was the place David chose for his headquarters. As soon as his family found out where he was, they went to stay with him.

People who were in trouble and afraid of King Saul's soldiers for many reasons began to find their way to the cave. Soon David had an army. Some of the men owed more money than they could pay. Some did not like the way King Saul was ruling the country. All of them were bold. They were known as "David's mighty men."

David felt that it was not safe for his mother and father to stay with them. So he took them over to Moab and asked the king to let them stay there until he could learn God's plans for him.

Those were the times when bands of Philistines would cross the border and raid the towns, stealing grain and burning fields and houses. But David and his mighty men fought them off. Many were the stories people told of David and his outlaw band.

One of his men fought alone against three hundred men and won the fight. One killed a lion deep down in a pit one snowy day. David's mighty men could shoot arrows or hurl stones as well with their left hands as their right. They could swim the Jordan River at flood time when the water was deep and flowing fast. They could fight as fiercely as lions and run as fast as deer.

From all round the country more men came to David.

"If you are friends who come to help me, then you are welcome," he greeted them. "But if you have come to play a trick on me, then may God punish you."

"We are on your side. We are your men. We come in peace to you and all who help you, for God himself is on your side," they would say.

So David took them all into his army.

One and all they loved him, and they gladly risked their lives to work for him and fight for him. One day when they were in the cave fort, David began to think about his home in Bethlehem. It was a good thing he had found a safer place for his mother and father, for the Philistine raiders were in the town, and no one could get in or out.

David was hot and tired, and he was thirsty.

"Oh, how I wish I had a drink of water from that well by the Bethlehem gate," he said.

Three of his men slipped away across the fields. Somehow they got past the Philistine guards, and they managed to draw up a jar of water from the well by the Bethlehem gate. Back to the fort they hurried, and they handed the water to their captain.

Thirsty as he was, David just held the jar carefully in his hands.

"I cannot drink this water. You risked your lives to get it for me."

In front of them all he poured it slowly on the ground—a gift he was offering to God.

Month after month Saul tried to track David down.

"Find all David's hiding places. Talk to all the people who have seen him. If he is in this land, I will find him among all the thousands in Judah," Saul gave his orders.

They were so near that Prince Jonathan met David in the woods.

"Don't be afraid. My father will not find you. Some day you will be king, and I will be there with you," Jonathan promised, and again they vowed that they would be friends forever.

"David is out there in the hills," some reported to the king. So Saul set out with three thousand men for the rocky hills where the wild goats lived. Now along the way there was a great cave where David and his men were hiding. Saul came to the opening of the cave, and he decided it was a good place to stop.

Far back in the shadows inside the cave, David and his mighty men were hiding. David slipped up behind the king so quietly that there was not a sound, and he cut off a piece of the king's robe.

A little later Saul and the soldiers were on their way. David followed close behind.

"My lord the king!" he called.

Saul turned around quickly and discovered David bowing before him.

"Why did you listen to all those tales that I want to harm you?" David asked. "Just now, back there in the cave, you were in my power, but I would not hurt you. See, I only cut off a piece of your robe.

"After all, what is the king looking for? Did he come all this way to catch a flea?"

For a moment King Saul was just the way he used to be when they were friends.

"Is that your voice, my son David? You have been good to me, and I have done my best to hurt you. Now at last I know that you are going to be king. Promise me, when that time comes you will not hurt my family."

David promised gladly, and Saul went home. But David and his men went back to their cave fort.

1 Samuel 22:1–4; 23:14–18,22–23; 24; 2 Samuel 23:13–23; 1 Chronicles 11:10–22; 12:1–2,8,15–18

A Shepherd Named "Foolish"

Nabal, whose name means Foolish, was a rich, important person. Thousands of sheep were in his flocks. A thousand goats found pasture on his lands. The Philistine raiders were just waiting for a chance to steal some of them. But as long as David and his soldiers were camping nearby, there was never a raiding Philistine or stealthy lion that made off with one of Nabal's sheep.

The time came for shearing the sheep, and the shepherds were hard at work. Whenever they stopped to rest, there was plenty of food and water for them, for Nabal took good care of his workers. But David was having a hard time finding enough food for his men, and so he sent ten of his soldiers to ask Nabal for a share of the food. This is what they said:

"Peace be to you, to your house, and all you have. While your men were near us not one of them was hurt. All you had was safe. Today is a holiday, and our captain, David, asks if you will give us a share of whatever you have to eat."

"Who is this David?" snapped Nabal, whose name was Foolish. "Shall I take my good meat and water and give it to people I don't know?"

So the men went back to report Nabal's rudeness to David.

"Put on your swords!" David ordered. Leaving two hundred men to guard the camp, he took four hundred with him to attack Nabal the Foolish.

While all this was going on, someone ran to tell Abigail, who was Nabal's beautiful wife. Now Abigail was wise, and she listened carefully.

"David's men were like a strong wall to guard us when we were out with the sheep. They were good to us. Do something now, for David will punish our master and all the household. And Nabal is so ugly no one dares to speak to him."

Abigail hurried to pack baskets of food. Bread, lamb, parched grain, raisins, and fig cakes, and something to drink were loaded on the donkeys.

"Go on ahead. I will follow," she told the drivers. But she said not a word to Nabal the Foolish.

David met her as she came riding over the hill on her own donkey. She dismounted and bowed.

"My lord, let me speak to you. Pay no attention to Nabal. Foolish is his name, and foolish are the things he does. Here is a gift for your men. Please take it, and forgive us for what has happened. Some day when you are king you will be glad you did not kill to get even."

"Blessed be God who sent you here," David said gently. "And blessed are you, for you are wise. You kept me from killing to get revenge. If you had not come to me, not one of you would be alive by morning. Go home now in peace."

So Abigail went back. She found Nabal the Foolish feasting and drinking, and so she said nothing about what had happened. But in the morning when he was sober she told him how near he came to being killed.

Suddenly Nabal was sick. He could not move or speak. Ten days later he was dead.

When David heard about it he was thankful again that he had not tried to get revenge. He kept thinking about Abigail, so wise and beautiful and understanding. And he sent word to her, asking her to be his wife.

So Abigail packed her things. Taking five of her maidens with her, she rode away from Nabal's great house to meet the outlaw soldier in the wilderness country. *1 Samuel 25*

How David Rescued His Family

David and his men hurried to Ziklag where their families had been staying. All they could see was smoke pouring from the burning buildings. No one was there. Their wives and children had been kidnapped by Amalekite soldiers.

At first the men turned on David, and they put all the blame on him. But David was asking God what to do.

"Shall I go after them?"

"Go on. You will overtake them and bring back all you lost."

So they set out, David and six hundred men, and they ran till they came to the brook called Besor. By that time two hundred men had dropped out, too tired to go any farther.

In the field across the brook they found a young man who was too weak to try to escape. David gave him bread and figs and raisins to eat and water to drink. Soon he could talk.

"Who are you? Where did you come from?" David asked him.

"I am from Egypt, servant of an Amalekite soldier. Three days ago I fell sick, and so they left me here. I have had nothing to eat. We were over in Judah, and we set fire to Ziklag."

"Can you take me to the Amalekites?" David demanded.

"Promise me that you will not turn me over to them or kill me."

So he led them quickly to the camp where the soldiers were celebrating their victory, eating and drinking and singing and dancing, with all their loot spread out before them.

David waited until it began to get dark. Then he attacked. It was a great victory. Only a few hundred men escaped.

David and his men saw their families and all their belongings. None of the captives had been harmed. So they packed up their own goods and whatever the Amalekites had left behind.

At the brook the others were waiting to welcome them.

"But don't think you will get any of the supplies we captured," the men with David threatened. "That all belongs to us."

But David would not allow it. "Share and share alike," was the order, and those who fought the battle and those who had to stay behind were to divide evenly everything that was captured. That became a law in Israel from that time on.

1 Samuel 30:1–25

David's Royal Prisoner

"David is hiding over there in the hills by the desert," the spies told King Saul.

So Saul took his soldiers and went out to the hills, and they pitched their tents near the desert. The soldiers built a barricade, and, safe inside, Saul and Captain Abner lay down on the ground and went to sleep.

But David was watching for them, and he sent out his spies to find where they were.

"Now who will go with me to Saul's camp?" he asked; and Abishai said, "I will go."

So when it was quite dark and everyone was asleep, the two men slipped inside the barricade. They could have stepped on the sleeping king before he had a chance to reach for the spear that was standing in the ground beside him.

"Let me strike him just this once with my spear," Abishai whispered. "I won't have to strike the second time."

"No, do not kill him. No one may harm the man God chose to be king. Pick up his spear and his water jug, and we will go."

The two men disappeared before anyone discovered them. Once they were safely out of danger on a hilltop, David shouted,

"Abner! O Abner, where are you?"

Sleepily Abner answered, "Who—who is that calling?"

"Abner, how brave you are! Who in all Israel is as brave as you! Why weren't you guarding the king just now when someone came over to kill him? You deserve the death penalty for not guarding your king. Look—where is his spear? Where is his water jar?"

By this time Saul was awake. He knew that voice.

"David! Is that you, my son?"

"It is my voice, my king. Why are you out here to capture me? Listen, my king, you are still trying to catch a flea. You are hunting a partridge in the mountains."

"I have been wrong," the king said soberly. "Come back, David, and I will not hurt you."

"Send someone over here after your spear. And remember that tonight you were in my power. But I would not harm the man God chose to be king."

"May God bless you, David. You will do great things, and do them well," said Saul. Then he went home. But David stayed in the wilderness country.

1 Samuel 26

When the King Died

Samuel, the wise old prophet, was dead. For the first time in his life King Saul was afraid. The Philistine army had come back, and it was bigger than ever.

"What must I do? Tell me how to fight," King Saul prayed to God. But he heard no answer.

"Who is going to win the battle I must fight?" There was no answer.

He remembered something Samuel had said years ago before ever he had heard of David.

"Because you have turned away from God, he has turned away from you. He has taken the kingdom away from you and has given it to a better man."

The Philistines came marching by hundreds and by thousands to Mount Gilboa, and the battle began. King Saul's men turned and ran, and the Philistines were after them. They killed Jonathan and two of his brothers. King Saul fell to the ground, wounded by a Philistine arrow.

"Draw your sword! Kill me yourself before the Philistines come," he begged his armor bearer. But the soldier could not kill his king, and Saul fell on his own sword. So Saul died, with his three sons and all his men, the same day, and the Philistines moved into their land.

The men who lived in Jabesh-Gilead heard what had happened, and for love of Saul, who once rescued them from the Ammonites, they slipped over in the night and took the bodies of the king and his sons, and they buried them under a tree at Jabesh. Then for a whole week they mourned because great King Saul was dead.

A man in torn, dirty clothes came running to David to bring him news of the battle.

"The soldiers have run away. Everyone has run away, and Saul and Jonathan are dead!"

David bowed his head, and he wept in his great sorrow for the king and for Jonathan his friend. Remembering them, he wrote:

How are the mighty fallen!
Tell it not in Gath,
Publish it not in the streets of Ashkelon,
For the daughters of the Philistines will laugh.
You mountains of Gilboa, let there be no dew,
No rain upon your slopes, no green fields,
For the shield of the great king was tossed away.
Saul and Jonathan were loved and loving while they lived,
And in their death they were not divided.
Swifter they were than eagles,
Stronger they were than lions.
You daughters of Israel, weep over Saul.
How are the mighty fallen in the midst of the battle!
Oh, Jonathan, slain on the high mountain,
I grieve for you, my brother Jonathan.

Very friendly you were to me,
Your love to me was wonderful.
How are the mighty fallen,
And all the weapons of war destroyed!

1 Samuel 28:3–6; 31; 1 Chronicles 10; 2 Samuel 1

How David Became King

Saul and Jonathan were dead. Now David was king. But his troubles were not over, for Saul's friends were insisting that Prince Ishbosheth, Saul's son, should be king.

So David stayed in the south country. He and all his family and Captain Joab and all the army moved to Hebron. Men came there from all the towns of Judah, and they hailed him as their king.

But in the north country Prince Ishbosheth was made king, and Captain Abner was head of his army. Now a long war began between David's men and those who were left of Saul's army, between the people in Judah and the people in Israel.

One day Captain Joab tricked Captain Abner and killed him. If he thought King David was going to reward him, he was greatly disappointed. David was horrified. He ordered all his people to mourn for the dead captain. On the day of the funeral he himself walked in the funeral procession, and that day he would not eat.

"A prince and a great gentleman is dead," he said. "Though I am king, I am weaker now that Abner is gone."

The people loved him for what he said.

Now Saul's son, the other king, was afraid. His captain was gone. There was no one whom he could trust, not even his own men. One day when it was very hot he was taking a noontime nap. Two officers in his own army slipped into his house and killed him. Then they reported to David,

"Ishbosheth, son of Saul, who tried to kill you, is dead. Today the Lord has helped King David to have revenge on Saul and all his family."

But David was far from pleased.

"Evil men, when Saul died someone brought me the news, hoping I would give him a reward. But he was punished. How much more you deserve punishment for killing a good man in his bed!"

And he ordered his soldiers to have them killed.

Now that Prince Ishbosheth was dead and Captain Abner gone, the whole country wanted David for their king. From all the towns of Israel, from the families and the tribes in the north, men came to meet him at Hebron.

"Even when Saul was king you were really our leader. You are one of us. Now be our king," they begged him.

So they all made a covenant-promise at Hebron. David promised to rule them justly and kindly, and they promised to obey him and fight for him. Then they made the sign that he was their king, pouring some oil on his hair, as Samuel had done years ago when David was just a young shepherd boy.

Then there was a great celebration. For three days the people feasted on roast beef and lamb, on figs and raisins. Not for a long, long time had the people been so happy.

2 Samuel 2; 3:22–39; 4; 5:1–5
1 Chronicles 11:1–3; 12:38–40

A New Capital for the New King

Where should the new king build his capital? This new city must belong to all the people, not just to those who lived in Israel, not just to those who lived in Judah.

High on Mount Zion there was a city that still belonged to the Jebus people. No army had been strong enough to climb the

203

steep roads and break through the high walls to capture it. That was the place David chose for his capital. So he sent messengers up to the Jebus people to ask for the city. They just laughed.

"Try and take it!" they mocked. "Why, our blind and lame folks could guard our city. No one can take it away from us."

David had a scheme. All the water for the city came from a spring far below the walls. In rocky tunnels it flowed below the city so that inside the walls people could lower their water jars and bring up their water.

"The man who leads through the water into the city and captures it, shall be commander-in-chief of the army," he said.

The plan worked. Joab led them, and they took the city.

High on Mount Zion the great walled city had a new name. The City of David they called it now, though they still used the old name, too, Jerusalem, City of Peace.

As soon as David and his people moved in they needed more houses. But who among the shepherds and the soldiers knew how to build a house? And where could they find enough wood for their houses?

King Hiram of Tyre, far to the north, offered his help. His mountain forests were green with cedar trees. David bought lumber from him. King Hiram had skilled carpenters and stone masons, too. He sent them to teach David's men to build with wood and stone.

The old, old city was growing. New homes and new streets were ready for the people moving in.

2 Samuel 5:6–12; 1 Chronicles 11:4–9; 14:1

Music and Marching Feet

Just about ten miles away from David's new City of Peace, in a house on a hilltop, Abinadab and his sons guarded the greatest treasure in the land. It was the ark of God's promise, holding the two stones on which were written the Ten Commandments. Covered with gold, with two beautifully carved angel figures on top, it had been made back in the wilderness country long ago when Moses had been leader of the Hebrews. No man must ever touch the ark; so it was made to be carried on men's shoulders by long poles slipped through rings at the four corners.

Once the Philistines had stolen the ark. But they became frightened, and they brought it back. All the days of the wars it had rested safely in Abinadab's house.

David was thinking about the ark and about all the priest people who were scattered here and there in all the towns. Long ago they used to help in the worship services when the people met God at the tabernacle. Now he had a plan, and he talked it over with his leaders.

"If you think this is a good idea, and if it seems to be what God wants us to do, we will send for all the priests. And then we will bring the ark here where we can take care of it."

All the people agreed that he was right.

So David sent messengers through the country to all the priests. He ordered a new oxcart made especially to carry the ark. Inside the safe, high walls of the City of Peace he had a tent set up to shelter it.

In Abinadab's house the journey began. Men lifted the ark by the long poles slipped through rings at each corner, and they rested the ends of the poles on their shoulders. Gently they carried it to the new cart which had never been used for anything else. Gently they lowered the ark on the cart. The drivers shouted to the oxen, and they all headed for Jerusalem.

The people sang as they went, following in a procession. The musicians played on their harps, their trumpets, their tambourines, and their cymbals. Everyone was glad because God's ark was coming home!

The road was long and rough, and there were troubles along

the way. But at last the oxcart came creaking slowly up the Jerusalem road, straight to the door of the tent tabernacle. Men lifted the long poles to their shoulders without ever touching the ark itself. Slowly and carefully they carried it to the place that had been made ready.

The trumpets rang out. The singers chanted joyously. And the happy people sang David's Song of Thanksgiving.

> Give thanks to the Lord; tell the people of his goodness.
> Sing to him; sing songs of praise to him;
> Tell of the wonderful things he has done!
> Let those who seek the Lord be glad.
> Seek for him, to be with him always.
> Remember all the wonders he has done,
> How he said, "To you I will give the land of Canaan."
> When there were only a few of you, unimportant,
> Wandering from country to country,
> He kept you safe, and none could hurt you.
> Great is the Lord God, greater than all the idols
>   of the heathen.
> For the Lord God made the heavens;
> Glory and honor, strength and gladness belong to him.
> Families of the people, give glory to God;
> Bring your gifts and come to him,
> Worship the Lord in the beauty of holiness.
> Let the heavens be glad! Let the earth sing for joy!
> Let men tell the world: "Our Lord is king."
> Let the great ocean roar; let the fields be glad.
> And the trees in the forest will sing for joy.
> Because the Lord is king.
> Oh, give thanks to the Lord, for he is good,
> Blessed be our God for ever and ever and ever.

2 Samuel 6:1–5,14–19; 1 Chronicles 13: 1–8; 15:1–3,25–28; 16

David and Mephibosheth

The Little Lost Prince

King David's army was strong, and his soldiers were brave. There was no country anywhere strong enough to fight against them. They conquered Moab, and the Moabite people came bringing gifts. They conquered the land by the great river. They conquered the Red Lands and the Valley of Salt. They captured horses and chariots. Treasures of silver and gold and shining precious stones, bronze shields and gleaming swords they brought back to Jerusalem and stored away in King David's treasure house.

In his strong, safe city David remembered his old friend Jonathan.

"You will be king some day, and I will be there with you," Jonathan had said that day when they promised to be friends forever. Now all Saul's sons were dead. Or was anyone left of the family? Someone suggested that Saul's old servant, Ziba, might know. So they brought Ziba to the king.

"Tell me, is there anyone left in Saul's family who needs my help?" David asked.

So old Ziba told his secret.

Jonathan had a little boy named Mephibosheth, who was just five years old that terrible day when messengers came running to Saul's house with the news that his father and his grandfather were both dead.

All the people had just one idea. They must run for their lives for fear of David's soldiers. Mephibosheth's nurse picked him up and ran with the rest. But she stumbled and fell, and the boy was hurt. He never walked straight again, for after that fall he was lame in both his feet.

"I can tell you where he is. He and his son have been living at Machir's house over in Lodebar."

So the king sent for his friend's son.

"I am your servant, sir," Mephibosheth said.

David helped him to stand.

"Don't be afraid. Your father was my friend, and I want to be your friend for his sake. You are to have the land that belonged to him. Now I want you to come here and live with me. You must eat at my table and be as one of my own sons."

So Mephibosheth and his young son, Mica, moved to David's house, and Ziba and all his fifteen sons took care of them.

2 Samuel 8; 9; 4:4; 1 Chronicles 18

Trouble at David's House

Even a king can do wrong, and there came a time when David sinned a great sin. Sorry at last for what he had done, he begged God to forgive him, and God answered his prayer. But from that time on there was trouble in David's house.

It all began when David wanted to marry Bathsheba. But Bathsheba was already married to Uriah, one of the soldiers in David's army. It was the time of the war with the people of Ammon, and David knew that there was going to be a battle. Just suppose Uriah should happen to be killed! King David wrote a letter to Captain Joab which said,

"Send Uriah to the front line where the fighting is fiercest, and then leave him to fight alone."

Before long the king's messenger came back to report,

"They were shooting down on our troops from the wall, and Uriah was among the men who were killed."

So now David could marry Bathsheba.

No one but the prophet Nathan had the courage to tell the king how great his sin was.

Nathan told him this story.

"There were two men who lived in the same town. One man was rich, and he had many flocks of sheep, many herds of cattle. The other man was so poor that he had just one little pet lamb that was almost part of the family.

"One day the rich man had a guest, a traveler who asked for something to eat. Instead of taking one of his own animals for meat for his guest's supper, he stole the poor man's lamb."

David was angry. "Why, the fellow must be punished," he broke in quickly. "At least he should give the poor man four other lambs to make up for the one he stole."

Nathan the prophet looked straight at the king.

"You are the man. And this is what God has to say to you:

" 'I chose you to be king. I rescued you from Saul. I have given you everything you have. If that is not enough, I would give you more. So why did you kill and steal to get what you wanted? The soldiers of Ammon killed Uriah, but you are the man who murdered him.

" 'You have brought trouble into your house, and trouble is here to stay.' "

David bowed his head.

"I have sinned against the Lord," he said miserably.

Now the great king could see that all his wickedness was ugly and shameful. He hated what he had done. He hated the sin that made him feel that he was far away from God. If only God would forgive him! David prayed:

"Have mercy on me, O God, in your kindness and love.
 Blot out the evil I have done.
 Wash me clean from all my sin.
 I know that I have sinned—I can think of nothing else—
 I have sinned against you.
 Wash me now, and I shall be clean, whiter than snow.

Wash me clean. Give me back a heart that is pure.
You do not ask for sacrifice offerings. I could give them.
All you ask is a broken heart.
Lord, truly I am sorry. Do not despise me.
Do not turn away where I cannot find you.
Let me hear laughing and singing again.
Let me speak, and I will praise you,
Tell all the people of your mercy and your goodness,
For happy is the man whose sins are forgiven."

So at last David knew that he was forgiven. But trouble never left his house. *2 Samuel 11:1–3,14–27; 12:1–13; Psalm 51; 32:1*

Traitor Absalom

Now the sons of King David were brave and handsome. But of them all Prince Absalom, with his long, beautiful wavy hair, was the handsomest. But Prince Absalom was a murderer.

Absalom and his brother Amnon quarreled, and Absalom killed Amnon. Then to save his own life he escaped out of the country. For three years he stayed away, and every day his father missed him and mourned because he was gone. Finally Captain Joab persuaded the king to let the young prince come home.

"But tell him to stay in his own house. I will have nothing to do with him," said David.

Two more years went by, and then Captain Joab begged the king to forgive his son. So Absalom came home at last to his father's house, and he bowed respectfully before David. But David threw his arms round his son and kissed him and welcomed him.

All the time Prince Absalom was plotting how to be king himself, and he had a plan to make the people choose him instead of his father.

Early every morning he went out to the city gate to meet the people who came to see the king. He would greet each stranger in a friendly way, asking, "From what town do you come?"

He would listen, and then he would say thoughtfully,

"It certainly is a shame the king has not appointed someone you might talk to. I wish I could be made a judge! Then anyone who needed help could come straight to me."

And whenever the stranger would bow before the prince, Absalom would take him by the hand and greet him like an honored friend. So he stole the hearts of all who came to see the king, and the people loved him.

That went on for four years. Then Absalom asked his father for permission to go to Hebron to worship God.

"Go in peace," the king told his son.

So Absalom left Jerusalem, and he took a small army of his own friends with him, and he sent word round the country, "As soon as you hear the trumpets, you will know Absalom is king in Hebron!"

Back in David's house a messenger brought the news: "All Israel is taking Absalom's side against you."

King David did not want to fight against his own son. And he would not run the risk of a battle inside his City of Peace if Absalom should decide to attack. So he and the men who were still loyal to him fled together for their lives. Zadok the priest tried to go with them, bringing along the ark of God's promise. But David refused to allow it to be carried into danger.

"Take the ark back. If it is God's plan, he will bring me back safely. I can trust him," said the king. "Go back and stay in Jerusalem until you can tell me it is safe to come home."

A little farther along the way, Prince Mephibosheth's servant, Ziba, came to meet them, leading two donkeys bearing baskets full of bread and fruit.

"What's all this?" asked the king.

"You will need the donkeys to ride on. And you will be needing the food when you get to the wilderness country," Ziba told him.

"But where is Prince Mephibosheth?"

"Oh, he's back there in Jerusalem telling everyone, 'This is the day I get my kingdom back,' " lied Ziba.

"Then everything that belongs to him I give to you."

"I thank my lord the king. I beg the king that I may always please him." Ziba bowed respectfully.

Farther along the way they came to the house of one of Saul's cousins, a man named Shimei. As they passed, Shimei came running out, shouting curses at David and throwing rocks at the king and his soldiers.

"Now you are getting what you deserve, and you brought it all on yourself. You killed Saul and his family. So God has taken the kingdom away from you and given it to Prince Absalom," he shouted.

"Why should this dead dog curse my lord the king? Let me go, and I will kill him," a soldier begged. But David stopped him. Then he spoke to all his men.

"My son is trying to kill me. What more could happen? Let him alone."

So they hurried on. Shimei followed as long as he could, hurling dirt and rocks, and cursing as he went.

At last the king and all his men came wearily to the Jordan River, and there they stopped to rest for the night. Next morning they escaped across the river. This time they were met by friends who brought them supplies—blankets and dishes and cooking pots, and grain and beans and meat and honey and butter and cheese.

So King David had time to get his soldiers ready for a battle. But he sent for his captains, and he told them,

"Be gentle with Absalom for my sake."

Fighting began in the woods. Absalom came riding toward his

father's camp, and as he stooped to ride under the low boughs of a great oak tree his head caught fast in the tree. His mule never stopped. Absalom was left hanging between sky and earth.

Someone raced for Captain Joab.

"Come quickly! I just saw Absalom hanging in a tree."

"Then why didn't you kill him? I would have rewarded you."

"I wouldn't harm him for any amount of money. I heard the king tell you not to touch him."

"I have no time to listen to you," Joab said. Taking three darts with him, he hurried out with his ten armor bearers. There under the tree, they killed Prince Absalom.

Two messengers raced back to the king with the news.

"All is well," the first man reported.

"Is the young man Absalom safe?" David wanted to know.

"News, my lord the king! Today you have revenge on all who rebelled against you!" the other reported.

"Is the young man safe?" David demanded.

"May all your enemies be as he is."

"Absalom, O Absalom, my son, my son! If only God had let me die for you!" David mourned. He went alone to an upstairs room. There he stayed by himself, and he would not come out. The great day of victory was turned into a day of mourning, and the soldiers who won the battle came sneaking back to their tents as if they were running away.

At last Joab went to the king.

"Today you have brought shame to those who love you and risked their lives for you," he said. "You are loving your enemies, but you are hating your friends. I really believe that if Absalom had lived and we had all been killed, you would be glad.

"Now go out and speak to your men. If you don't, they will desert you this very night."

So David went to meet his men as a king should go.

At last it was safe for them to begin the long journey home. This time they could travel more comfortably, and when they came to the river a ferryboat was waiting for them.

Across the river David could see a crowd of people. He saw Shimei, who had chased them along the road with rocks and curses; and now Shimei had a thousand men with him. Now he was bowing as a man bows before his king.

"I beg my lord to forgive what I did. I want to be the first to meet my king as he comes home," he said.

One of the king's officers would have killed him, but David would not allow it.

"There has been enough killing. You shall not die," said David.

Back in Jerusalem one of the first men to welcome him was Prince Mephibosheth. David remembered what Ziba, the man's servant, had reported to him when he and his men were escaping from Jerusalem.

"Where were you when we left?" he asked.

"My lord, my servant tricked me. He asked me for donkeys and food so that he could go to help you in my place since I am lame. Why, the king is like an angel of God to me. My father and all my family were dead, and you brought me here and invited me to be like one of your own sons. But now do to me whatever you think should be done. I have no right to ask for more."

"We will forget the whole thing," David told him. "You and Ziba divide the land I told him should be his."

"No, let him keep it all. It is enough for me that my lord the king has come home in peace."

2 Samuel 14 to 19

Temple Plans and Treasures

The city of the great king had grown bigger and stronger every day. People were building houses, making streets. The walls of the city were high and strong. But David was not satisfied. One thought kept coming to his mind.

"Here I am living comfortably in a house built of cedar wood. But the ark of God's promise is still over there in a tent," he said to his friend, the prophet Nathan. Surely, thought David, an earthly king's house should not be finer than God's house.

Nathan knew what he was thinking.

"Do what is in your mind. You have a good idea," he said.

But David never built a house for God. That night Nathan heard a message for the king. God told him,

"David is a soldier, a fighting man. He is not to build a house for me. Go and tell David,

" 'Remember that I chose you and took you away from the sheep to be king over my people. I have been with you wherever you have gone. I have protected you from your enemies, and I have made you famous. You have led my people in the country I have given them for their own.

" 'Now your God will make you a strong house, a house not built with hands. Your house will be a strong family, and when your life is over, your son Solomon will be king. I will be his father, and he will be my son. If he does wrong, I will punish him. But I will forgive him and be merciful to him.' "

David listened, and he wondered at the love of God for him.

"Who am I, Lord God, that you should think so much of me and of my family—all my house?

"You are great and wonderful. There is no other God like you. There is no other nation like your people whom you have chosen to be your people forever.

"Now, Lord God, may it please you to give your blessing to this house of mine, the house of my family." That was David's prayer.

And God blessed the family of David in his house.

Now David began to make other plans. He went to work to collect materials so that someday Solomon might build a house beautiful enough for a place to worship God.

He collected cedar wood, gold and silver, brass and iron. He stored away shining precious stones. He hired masons to cut and shape the stones for the building. He made iron ready for the nails to be used in the doors of the gates.

David even chose the place where the Temple was to be built. It happened this way: He had disobeyed God and wanted to make a special sacrifice gift to show God that he was sorry. He climbed a hill in the City of Peace, and he came to the level land on the top where the farmer Araunah was threshing his grain. That was the place he wanted.

"My lord the king is welcome to the land. Here are oxen for the sacrifice, and take my wood to build the fire," Araunah offered generously. "And may God accept your sacrifice."

But David would not take the land as a gift.

"How can I offer to God a gift that cost me nothing?" he asked. And he paid the farmer fifty silver pieces, full value for the land.

2 Samuel 7; 24:18–24; 1 Chronicles 17; 21: 18–26; 22:1–5

A Commission for Solomon

Now that David had the blueprints for the Temple and the materials to build it, he had an announcement to make. He called all his army, all his leaders, all the princes of the land together, and this is what he told them:

Heaps of Treasures

"My brothers, my people, it was in my heart to build a house for God where the ark of his promise might rest. But God said to me,

"'You shall not build this house, for you have been a fighting man. Solomon your son shall build my house. He will be no soldier, for when he is king there will be peace in the land. If he keeps my laws as they are kept this day, I will be his father, and I will make his kingdom strong.'

"Now I say to you, while Israel is watching and God himself is listening: Learn the laws of God. Obey his commandments so that you and your children and their children's children may enjoy this good land forever."

The king turned to Prince Solomon.

"My son, remember to keep the laws of your father's God. Serve him with a perfect heart and with a willing mind, for he knows all that is in your heart. Whenever you need him you can be sure that you will always find him. When you forget him he will turn away from you."

Then he handed to Solomon the plans for the house, with its porch and its treasure rooms and the place for the ark.

"Go ahead now with the work. Do not be afraid. Do not get discouraged. The Lord God who has led me will guide and teach you till you finish the work, and you will worship him in his own house."

Then he gave Solomon gold and silver for the lampstands and the lamps, for the tables, for cups and bowls, for the altars, for everything that was to go into the Temple. Now he spoke to the people again.

"My son Solomon, whom God has chosen, is young, and the work is great. So I have collected all these things for the house he will build. And because I love that house, I have added from my own treasure enough silver and gold to cover its walls.

"Now who of you will offer your gifts? Who will volunteer to work on the house?"

Princes and captains and soldiers willingly offered to work. And they brought their own gifts of gold and silver and jewels, brought them gladly, because with all their hearts they wanted to give.

Then David led them all in a thanksgiving prayer:

> "Blessed be the Lord God, our Father, forever and ever!
> Yours, O Lord, is greatness and power and glory,
> All things in heaven and on earth,
> Riches and honor are gifts from you.
> So now, our God, we bring our thanks, our praise.
> But who am I—who are all these people—that
>   we should talk of gifts for you?
> For all things come from you, and of your own we
>   have given you.
> Gladly we give with all our hearts.
> Hear my prayer for Solomon my son.
> With all his heart may he keep your laws,
> And build for you this house I planned."

Gladly the people joined in thanksgiving, and they worshiped together.

Afterwards there was a great celebration. First they offered their sacrifice gifts, and smoke rose from hundreds of altar fires. Then there was feasting and laughing and singing for love of King David and the new king, Solomon his son, and the house the people were going to build for God. *1 Chronicles 22; 28; 29:1–19*

"God Save the King!"

King David was an old, old man. The time had come to announce to all the people that Solomon was to take his place. He sent for Zadok the priest and Nathan the prophet. They made plans.

An important procession went riding down the road from Jerusalem. There was Prince Solomon on David's own mule, and Zadok the priest and Nathan the prophet and the king's own bodyguard. They rode till they came to the spring named Gihon.

Zadok the priest poured the king's oil on Solomon's hair, anointing him king. The trumpets sounded and the people shouted,

"God save the king! Long live King Solomon!"

Then they rode back up to the city, and as they went the people joined in the procession, and they shouted and cheered while the flute players made the earth ring with their music.

So they all came to the king's house. King Solomon took his place on the king's throne, and all the king's bodyguard came to him.

"May God make King Solomon more famous than King David, make him even greater than the king," they said.

And the old king, his father, said,

"Blessed be the Lord God of Israel who has given us a man of Israel to sit on my throne this very day and has let me see it for myself."

He knew that he had not much longer to live, and there was so much he wanted to tell the new king.

"You must be strong," he warned again and again. "Keep the charge of the Lord your God, and remember his ways. Keep his laws and his commandments. Then will the Lord God keep his promise to me,

" 'If your children take heed to their way, to walk before me in truth with all their hearts, with all their souls, there will always be a king from this house in Israel!' "

So David died, and they buried him in the City of Peace.

1 Kings 1:32–40; 2:1–11

SOLOMON, THE SPLENDID

The Young King's Prayer

THE FIRST THING young King Solomon did was to call together all the governors and the judges and the leaders of the tribes for a great sacrifice worship service. Smoke from a thousand altar fires on high Gibeon curled into the air as the people prayed together. For Solomon loved God as his father David had loved him, and he remembered to worship God as his father had taught him to worship.

After the great service Solomon dreamed that God was standing beside him, saying,

"Ask me now for what I shall give you."

"Lord, you have shown great kindness to my father, and you have saved this last kindness for him—you have allowed his son to be king in his place.

"Now I am king. But, Lord God, I feel like a little child. I hardly know how to go out or come in. Yet I am to be the leader of all these people—so many that no one can count them.

"So give me an understanding heart, that I may be able to tell the difference between good and evil and lead these people wisely."

The unselfish answer pleased God, and he told Solomon,

"A wise and an understanding heart you shall have. You did not ask to be rich or honored or to win all your battles or to live a long time. But rich you shall be, and honored you shall be.

"And if you remember to keep my commandments as your father kept them, long life, too, will be yours."

Then Solomon awoke and knew that God had spoken to him in the dream.

1 Kings 3:1–15; 2 Chronicles 1:1–3

Building the Temple

A House for God's Honor

King Hiram of Tyre heard the news that the son of his old friend David was the new king in Israel. So he sent messengers to Solomon with his good wishes. They came back home to Tyre with a letter from Solomon:

"You remember that my father could not build a house for God while he was busy with so much fighting. Now our God has given us peace. So I am going to build his house, just as my father planned.

"It will be a great and wonderful house, for our God is very great. But who am I to try to build a house for him? The highest heavens are too small for our God. But I will build a house where men can bring their gifts and worship him.

"You know yourself that none of us can cut wood like your woodcutters. So hire men to work for me. I will pay them, and I will send my own men to work with them."

King Hiram was glad to help. Back to Jerusalem came his answer:

"The Lord God showed how much he loves his people when he made you their king. You shall have all the cedar and cypress wood you need. My men will cut the wood and bring it down the coast, then load it on barges to take it to Joppa. You can pay me by sending me grain and oil."

So the two kings worked together on the project. Solomon drafted woodcutters and stone masons and porters and overseers, and he sent them to help Hiram's men. Each crew would work a month in the forests, then come back home for two months.

Lumber for the new house was piled high. Stones large and small were carefully cut and shaped. Never a hammer nor an ax would be needed when the work began.

Early in May, on the threshing ground David had bought from Araunah, they laid the stone foundations for God's house. Walls and ceilings they built of cedar wood, and walls and doors and pillars they covered with gold.

Then another Hiram came to help. This man was an artist who could carve stone, engrave silver and gold, make beautiful things of brass, and dye fine linen blue and purple and crimson. The king had sent him to work for Solomon, for he was the best artist in Tyre. He knew how to carve palm trees and flowers on the walls. He could make the cherubim for the quiet, holy room built just for the ark of God's promise. Two great carved figures they were, like golden angels with their wings spread wide, just touching above the place where the ark was kept and reaching far across the room till they touched the walls. Safe under those wings was the place for the ark.

For the court outdoors where the sacrifice gifts would be burned, Hiram made the altars and the huge bowls to hold water for washing the gift animals. One was so big it rested on the backs of twelve carved oxen. Three of them faced the east; three faced south; three faced west; and three faced north. The sides of the bowl were thick as a man's hand, and round the brim of it were lilies made of bronze.

Lampstands and snuffers Hiram made of gold, and tongs and cups, and everything the priests would need for the Temple services.

Seven years they were working on the Temple, and Solomon knew in his heart that God was pleased. He had heard God plainly say:

"About this house you are building for me—if you will keep my laws, then I will live with my people. I will never leave them alone."

By fall of the eighth year the work was finished. All the doors and windows were in their places. All the treasures of gold and silver and jewels David had saved were carried in. But the greatest treasure, the ark, was still in the tent tabernacle where David placed it.

King Solomon sent for all the governors and judges and leaders of the tribes, and he called the Levites who were the only men allowed to carry the ark.

For the last time the priests picked up the ark by the poles that went through the rings at each corner. Out of the tent they marched, up to the shining new Temple. Past the altars in the court they went, up the steps of the porch, past the beautiful carved pillars, through the olive wood doors that were covered with gold, into the Temple itself. Back to the quiet, holy room they went, and there they lowered the ark gently under the wide, touching wings of the cherubim.

Outside, the people were crowding in the courts, waiting. As soon as they saw the priests coming back from the holy room the singing priests all dressed in white began their chanting. The musicians were playing their harps and cymbals. One hundred and twenty trumpeters joined in.

"Praise, oh, praise the Lord, for he is good;

"In his mercy he loves us forever."

Glory like a cloud filled the whole house, and smoke from the altar fires began to rise from the court.

King Solomon stood beside the altar on a high platform where all the people could see him. First he gave them his blessing. Then he reminded them how God had led them every step of the way to Jerusalem, how he chose David to be their king, and how David had wanted to build the Temple.

"Now I have built a house for God, a place for him forever," said the king. Then he knelt and, lifting his hands, he began to pray:

"Lord God of Israel, hear my prayer that you will watch this house day and night, that you will be listening when your people come here to pray. Hear them, and when you hear, forgive.

"If your people are in trouble when they have done wrong, and they come back here to pray and ask to be forgiven, then hear them from the heavens and forgive.

"When there is no rain, when there is famine or sickness, whatever may happen, and they come here to pray—one person in his trouble or all the people together—then hear them from the heavens and forgive them. Give to each one what he needs, for only you can know.

"As for the stranger—not one of our own people—who comes from far away to pray in this house, hear him from the heavens and answer his prayer, so that all people everywhere may know you, and know that this is your house.

"And if the people go to war and they pray to you, then hear them from the heavens and make them strong. If they should sin and for punishment they are taken away captive to some far land, then if they remember and come back to you with all their hearts,

"Hear them from the heavens and forgive them.

"Hear, Lord God, these prayers we pray in this house."

Solomon finished his prayer. Now he stood up, looking at all the crowd of waiting people.

"Thanks be to God who has given peace to his people. Not one word of all the promises he made to Moses has failed," he said.

"May God be with us as he was with our fathers.

"May he draw our hearts toward him to make us choose to keep his laws, make our hearts perfect, teach us to keep his commands.

"May all the people of the world know he is the one God. There is no one else."

Then the king and the people together brought their offering gifts, so many that the altars could not hold them all.

And so they gave God's house to him.

Then there was a celebration that lasted for days. After that they all went home, proud of their Temple, proud of their king, and grateful to God for all his love and mercy.

In those days King Solomon listened for God's voice, and so one night he heard another message:

"I have heard your prayers, and I have chosen this place to be my house.

"If my people who are named for me will pray humbly and try to find me and turn away from their wicked ways, then I will be listening from heaven, and I will forgive their sins, and I will help them.

"As for you, if you will keep my laws as David your father did, I will make you strong, remembering my promise: There will always be a king of the house of David for my people.

"But if you forget, if you go away and worship other gods, I will pull my people up by the roots out of the land I gave them. I will forget about this house I have blessed. Its high walls will be a ruin that will make people passing by stop and say,

" 'Why did the Lord let this happen?'

"And they will be told, 'They forgot the God of their fathers who rescued them in Egypt. They worshiped other gods, and this was their punishment.' "

1 Kings 5 to 9; 2 Chronicles 2 to 7

Rich and Wise Was Solomon

From the Euphrates to the land of the Philistines by the sea, far away as Egypt, Solomon was king. There was peace in all the land, for no other country was strong enough to fight his army.

People were busy building, and there was work for all. No one who was willing to work went hungry. There were homes for all the people where they lived safely in the shade of their own vines and trees.

After the Temple was finished, Solomon put the builders to work on his own house. Then he built the House of the Cedars of Lebanon where the king's throne was and a house for his wife, the daughter of the Pharaoh of Egypt. For twenty years the building went on.

Solomon built cities with strong, high walls. Some were storehouse cities, and some were for the chariots, some for the riders of horses.

No other king was as rich as Solomon. The ships in his navy brought gold and silver, spices and ivory, apes and peacocks from far countries. Merchants brought him linen from Egypt. His dishes were made of gold, and there was so much silver it was as common as the stones in the streets of Jerusalem.

He had horses and chariots from Egypt, and mules and camels for traveling across the desert. Spices and flour and meal, oxen and sheep, deer and fat chickens were brought to the palace for the king's cooks. There was plenty of barley and hay for the horses and the camels.

In the House of the Cedars of Lebanon a great ivory throne covered with gold had been built. Six steps led up to the throne, and there were twelve carved lions guarding it, two on each step. Even the footstool was made of gold. There was nothing like it in all the country.

Now God answered Solomon's prayer and gave him wisdom and an understanding heart so that he became wiser than any man alive from the east country all the way to Egypt. And he wrote three thousand proverbs and a thousand songs, all about trees and vine-covered walls and beasts and creeping things and birds and fish, about people and their ways. From all the country round, the people came to hear the songs and the wise sayings of Solomon.

One day two women came to him because they had been quarreling, and they needed a judge.

"We live together in the same house," one of them told him. "My baby was just three days older than this woman's child. One night her baby died, and while I was asleep she stole my baby and left her dead child beside me."

"No, the living baby is mine. Hers is dead," the other woman insisted.

Solomon interrupted: "So, this one says, 'This is my son, the living child.' The other says, 'Your son is dead.' "

Then he turned to his guard. "Bring me a sword," he ordered. "Divide the living child in two and give half to one mother, half to the other."

"My lord, give her the living child. Don't hurt the baby!" one mother cried out.

"Let him be neither yours nor mine. Go on and divide him," the other mother said agreeably.

The king pointed to the first woman.

"There is the mother of the living child. Give him to her, and see you do not hurt him."

The story was told from one village to the next. Soon everyone was talking about their king who was so wise a judge.

Stories about Solomon, the richest king, were being told in faraway lands. Travelers reported to the Queen of Sheba what they had seen and heard about the king who drank from golden cups and lived in a house with walls of gold, who had forty thousand horses in his stables and was so wise he could answer the hardest questions.

"I will go to see whether it is so," she decided.

She and her servants set out with a long caravan of camels loaded with gifts for the king—spices and gold and jewels. So she came to the City of Peace, and the king welcomed her, and he showed her all the beautiful shining city. She saw his house. She saw the servants dressed in their fine clothes. She ate the good food his cooks prepared. She watched him working with his governors. She saw him go to the beautiful new Temple to worship God. She asked him questions, and he knew the answer to every one. At last there was nothing more for the Queen of Sheba to see, nothing more for her to ask.

"All that I heard about you is true," she told him. "I could not believe the stories until I had seen and heard for myself. They did not tell me the half of it.

"Happy are your subjects, and blessed be your God who loved you and made you king."

Then, with all the gifts she could carry, she went back home to her own country.

2 Chronicles 1:13–17; 8; 9; 1 Kings 3; 16–28; 4:20–34; 7:1–12; 10

When the King Lost His Kingdom

King Solomon was rich and he was wise, yet for a foolish thing he lost his kingdom. He had not one, but dozens of wives, for he married many a princess from the outer lands where no one worshiped God.

"Do not go among them or let them come to you, for they will persuade you to worship false gods." That had been God's warning. Plainly he had said, "You must not."

Each new wife came to live in Jerusalem, bringing along her favorite images, and soon Solomon was worshiping them, too. So there came a day when Solomon heard this message from God:

"You have broken my laws. So I will take the kingdom away from you. For your father David's sake I will let you rule as long as you live. But when your son is king, ten of the twelve tribes of Israel will be lost forever."

Trouble began in the neighbor lands David had conquered. Hadad had escaped from Edom and found friends in Egypt. Now he went home to take back his land. So Solomon lost a part of his country. Rezon had escaped from David, and gone north to Syria. Now he rebelled against King Solomon, and so Syria was lost.

Even at home trouble was beginning. When King Solomon was so busy building cities, he had needed a strong man to put in charge of the work, and he had chosen Jeroboam. One day that young man was on his way out of Jerusalem when a strange thing happened. Out in the country he met the prophet Ahijah. Now Ahijah was wearing a new robe, and when he saw Jeroboam he began to tear it up. He did not stop until he had torn it into twelve pieces.

"You take ten pieces," he told Jeroboam. "It is a sign from God who says,

" 'I will take the kingdom away from Solomon because he has gone away from me. Not now, for I have made him a prince for life for his father's sake. But I will take it away from Solomon's son and give ten tribes to you.

" 'You are to be king of Israel. If you will listen to me, if you will keep my laws as David did, I will be with you, and I will build the house of your family strong and sure.' "

Somehow Solomon heard about Jeroboam's adventure, and he did his best to kill him. But Jeroboam slipped away and escaped to Egypt. There he stayed as long as Solomon lived.

And then at last Solomon the rich, Solomon the wise died, and he was buried in the city of Jerusalem where his father was buried.

1 Kings 11; 2 Chronicles 9:29–31

A KINGDOM DIVIDED

How the Kingdom Was Divided

THE ROADS to Shechem were crowded with travelers on their way to the coronation.

Prince Rehoboam, son of Solomon, was riding to Shechem to hear the people shout, "God save the king," when they placed the king's crown on his head.

The wise old men who used to talk over government business with King Solomon were riding north from Jerusalem to stand beside the young prince when he became their king.

Young men who had grown up with Prince Rehoboam were riding to the coronation service, hoping to have important positions in the new king's government.

Jeroboam, who had escaped to Egypt when Solomon tried to have him killed, was back home now that it was safe, and he was riding to Shechem.

Then there were the people, the king's subjects. Tired they were from working day and night building Solomon's houses and roads and high walls and watchtowers. Poor they were because of all the taxes Solomon had made them pay to give him money for the building.

A committee came to the new king. Jeroboam spoke for them.

"Your father, the king, made our work heavy and our lives hard. Now give us easier work, and we will gladly serve you."

"Give me three days to think it over," said the new king.

He sent for the wise old men, and he asked their advice.

"Be kind to your people and speak fairly with them, and they will be loyal to you forever," they told him.

Rehoboam sent for his young friends and asked their advice.

"Don't give in to them. Show them who is king. Tell them you can do more with your little finger than your father could with his whole body."

The third day the people came back for their answer, and King Rehoboam was waiting. Proudly he looked at them, and roughly he spoke:

"My father made you work. I will see that you work harder. He had you punished with whips. I will have you beaten with barbed whips."

Wearily the people went away, and the men of Israel, who were from the ten northern tribes, said,

"It seems we do not belong to the family of David any more. To your tents, O Israel! Home to your tents!"

But when the king sent an officer to collect taxes from the Israelites, they stoned him until he died.

King Rehoboam rushed to his chariot and escaped to Jerusalem. That day the great kingdom of David disappeared. The northern tribes of Israel rebelled, and they chose Jeroboam for their king. Solomon's son was king in Jerusalem, but only the people of the tribes of Benjamin and Judah were left in his kingdom.

1 Kings 12:1–20; 2 Chronicles 10:1–19

Two Kingdoms and Two Capitals

King Jeroboam needed a capital city, too. So he built strong walls around Shechem and called it the capital of Israel. But he began to worry. What if his people kept on going to Jerusalem to worship in the Temple?

"They might go back to Rehoboam. They might even kill me," he decided. So he built two places to worship in his kingdom, one in Bethel and one in Dan.

"It will be too hard for you to keep going all the way to Jerusalem," he explained to his people. He himself appointed men to be priests, and evil men they were. He even dared to be a priest himself, and wicked were the ways of them all. He chose new feast days, different from the days which God had planned. And he had great golden calf images set up in Bethel and in Dan.

"Here we will worship," he ordered.

Now it happened that young Prince Abijah, son of King Jeroboam, was very sick, and his father said to his mother,

"Go quickly to the prophet who told me I was to be king. Disguise yourself so he won't know you, but take him a gift—some bread and crisp cakes and honey—and ask him what will become of our boy."

Now the prophet was very old, and he could hardly see. But when he heard the mother's footsteps, he knew who she was.

"Why do you pretend to be someone else, wife of Jeroboam? Come in. I have bad news for you. To the king God says this:

" 'I took the kingdom away from the family of David and gave it to you. I made you king. But you have not been like David. You have made yourself idols to worship, and you have turned your back on me. The boy is not like you. He alone of all your family is good, and I will not let him suffer as the rest of you will suffer because of your evil ways.'

"Go back to your home," said the prophet. "When you step inside the city the lad will die."

And so it was.

In the south, in Judah there was trouble, too. King Rehoboam was busy arming his troops and building walls to keep his country strong. He was busy setting up worship places for idols on the hills as the heathen neighbors did, and his people liked what he did.

Down in Egypt King Shishak heard reports that Solomon's great, strong kingdom was weak and divided. So he came marching with his soldiers. Straight into Jerusalem he went, into the beautiful Temple. He stole the golden treasures of King Solomon and the shining golden shields that hung on the walls, and he carried them all away to Egypt.

King Rehoboam had no more gold. So he had copper shields made, and he hung them on the walls. The wonderful Temple was never quite so beautiful again.

After that, the people of Israel began to fight their cousins in Judah, and there were battles between the two kings as long as they lived.

*1 Kings 12:26–33; 13:33–34; 14;
2 Chronicles 11 and 12*

In the Days of Good King Asa

The stories of the kings of Israel in the north and of Judah in the south are stories of wise men and foolish, of men who loved the Lord God and men who built shrines for idol gods.

This is the story of Asa the Good, King of Judah.

The first thing Asa did was to break up all the altars where his people prayed to idols. He smashed the heathen statues which they worshiped. He gave orders that in all the land his people were to honor God, to try to find out his will for them, and to serve and obey him.

Then he built walls around his cities, and watchtowers and gates to keep them safe from attack. In his army he enlisted the bravest men in the land, and he supplied them with bows and arrows, spears and shields.

Up from Africa General Zerah came riding in his chariot with an army of Ethiopian soldiers. But King Asa was ready for them. He marched out at the head of his army, and as he went he prayed, "Lord God, it is as easy for you to help the weak as the strong. Help us now, for we need you."

That day Asa's army won a great victory. The Ethiopians tried to escape, but they were completely defeated.

King Asa's work for his country was just beginning. The prophet Azariah came to talk with him.

"Hear me, King Asa," he began. "The Lord God is on your side as long as you are true to him. If you go off by yourself, he will let you alone.

"For a long time now the people of Israel have had no teaching priest, and they have forgotten the laws of God. But as soon as they go back to look for God they will find him.

"Lead them, my king. Be strong. Keep on as you have begun."

King Asa decided on a great crusade. He made his people throw away every idol. He rebuilt the broken-down altar by the entrance to the Temple. Then he called together all his people for a great sacrifice and worship service.

There beside the altar they promised to love and serve God. And the music and the glad shouting sounded like the old times when Solomon first was king.

But even wise King Asa made a foolish mistake. It happened during one of those wars when the people of Israel were fighting against their cousins in Judah. The king of Israel began to build a strong fort that would keep anyone from traveling in or out of Judah. King Asa was frightened, and he decided that he must have help. So he collected all the gold and silver treasures that were left in the Temple, and he sent them off to King Benhadad in Syria, beyond Israel.

"You and I have been friends for a long time. Here is a gift for you. Now go and drive the king of Israel away for me," he wrote in the letter he sent with the gift.

The plan seemed to work, for King Asa and his people were safe again. But Asa had a visit from Hanani, the wise one.

"Why did you depend on the king of Syria instead of God? Weren't the Ethiopians a great, strong army with chariots and horsemen? You trusted God when they came. This time you trusted a man instead. You may have peace now, but there is going to be war later."

Angry King Asa had the wise one put in jail. But wars he had until he died.

1 Kings 15:9–24; 2 Chronicles 14 to 16

Elijah, the Fighting Prophet

Somewhere east of the Jordan River a man named Elijah was hearing grim stories about the new king of Israel. He heard that King Ahab's capital city, Samaria, was the wickedest city in all the land. People said that King Ahab was the worst king Israel ever had. They said that his queen, Jezebel, had brought her heathen idol, Baal, with her when she left her home in Zidon to marry the king. They said that the queen was doing her best to get rid of all the prophets of God.

Elijah listened to the stories, and he talked it over with God, and then he knew that he must go to the palace. So one day there he was, standing before the king. He had a strange message. It was the one thing he could say that would frighten even a soldier king like Ahab.

"There will be no more rain, not even dew, for years. Not until the day I tell you it will come back."

Elijah and the Widow of Zarephath

As quickly as he had come, Elijah disappeared, for no prophet of God would be safe around Queen Jezebel.

"Go east," were God's directions. "Just before you come to the Jordan River, stop by the brook Cherith and hide there."

So Elijah slipped away to his hiding place. He found plenty of water in the brook. And every morning and evening ravens flew by to drop him bread and meat.

Week after week went by, and the sun baked the earth. There was no rain, no dew. At last even the brook dried up, and Elijah had no more water.

"Go to Zarephath in Zidon," God told him. "A widow who lives there will see that you have a place to stay."

Just outside the town Elijah met the woman picking up sticks for firewood.

"May I have a drink of water?" he asked her. As she went to get it he called,

"And please bring me a little bread."

She turned around, and she said sadly,

"I have none. There is a little meal in the jar, a little oil in the bottle, enough to make bread for my son and me. I came out for wood to make a fire to bake it. That is all we have. When it is gone we must die."

"Don't be afraid," Elijah told her gently. "Just share what you have with me. For the Lord God of Israel promises that the jar of meal will be full and the bottle of oil will be brimming over till the day he sends rain on the earth."

It all came true. Elijah stayed with the woman and her boy, and there was always something to eat in the house.

His chance to do something for them came when the boy suddenly became sick, so sick that he died. Elijah picked him up and carried him to his room. Laying him on the bed, he warmed him with his own body, and he prayed,

"Lord God, let this child live again."

Life came back to the still body. Elijah carried him down to his mother.

"Look, your son is well."

"Now I know—I know God keeps his promises. Surely he sent you here to us," said the happy mother.

The hot, dry months went by, until more than two years had passed. Still there was no rain, just as Elijah had said. People had no food, for vegetables and fruits could not grow. Grain crops were ruined, so there was nothing to use for making bread.

The grass had almost disappeared. Horses and other animals were starving.

King Ahab sent for his prime minister, Obadiah. He was desperate enough to go to work like any ordinary man.

"We will divide the land. You go one way, and I'll go the other, and we'll check on every fountain, every spring. It may be we can find enough grass somewhere to save the horses and the mules," he told Obadiah. So each man set out alone to search for grass and water to save the animals.

Now Obadiah secretly loved God. When the queen had tried to kill all the prophets, he had rescued a hundred of them and had hidden them safely in a cave, where he carried food and water to them.

Walking slowly over the hard, dry ground, Obadiah came face to face with Elijah. At first he could not believe his eyes. He certainly could not believe his ears when Elijah said,

"Go tell the king where I am."

"But—but he has been looking everywhere for you. If I tell him I have seen you, how do I know you will not disappear again? When he can't find you he will surely kill me. And you know I have always been a friend of the prophets."

"I will be here, for I am going to see the king today," Elijah promised.

1 Kings 16:29–33; 17; 18

The Battle with the Baal Priests

King Ahab could hardly wait to see the man he blamed for all the hard times.

"So there you are, you troublemaker!" he called.

Elijah answered quickly,

"I have made no trouble for Israel. But you have, you and all your family. You have worshiped Baal instead of the Lord God. Now send for your people. Send for the Baal priests and the priests who live in your palace. Tell them to meet me on Mount Carmel."

The king obeyed without an argument.

Up on the mountain Elijah began to speak to the people.

"How long are you going to go on limping between two sides? If our Lord is God, then listen to him. If your Baal is god, then be on his side."

The people said nothing at all.

"Here I am alone of all the prophets of God. You priests of Baal, there are 450 of you. Now I want two bulls. You take one for a sacrifice to Baal, and I'll take one for a sacrifice to God.

"But none of us will touch fire to the altar. You pray to Baal. I will pray to God. Whichever answers with fire, he is God."

"Well said!" the people agreed.

So the Baal priests began their service.

"O Baal, hear us! O Baal, answer us!" they began shouting in the morning. There was no answer, no flicker of fire on the altar.

"O Baal, hear us! O Baal, answer us," they kept on till it was noon.

"Call out to him," Elijah mocked them. "Perhaps he is talking to someone. Perhaps he stepped outside. Maybe he is away on a trip. Or he might be asleep. Why don't you wake him up?"

"O Baal, hear us! O Baal, answer us!" the priests of Baal called all afternoon.

There was no answer.

Elijah stepped out before all the people, and he beckoned them to step up and watch. He picked up twelve stones, one for each tribe of God's people, and he built up the old broken-down altar. Round it he dug a deep trench. On the altar he laid wood, then the meat to be roasted. And then he called for water. Four barrels of water he poured on meat and wood till everything was soaking wet. He did it again and again. The trench was running over.

It was the time for the evening sacrifice. Now Elijah began to pray to God.

"Lord God of Abraham, of Isaac, and of Israel, let all the people know today that you are God, that I am your servant obeying you. Hear me, Lord, so that all these people may know who you are."

Fire flashed high over the wet wood, and smoke rose from the steaming sacrifice. Flames blazed up against the evening sky. There was no sound but the hissing steam on the wet rocks and the crackling of the fire. Then the people began to shout,

"The Lord, he is God. The Lord, he is God."

"Now you can celebrate, for I can hear the sound of pouring rain. Now you will have all you want to eat," Elijah told King Ahab, though all the ground around was still bare and hard.

He climbed to the top of Mount Carmel, and there he told his servant to watch the sky off in the direction of the sea. He himself sat down to wait, resting his head on his knees.

"I see nothing, only the clear sky," the servant reported.

"Look again. Keep watching."

"A little cloud—a very small one, no bigger than a man's hand, coming up over the water!" the man said at last.

"Here it comes. Go tell Ahab to get in his chariot and hurry home before he is caught in the mud."

Black clouds covered the sky, and the wind whipped round the mountain. Then the rain came, drenching the hot, dry earth. Elijah ran ahead of Ahab's chariot all the way back to town.

1 Kings 18

God's Quiet Voice

In the palace Queen Jezebel was too angry to listen to the sound of pouring rain. Her priests had failed, and Elijah had ordered them all to be killed.

"May the gods kill me if I don't kill you, too, by this time tomorrow," she warned Elijah.

This time the fighting prophet was frightened. He did the only thing he could. He escaped by the road to the south. When he crossed the border and came to Beersheba, which belonged to the land of Judah, he told his servant to wait for him. Then he traveled on alone for a day.

Tired and hot and lonesome, he sat down to rest in the shade of a scrubby tree.

"Lord God, I've had enough. Let me die now, for I'm nothing but a failure," he said miserably. Then he fell asleep. While he was sleeping an angel touched him.

"Get up now and eat."

Elijah could smell a cake baking over hot stones, and he saw a bottle of water. He ate a little and took a drink. Then he fell asleep again. The angel was still there beside him.

"Get up, Elijah, and eat, for you will be going a long way. You need your strength."

So he ate a good meal. Then he walked on for days until he came at last to a cave high on Mount Horeb, and there he stayed. He still felt lonely and discouraged, and all he could think about was poor, tired Elijah.

"What are you doing here, Elijah?" He heard the Voice he knew so well.

"I have been doing my best for you, Lord God. Your people have thrown down your altars. They have killed your priests. I'm the only one left, and they are trying to kill me, too."

"Elijah, step outside and watch."

Then the Lord God himself came by, but at first Elijah could not find him.

He heard a stormy wind whip round the mountaintop. He saw rocks it tore loose hurtling down the valley. But he could not find God in the windstorm.

He felt the ground shaking in an earthquake. He saw fire break out after the earthquake was over. But he could not find God in the earthquake, nor in the fire.

Then he heard a quiet voice, like the sound of a breeze in the leaves.

"What are you doing here?"

"I have been doing my best for you, Lord God," Elijah said. "Your altars are broken down. Your priests have been killed. I am the only one left, and they are trying to kill me, too."

"I have work for you to do, Elijah," the Voice said quietly, patiently. "First go to Damascus and anoint Hazael to be king of Syria. Then go to Israel, and when it is time, you are to make Jehu king. And find Elisha, son of Shaphat. Tell him he is to take your place as my prophet. Remember, there are still seven thousand men in Israel who are true to me."

Back to work went the fighting prophet. In the valley, moist now after the rains, the land was ready for plowing. Elisha and his father's men were busy. Twelve plows, each drawn by two oxen, were making straight furrows across the field. Elisha looked up from his work to see the great prophet Elijah standing beside him.

The young farmer watched the older man take off the mantle he was wearing. He felt it thrown around his own shoulders. As plainly as words could say it, Elijah was telling him,

"You will be taking my place as prophet of the Lord God."

Gladly Elisha left his team. "Let me tell my family good-by, and I will be ready. But come home with me first," he invited Elijah.

And that day there was a great feast in honor of Elijah.

1 Kings 19

The Royal Thief

King Ahab was sure that just because he was the king he could have anything he wanted. One day he noticed some land he liked. Now that land belonged to Naboth, and on it were Naboth's grapevines. But Ahab decided to get it.

"Give me your land. It's near my house, and I want it for an herb garden. I will pay you for it, or I will give you more land in exchange for it," he told Naboth.

"But this is my family's land. It belonged to my grandfather and to his father before him. Now it has come to me, and I don't want to sell," Naboth objected.

The king went home sulking, and he went to bed and refused to eat.

"Whatever is the matter?" Queen Jezebel wanted to know.

So he told her about Naboth who wanted to keep his land.

"Is that all? Who is king of Israel? Get up now and eat. I'll get you your land."

She wrote some letters, and she signed the king's name to them, and she sealed them with the king's seal, and she sent them to the important men in Naboth's town.

"Get ready for a celebration. Be sure that Naboth is one of the leaders and that everyone will see him. Then get a couple of worthless fellows to talk about him. Have them go around saying he cursed God and the king."

It was done, of course. Did not the letters come from the king, signed with his name? And the people believed the stories about Naboth, and they dragged him out of town and stoned him until he was dead.

Jezebel went to tell the king,

"You can go out to your land now. Naboth is dead."

Somewhere off beyond the hills Elijah knew that he must go on another mission for God. In Naboth's vineyard he met King Ahab face to face.

"Have you killed and stolen, too?" the prophet asked the king.

"Have you found me out, my enemy?"

"I have found you because you sold yourself to do evil and make your people do evil. This the Lord says,

" 'Evil shall come back to you.' "

And it was so. Several years later Ahab and Jezebel died miserably and no one mourned.

1 Kings 21

Two Kings Who Went to War

In the southern country, in the land of Judah, there was peace. Good King Jehoshaphat ruled his country well. His people were safe, for his soldiers patrolled the borders to keep the enemies out. He loved God with all his heart, and he tore down the heathen altars. He studied the law of God, and he sent men out on a teaching mission so that all around his country people might learn God's will for their living.

The news spread to the neighboring countries. Citizens of Judah were happy, people said. The king was strong and powerful. His army was brave. So instead of trying to raid the border towns, the neighbors wanted to be friends, and they came to King Jehoshaphat with fine gifts. Philistines brought silver. Arabians came with flocks of rams and goats. Rich and honored was King Jehoshaphat in his country.

He decided to go on a friendly visit to his neighbor, King Ahab, in Israel. So to Samaria he went, and King Ahab welcomed him with a great feast.

The two kings must have talked together about wars and armies. King Jehoshaphat knew that his neighbor's old enemy, Syria, had not attacked Israel for three years.

"Why don't we go together and take back my city, Ramoth-gilead, from the Syrians?" King Ahab asked.

"Why not? Our people are cousins. My men are yours to command. We will go to war with you. Just one thing I want you to do. Won't you find out what the Lord wants done about this?"

So Ahab sent for his four hundred prophets.

"Shall we go to Ramoth-gilead?" he asked.

"Go ahead. God will give you the city."

"Just a minute. Isn't there another prophet—one of God's own prophets? I would like to hear what he says."

"There is one other man, Imlah's son, Micaiah. But I hate him.

In Naboth's Vineyard

He is always telling me I am going to have trouble."

"Surely the king does not say so," the other king said politely.

"Send for Micaiah," Ahab ordered.

When the prophet came, he saw the two kings, each sitting on a throne, and the four hundred prophets nodding their heads. Prophet Zedekiah had made himself a small pair of iron horns. Now he held them to his forehead.

"With these you will push back Syria's army till every man is destroyed."

And all the prophets chanted,

"Go up to Ramoth-gilead, for the Lord gives it to the king."

The king's messenger who had brought Micaiah whispered to him,

"You hear what they all say. You go on and say the same thing."

"I tell what God says to me," said Micaiah.

"Come now, give me an answer. Shall we go to Ramoth-gilead?" asked Ahab.

"Go on to Ramoth-gilead, for the Lord gives it to the king," Micaiah mocked the words of the prophets.

"I want the truth," Ahab insisted.

"I can see Israel's people scattered over the mountains like lost sheep without their shepherd. I can hear the Lord say, 'Their leader is gone, and they must go home.'"

"What did I tell you! He is always talking about trouble," Ahab told his friend.

"And this is what I saw. There was the Lord on his throne, and he said, 'Who will send Ahab to fight and be killed at Ramoth-gilead?' Then I heard a voice say, 'I will go and be a lying spirit, talking like a prophet.' And the Lord said, 'You will go.'

"Don't you see? A lying spirit has spoken by these men. The Lord himself talks of trouble."

Zedekiah stepped over and slapped Micaiah on the cheek.

"Which way did he go—that lying spirit?" he asked.

"You will see, the day you run from room to room hunting a place to hide."

King Ahab had heard enough. "Take this fellow away. Put him in jail and give him bread and water till I come back in peace."

Micaiah had one more thing to say.

"If you come back at all, then it was not the Lord who spoke."

So the two kings rode off to war.

"I am going to wear a disguise. You put on my robes," Ahab said to his friend.

In the meantime the king of Syria was giving his final orders to his men. "Don't waste time on ordinary soldiers. Aim at the king of Israel."

So when Jehoshaphat came riding in his chariot wearing Ahab's robes, they surrounded him.

"That's not the king! Aim at the king of Israel!"

No one was watching an ordinary chariot in which two men were riding, but a Syrian soldier happened to shoot an arrow just once at the men as they went speeding by. His arrow flew straight at the man who stood by the driver, and it struck him between the pieces of his armor.

"Take me out, for I am wounded," he gasped.

But the battle raged all around them, and they could not escape. All day the wounded man stood up in his chariot, but at sunset he died. The king of Israel never went home.

1 Kings 22; 2 Chronicles 17 and 18

Victory Before the Battle

Back to his home in Judah went King Jehoshaphat, and again he set about the business of being a good king. He sent his judges to all the towns, and he told them,

"Be careful how you judge the people. You speak for God, not for men, and he will teach you what to say. Be fair to all, both the rich and the poor, and take no bribes at all."

He brought the Levite priests to Jerusalem to serve in the Temple, and he told them,

"Serve the Lord faithfully. Warn the people that they must not break the laws of God. Be brave enough to do right, and the Lord God will guide you."

One day messengers brought bad news to the king's house.

"They are coming from beyond the sea, all Moab and Ammon. They are marching on us. They are at Engedi already."

The great king was afraid, and his people were afraid. But they did not give up. They all met together by the house of God, and the king led their prayer.

"Lord God of our fathers, are you not king over all heaven, king over all the lands of the earth? Aren't you more powerful than all the people? Aren't you our God? Did you not rescue us and tell us you will listen whenever we are in danger and come to you for help?

"Now, Lord God, this enemy army is coming our way. We do not know what to do, and we need your help."

They all stood praying together, mothers and fathers and children. One priest stood and spoke to them all.

"Do not be afraid. Do not let this huge army terrify you. This is not your fight but God's. Tomorrow go out after them. You will find them all at the far end of the valley, but you will not need to fight. Just stand quite still. The Lord himself will be with you. You will see how God will rescue you."

The king bowed his head, and all the people bowed low, and they worshiped God together.

Early the next morning the army went out, but instead of soldiers they were singers chanting,

"Praise the Lord, for he guides and guards us forever."

They came as far as the watchtower that looked out over the valley. There was the enemy army, dead—every soldier of them—for there had been a battle with the people of the valley, and both sides had lost.

So the people of Judah came marching home to the music of harps and trumpets, and they sang as they marched along the road:

"Praise the Lord, for he guards and guides us forever."

2 Chronicles 19 and 20

The Prophet Who Took Elijah's Place

Two men were walking down the road together. One was Elijah, the fierce prophet who had fought and won many a battle for God, and the other was Elisha, the younger man who was busy at his plowing when he first met Elijah.

"You wait here. The Lord has sent me on to Bethel," Elijah said when they came to a good place to rest.

"As the Lord lives, and as you live, I will not leave you," Elisha told him. So they went on to Bethel.

There they met a group of prophets who said to Elisha, "Did you know the Lord is going to take your master away from you today?"

"I know," Elisha said.

"Wait here. The Lord has sent me on to Jericho," Elijah said.

"As the Lord lives, and as you live, I will not leave you."

So they went on to Jericho. And the prophets at Jericho said to Elisha, "Did you know that the Lord is going to take your master away from you today?"

"I know," Elisha told them.

"You wait here. The Lord has sent me on to the river," Elijah said.

"As the Lord lives, and as you live, I will not leave you."

So they went on to the Jordan River.

Elijah took off his mantle. Folding it together, he struck the water with it so that it flowed this way and that, and they could cross over safely on dry land.

When they were on the other side, Elijah said, "What can I do for you before I am taken away?"

"Let me be strong. Let me be wise. Let me be able to work twice as hard for the Lord our God."

"That is a hard thing," Elijah told him. "If you can see me when I am taken away from you, it shall be as you ask. If not, it cannot be."

They walked along, still talking. Suddenly a flaming chariot drawn by horses of fire swept between them. A storm cloud swirled round, and in the cloud Elijah and the chariot disappeared. Elisha stood watching.

"My father! My father! Chariot of Israel and driver, too!" he called after the great man who had been his friend.

On the ground at his feet lay Elijah's mantle. Elisha picked it up and he walked back to the river.

"Where is Elijah's God now?" he wondered. He struck at the

water the way he had seen Elijah do it. Before him stretched a dry pathway across the river.

He went back the way he had come. At Jericho the prophets came to meet him. They recognized him, but something about him was different.

"This man is like Elijah," they said, and they bowed respectfully as they greeted him.
2 Kings 2:1–15

Water Safe to Drink

In Jericho, Elisha did first of all the kindly, helpful things that were to make the people love him.

"This is a pleasant town," the men of Jericho told him. "But the water supply is bad. When we water growing things with water from the spring, they die."

"Bring me a bowl filled with salt," Elisha said. He carried the salt to the spring and threw it into the water. From that time on water from the spring was good to drink and safe for growing things.
2 Kings 2:19–22

Soup Fit to Eat

When Elisha and his servant Gehazi came back to Gilgal, it was in a time of famine, and there was little to eat in all the land. The young prophets came to study with Elisha, and they stayed with him.

"Put the big pot on the fire, and make soup for everyone," Elisha told Gehazi.

Someone went out to the fields to look for roots, and he came back with an armful of vines and herbs, wild gourds, things no one knew much about. But they were hungry, and they chopped it all up for soup. At last it was ready, and all the young prophets began to eat.

One man choked and cried out,

"Prophet! There's poison in the pot."

Elisha sent for meal, and he poured it into the soup.

"Now try it," he said.

So they ate their soup, and there was nothing harmful in it.

2 Kings 4:38–44

Money for a Mother's Debts

A woman came to Elisha to beg for help.

"What shall I do for you?" he asked.

She told him that her husband had borrowed a great deal of money, but before he could pay it back, he died. Now the man who made the loan wanted his money, and he was threatening to take away her two boys to be slaves if she did not pay him right away.

"Tell me what you have at home," Elisha said.

"Not a thing—nothing but a jar of oil."

"Go home, and go to your neighbors and borrow all the empty jugs and bottles you can find. Take them home and close the door. Pour, and keep on pouring oil from your jar. As soon as one jug is full, set it aside and fill the next."

So she did exactly as Elisha told her. The house was full of empty jars and jugs when she shut the door. The boys handed her bottle after bottle. As fast as each was filled they set it aside.

"Bring me another," she said.

"There are no more," the boys finally reported. Every bottle was full to the brim.

So the mother hurried to tell Elisha.

"Now go to market and sell your oil," he told her. "Pay your debt, and save the rest for yourself and the boys."

2 Kings 4:1–7

Prophet's Room at Shunem

The Most Welcome Guest

In the town of Shunem, where Elisha and Gehazi sometimes stopped to rest as they traveled round the country, there lived a friendly woman and her husband. They used to ask Elisha to stop for lunch. His visits gave the woman an idea. She talked it over with her husband.

"Let's build a small room for this man of God who travels this way so often. We can furnish it with a bed and a table and a stool and a lampstand, and it will be his own whenever he comes."

So Elisha was their guest, and it pleased him very much that they had gone to so much trouble for him.

"How can we thank her?" he asked Gehazi.

"She says she lives here comfortably with her people. She needs nothing. But I know that she has no son."

"Ask her to come here," Elisha told him.

Soon she was standing in the doorway.

"About this time next year you will be holding your own son in your arms," he promised.

"My lord, you are a man of God. Don't tell me what is untrue," she cried. But a year later she had a baby son.

The boy grew up. He was tall now, and old enough to walk with his father in the fields. It was harvest time, and the sun burned fiercely hot in the fields where the harvesters were at work.

Suddenly the boy stopped his work.

"My head! Oh, my head!" he moaned.

"Take him to his mother!"

The boy was carried back to the house, and all morning his mother held him in her arms. At noon he died.

She laid him gently on the bed, closed the door, and called her husband.

"I must go and find Elisha. Hurry! Send for one of the servants. Get one of the donkeys," she said.

"Go straight ahead. Don't stop for anything. Hurry!" she told the man as they set out for Mount Carmel.

Elisha saw her coming when she was still far down the road, and he sent Gehazi out to meet her.

"Are you all right?" Gehazi wanted to know. "Is everything all right with your husband? The boy—is he all right?"

"Everything is fine," she said, but she pushed on past him and ran to Elisha and caught hold of him.

"Did I ask you for a son? Didn't I beg you not to trick me?"

Elisha understood. Something was wrong at home. He turned to Gehazi.

"Take my staff with you and go as fast as you can. Hurry! Don't stop to talk with anyone along the way. When you get there lay my staff on the lad's face."

"I will not leave you," the mother warned Elisha. He went along with her, but before they reached the house, Gehazi met them.

"It did no good. He has not waked up," he reported.

As soon as Elisha saw the boy he shut the door, and then he prayed. He blew his own breath into the boy's lungs. He stretched his body on the lad's body and gave him warmth. And all the time he prayed.

Suddenly the boy sneezed. He opened his eyes.

"Go call his mother," Elisha told Gehazi.

When she came, she found her boy was well.

2 Kings 4:8–37

Help for the Great Captain

Captain Naaman of the Syrian army was a great man and bravest of the brave, but he was sick with leprosy. In his big house there was a little girl, stolen from her home in Israel in a raid by the Syrian soldiers. Now she was a maid, working for Naaman's wife.

"I know how the master could be cured," she told her mistress. "I wish he would go and see the prophet in Samaria."

Someone told Naaman, and Naaman told the king.

"Go to him at once," the king ordered his captain. "I'll write a letter for you to carry to his king."

So Naaman set out with the letter and with silver and gold and fine robes for a gift.

The king of Israel read the letter.

"When you receive this, you will know that I have sent my servant Naaman to you to be cured of his leprosy."

The king was furious. "It's nothing but a trick to stir up trouble. Am I God? Can I cure leprosy?"

Elisha heard about it, and he sent word to the king: "Let him come, for he will find out there really is a prophet of God in Israel."

So Naaman's chariot drove up to Elisha's house, and Naaman stood at Elisha's door.

Elisha sent a man out to tell the captain, "Go and bathe in the Jordan River seven times. You will be well."

Now Naaman was furious. "He might at least have come out to meet me. I thought he would pray to his God and wave his arms and do something about curing me. Aren't my two rivers back home better than all the rivers in Israel? Can't I wash clean in them?"

He turned away, but his men said quietly, "Sir, if the prophet had ordered you to do some really hard thing, wouldn't you have done it? Why not try this little thing?"

So the captain went down to the river, and he dipped his sick body seven times in its water. When he came out, his skin was healed. The disease was gone.

Back he hurried to Elisha's house, and gratefully he thanked the prophet.

"Now I know that your God is the only God in all the earth. I will pay you well for what you have done," he said.

"I will take nothing from you. Go in peace," Elisha told him.

So the captain's chariot headed north, back up the road leading to Syria.

But Gehazi kept thinking about those gifts Naaman had brought. What a pity no one was going to use them!

"I'll just run after them and get a share," he decided.

Naaman saw him coming, and he stopped.

"What's the trouble?" he asked.

"Nothing, but my master sent me to tell you he has two guests, young men who are sons of the prophets. Would you give them some silver and a change of clothing?"

"Of course. Take twice that much, and my servants will carry everything home for you."

Gehazi put the gifts in the house and told the servants good-by before he reported to Elisha.

"Where have you been, Gehazi?"

"Nowhere."

"Gehazi, did you think I would not find out? This is no time to be taking money and gifts. Look now. You have something else from Naaman."

Gehazi looked at his hands. His skin was white with leprosy.

2 Kings 5

"Tomorrow About This Time"

For a long, long time the raiders from Syria had stayed out of Israel. But the king of Syria came back with his army to attack Samaria, and the people of the city guarded all the roads so that no one could go in or out.

Inside the city the people ate up all the food, and the hungry time came. A donkey's head sold in the market for fifty dollars, and people were fighting for scraps of food. When they went complaining to the king about their troubles, he blamed Elisha for not taking better care of them.

"I'll have his head off this very day," he stormed.

But while his guard was on the way to Elisha's house, the prophet sat talking with the wise ones.

"When the messengers from that murderer get here," Elisha said, "lock the door. All this war and trouble has been his punishment. But it is over now. Tomorrow about this time you will go to market and buy a peck of flour or two pecks of barley for sixty-five cents."

"That I'll believe when the Lord makes windows in heaven!" laughed one of the king's friends.

"You will see it, but you will not eat any of it," Elisha answered him.

Just outside the city gate four lepers sat hopelessly talking over their troubles.

"If we go into town we'll starve. If we stay here we'll starve. We might as well go out to see the Syrians. They may give us some food. The worst they could do would be to kill us."

It was getting dark when the lepers walked out toward the Syrian camp. Not a sound did they hear. There was no guard to stop them. Not a single soldier did they see. They went into a tent and stopped to eat and get something to drink. Then they helped themselves to gold and silver and silken robes and went on to the next tent. Horses were tied up. Donkeys were tethered. Tents were left as if the soldiers had just walked out.

But they had not walked out at all. They had run. Suddenly the soldiers had heard a thundering noise—the sound of chariots and stamping hoofs.

"What's that? The king of Israel must have hired all the Hittites and the Egyptians to attack us!"

The thundering noise had grown louder. In the twilight the Syrian soldiers fled, leaving tents and horses behind.

The four lepers were helping themselves, hiding their loot, going back for more. Suddenly one man stopped.

"This is a night of good news. We can't keep it to ourselves. Let's go and tell the king."

So they went back to the city gate, and they told the watchman that there was no man in all the Syrian camp, no sound but the sound of sleepy horses and donkeys.

"It's only a trick," said the king. "Those Syrians know how hungry we are. They have just gone out from camp a way to hide in the fields so we will go out where they can capture us and get into the city."

"Just go and see," begged one of his guards. "Let's take some of those old starved horses of ours and ride out to their camp."

So out they went, and not a soldier was there to stop them. All the way to the Jordan River they rode. No soldier did they see, only heaps of baggage and clothes, even pots and pans the soldiers had dropped as they ran.

Hardly had they come home with the good news than the people piled out to plunder the tents, and they found so much food that in the morning a peck of flour or two pecks of barley were selling in the market for sixty-five cents.

2 Kings 6:24–33; 7

Choosing the New King

Evil was Ahab, king of Israel, and evil was his wife, Jezebel, who built altars to the heathen Baal and led the people when they prayed their heathen prayers. And evil was Jezebel's daughter, Athaliah, who married Jehoram, the son of good King Jehoshaphat of Judah. So both in Israel, land of the north, and in Judah, land of the south, the people of the true God said their prayers and brought their sacrifice gifts to idols made of wood and stone.

The prophet Elisha waited patiently, for well he knew that, when it was time, God would show him what to do.

Athaliah's son, King Ahaziah of Judah, as wicked as his mother, was a good friend of his Uncle Joram, king of Israel. They had fought many a battle together against the Syrians and some of the other unfriendly neighbor countries. When news came that King Joram was wounded, King Ahaziah went to Jezreel to visit him.

Now was the time. Elisha worked fast. If his plans worked, he would rid the country once and for all of the wicked family of Ahab. He sent for one of the younger prophets, and he gave him a jar of the oil that was used for anointing kings.

"Go and look for a man named Jehu. When you find him you will know what to do," were Elisha's instructions.

The young man went to army headquarters where he found the captains sitting around talking. He passed them by, but he beckoned to Jehu, and the two went indoors together.

Solemnly the young prophet poured the oil on Jehu's hair.

"You will be king by the will of the Lord God who says, 'I have chosen you. Now go and fight the family of Ahab to the last man. Not one of them is to be left.' "

The prophet slipped quietly away, and Jehu went back to his friends.

"What happened? What did that fellow want?" they all asked.

"He made me your king," Jehu announced.

The captains jumped to their feet. The evil days were over! The king they hated would have no more power over them.

"Long live King Jehu!" they shouted. And as the trumpets sounded a long salute, the captains tore off their cloaks and threw them on the stairs to make a carpet for their king.

Jehu strode out to his chariot, leaped into it, and drove furiously away. After him came his army.

On the wall of Jezreel, a guard stood watching the road.

"A great crowd rides this way," he called to King Joram.

"Send a messenger out to see if they are coming peaceably."

The messenger rode out, but he never came back. He had joined the rebels.

So the king sent another man.

"He does not come back," the guard reported. "I can see him going over to their side. Now I can make out the riders in the first chariot. That's Jehu. I know him by the way he drives."

The two kings climbed into their chariots and rode out to meet the visitors, and they all met on the very land King Ahab had once stolen from Naboth.

"Are you coming peaceably?" King Joram shouted.

"There can be no peace as long as your mother is queen."

"Treason!" King Joram shouted angrily. But he ordered his driver to turn around and ride away as fast as he could. At that very moment Jehu aimed an arrow, and his aim was true. King Joram fell dead in his chariot.

"Throw him over there in Naboth's vineyard," Jehu shouted.

King Ahaziah swung his chariot round by the garden house as he tried to escape. But Jehu's sharpshooters caught him. And so the other king died.

King Jehu and his men went on into the city. Queen Jezebel was waiting for him. She had painted her face, and she had combed her hair, and she was leaning far out of the window.

"Greetings, murderer of your king!" she called to Jehu.

The new king looked up.

"Is anyone up there on my side?" he called.

Two serving men came to the window.

"Throw her down!"

They tossed her out, and her body fell in front of Jehu's chariot.

"Go bury the woman," he ordered as he went inside.

There was a great house-cleaning in Israel. The people threw broken idols on the trash piles. They tore down the worship places on the hills, and they swept the shrines from the rooftops. Jehu did not rest until the last idol was gone.

2 Kings 8:25–29; 9; 10:26–28; 2 Chronicles 22:1–9

The Baby King in the Secret Room

In Judah, Queen Athaliah went on building altars to Baal. When they told her that her son Ahaziah was dead, she ordered all the young princes, her own grandsons, killed. She, and she alone, was going to be ruler in Judah.

But she did not know that one young prince escaped, a very small prince named Joash. He was just a baby whose nurse hid him, first in a bedroom, and then in the safest place of all, a room in the Temple, where neither his heathen grandmother nor her priests ever went.

A year went by, and another and another. The small prince Joash learned to walk and talk, very quietly of course, for no one must discover him until it was the right time.

Six years went by. Ahaziah's sister, the small prince's aunt, and his Uncle Jehoiada, the high priest, guarded him well. The young prince was nearly seven now, old enough to be crowned king if the people could find out who he was before the queen discovered him.

Jehoiada quietly called the priests from all the cities round about. He sent for the officers of the guards. He took them into the Temple, and there he showed them their boy king.

"A prince of the family of David shall be king again," he promised. "It will be on the sabbath day at the time of the changing of the guard. One third of you who are coming on duty are to guard the doors of the Temple. One third of you are to keep watch by the queen's house. One third are to guard the outer gate while the people will be coming inside the Temple court.

"Now, you who are going off duty—two thirds of you are to guard the king. If anyone comes too close, shoot at once."

From stores of King David's weapons hidden away in the Temple, Jehoiada brought spears and shields, enough for every soldier. Now the armed soldiers lined up around the small prince from one corner of the Temple to the other, along by the altar.

Joash stood quietly waiting. Before the army and the people, Jehoiada put the crown on the boy's head and anointed his hair with the king's oil. They all made a covenant promise together, the people and their king, that they would obey the Lord God forever. The people shouted, "Long live the king!"

In the palace Queen Athaliah heard the shouting, and she came running to the Temple. Suddenly she saw the small king standing by a pillar. Round him the king's trumpeters were sounding a salute, and the people were cheering and shouting.

The queen's face grew dark with anger.

"Treason! Treason!" she screamed at the guards.

No one came to her rescue. No one tried to stop her.

"Let no one harm her in the Lord's house," the priests had warned them.

Quickly she turned and hurried toward the Horse Gate. But the guards followed her, and just outside the Temple they killed her for her wickedness.

When she was gone, there was peace again in the land, for she was the last of all the family of wicked King Ahab.

2 Kings 11; 2 Chronicles 22:10–12; 23

A Chest Full of Gifts

Small Joash was only seven, but he was big enough to listen, big enough to learn, and his uncle, the good priest Jehoiada, taught him to be a good king.

While he was growing up, he discovered how shabby the Lord's house was looking.

"Why doesn't some one fix the leaky roof and the holes in the floor?" he wanted to know.

As he grew older he discovered that people were supposed to bring gifts to the priests every year to keep the Temple repaired.

"What are the priests doing with all the money?" he wanted to know.

By the time he found out how much it cost to do all the work that was needed, he had a plan, and he talked it over with his uncle.

He ordered the carpenters to make him a wooden chest, big and strong, with a hole in the top. He placed the chest beside the altar, just to the right of it, as people walked into the Lord's house.

Next, he sent his messengers through all the land to tell people why their gifts were needed. And they came hurrying to the Temple, gladly dropping their gold and silver in the chest as they walked by the altar.

As soon as the chest was full, the priests carried it to the king's office and counted the money. Then they took it back to be filled again. Soon there was money a-plenty for the work.

Carpenters and stone masons were busy on the walls and the floors and the roof. All the iron and brass work was repaired. There was enough money left to replace the gold and silver bowls and spoons and pitchers Queen Athaliah had stolen for her idols years before.

So Joash ruled his people wisely and well all the days that his Uncle Jehoiada lived to give him good advice.

2 Kings 12; 2 Chronicles 24:1–14

Uzziah, Who Wanted His Own Way

Kings good and bad ruled in the land, but it seemed there were more who were bad, more who led their people into evil—to worship idols, to steal from the poor, to forget the laws of God. Sometimes the men of Judah fought against the men of Israel, though one time they had all belonged to the same nation. Sometimes the armies of the north countries came marching south to steal a town or two and burn the fields and kill the sheep and cattle.

Prince Uzziah was just sixteen when his father died and he was crowned king of Judah. Good he was and wise he was, and at first he led his people wisely. He fought against the Philistines and drove them back from Judah, and he fought the Arabians. The Ammonites hurried to send him presents before he could fight them. He captured Eloth far down on the Red Sea where trading ships stopped with their cargoes of spices and perfumes, gold and silver from faraway lands, and he rebuilt the town. As far away as Egypt, people were talking about the great king of Judah.

In Jerusalem he built watchtowers high on the city wall, and he repaired the gates to keep the city safe. He was a farmer, too, and his herds of cattle grazed on the plains of the low country near the sea. He dug wells for them, and he built towers for shelters for his herdsmen. Higher on the fertile hillsides his vineyards stretched as far as a man could see.

His army was strong and brave. His soldiers had shields and helmets and bows and slings. His men invented a kind of catapult to shoot arrows and rocks a long distance.

While he was loyal to God, all was well, for God helped him in everything he did. But after he became strong and famous he grew proud, and trouble began.

One day he decided that he would go into the Temple and burn incense on the altar of God, though well he knew that not even a king might do the work of a priest.

Azariah, the priest, and eighty others rushed in to stop him.

"You must not, my king! Leave this holy place at once! This is a sin against God. You must not!"

Angrily the king raised the incense in his hand. So angry he grew, so red his face, that the telltale spot showed white and clear on his forehead. King Uzziah was sick with leprosy, and everyone could see.

From that day on he was quarantined, and his son Jotham became the king.

2 Chronicles 26; 2 Kings 15:1–7

GOD'S WATCHMEN

They Spoke for God

EVEN MORE IMPORTANT than the kings of Judah and Israel were the prophet-preachers like Isaiah, Amos, Hosea, Ezekiel, and the others.

Each of them heard God's call to preach, and each obeyed. Each of them went to the people with a special message from God. They dared to tell the king himself when he was doing wrong. They dared to stand before the most important people of the town and tell them that they were cheating and stealing.

Over and over these prophets begged the people to love and serve and trust the Lord God before it was too late.

For God must punish when his laws are broken, they said, and the punishment would be capture by a foreign nation in a war they could not win.

But God who loved his people was only waiting to forgive when they came back to him, trusting him for help and sorry for what they had done. Over and over the prophets spoke.

Some of the prophets were beginning to understand God's special plan to save his people. When the right time came, he would send the one they knew only as the Messiah or the Christ. No one knew when it would happen, but certain prophets were able to look ahead and understand certain things about his coming. They told the people.

The prophet Micah said that he would be born in Bethlehem.

The prophet Isaiah said that people would misunderstand him and hate him—and even kill him.

Amos, the Shepherd Preacher

In the northern land of Israel, Jeroboam was king. His capital city, Samaria, was rich and beautiful. The house of God at Bethel where the people brought their gifts was as fine as they could make it. Rich people lived in fine stone houses with walls of ivory—winter houses with thick, strong walls to keep out the cold winds and summer houses open to the cool breezes. Their soft beds were made of ivory. They spent their time feasting and drinking. Their musicians played so loudly in entertaining the rich that they could not hear when poor folks cried out for help. And when the sabbath day or a holiday came round, the merchants counted the hours till they could go back to their businesses where they cheated the poor, sold bad food, and shortchanged them for food weighed out on dishonest scales.

In the hill country a shepherd named Amos was hard at work taking care of his sheep, stopping only long enough, when the wild figs were ripe, to harvest his crop.

Up there in the hills he heard the Voice:

"Amos, go and preach to my people in Israel."

Amos had never been a preacher. His country dress and ways would look strange in the city. But he knew that Voice, and he knew that he must obey an order that came from God.

Straight to Bethel he went, to the king's chapel, and before the priests could stop him he began to preach.

At first the people liked the stranger who was dressed like a country shepherd. At first they liked the way he was talking.

" 'Three times, four times Syria has sinned, and I will not forget,' says the Lord. 'Fire will burn down the house of the king of Syria, and his people will be captured.

" 'Three times, four times the Philistines have sinned, and I will not forget. Fire will burn down the wall of Gaza, and the people will be destroyed.

" 'Three times, four times Tyre has sinned, and I will not forget. Fire will burn down the walls of Tyre, all the wall around the city.' "

The preacher went on. The enemies of Israel were to be punished for their sins—Edom and Ammon and Moab. The new preacher was very great indeed.

" 'Three times, four times Judah has sinned.' "

This was interesting, too, to the people of Israel who liked their neighbor cousins little better than their neighbor enemies.

" 'They have despised the commandments of God. They have broken his laws.' "

Would Jerusalem burn up, too? No one felt too sorry.

The new preacher spoke fearlessly for God.

" 'Three times, four times Israel has sinned. You have been my people, chosen from all the earth. But woe to you now for your sins! You cheat the poor. You break my laws.

" 'I won your battles for you. I brought you away from the land of Egypt and led you forty years through the desert lands. I destroyed the Amorite soldiers, tall as cedar trees, strong as the oaks, when they would have conquered you.

" 'I sent you hunger for a warning, but you did not come back to me. I held back the rain for a warning, but you did not come back to me.

" 'So now your punishment will come to you, and you will discover who your God is.

" 'For he who made the mountains,
   He who made the winds,
   Who tells a man what he is thinking,
   Who makes the morning darkness
   And walks upon the mountain peaks,

© 1963, Broadman Press

Amos and the Cheating Scales

> The Lord, the God of earth and heaven is his name.
> Listen! For he speaks to you:
> "Look for me, and you will live."

" 'Never think you can escape by saying prayers in Bethel or in Gilgal, for when the enemy comes marching, Bethel and Gilgal will both be gone.

" 'I know your evil ways, how you cheat and steal;
I hate, I despise your palaces.
I hate, I despise your gifts and prayers.
Though you bring me gifts I will not take them,
Though you sing to me I will not listen,
You who laugh and sing and forget the troubles
  of the poor.

I will give your cities to your enemies, let you be taken
  to far lands beyond Syria.
Look now for God who made Orion, who made the stars,
Who turns the shadows into morning light,
Who darkens day with evening,
Who calls the ocean waves and pours them out
  against the shore.
The Lord God is his name.

Seek for good and not for evil,
Hate the evil and love the good.
Let justice roll down like a river;
Let goodness flow like a mighty stream.
Then shall the Lord be with you, and help you
  in your time of trouble.'

"So says the Lord, who is God of all the world."

About that time the high priest of Bethel hurried up to Amos.

"Go away. Go back to Judah and earn your living preaching there. Just don't preach any more here in Bethel. This is the king's chapel. This is the king's court."

The shepherd preacher from the country said quietly, "I am no prophet trained to preach. The Lord sent me on this mission while I was still tending my sheep. He told me,

"'Go and preach to my people in Israel. Their ways are evil, and I cannot forget what they have done. Tell them even the land will shake for fear. The people will weep for their troubles. For I will turn your celebrations into mourning, your songs to sadness.

"'For the time will come,' says the Lord God, 'when I will send a famine in the land. Not a famine when people are hungry for bread, thirsty for water, but hungry to hear the word of God. They will be wandering this way and that, from Dead Sea to the Great Sea, hunting for the sound of the Lord's voice.'

"Are you laughing?" asked Amos. "Do you think nothing like that could ever happen?

"'For their sins my people will die,' says the Lord.

"'But I will sift out the people of Israel, separate good from bad, the way grain is separated from chaff in a sieve. Not one good grain will fall away to the ground. One day I will bring my people back to their homeland again. They will build their cities and plant their vineyards, make their gardens, and settle down to live comfortably. Never again will they be taken from the land I gave them.'

"Hear the words of the Lord God," said the prophet Amos.

2 Kings 14:23–29; the Book of Amos

Hosea's Discovery

There was one king in Israel, then another and another—Zechariah, and Shallum, and Menahem, and the rest. Evil they were, and evil they did all the days of their lives. Again and again God warned that punishment was coming to his people if they insisted on doing as they pleased and did not obey him.

The preacher-prophets scolded and they warned. God insists on being obeyed, they said. God punishes everyone who disobeys, they said over and over again. Amos preached on playing fair.

It was the prophet Hosea who discovered how much God loves people, and so he preached about love.

When he had trouble in his own family Hosea discovered what God is like. His wife, whom he loved dearly, left their home, left him to take care of their three children, two small boys and a little girl. In spite of that, he continued to love her and he wanted her to come back.

At last he went to find her. Poor she was now, and sick and dirty and ragged. But he loved her so much he brought her safely home where he could take care of her.

That is how God loves, Hosea taught the people of Israel.

Hosea took care of the children, and he discovered how much a father loves a child even when he tries to have his own way.

God loves the way a father loves, Hosea taught the people.

"When Israel was a child, then I loved him.
    I called my son out of Egypt,
Taught Ephraim how to walk,
    Took the small boys by the hands,
I drew them with soft reins of love.
    How shall I give you up?
    How can I cast you off?
I will listen, says the Lord God. I will hear them calling.
    I will have mercy,
    I will say to those who forget they were my people,
    You are my own,
    And they will say,
    You are the Lord our God."

2 Kings 15:8–18; Hosea 1; 2; 11

Jonah, the Unwilling Missionary

"I am a Hebrew, I serve the Lord, God of heaven and earth," Jonah boasted proudly. Very sure he was that God was not the least interested in any other country but his own.

So God's orders were strange and surprising.

"Jonah, go up to Assyria, to Nineveh, and preach to the people, for their wickedness troubles me greatly."

The Lord himself was speaking, but Jonah hurried to get away. Why would God be interested in those foreigners off there in Nineveh?

He hurried the other way, to Joppa by the sea, and there he found a ship just ready to sail for Tarshish. So he paid his fare and went on board, to get as far away from God as he could.

Before the ship had gone far, a great storm broke. The wind pitched the small boat this way and that until it seemed she would surely be wrecked. The terrified sailors began to pray, each man to his god. To make the ship lighter they threw overboard every piece of baggage and freight.

Jonah had gone below to take a nap, but the captain went down and woke him up.

"What do you mean, you sleeper? Get up and start praying. Maybe your God can save us."

Up on deck the sailors were saying, "One of us must be to blame for this storm." Someone pointed to Jonah.

"Who are you? Where do you come from? What do you do?"

"I am a Hebrew. I serve the Lord, God of heaven and earth, who made the sea as well as the dry land."

"But you are running away from him. You said so yourself."

The wind struck with sudden force. The ship was pitching badly.

"It is my fault," Jonah said. "Take me and throw me overboard."

The men tried harder than ever to row against the wind, but they could not get the ship to shore. They prayed again.

"Lord God of Jonah, do not make us die because of this man."

And then they did throw him overboard.

The storm died down. The little ship went on its course.

Deep water closed over Jonah. The waves tossed him, rolled him round. Far down below the surface seaweed tangled round his head. Sent by God, his rescuer was a great fish out of the depths of the sea, and the fish swallowed him and carried him for three days till it took him safely to dry land. Jonah said,

"I called to the Lord in all my troubles,
And he answered me.
When my heart gave up within me,
I remembered the Lord.
Then my prayers reached him.
The Lord himself rescued me."

Now Jonah heard his orders again.

"Get up and go to Nineveh and preach my message."

This time Jonah went.

He found that Nineveh was a big city, so big it took three days to walk across from one side to the other. So he walked a day, and then he stopped to preach.

"Turn back from your evil ways. Stop your wickedness. Listen to the teaching of the Lord God. Or else in forty days' time your great city will be destroyed," he began his sermon.

The people stopped to listen. They began to worry about their meanness, and they believed every word he was telling them about God. Even the king listened, and he ordered his people to go into mourning for sorrow over their sins.

"Who knows? Perhaps it is not too late. Maybe God will forgive us."

So God did. And the great city was saved.

But Jonah grumbled, "I knew it would happen. I knew the Lord God is as loving as he is just. I knew how ready he is to forgive and love everyone. That's why I ran away." (Why did he have to love foreigners? was what Jonah meant.)

"Lord God, I'd rather be dead. Take my life, and I'll not have to see these foreigners forgiven."

"Are you really so angry?" God asked.

Just outside the city Jonah stopped to rest. After all, something might happen to Nineveh. It was hot, and he made himself a shelter of branches and leaves, and he sat down to watch.

While he was sitting there, up shot a gourd vine with thick green leaves. It made cool shade for him, and he liked it. But the next day a worm killed it. When the hot east wind blew and the sun beat down on him, Jonah felt sick.

"Oh, let me die. I'm better off dead than alive," he mourned.

"Are you really so angry about the gourd?" he heard God ask.

"Yes, I am—angry enough to die."

The Voice went on talking.

"You were sorry for the plant that died. You did not make it or help it grow. It just sprang up, and then it died. But think of Nineveh, that great city with 120,000 people in it. Just babies they are. They need help in choosing right from wrong. Would I not be sorry for them?

"Would I not want to save those people?"

Jonah did not need to answer. At last he understood that God loves all people.

The Book of Jonah

Isaiah, Messenger to Kings

A boy was growing up in Jerusalem. His family was important at the king's court, and they lived like princes. There was plenty of silver and gold in the land. It was full of treasure, full of fine horses and chariots. But it was full of idols, too, and people bowing to pray to things their hands had made.

The boy had been taught to choose what was right. But he discovered that people he knew were calling good the things he knew were evil, calling evil what he knew was good. He saw princes making friends with robbers. He watched judges taking bribes and letting criminals go free for a gift. He saw the beautiful ladies of Jerusalem go walking down the street, bells tinkling on their fine shoes, with never a care for the poor and the sick. He saw proud noblemen taking the best of everything for themselves, with never a thought for people who were hungry.

He watched dry, dead leaves fall from the tall oak trees, watched a garden curl up and wither away when no one watered it. God's people were like dead leaves in a garden, he realized.

"Jerusalem is ruined!" he wanted to shout. "Run and hide in the caves, behind the rocks, before the Lord God himself judges his people and they get the punishment they deserve."

But the walls of Jerusalem stood strong and high, and the people went on about their business. The boy went on thinking.

The boy, Isaiah, grew to be a man, still thinking about his people and their danger. One day in the year that King Uzziah died, he discovered that God had special work for him to do.

He was in the Temple when it happened. Suddenly he could see the Lord God on his throne, and glory filled the Temple. Above the throne he could see the golden figures of the seraphim that always rested just above the ark. But now they were great tall angels, and

© 1948, The Sunday School Board, S.B.C.

Isaiah's Vision

each of them had six wings. With two they covered their faces from the glory. With two they covered their feet for reverence. With two they were flying. And one was chanting to the other,

"Holy, holy, holy is the Lord of hosts!

"All the earth is filled with glory."

The walls seemed to shake with the sound of their voices, and all the house was filled with the glory cloud. Isaiah was frightened.

"What is to become of me?" he cried out. "I am just a man, and I have sinned. I live with people who have sinned. Even my lips are unclean for the evil words I have said. And with my own eyes I have seen the King, the Lord of all."

One of the golden seraphim picked up the tongs from the altar, lifted a burning coal from the altar fire. Flying over to Isaiah, he touched his lips with the fire.

"Now you are clean, for the evil is burned away," he said.

Isaiah could hear the Lord God speaking.

"Whom shall I send?"

"Here I am. Send me," he answered quickly.

"Go and teach my people. But they will not listen. Show them. But they will not see. Teach them. But they will not understand."

"How long will it be until they listen?" Isaiah asked.

"Not until the towns are ruined and empty, and the houses are no longer homes, and the people have been taken far away.

"But a remnant of them will be left. When they have learned to trust their God they will come back home, like the green shoots growing from the stump of a tree long after it has been cut down."

So the prophet Isaiah went to work, telling the people God's ways, learning from God his will for the people.

"Hear what the Lord God is saying," he would preach.

" 'I have no time for your feasts and your sacrifices when you come trampling into my house with stained hands and evil hearts. Put away your wickedness. Help your neighbor instead of stealing from him.

" 'Come, let us talk it over,' says the Lord. 'Your sins may be so bad they are stained blood-red, but they can be washed white as snow.' "

For Isaiah understood something most people did not understand:

God was depending on his own people to tell their children and their grandchildren and their many great-great-grandchildren about him, and some day to spread the news of the one true God to all the world.

So, even though the people must be punished for their evil ways, God would keep safe all who wanted to change their minds and live like his children again. Their punishment might mean losing their homes and being prisoners of war in some strange land far away. But some day, when they learned their hard lesson and gave up their foolish idols forever, he would bring them home again.

But now, Isaiah knew, his people must not fight a strong enemy and run the risk of being killed while they still had a chance to carry out the mission God had given them. So he knew that he must do more than preach to the people. He must work for his country, too.

There came a time when Isaiah knew that the king was about to make a big mistake.

When Menahem was king, great Tiglath-pileser from far-off Assyria sent his army to capture Israel. But King Menahem offered him money to let them alone. The king agreed and took the money—nearly two million dollars—and then he collected a tax from every citizen, too.

About that time King Ahaz in Jerusalem heard news that was making the people shiver like trees swaying in the wind. Pekah, who was king of Israel now, and his friend the king of Syria, decided that all the little countries should get together to fight the Assyrians. Even now they were on their way to force the people of Judah to join them.

King Ahaz made his plans to guard Jerusalem against any attack, and he himself went out to inspect the waterworks. He was standing on the road to the fields where the cleaners were at work on the soiled clothes when he saw a man and a boy coming to meet him.

The man was Isaiah. The boy was his son who had the strange name, Shear-jashub, which meant, "Remnant will come back." Even his son's name showed how sincerely Isaiah was working on his mission. Now he must give the frightened king courage and persuade him not to get mixed up in a war against Assyria.

"Don't be too alarmed," he begged King Ahaz. "Just be quiet. Don't do anything to attract attention, and the great nations will let us alone. Don't be so worried about Israel and Syria. They are just two pieces of half-burned, smoking firewood, and they can't last long.

"Don't you see—if you have faith you can hold on."

King Ahaz said nothing at all.

"If you don't believe me, ask the Lord God himself. Ask him now for a sign to show you I am right."

"I will not," said King Ahaz.

Isaiah's heart was heavy, for he could see what was sure to happen, see the land growing wild with briars and thorns. So next he tried to get his message to the people. He put up a mysterious sign which read:

"For Maher-shalal-hashbaz."

This word means "For Swift to the Plundering Quick the Booty Captured in War."

But he did not explain what it meant.

Then after a time Shear-jashub's little brother was born, and Isaiah told everyone his name was Maher-shalal-hashbaz.

"Before that baby is old enough to say 'Mother' and 'Father,' both Israel and Syria will be prisoners of Assyria, who comes plundering swiftly, capturing quickly. Take counsel together, you people, and think well what you are doing before you get into a war."

But they would not listen.

So for a time Isaiah gave up his preaching. But he wrote out his message, sealed it, and gave it to a group of his students.

"I will wait, with the children the Lord God gave me, for him to speak," he told them. *Isaiah 1 to 8; 2 Kings 15; 16; 2 Chronicles 28*

Farmer Micah

Now another prophet was busy working and teaching and preaching God's plan for his people. He was Micah, one of the farmer people who lived in Israel, near Gath. Idols he hated, and all the cheating, lying ways of God's people he hated.

"You lie awake at night plotting, and as soon as it is light you hurry off to steal a man's land and cheat him out of his house. You hate the good and love the evil, you who are named for the Lord God himself.

"Now for your sins your cities will be turned into heaps of rubble. Your children will be prisoners of war."

The people just kept on sinning.

"But who forgives sins like our God? Who else would forget the evil ways of the few who still love him?" Micah's voice rang out, though his heart was breaking. "He does not stay angry forever. When his own come back to him he gladly offers them his love.

"He has taught you, man, what is good. This the Lord will have of you:

"Do justly. Love mercy. Be not proud, but walk humbly with your God." *Micah 2; 6; 7*

PROUD ISRAEL'S END

The trouble between Israel and Judah grew worse. First the Syrians took the town of Elath away from Judah. Then the men of Israel invaded Judah and captured their own fellow countrymen, soldiers and women and children, and they carried them home to Samaria.

But there in Samaria the gentle prophet Oded was waiting when the prisoners came in, for he had something to say to the officers of the army.

"So you have won your battle, and you have taken the people of Judah to be your slaves. Just stop and think what you are doing. Have you no faults of your own to trouble you? Listen to me, and let these people go home, for I tell you the Lord God is angry with you."

Then the leaders of the people themselves rebelled against the army. So the prisoners were released and the men of Israel gave them food and clothing. They found donkeys for the tired ones to ride, and they went home with them as far as Jericho.

Glad as the prisoners were to be returned, they found little joy at home in Judah. Soldiers came marching from the Red Lands to steal and carry away prisoners. Philistine raiders moved into the towns in the south and settled there to live.

King Ahaz knew he had to have help, and he was determined to get it his own way. So he quickly wrote a letter to the king of Assyria:

"Help me. I'll send you gold and silver. I'll be your servant. I'll do anything you say."

He hurried to the Temple, and he packed up all the gold and silver he could find. He added the treasures in his palace. He sent these gifts to Assyria to buy the king's help. The Assyrian king took the gifts gladly enough, but he did not help.

Then King Ahaz tried something else.

"Up in Syria the gods help the people. I will pray to the Syrian gods, too, and maybe they will help me."

But that was the ruin of King Ahaz and of all the country with him. He died in his trouble, and so evil had he been that the people would not bury him with the hero kings of other days, but outside the city in a lonely tomb.

Evil they were in Israel, and King Hoshea was more wicked than the kings who had gone before him.

From far Assyria the army of King Shalmaneser came marching, and they captured the king's city, Samaria. Quickly Hoshea made peace, and he offered the enemy king presents and promised to pay him more money every year.

Easily he made his promise. Quickly he broke it. His messengers hurried to Egypt to ask King So for help. Then one year he sent no money at all to Assyria. All the time his people just went on breaking God's laws and praying to their heathen gods on the hilltops.

"Give up your evil ways," the prophets begged.

But the people kept on saying their prayers to the idols, worshiping golden images, and making magic. In all the land of Israel they had forgotten God.

Back came the Assyrian army. Outside the walls of Samaria they camped. No one could go out for food. No one could get in to bring help. For three years the people of Samaria tried to fight them off, and then they were too tired to fight any longer.

Out from their homes the soldiers drove the proud people of Israel. They herded them together like cattle and marched them to far-off Assyria. The people of Israel were captives of the Assyrians. Never again would there be an Israel.

The great king sent other prisoners from other lands he had conquered to live in Israel. But the walls were broken down. Mountain lions prowled around the ruined streets. The foreign people who moved in worshiped all kinds of gods. They even tried to worship the Lord God of the Israelites, too, for they wanted to be sure to please everyone.

So proud Israel was gone from the land. And only the families of Judah in the south were left of all the nation God chose to be his own.

2 Kings 16; 17; 18; 2 Chronicles 28

LONELY JUDAH

Housecleaning in the Temple

WHILE ALL THE TROUBLE was happening in Israel, there was trouble of a different kind in Judah.

High on the mountain in Jerusalem the great Temple was dark. No one opened the doors of the porch since wicked King Ahaz ordered them shut. Round the broken altars, trash and pieces of broken idols cluttered the court. And the priests of the Lord God were far away.

Then Hezekiah became king of Judah. Now Hezekiah trusted God and kept his laws, and God was helping him.

The first thing he did was to call back all the priests. When they met together in East Square he told them what he wanted.

"Make yourselves ready to serve in the Temple of the Lord God. Then get in there and clean it up. Carry out all the trash. Repair the altars, for we are all going in there to worship our God."

So the priests went to work—Mabath and Joel and Kish and Joash and all the rest. They swept up the dirt and carried it all out and threw it into the Kidron Brook. They mended the altars and cleaned them up. They shined the lamps and lighted them. They hunted for the bowls and altar things King Ahaz had lost. They mended and they polished until everything was ready. And then they went to King Hezekiah.

"The Temple is clean and ready for worship," they reported.

Early next morning was the time for the big worship service. The priests made the sacrifice gifts ready for the altars. Then the musicians led the singing with harps and cymbals and trumpets sounding loud and clear, and the people chanted:

"Sing a joyful song to the Lord, you people of all the lands;

Serve the Lord with gladness; come singing as you meet him." They brought their gifts, and they bowed their heads, and they worshiped all together.

The next thing King Hezekiah did was to plan a great Passover celebration. To north and south, along the highway, the king's messengers carried the news.

"Come back to God who loved your fathers and their fathers' fathers. Come back to him, and he will come to you. Enter into the Temple, and serve him."

Far in the north country people who had escaped from the king of Assyria heard the message. Some of them laughed. How could anyone rescue them from the king they hated? But others listened, and they believed. Back they went to Jerusalem, glad to be going back to the Temple at last, and sorry, too, because they had forgotten God so long.

So they all met in Jerusalem, great crowds of people, and they kept the Passover feast the way Moses had taught them years and years before.

King Hezekiah stood by the altars, and he prayed,

"The good Lord pardon every one

"Who in his heart will truly seek him."

And God answered the king's prayer.

When the people returned home, they went to work to clean up the rest of the country. They tore down every heathen altar. They broke the images in pieces, and they swept the trash from the hilltop worship places.

King Hezekiah planned with the priests to keep up the worship services at the Temple. He sent word to the people to bring their gifts for love offerings and for the priests' food. So they brought their gifts, a tenth of all they had, corn and wine, oil and honey, sheep and oxen. There was plenty of everything that was needed and enough to put away in the storerooms.

The walls of Jerusalem were high and strong. Every broken place was repaired. King Hezekiah had worked out a new way to bring running water inside the city. The Temple was clean, and a man could go there to worship God as he should. But the people of Jerusalem were frightened. Some who knew no better wasted their money on chirping wizards and muttering magicians as if magic could keep them safe. For they knew what the Assyrian soldiers had done to their cousins in Israel. Any time now those fearful chariots and horses and soldiers could come thundering up the road to Jerusalem.

King Hezekiah and his men set to work to keep Jerusalem safe. They stopped up the fountains and the brooks down in the valley. After all, why should the Assyrian soldiers find all the water they wanted? They built the city wall higher, up as high as the watchtowers, and they made more swords and shields, plenty for every soldier to be armed.

Then the king called his people together in the street by the city gate.

"We do not need to fear the king of Assyria and all his army, for we have the Lord God to help us. Keep up your courage!" he told them.

Because the people trusted their king, they forgot their worries for a while. *2 Chronicles 29; 31; 32:1–8; 2 Kings 18:1–7; Psalm 100:1; Isaiah 8:19*

Dangerous Neighbors

A few years later the Assyrian army came back and captured some of the border towns. Quickly Hezekiah sent a letter to the Assyrian king:

"I must have done something to make you angry. Just tell me what you want me to do."

The king of Assyria promptly sent back word,

"I want gold, and I want silver."

Hezekiah sent him gold and silver, all he could find, even the gold from the doors and the pillars of the Temple, along with ivory couches and ivory thrones and elephant skins.

Then Hezekiah lost his courage, and he decided that it was time to get help. He would beg his neighbor, the king of Egypt, to drive the Assyrians away.

But Isaiah had something to say about that. Back he came from his home where he had been living quietly with his wife and the two boys. Once again he was busy giving advice to the king.

"Not Egypt! Egypt is weak and God alone is strong. Trouble will surely come to anyone who trusts Egyptian horses and chariots and their drivers. Egyptians are just men, not gods. Their horses are just animals. When the Lord God reaches out his hand, both he who helps and he who is helped will fall down together."

Then he tried teaching by signs again. For three years he walked barefoot in the Jerusalem streets to remind the people how prisoners of war look.

"Don't trust Egypt," he warned over and over again. "Trust in the Lord God, who is forever strong. You will hear his voice close behind you saying,

" 'This is the way you are to go.' You need not worry when you can hear that voice."

Nearer and nearer came the Assyrian army, bigger than ever. The soldiers were cruel. The captains had no pity. All the travelers told the same story. About that time King Hezekiah fell sick. On his body he could feel the hot, sore swellings that came with the great sickness.

His friend Isaiah told him sorrowfully, "You had better make your will."

Hezekiah turned his face to the wall.

"Lord, O Lord, remember me," he begged. "I have worked for you with all my heart." And he cried because he did not want to die, and he prayed that God would let him live a little longer.

Isaiah left the room, but he had gone only as far as the courtyard when he heard God say to him,

"Go and tell Hezekiah that I have heard his prayer. I saw his tears. And I will add fifteen more years to his life. Tell him, too, that I will save the city from the Assyrians."

Isaiah hurried back to tell the king the good news.

"Make a fig poultice and put it on the swellings," he told the servants. "He will be better soon."

"All the days of my life I will sing my praise to God in his house," said the king.

One day splendid visitors from faraway Babylon came to Jerusalem. Their king had heard about Hezekiah's sickness, and he had sent messengers with letters and a present for the king of Judah, so they said.

King Hezekiah was pleased, and he welcomed them, and he invited them to stay. He showed them all the fine buildings of the city, and he took them into the treasury. They could see for themselves how much silver and gold he had. He took them into his armory, and they could see for themselves just how many swords and spears and shields he had—all his treasures. He told them all his secrets, as if they were his trusted friends and friends of his country.

As soon as Isaiah heard what had happened he hurried to the king.

"Who are these men? Where did they come from?"

"From a far country—all the way from Babylon."

"What have they seen here in your house?"

"Why, all that I have."

Isaiah shook his head. "In the days to come," he told the king, "your people and everything you have will be carried away to Babylon. Nothing at all will be left."

2 Kings 18:13–16; 20; Isaiah 8; 20; 26; 39

The Army That Disappeared

The Assyrian army came closer and closer. Now the watchmen on the Jerusalem wall could see their tents and their flags down in the valley. The worst days had come.

Up the winding road that led to the city gate the chief of the Assyrian captains, the Rabshakeh, came marching with his troops. Just outside Jerusalem, by the tunnel where water came into the city, three of Hezekiah's officers came to meet them—Eliakim, in charge of the palace and all the king's business, and Shebnah, the king's secretary, and Joah, his recorder. People came crowding to the wall to see what was going on.

"Go ask your king who is helping him now. Didn't he persuade you to stay in there and starve to death? Do you think Egypt is going to save you? Egypt is nothing but a dried-up weed stalk.

"Do you think your God will help you? Why, your king has just torn down all the altars out there in the country. He told you so himself. You must say your prayers right here in Jerusalem. And who is going to take care of you when you go to the country?

"You can see that the only thing to do is to give up now. If you do, I'll ask my master to send you two thousand horses—if you have men enough to ride them."

"Just a minute!" Eliakim and Shebnah and Joah interrupted. "You keep talking in our language, and the people are listening. Speak to us in the Syrian language. We can understand it."

"They are the very people I want to listen. You—on the wall—listen to me. Your king can't save you. Just agree quickly to make peace, and you can all live safely here at home till I come back to take you to another country like your own, where there is always plenty to eat."

The people said nothing at all, for their king had warned them not to quarrel with the enemy. But three sad and worried men went back to report to King Hezekiah.

The king listened quietly to the bad news. The generals were laughing at him, laughing at his high, strong wall and his army. They were laughing at the Lord God.

"Go tell Isaiah it is a day of trouble and shame. Pray for us, the few who are left. It may be God will hear."

"Do not be afraid. No harm will come to you. That is the word of the Lord," came back Isaiah's answer.

Then the Rabshakeh wrote to King Hezekiah.

"Don't let your God trick you when he says Jerusalem will never be taken. Haven't you heard what we did to other countries? What makes you think your God can save you now?"

King Hezekiah went straight to the Temple, and he spread the letter out for God to see. At last he realized that only God could help. And so he prayed.

Isaiah came to him bringing him God's answer.

" 'They will not come into this city nor shoot one arrow here. They will go the way they came, for I will defend the city and save it. Tonight's trouble will be gone in the morning.' "

Down in the valley the Assyrian soldiers were sleeping in their tents. All they had to do was march up the hill in the morning and take the city. But that night something happened. One hundred and eighty-five thousand soldiers died. The king of Assyria packed up and hurried home with his little army. Jerusalem was safe.

Next day all Jerusalem celebrated. People climbed up on the roofs of their houses to see where the Assyrians had gone, and everywhere they were laughing and shouting for joy that they were still alive. And there was feasting and drinking and forgetting who it was who saved them.

Sadly Isaiah watched and listened.

"You should be counting the broken places in your walls, the houses you tore down to get bricks to patch them. You should be giving thanks to God for the water you stored up there between the walls." It was a time for thanksgiving and praying, and for sadness over failures and sins, he was saying.

"Here you are killing your sheep and your cattle for the feasts. 'Let's eat and drink, for tomorrow we die,' you say. You will die," he warned, "but this thing you have done will be remembered as long as you live."

But there was peace in the land as long as King Hezekiah lived. And when he died they buried him lovingly and with honor.

2 Kings 18; 19; Isaiah 22; 36; 37

The King Who Had a Second Chance

Prince Manasseh was just twelve years old when his father, King Hezekiah, died. No sooner did he become king than he began to undo all the good his father had done.

Back came the idols and the shrines. Back came the heathen

altars where the people worshiped the stars. Right in the Temple they set up altars to the stars. Back came the magicians and the wizards and the king's wise men.

Then God was angry.

"I will bring so much trouble to Jerusalem and to Judah that the very story of it will make a man's ears tingle. I will wipe Jerusalem as a man wipes a dish and turns it, empty, upside down."

Back came the army of Assyria, marching on Jerusalem, and this time there was no help from God. They captured King Manasseh, and they bound him with chains and carried him off to Babylon.

Far away from home, the miserable king realized what he had done, and humbly he prayed that God would forgive him. And so he had a second chance, for the Assyrians let him go home.

Then he went to work to clean up Jerusalem. He took away the idols, with the altars he made for the stars, and he threw them all outside the city. He cleaned up and mended the altar of the Lord God. Then he himself led the people as they brought their thank offerings to the house of God and prayed to him as God's own people.

2 Kings 21; 2 Chronicles 33

Message from Isaiah

The Lord's hand is not shortened that it cannot save,
Or his ear dull, that it cannot hear.
But your sins have made a separation between you and God.
They have hid his face from you so that he does not hear.
When God called no one answered,
When he spoke no one listened.
Seek the Lord while he may be found,
Call upon him while he is near.
Let the wicked man forsake his way, the sinful man his thoughts.

Let him return to our God, for he will abundantly pardon.
Before you call he will answer,
While you are speaking he will hear.
Since the beginning of the world men have not heard
Nor have they seen one like our God
Who works for those who love him.
For as the heavens are higher than the earth,
So are his ways higher than our ways
And his thoughts higher than our thoughts.
I will trust him. I will not fear,
For the Lord God is my strength, my song.

Isaiah 59:1–2; 66:4; 55:6–7; 65:24; 64:4; 55:9; 12:2

Idols in the Temple

"Earth, earth, earth, hear the word of the Lord," the great prophet Jeremiah pleaded as he preached. But people just laughed at him. Or they turned away to talk about something else. Or they had him arrested and put into prison.

It all began in Anathoth, just an hour's walk north from Jerusalem, where Jeremiah was growing up. His father and his uncles —all of them priests—taught Jeremiah to love God and to hate and despise the idols the people worshiped on every hilltop.

In the king's house Josiah was growing up, and he became the king when he was only eight years old, the day his father, Amon the Evil, died.

One thing he was learning, because his teachers were wise and good: "Love the Lord God, and serve him only."

As he was growing up he was wondering. Why were there smoking altars to the idols on the hilltops? Why did worship fires glow in the night from the roofs of the houses where people prayed to the stars? Why were the chariot and the horses of the sun-god kept right by the gate of the Temple? Why were there altars to the idols in the court of the Temple? And why was the Temple dark and lonely, its floors so rotten that it was dangerous to walk on them? Why did no one go inside?

But the men of the city, when they wondered at all, were asking, "When will the next war begin?"

There was really no fighting at all. But Egypt in the south had a strong army. The faraway Assyrians, Judah's ancient enemy, no longer sent soldiers to collect tax money.

But from time to time travelers told strange tales of wild warriors from the north. Some day, they said, these warriors were sure to come sweeping down toward Judah, and there would be war again. Most people just said carelessly, "What does it matter? The Lord God will do us no harm—no good either."

Then the prophet Zephaniah began to preach, and he had one text: "The day of the Lord is coming!

"On the day of the Lord's judging he will come with a lamp in his hand, looking for the wicked ones in every house in Jerusalem. Their silver and their gold cannot save them, for he will punish the princes and the king's children, the judges and the prophets.

"Go and look for God if you are not too proud. Discover how good he is, how fair, and in the day of the Lord's judging he may hide you safely away."

A few people listened to the prophet. But most of them just went on about their business.

2 Kings 22; 23:11–12; Jeremiah 22:29; Zephaniah 1:12,14–18; 2:3

Jeremiah's Call

Busy at work on his family's farm near Anathoth, young Jeremiah used to worry about all the troubling ways of his people. He knew that for him there was nothing to do but obey the Lord God loyally. Early one spring when the almond trees were blossoming, he discovered what he had to do. He heard God say to him,

"Go and preach. Before ever you were born I knew who you were, and I chose you then to be my prophet."

"But, Lord God, how can I speak for you? I'm too young," Jeremiah objected. He felt the touch of a hand on his mouth.

"See, I have given you the power to speak to many people. You will destroy and tear down what they have built in their wickedness. You will build up what they have destroyed.

"Look in their faces, but never be afraid. They will fight you, but I will be there beside you."

Jeremiah 1

An Old Book in a Dusty Corner

There were strange sounds in the quiet, darkened Temple. By the order of King Josiah, the last good king in Judah, carpenters and masons were at work repairing the broken floors, the leaking roof, and the crumbling walls. Hilkiah, who was chief priest, was overseeing the work. One day he happened to see an old, old book, long forgotten, lying in a dusty corner.

"The lost Law Book of God!" the workmen whispered, and great was the excitement. Hilkiah sent the dusty book straight to King Josiah by Shaphan, the scribe, and the king listened while Shaphan read aloud words the people had almost forgotten:

> Hear, O Israel, the Lord our God is one Lord.
> Love him with all your heart, all your soul, all your might.
> For if you heed the laws of God and keep them,
> If you love him only, serve him,
> The Lord will open for you his good treasure.
> Blessed shall you be in the city,
> And blessed in the fields,
> Blessed when you go out, blessed when you come home.

But if you do not listen, if you disobey,
Cursed shall you be in the city,
And cursed in the fields,
Cursed when you go out, and cursed when you go home.

The great king cried as he listened. His people had failed so terribly.

At once he called them all together to a great meeting in the Temple. Clean it was, and beautiful again after the workmen had finished the repairing. The king stood by one of the pillars, and he read aloud from the Law Book all the cursings and the blessings and the great law, "Love God only." Then the people mourned with him for all their wickedness. Together they all promised to keep the laws of God, to worship him only, and they all chanted together, "We will obey."

In the streets of Jerusalem, along the hilltop roads, smoke began to swirl in clouds, not smoke from altars to the idols, but from bonfires.

"Break down the altars and the images. Tear down the carved idols. Grind them to dust. Beat them into powder," was the king's order, and at first the people obeyed him.

There was a great Passover feast, kept by the rules in the lost Law Book. And for a while the people remembered gratefully the Lord their God. Then they began to go about their business again.

2 Kings 22; 23; 2 Chronicles 34;
Deuteronomy 6:4–5; 28:1–19

No One Was Listening

Now the young prophet Jeremiah was going up and down the streets of Jerusalem preaching wherever people would listen. Sometimes he would look far away toward the highway as if he might be waiting for danger.

Hilkiah Finding the Scroll

"Hear and listen! For it is the Lord speaking.

" 'Why have you deserted me, forgotten how I led you through the desert where no man could travel, brought you here to food and plenty? You have disgraced yourselves, spoiled the land with your evil ways.

" 'Look to the farthest west, the farthest east, and see whether any of the heathen nations have changed their gods. But my people have changed their glory for trash. You call a stick of wood your father. You call a stone your child. But you call upon me in your trouble. See whether your handmade gods can help you when trouble comes.

" 'It is a bitter thing to desert the Lord your God, to promise and promise, all the time lying. I can see the stains on you, though you scrub with soap and lye.

" 'Jerusalem, wash the wickedness from your heart. Stop where you are and ask where are the old paths, the good roads, and choose the way you go.' "

The more the lonely preacher talked, the more he knew the people did not care. They still climbed the hill to worship in the Temple, but they hurried back to the hilltops in the country to pray to Baal and the stars. They cheated and they lied, and they stole just as they did before Hilkiah discovered the lost Law.

Jeremiah went on preaching.

" 'A horrible thing, a thing of wonder—the prophets lie, and the priests get rich, and this is the way my people like to live. Will they give up their wicked ways? Can the man from Africa change the color of his skin? Can the leopard change his spots? Your hearts are false and desperately wicked.

" 'Sound the trumpet alarm! Light the signal fires!

" 'Danger and destruction are coming from the north, for I am bringing a nation from far away to punish you. It is a strong nation, an old, old nation. The people speak a language you do not understand. Cruel they are, and they have no mercy. They will eat up your grain and all your bread, feast on your sheep and your cattle, eat up the fruit from your vines and your trees, destroy your towns where you think you are so safe.

" ' "Why did the Lord let it happen?" you will be asking.' "

Jeremiah 2; 4:14; 5:15–19,30–31; 17:9; 6:23

Dangers Far and Near

Who would believe Jeremiah, the loneliest prophet, when he kept saying, "The soldiers come marching, marching from the north"? Once the armies from the north, from Assyria, had come marching on Jerusalem. Straight to the walls of Jerusalem they had come, and God had rescued his people.

Now the prophet Nahum, whose name meant Comforter, was saying that God would punish Assyria for the wickedness and cruelty of its people. The great, rich city of Nineveh, most beautiful in all the land, would be destroyed. Soldiers in scarlet uniforms, armed with spears and scarlet shields, would race their shining chariots, cracking their whips over their prancing horses, crashing into one another in the streets like flaming torches. After the battle there would be no sound in the ruined houses along the ruined streets.

"So keep your feasts in the Temple, you people of Judah, for the wicked ones are gone. They will not come back," said Nahum.

"Now we have nothing to worry about," the people said, and they went on carving idols from wood and stone. "The Lord God will do us no good, no evil, either." The priests said, "Now there is peace." But there was no peace, not then nor afterward, when messengers brought the news that Nahum's report was true. Nineveh was in ruins.

Down in Egypt King Neco decided that Egypt was going to be the biggest country in the world, and now was a good time to go after some of the land that used to belong to Assyria. Little Judah up there across the desert did not worry him. But far, far away in the land by the rivers there were people he must fight if he would make Egypt strongest of all.

So off he went to war, and he marched along the coast, close to Judah because the road went that way. Then he turned east through the Valley of Megiddo.

But King Josiah would not have it, and he set out to stop the great Egyptian army.

"Go back! Go back! I'll have no fight with you," King Neco's messengers sent him word.

King Josiah refused to go back. Heading north, past Bethel, past the ruins of the beautiful city of Israel, Samaria, he caught up with the Egyptians in the Valley of Megiddo. And there they fought.

An Egyptian soldier shot him, and sadly his men carried him back to Jerusalem where he died. All the city, all the country round, mourned for love of the good king.

After King Josiah died, trouble after trouble came to Judah. Prince Jehoahaz was crowned king, but he reigned only three months. Back came King Neco from his war, and he took the new king prisoner and carried him off to Egypt. He made Jehoahaz' younger brother, Jehoiakim, king, and he fined the people of Judah for attacking him. Silver and gold they had to pay out of the treasury. And heavy taxes had to be laid on the people to pay the King of Egypt.

Now there were dangerous times in Judah, for the new king cared nothing at all about the Temple of God, and he gave no thought to Jeremiah's warnings. Once more the altars to the idols smoked with offering fires.

Off in the east a new nation, Chaldea, sometimes called Babylon, was growing stronger and stronger.

Nahum; 2 Chronicles 35:20–27;
2 Kings 23:28–37

Prophet on a Watchtower

That was the time when the prophet Habakkuk made a discovery. He used to worry about the evil ways of his people, worry because he could see the Chaldeans coming, like God's messengers of punishment, riding on horses swifter than leopards. Why should God allow those cruel Chaldeans to grow so powerful?

"I will climb up to my watchtower and ask the Lord God what it all means," he said. "Why must we be punished when our enemies are not punished?"

High in his watchtower Habakkuk learned God's answer, and he wrote it down for all to read:

"The Lord is in his holy Temple. Let all the earth be still and listen. Trust God. As for the wicked, their crooked souls are doomed. The good man who trusts God lives by his faith."

Habakkuk could see so clearly that punishment must come to his country. But he knew that some day all the world would understand the glory of God. And he could say:

"Though there is no blossom on the fig tree, no fruit upon the vine, though the olive trees are bare and no grain is growing in the fields, though the flocks of sheep and cattle die, I will trust God. I know that he will save me, keep me strong, keep me walking without stumbling on the hilltops."

The Book of Habakkuk

The Prophet No One Liked

Now lonely Jeremiah looked out sadly on the streets of Jerusalem. He watched the children picking up sticks so their fathers could build fires for their mothers to bake cakes for the goddess of heaven. He saw men who cheated their neighbors parade up to the Temple to pray. He heard them boast,

"No harm can ever come to us in Jerusalem. We have the Temple of the Lord here to keep us safe."

Up to the Temple Jeremiah went, and standing in the court he preached a sermon. But no one listened.

"You with your offerings to God! Take them home and eat them yourselves. You have turned the house of the Lord God into a robbers' den.

"You think you are safe here, but go look at the house of the Lord in Shiloh. For the wickedness of the people he let the Assyrians destroy it.

"Is anyone honest enough to ask, 'What have I done?'

" 'Come back,' he says to you, 'before it is too late and not even the Temple is left in Jerusalem.' "

The people began to listen.

"He can't talk that way about the Temple! For that a man deserves to die."

Jeremiah went on talking.

"I obey the orders of the Lord God who sent me. If you kill me, you kill an innocent man."

The priests and the prophets and the people all talked it over.

"After all, he did say he was speaking for God."

"I remember how Micah used to preach when Hezekiah was king. 'Jerusalem will be plowed up like a field,' he said. Did the king have him killed? No, we all prayed to the Lord God, and he himself saved us from our enemies."

"But I remember how the prophet Urijah was killed for saying the very same thing. Right here in Jerusalem it happened, and they buried him without even a proper burial."

While they were all busy talking, Jeremiah's friend Ahikam helped him to escape from the mob. For a time he was safe.

Jeremiah's heart came near to breaking those days. When he tried to pray for his people's forgiveness, he learned the terrible truth from God. It was too late. Punishment was coming.

"If Moses and Samuel themselves prayed for them, I would not listen. Mount Zion will be plowed up like a field. Jerusalem will be a heap of ruins. Trees will grow in the streets. This will be the lonely land where no one laughs."

Discouraged, without any friends, Jeremiah went home to Anathoth only to discover that his own family was plotting to kill him. Traitor to his country, they were calling him. He would have given up gladly. But the Voice would not let him.

"If you are tired now from racing with the runners, how can you race the horses? If you are discouraged now while there is peace in the land, what will you do when war comes?"

Jeremiah went back to work. *Jeremiah 7; 8; 3; 11:18–23; 12:5–6*

The Teacher in the Street

"Hear and listen, and be not proud, you people. Hear the word of God while you can still see where you are going, before he takes the light away and you stumble in the dark mountains.

"I go walking in the fields, and I see soldiers dying in battle. I walk in the streets, and I see them sick with hunger. Those who are left are marching, marching, far away."

The king did not like Jeremiah any more than the people

did. He had been busy rebuilding his palace, making it bigger, with wider windows and a high roof of cedar wood. All that cost money, and he was already paying the king of Egypt more than he could afford. So he decided to make the people work for him without pay.

"Trouble and sorrow come to you," warned Jeremiah. "Your father lived well, but he was just and fair. No poor man went hungry because of him. But you want everything for yourself."

Jeremiah 13:15–16; 14:18; 22:13–19

The Lesson of the Broken Pot

Far away to the east the Chaldean king was winning battle after battle. Nineveh was gone. Assyria was beaten. Now Egypt was next.

Jeremiah knew now who God's punishing power was to be. Chaldea was coming, and Judah could not escape.

"Hear and listen!"

Jeremiah called the wise old men and the priests. In his hands he carried an empty clay pot. He led them down the street, out of the city, by Broken Pot Gate, to the dumping ground where people threw away their broken dishes.

"The Lord is speaking," he told them.

" 'I will bring so much trouble to this place that even hearing about it will make your ears tingle.

" 'Here you burned your fires to idols. Here you prayed to Baal.' "

He pointed toward the beautiful Temple, and no one said a word.

" 'When war comes, all the city will be a ruin. The tall houses will burn, and the roof tops where they worship the stars. The people will starve, and no one will care.' "

Jeremiah lifted his clay pot high and hurled it down. It lay there smashed, and no one could put the pieces back together.

" 'That is the way I will break Judah—houses, people, and all.'

"Hear and listen," Jeremiah pleaded.

Jeremiah 19

The Family That Kept Its Promise

When the army of the king of Babylon came marching through the land of Judah, no one living in the country was safe from the raiding soldiers. So all the sons and grandsons of Rechab and their families and their servants packed up and moved into the city. They were living safely inside the high walls when Jeremiah heard a message from God.

"Go and call the sons of Rechab to the Temple, and offer them wine to drink."

He brought them all to an upstairs room and gave them each a cup. But the family of Rechab refused the wine.

"We cannot drink it," they told him. "Our grandfather told us, 'You are to drink no wine, you or your sons or their sons forever.' Our grandfather also said,

" 'You are to build yourselves no houses, but live in tents. Plant no gardens, but live all your lives as strangers in the land.' And we have obeyed him."

Now God was speaking again.

"Go to the people of Jerusalem and tell them,

" 'Will you never listen to my teaching? To this day the family of Rechab obeys his command. But again and again I have spoken to you.

" 'I have sent you my teachers and my prophets. But you do not listen.

" 'So now I will give Jerusalem to the king of Babylon, and all the country roundabout.

" 'No more will anyone hear the sound of the millstones grinding meal. No more will anyone see the light of a lamp in the city. For seventy years it will be so, while my people serve the king of Babylon.' "

Jeremiah 35; 34:21–22; 25:10–11

The Message in the Book

The days of good King Josiah were all but forgotten. Some of the people still went to the Temple to worship. They kept the gay feast days and the solemn days when they were careful to eat nothing at all. But they grew more and more careless about God's laws.

After his sermon in the Temple court, Jeremiah was so unpopular that he was forbidden to come back. But he could still go on preaching. This time he wrote a book. He called for his secretary, Baruch, and he dictated the book of the Lord's words so that Baruch wrote a big scroll, all the message of trouble and punishment to come, and of God's love for his people forever.

There was a day of celebration at Jerusalem, and people came from all the towns around to join in the worship service at the Temple. Baruch went, too, the scroll under his arm. Standing in the upper court by the new gate of the Temple where everyone could see and hear, he began to read aloud,

"The king of Babylon will come to destroy the land, to kill man and beast. For the evil we have done, the Lord God will punish us all."

A man named Micaiah listened thoughtfully. Then he went running to the king's house where all the princes were sitting together and reported what was happening.

"Bring Baruch here. We will find out what this is all about," they said. So Baruch brought his book, and he began to read it aloud to them.

"Where did you get this?" the princes demanded.

"Jeremiah gave me the words, and I wrote them."

"Give us the scroll. The king must hear about this. And you and Jeremiah had better hide where no one can find you."

Sitting comfortably by a charcoal fire in his winter home, King Jehoiakim heard about the strange scroll and its frightful message.

"Read it to me," he ordered.

So Jehudi began to read aloud:

"The king of Babylon will come to destroy our land, to kill man and beast."

"Enough of that!" The king slashed out with his knife and cut the scroll through and through. Then he tossed it on the fire.

Jeremiah, hiding safely where no one could find him, knew that he must do his work again. Another scroll, another chance to warn the people. The king might burn a book, but he could not destroy the word of God.

But no one listened, not the king, nor the princes, nor any of the people.

At last the king died, and no one mourned for him. In fact, they did not even give him a proper funeral. Young Prince Jehoiachin was the next king, but he was king for just three months.

Jeremiah 36

Then It All Came True

Then the terrible years began. King Nebuchadnezzar's soldiers attacked Jerusalem, and the young king surrendered with hardly a fight. They carried him off to Babylon, and they carried off the golden treasures from the king's house, from the Temple.

Along with the king, they carried away the princes and the soldiers, the queen mother and the ladies of the court, and the artists and skilled workers in metal. They took the young men to grind their grain in faraway Babylon, took the children to carry wood, took away the leaders and left behind the poor and the unskilled workmen.

Far, far from Jerusalem the lonely people of Judah grew more homesick every day for their fair city on the hill. King and queen mother, princes and carpenters and blacksmiths, and all the rest sat around mournfully and counted the days they had been prisoners in Babylon. Some of the priests kept promising they would go home any day now. But, back in Jerusalem, Jeremiah knew this was not true.

One day messengers went riding down the caravan road from the wide desert that stretched between Babylon and Judah.

"Letters! Letters from Jerusalem!"

The news spread fast, and the prisoners came running.

There was a letter addressed to them all, and it began, "Hear and listen! It is God who is speaking."

They all knew those words. Jeremiah always used to begin his sermons that way. Now he was giving them a message from God.

"Build yourselves homes, and settle down to live in Babylon. Plant your gardens. Settle down with your families. Don't expect to come home for a long, long time—not for seventy years.

"Then you will pray to me, and I will be listening. When you search for me with all your hearts you will surely find me.

"I will bring you back together again, bring you home. For I have loved you with an everlasting love, and with my love I will bring you home to me."

After Jehoiachin, Zedekiah was the last sad, evil king of Judah. Though the Assyrians chose him to be king, he thought he was strong as Nebuchadnezzar himself. Now Jeremiah's advice had been for everyone to live peacefully as subjects of the king of Babylon. But Zedekiah liked the advice of his friend, Hananiah, for Hananiah was very sure that his people would soon be free.

"Two years, and the prisoners will all come home. Two years, and all the treasures of the Temple will be back in their places."

"You make these people believe a lie," Jeremiah warned.

"Egypt is getting stronger. Egypt will help us get free," said Zedekiah's friends, and he listened to them. So he refused to pay the regular tax to Babylon.

King Nebuchadnezzar came back with his army, and they camped in the valley just below Mount Zion. They began to build forts, and they spread out as far as a man on the watchtower could see. No one could get into Jerusalem.

Then as suddenly as they had come they were gone. The people of Jerusalem looked out from their windows, and they shouted the good news from house to house. What they did not know was that the Assyrians had heard that the Egyptians were getting ready to revolt, and they had just gone away to settle the trouble.

Jeremiah 28; 29; 30:10; 31; 33; 37:1–10;
2 Kings 24; Lamentations 2

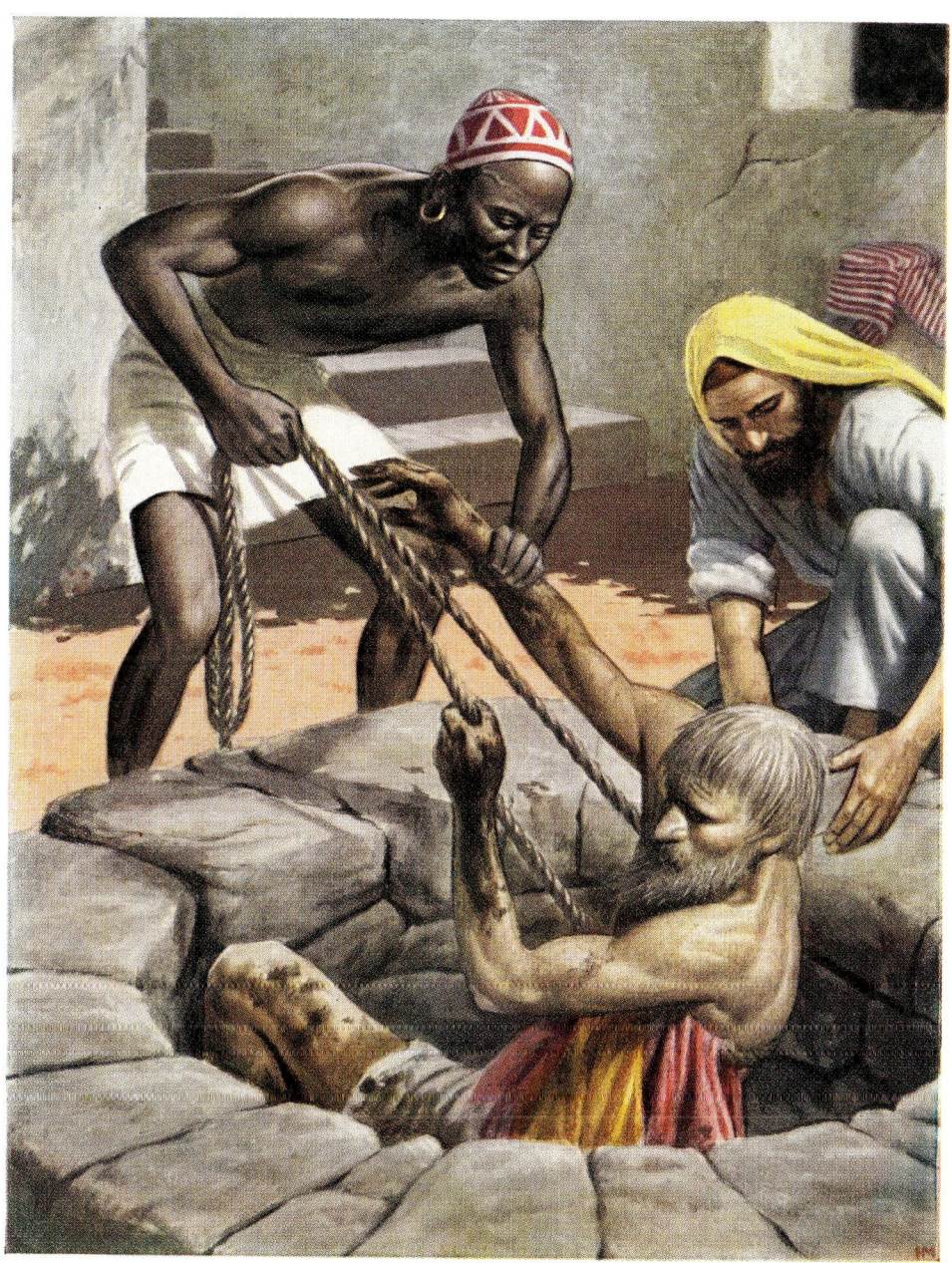

© 1962, The Sunday School Board, S.B.C.

Jeremiah and the Ethiopian

Prisoner in the Slime Pit

Now that the Assyrian guards were gone, Jeremiah decided it was a good time to go back home to Anathoth. But as he was slipping out the Benjamin Gate, one of the guards arrested him.

"Deserting to the enemy? Let's see what the princes will say to this!"

So Jeremiah went to jail. But he went on preaching, and people were listening.

"Stay here in the city, and you will die. You will starve, or you will die of the deadly sickness, or the soldiers will kill you. But go quietly away with the Assyrians as their prisoners, and you will stay alive."

This had to stop. The princes hurried to tell the king.

But the king was terrified. He was afraid of the Chaldeans, afraid of Jeremiah. Now he was afraid of his own leaders.

"Do whatever you like with him," he said weakly.

So the leaders took Jeremiah from prison where he was fairly comfortable and had a piece of bread every day as long as there was any bread, and they dropped him into an old cistern half filled with mud and slime.

Jeremiah had one friend in the king's house, a black man from Ethiopia, whose name was Ebed-melech. Now he hurried to the king.

"My lord, these men have done an evil thing. Jeremiah will die unless he gets help."

So the king gave his permission, and Ebed-melech took thirty men with him and went to rescue his friend. With long ropes and old rags they hurried to the edge of the dungeon.

"Jeremiah! Can you hear? Catch these rags when we lower the

ropes. Put the ropes under your arms, and pad them well with the rags. Let us know when you are ready."

Slowly, carefully they drew him up out of the mud and carried him back to the prison where he had been safe and comfortable.

King Zedekiah was still terrified. Now he called for Jeremiah, and the two went together to the Temple.

"Tell me the truth. Don't hide anything from me," he said.

"If I tell you the truth you will have me killed. If I give you advice you will not listen," the patient prophet told the king.

"I swear I will not harm you."

"Then this is the word of the Lord: If you will surrender to the king of the Chaldeans you will live, and the city will not be burned. If you fight, you cannot escape, and they will destroy all that is left of Jerusalem."

"Don't say anything about this to anyone," the king whispered. "I promise that you will be safe."

Jeremiah 37; 38

Captured King, Ruined City

Round about Jerusalem the soldiers of King Nebuchadnezzar's army were camping again in the valley and up and down the hills. In the streets there was talk of the battle—frightened talk—and the crying of hungry children.

But there was no talk of doing business, of buying land or selling houses. For who knew where they might be tomorrow? Then someone brought news to Jeremiah's prison cell. Back in Anathoth, his home town, there was some land for sale. It used to belong to Jeremiah's cousin, and so Jeremiah had first right to buy it and keep it in the family. But who wanted to buy land now? Any day it would belong to the Chaldeans and be ruined.

The people would not believe what Jeremiah knew. For he had heard God say,

"I will bring them back to this place, and here they will live safely. They shall be my people, and I will be their God."

"I will buy the land," Jeremiah decided. So the owner and Baruch, Jeremiah's secretary, and all the witnesses came to the courtyard of the prison. There Jeremiah paid the money. The land was his, and the deed was recorded and sealed away in a clay jar.

Month after month the people tried to hold out against the Chaldean army. Every gate was guarded. The high walls seemed safe and strong. But inside the walls the people were hungry and sick. Month by month the food was being used up.

Then the Chaldean soldiers came storming over the walls. They burst open the doors of the palace. They tramped through the court of the Temple. Everything that was golden or silver or bronze they carried home with them—all the bowls and spoons and lampstands—and they smashed the rest. Then they set fire to the city.

In the night King Zedekiah and his princes slipped out of the palace through the garden, out the gate, and they hurried down the steep road to the valley. But they could not run fast enough, and the Chaldean soldiers arrested them near Jericho.

Smoke and flames swept through the heights of proud Jerusalem. The cedar beams of the Temple crackled and crashed in a shower of sparks on the altars. Not a house, not a wall was left standing in the ruins where foxes soon came to prowl at night.

But there was no one left to need a house. For all the wise ones, all the strong ones were sent to Babylon in the long, long lines of prisoners traveling the road to the north. Only a few of the poorest and weakest were left behind, and Gedaliah was to be their governor. They were given land of their own where they could grow their own food, but they never went back to ruined Jerusalem.

The Chaldeans were kind to Jeremiah. "Take him out of prison, and let him have whatever he wants," was the order. The captain of the guard himself took off his chains, and he told Jeremiah,

"You are free to go with us if you like, but you will be treated well if you stay in Jerusalem."

Jeremiah chose to stay with the people who were left. Soon others joined them. There were a few troops of soldiers who had been fighting farther away and had escaped the Chaldeans. There were some Jewish families who had escaped to Moab and the Red Lands. It looked as if their troubles were over, at least for a time.

Then they began to fight among themselves and the governor was killed. That frightened them all, and they decided to move away to Egypt for fear of punishment from the Chaldeans.

All the families met at Bethlehem, ready to move. But before they set out they talked it over with Jeremiah.

"There is no war in Egypt, and there is plenty to eat. Come on with us," the people begged.

For many days the tired old man thought it over and prayed. Then he knew.

"Hear and listen, for the Lord God is speaking. Stay here in this land. There is war in Egypt. There is sickness and hunger. If you go you will not come back."

But the people laughed.

"The Lord God said nothing of the kind, and even if he did, we won't listen. When we burned incense for the goddess of heaven, we had everything we wanted, and look at us now."

They picked up their baggage and headed south for Egypt. And Jeremiah, loneliest of the prophets, went along with them. Sorrowful and tired, he went on warning them, giving them counsel. But there were few who listened.

"Hear and listen, for the Lord God speaks:

" 'In the days that are to come you will understand. You cannot blame your fathers or your brothers or your country. You are the ones who are being punished, and yours are the sins.

" 'But in the days to come I will make a new covenant promise with my people—not the old agreement that I made when I took them by the hand to bring them away from Egypt, the agreement they broke.

" 'This will be the new promise: I will be their God, and they will be my people. This I will write in their hearts, and they will choose to keep my laws.' "   *Jeremiah 31; 32; 39; 43; 52; Lamentations 5:18*

EZEKIEL'S PICTURE SERMONS

God's Shining Glory

BY THE RIVERS of Babylon we sat down and cried,
For we remembered the city of Zion.
We hung our harps on the branches of the willow trees.
They carried us away, and we were their prisoners. They said,
"Sing for us! Laugh for us! Sing us a song about Zion!"
How could we sing the Lord's songs in the stranger's land?

Far, far away from their homes in Jerusalem the captive families in Babylon were homesick for their shining Temple on Mount Zion, homesick for their shops and houses, and lonely because it seemed as if their God were far away, too.

"Are we being punished just because our grandfathers did wrong?"

"Can't we ever go back to Jerusalem?"

"Why did God let this happen to us?"

These were the questions the captives were asking. No one knew the answers. Not until Ezekiel made a discovery.

Perhaps Ezekiel missed the beautiful Temple more than anyone. He was one of the priests, and he was a leader among his people. The wise, older men used to meet in his house. One day down by the river Ezekiel discovered that God was in Babylon, too.

He saw wonders he could hardly describe. Bright with the colors of the rainbow, in light all gold and scarlet like flame, God was there in all his shining glory.

Out of the north the vision came, from the direction the weary captives traveled after they crossed the desert lands. Four great shining creatures Ezekiel saw, and their faces were the faces of the creatures of God's world—the eagle, king of birds; the ox, king of farm animals; the lion, king of beasts; and man, ruler of them all—and they were traveling fast as lightning.

Now Ezekiel heard the voice of God:

"Son of man, stand up!"

As he stood, he listened to the words that were his commission.

"I am sending you to be a teacher to the children of Israel. Hard of face and hard of heart they are. They may listen to you, and they may not. But they will know that there has been a prophet among them.

"Never be afraid of them, of the way they look or the words they say, for they are rebels, all of them.

"You will not be preaching to strangers who never heard the

word of God. Strangers might listen to you. But these people will not listen. They do not listen to me. But go to them. Teach them, and tell them, 'Hear the words of the Lord God.'"

Ezekiel felt the glory of the Lord God all around him, but he was bitter and unhappy, for it was a hard thing God was asking him to do.

"Now take the word of God in your hands. Eat it, and make it your own."

He seemed to see the scroll of the word of God pressed against his lips, all the words of God's commission which sounded so bitter. But as he obeyed the strange order, the bitter words seemed sweet to taste.

So he hurried to the meeting place by the river, and he sat down with his friends. But he could not say a word. He simply could not speak. A week went by, and he did nothing at all. Then he heard God calling him again.

"I have made you the watchman for the family of Israel. Warn them quickly. Come out to the plains now, and I will talk to you there."

Psalm 137:1–3; Ezekiel 1 to 3

The Horrors in the Temple

Far outside the city, in the flat plain country, Ezekiel found the glory of God again, and he heard the voice speaking plainly.

"Stand up! When you go home you will stay there quietly by yourself. You will know when it is time to begin your work, for I will teach you what to do."

It seemed to Ezekiel that a hand touched his hair, and he felt himself being lifted high above the earth, traveling swiftly back to Jerusalem. He stood inside the high wall in the very court of the Temple. He could see a hole in the Temple wall, and when he dug through the hole he saw a door. Beyond the door he saw a room of horrors—idols big and little, images of snakes and animals and all kinds of queer gods. And there before them in the dark stood the seventy wise old men of the city, worshiping idols in the Temple of God.

"The Lord God cannot see us here. The Lord God has gone away and left us," they whispered.

In another court of the Temple he saw women worshiping the heathen god of harvest time. And by the altar of the Lord God, right in the open, men were bowing as they prayed to the sun.

"See for yourself, Ezekiel. I can have no pity for them. Though they call to me for help I cannot listen."

"Must this be the end of your people? Will none of them be left?" he asked anxiously.

Then the loving God who has ever been ready to bring his people back to him answered,

"Though I have deserted them and scattered them through all the lands of the world; though they live among the heathen, I will be with them wherever they are. Go and tell my people that when they throw away these filthy things, I can bring them home. Then I will put a new spirit in them. I will take away their cold, stony hearts and give them hearts that are warm and loving. Then they will be my people, and I will be their God."

Ezekiel 8; 11

The Toy War

As time went on the people of Judah had settled down in Babylon, and they began to be comfortable, though they were so far away from home. They learned to live as the people of Babylon lived, and they were forgetting the teaching and the law of God. Most of the time now they were doing just as they pleased.

"Nothing more can happen to us. We always have Jerusalem

for our real city, and God won't let anything happen to Jerusalem. So everything is going to be all right," they said.

"Jerusalem is going to be destroyed." That was the first lesson Ezekiel taught.

First he set a flat brick on the ground. That was the city. On the brick he set an iron skillet for the wall about the city. Outside the wall he built a toy fort and the camp of the enemy, and he stationed battering rams like great cannon to fire at the city walls.

How long would the battle last? He showed them by lying on the ground beside his toy city. A day stood for a year, and he lay there forty days. He showed how it felt to starve to death while the city was being attacked. He measured out bread, just a little for each day, and he measured out water, just a little for each day. Now and then he would eat a crumb or sip some water carefully, just a little at a time.

"Stop and listen! The Lord God speaks. 'This is Jerusalem where the people broke my laws and refused to listen to me. You have dirtied my house with your sins, and I will not save it now.

"'Listen! They have blown the trumpets for the battle, but where are the soldiers marching out to fight? Inside the city they are lying sick with the deadly fever. Their hands are feeble, and their knees are shaking. They are pouring out their money in the streets, but they cannot buy peace. They have the punishment they deserve, and at last they will know that I am the Lord who punishes all who do evil.'"

But the people began to whine.

"God is not fair. He is punishing us for something our fathers and mothers did."

"Each man pays for his own sins," said the Lord God. "But I have no pleasure in your punishment. Throw your sins away from you. Make your hearts clean again. Turn back from your wicked ways. Turn back now while you can see the way to go."

Ezekiel 4; 7; 18; 33

The Bad Shepherds

"Preach now to the leaders of the people, those bad shepherds of my sheep," said the Lord God.

So Ezekiel began to teach.

"Should not the shepherds feed their sheep? But you have eaten your own lambs for meat. You have made yourselves coats from their wool. But you never nursed the sick lambs or set their broken bones. You never went out to look for the strays. You just whipped them and drove them wherever you wanted them to go.

" 'So my sheep went wandering over the mountains, scattered over the earth, with no one to look for them.

" 'But I will go to hunt my sheep,' said the Lord God. 'I will go after my people the way the good shepherd goes to look for the scattered sheep. I will rescue them from all the places they hid when it was dark and stormy and they were afraid.

" 'I will find the lost ones, nurse the sick, and bind up the broken bones, lead them to green fields, and bring them to their own pastures where they can go to sleep, safe from every prowling animal.

" 'So I will bring my people home, never to be hungry any more, for fruit will be growing on every tree and grain in all the fields, watered by showers, showers of blessing in the season of rain. They will be safe, for no one will make them afraid. So at last they will know that I, the Lord God, am with them, and they are my people forever.' "

Ezekiel 34

The Dead and Dusty Valley

Ezekiel stood looking out over the valley. Dusty and dry it was, where nothing could live, and as far as he could see there were only dry bones where people used to live.

"Tell me, can anyone live here? Can Israel live again?" Ezekiel heard a voice asking.

"No one but you knows that, Lord God."

"Speak to the dry bones. Tell them to live again," the Lord said to him.

Ezekiel obeyed. He heard a rattling, shuffling noise as the bones came together to form skeletons, and then flesh covered the bones so that bodies without breath stood there in the valley.

"Call the wind."

So Ezekiel called.

"Come from the four winds. Breathe on these murdered ones that they may live."

Then the wind came blowing, and they stood tall and strong, a great army of living men.

The Voice was speaking again.

"You have seen the people of Israel, dead as the bones in the dusty valley. Hopeless and lost and dead in their spirits they were.

"Tell my people how I will bring them back and give life to their nation again. Tell my people how I will put my own spirit in them, and I will take them home again to their own land."

Ezekiel 37

The Picture of the New World

"When you come back home again, leaving all your evil ways behind you, you will build your homes again. All the dusty hills and valleys will be green again, and crops will grow in the fenced lands. People will say, 'This desert land has become like the Garden of Eden.'"

Ezekiel often remembered the promise of the Lord God. He could see the shining new city on Mount Zion, see the beautiful new shining Temple rising where Solomon's Temple used to be, all the courts and gates, the windows and arches, the altars and doorways and walls with carved palm trees and winged lions. Through the eastern gate he watched the shining glory of God come back to his house, there to stay forever.

"Take the blueprints of the house to the people of Israel. Give them the measurements and show them how to build. If they are ashamed of what they have done, teach them how to begin again. For when they have thrown out their idols forever, I will come to stay with them."

Then Ezekiel could see a healing river flowing from beneath the eastern door of the Temple, shallow enough for wading at first, then deeper and deeper. All the way to the sea the broad, clean river was flowing, and it flowed into the Dead Sea and made the salty water safe for living creatures again. Only the salt marshes near the sea were left to give salt to the people.

Along the banks of the river tall trees were growing, and the fruit of them ripened all year round. Leaves of the trees were good for medicine for the sick of all the land, and the fruit of the trees was good for food.

And this was the name of the city: The Lord Is Here.

Ezekiel 36; 40; 41; 43:10,11,17; 47:7–12; 48:35

STORIES OF DANIEL

Four Young Men in Training

ONCE LONG AGO the prophet Isaiah had stood before good King Hezekiah, and he had warned the king with a fearful warning.

"In the days to come your family will all be carried off to Babylon. Nothing will be left. So says the Lord God.

"Your sons, too, will be taken away, and they will be servants in the palace of the king of Babylon."

Now the prophecy had all come true. In Babylon by the great river, far away in the land of Shinar, King Jehoiakim was a prisoner of war. In the temple in Babylon the golden treasures from the Temple in Jerusalem were spread out before the heathen idols. The boys of Jerusalem, king's sons and all, were prisoners with the rest.

King Nebuchadnezzar had a plan for training those young men, for he wanted them to become captains and judges and doctors and teachers. He gave them the best education possible. He sent them to the palace college for three years. There they studied all the wisest books in the land. They had the best food—wine like the king's wine, and rich meats and desserts, the kind the king ate.

Among the young men who were chosen were Daniel and Hananiah and Mishael and Azariah. First of all they were given new Babylonian names. Daniel became Belteshazzar. The others were called Shadrach, Meshach, and Abednego.

Daniel decided that he would have nothing to do with the king's wine or the king's rich food. So he and his three friends asked permission to eat vegetables and to drink water. The steward, who was in charge of the students, shook his head. He loved Daniel especially, and he wanted him to succeed.

"You won't be fit for anything on a diet like that," he warned. "And if the king sees you looking pale and thin, what is going to happen to me?"

"Just let us try it for ten days. Then check us and see what you think," Daniel persuaded him.

So for ten days Daniel and Shadrach and Meshach and Abednego ate their vegetables and drank their water while the other young men ate the king's rich food and drank the king's wine.

Then the steward examined them all. Daniel and his friends had gained weight. They looked stronger than all the others. So the steward let them have their way.

As for the young men, God helped them to learn. He gave Daniel a special understanding of the meaning of dreams. When the years of school were over, the young men reported to the king, and he found that they were wiser, more understanding than all the wise men of the land. *Daniel 1; 2 Kings 20:17–18*

The Image in the Dream

King Nebuchadnezzar could not sleep at night. He kept on dreaming a strange, troublesome dream, and he would wake up too troubled and worried to go back to sleep. Every night the same thing happened.

So he sent for his wise men, whose business it was to tell what dreams meant.

"O king, may you live forever! Tell your servants what you dreamed, and we will tell you what the dream meant."

"It's gone. I can't remember. But you tell me what I dreamed and what the dream meant, or you shall be cut in pieces," thundered the king. "Tell me, and I will pay you well."

"Just tell your servants what you dreamed," they begged.

"Stop wasting time. Tell me at once."

The wise men shook their heads.

"No man on earth can do what the king asks."

They made the king so angry that he ordered every wise man in Babylon killed.

By this time Daniel was one of the wise men, too. When the captain of the king's guard came to arrest him he demanded,

"Why is the king in such a hurry? Let me speak to him."

So Daniel was allowed to go to the king. He asked for time to study about the mysterious dream. Then he went home and talked it over with his three friends, and all four of them prayed that God would teach them what to do.

That night God himself told Daniel the secret, and Daniel thanked him in these words:

"Blessed is God's name for ever and ever,
> For he is wise, and he is powerful.
He sends the winter, the spring, summer, and the autumn,
He takes kings from their thrones and chooses men to be kings.
He sees the things that are hidden in darkness, for where he is there is always light.
He teaches and he gives understanding.
I thank the God of my fathers, for he has taught me secret things."

In the morning he went to Captain Arioch with the good news.

"Wait! Don't carry out the king's order yet. Let me go to see the king."

Arioch reported to Nebuchadnezzar.

"I have found one of the captives from Jerusalem who knows your dream."

"Can you really tell me what it was?" the king asked Daniel anxiously.

"No man can tell you, O king, not the wisest man in all the land. But there is a God in heaven who can tell secret things. He is telling the king something that is going to happen.

"O king, you dreamed you saw a huge shining image, and it was frightful. Its head was made of gold. Its chest and arms were silver. Its sides were brass. Its legs were iron. Its feet were part iron, part clay.

"A great stone fell, with no man's hands to throw it, and it struck the image in the feet, smashing them in pieces. With that, the huge idol fell down and crumbled into iron and clay and silver and brass and golden dust that blew away with the wind.

"But the stone began to grow, and it grew and grew till it became a great mountain, big as the earth.

"That was your dream, O king.

"And this is what it means:

"You are king of kings, for the Lord God of heaven has given you a kingdom and, with it, power and glory. Wherever people live they know that you are their king. You are the head of gold.

"Some day there will be another kingdom, not quite so strong as yours, as silver is not quite so fine as gold. Then there will be a third kingdom, like the brass, and another, like the iron. This kingdom will be partly strong, partly weak, like the clay-iron feet of the image.

"But after them all the Lord God of heaven will build his kingdom stronger than all the rest of the kingdoms made by men, and it will last forever.

"The great God has told the king what is going to happen. This was the dream. That is what it means."

King Nebuchadnezzar bowed before Daniel.

"Now I know that your God is greater than all the kings of earth."

Then he gave Daniel gifts, and he made him governor over all the state of Babylon and chief wise man of the kingdom, and he let Daniel have his three friends for his assistants.

Daniel 2

Four Who Walked in Fire

King Nebuchadnezzar made an idol image, and a very great image it was. Ninety feet high, of shining gold, it stood out on the Plain of Dura where crowds of people could come to worship it. The king sent for all the important people the princes and the governors and the captains and the judges and the treasurers and the counselors and the sheriffs—to come to the dedication of the image. And when they came together from all the farthest provinces of the land, the king's herald proclaimed,

"O people from all the lands, whatever languages you speak, it is commanded that whenever you hear the music of the cornets and flutes, the harps, and the sound of singing, you must kneel down and worship King Nebuchadnezzar's golden image. Anyone who refuses will be thrown inside a burning fiery furnace."

So when all the people heard the music of cornets and flutes and harps and the sound of singing, they did kneel down to worship the king's golden image.

Some of the wise men were always watching the king's new favorites, Daniel and his three friends, hoping to catch them in some kind of trouble. Now they made a discovery, and they hurried straight to tell the king.

"O king, live forever.

"You have made a law, O king. At the music of cornets and flutes and harps and the sound of singing, every man is to kneel down and worship your golden image. And whoever refuses is to be thrown inside a burning fiery furnace.

"Now there are some Jews whom you made rulers in the province, O king, and these men—Shadrach, Meshach, and Abednego—have disobeyed you. They do not pray to your gods nor worship your golden image."

King Nebuchadnezzar was furious.

"Is this true?" he demanded when the three men were brought to him. "You do not pray to my gods? You do not worship my golden image? You know what to do when you hear the music of cornets and flutes and harps and the sound of singing. Go on and keep my law, and everything will be all right. If you do not, you will be thrown inside a burning fiery furnace. And who is this God of yours to save you?"

The three young men looked steadily at the king.

"O king, we are not afraid to answer you.

"If it must be this way, our God whom we obey is able to rescue us from the burning fiery furnace, and he is able to save us from you.

"But if he will not, even then we will not pray to your gods or worship your golden image."

King Nebuchadnezzar was so furious that his face was ugly to see. He ordered his furnace heated seven times hotter than usual, and he ordered his guards to bind Shadrach, Meshach, and Abednego and throw them inside. The flames blazed up so high and hot that the heat killed the guards who threw them in. The king stood watching. He called his counselors to see.

"Did we not throw three men in there—three men bound with ropes?"

"That is true, O king."

"Look! I can see four men walking around in the fire. They are not even hurt. And the fourth man looks like—the Son of God!"

He walked up to the door of the furnace.

"Shadrach! Meshach! Abednego! You who worship the Most High God, come out! Come here!"

Three men walked out of the fire. And all the king's court was amazed to see that they were not hurt. Their clothes were not burned. There was not even the slightest smell of scorched cloth about them.

King Nebuchadnezzar bowed his head.

"Blessed be their God who sent his angels to save them.

"Now I make this decree," he went on. "If any person—no matter what his country is or what language he speaks—says one word against the God of Shadrach, Meshach, and Abednego, he shall be cut to pieces and his house shall be torn down. None of our gods can do things like this."

Then he promoted Shadrach, Meshach, and Abednego to higher places in the state of Babylon.

Daniel 3

A Dream About a Tall Tree

This is my story. I am Nebuchadnezzar, king of Babylon. Let me tell you how I learned about the great Lord God. I was living safely in my palace. One night I had a dream that made me afraid, and so I sent for my magicians and all the wise men, and I told them about my dream. But they could not explain it.

Then Daniel came, my favorite wise man whom I call Belteshazzar. Truly the spirit of the holy gods is in his heart.

"Belteshazzar, no secret bothers you. Tell me what my dream means," I asked him.

"I dreamed that I saw a tall tree growing till it reached the sky and its branches covered the earth. Its leaves were fair to see, and its fruit was good to eat. Animals came to rest in its shade, and birds made their nests in its branches.

"I dreamed that I saw a watchman coming down from the sky, and he called loudly,

" 'Cut down the tree! Cut off its branches. Shake off the leaves. Scatter the fruit. Chase away the animals and the birds.

" 'But leave the stump and the roots there in the field where the dew falls on the grass.

" 'Then let this man's heart be changed from a man's heart to a beast's heart. And let it be so until he learns that the Lord God rules the kingdoms of men and gives them to whom he chooses.'

"This was my dream. Now tell me what it means."

Daniel, whose other name was Belteshazzar, studied sadly for an hour. At last he said to me,

"My king, may the dream be only about those who hate you.

"The tall, strong tree, O king, is yourself, grown great and strong and ruling all the earth.

"And this is the word of the Most High God:

"They will drive you out of your house, and you will live among the wild beasts. You will live on grass like the oxen, and the dew will fall on you. It will be that way until you learn that the Lord God rules the kingdoms of men and gives them to whom he chooses.

"May I give the king my advice?" Daniel asked. "Break away from your sins. Give generously to the poor. Choose the right way to live, and it may be a much longer time before your sickness comes upon you."

Everything happened just as Daniel said it would. A year later I was walking about my palace, and I was saying,

"What a great, strong country my Babylon has become since I have been king!"

Suddenly I heard a voice that spoke from heaven.

"King Nebuchadnezzar, your kingdom has been taken away from you. Men will drive you out to the fields where you will live with the animals, eating grass like the oxen. It will be that way until you learn that the Most High God rules the kingdoms of men and gives them to whom he chooses."

So they drove me out of the palace. I was no longer a man, but I lived like one of the animals, and I ate grass with the oxen. My hair grew long, and my nails were like birds' claws, and I was soaked with the dew of heaven.

The weeks and the months went by.

One day I looked up from the ground, and I remembered that there was a God in heaven. Then I was a man again, and I gave thanks to the Most High God whose kingdom takes in all the world and lasts forever.

So I came home. My counselors welcomed me back, and all my

kingdom and its brightness and glory belonged to me again.

Now I, King Nebuchadnezzar, praise the King of heaven, whose work is true and just, who brings low the proud and mighty.

Daniel 4

Mysterious Message on the Wall

Great King Belshazzar gave a feast, and a thousand guests were invited.

"Bring me the golden cups and the silver bowls my father captured from the Temple in Jerusalem," he ordered. "Bring them here, for my guests will drink their wine from them."

So the guests drank from the golden cups and the silver bowls that had been dedicated for the worship and sacrifice services in the Temple. And while they drank they sang to their idols made of gold and silver and brass and wood and stone.

While they were celebrating, the revelers saw something so frightening that even the king began to tremble. Over by the light a hand appeared and began to write on the wall. But no one was there—just a hand, writing words no one could read.

"Bring the magicians! Bring the wise men! Quickly!" shouted the king.

So the wise men and the magicians hurried in.

"What do those words say? Tell me, and you shall have a scarlet robe and a golden chain to wear round your neck, and you shall be third ruler in my kingdom," he offered.

The king's wise men studied the writing, and they shook their heads, for who could read such strange words?

The king was looking stern and worried when the queen came to him.

"O king, may you live forever! Don't be so troubled. Right here in your kingdom you have a man who knows everything. Your father, King Nebuchadnezzar, made him chief of the wise men.

Call for Daniel now. I know he can explain what the words mean."

So Daniel came to stand before the king.

"Are you the same Daniel who came with the prisoners from Judah? I have heard about you, how God gave you his spirit so that you are wise and understanding.

"Now tell me what that writing says, and I will give you a golden chain to wear around your neck and a scarlet robe and make you third ruler in my kingdom."

"Keep your gifts for yourself, O king," answered Daniel. "I do not want any reward. Give the pay to someone else. I will read the writing.

"O king, the Most High God gave to your father Nebuchadnezzar a great kingdom and glory and honor. But when he became too proud, God took his kingdom from him, and he wandered in the fields like an animal until he learned that the Most High God rules the kingdoms of men and gives them to whom he chooses.

"You are proud, and you have dared the Lord of heaven. You have used the golden cups and silver bowls from his Temple in your own feasting. You have worshiped gods of silver and gold, of brass and iron and wood, and you give no heed at all to God who gave you life. The hand you saw was sent by him, and this is the meaning of the words on the wall:

"God has counted the years of your kingdom and ended it.

"You have been weighed on the scales, and you are too light.

"The Medes and the Persians will take your kingdom from you."

Servants brought the scarlet robe and the golden chain to Daniel, and Belshazzar made a proclamation that he was to be the third ruler in the kingdom.

That very night the armies of the Medes and Persians attacked Babylon and captured it. King Belshazzar was killed, and Darius the Mede became king of his country.

Daniel 5

Into the Lions' Den

King Darius changed the government of Babylon. There were 120 princes in charge of the whole country, and over them he appointed three presidents. One of the three, and head of them all, was Daniel.

The others were envious, and they began to plot a way to get Daniel in trouble. But he was so faithful in his work that they could find nothing to report against him.

"Nothing he does is wrong, unless it's this business of his God."

They all went hurrying to the king.

"King Darius, may you live forever! We have all been talking together, and we have something to ask of you. We want you to order that for a month no one shall ask anything from any god or man but you. If anyone does, let him be thrown into the den of lions kept to punish criminals.

"Give the order, and sign it with your name, King Darius, and make it one of the laws of our people that cannot be changed."

King Darius nodded his head, and the law was made.

Now when Daniel heard about the new law he went straight home. By the open window, looking toward Jerusalem, he knelt to pray and give thanks to God. Morning, noon, and night he prayed just as he had always done.

It was not long before the presidents and the princes caught him at his prayers. So they reported to the king.

"That Daniel who came here with the prisoners from Judah has no respect for you, King Darius. He breaks your law and prays to his God three times a day."

The king was worried and troubled. All day he tried to think of some way to save Daniel. But the men came back.

"You know the law of our people, the law of the Medes and the Persians, King Darius. No order you make can ever be changed."

So King Darius unwillingly gave the order.

"Daniel is to be thrown to the lions."

But to Daniel he said,

"Your God whom you serve will save you."

That night the king could not sleep. Early in the morning he hurried out of the palace. Standing in front of the great stone door that barred the entrance to the lions' den, sealed shut with the king's own seal, he called,

"Daniel! Daniel, *is* your God able to save you?"

"King Darius, may you live forever!" Daniel's voice was clear and strong. "My God closed the mouths of the lions, and they have not hurt me. He knew that I have been true to him and to you, my king."

Gladly the king welcomed his friend. And when he looked to see whether Daniel was hurt, he saw that there was not a scratch on him.

So Darius gave another order—punishment for all the men who accused Daniel. And he ordered that Daniel's God should be worshiped everywhere in all the land.

"God rescues and saves. God is king in heaven and earth, God who rescued Daniel from the lions."

So Daniel was great and famous as long as Darius was king, and after Darius, when Cyrus became king.

Daniel 6

The Dream of the Shining Kingdom

The four winds blew across the ocean, from north and south and east and west. Up from the sea, tossed by the whirlwinds, came four great beasts, each stronger than the last. The first was like a lion, and it had eagles' wings. Upright it stood and walked like a man, strong like a conquering nation. The second looked like a bear, and its teeth were long fangs. The third was a winged leopard with four heads. And the fourth beast, dreadfully, terribly strong, had teeth of iron so strong that it attacked all the others, then stamped them to pieces beneath its feet.

Lands of the north and south and east and west they were, and the strongest country conquered all the rest.

So it was till all the thrones of all the kings of all the world were gone. Then the Ruler of heaven and earth, the Ancient of Days, in robes white as snow, looked out on his world from his dazzling throne. A thousand, thousand servants waited on him. Ten thousand times ten thousand stood before him. The heavenly court was in session, and the book of records of the deeds of men was opened.

Then there came to the dazzling throne, one they called the Son of man, and the clouds of heaven swirled about him.

To him was given all the world, with glory and power. All the people of all the world belong to him, and his kingdom will last forever.

There would come times of trouble, such as never were in all the history of the world, but the people of the Lord God—everyone whose name was written in his book—would be rescued. From the dust of the earth the sleeping dead would awake, some to live forever with him, some to shame that never ended. And the wise ones would shine in his glory. And those who had taught people about his love would shine as the stars forever and ever.

Daniel 7; 12:1–4

QUEEN ESTHER

A Jewish Girl Chosen Queen

BEAUTIFUL TO SEE was the great palace of King Ahasuerus, king of all the Medes and Persians and the lands from India to Africa. The floors were made of marble, red and blue and white and black. Curtains of white and green and blue, hanging from silver rings, covered the walls. The beds were made of gold and silver. The cups were golden, and no two of them were just alike.

So large was the palace that when the king gave a feast and invited all the nobles and princes of the land, they came and stayed for days while he showed them all his treasures, gold and silver and jewels, while they feasted and drank the royal wine.

Meanwhile, in her own apartments, Queen Vashti was giving a feast for all her friends. The merrymaking went on for a week. Then, although a queen would hardly ever appear in public, the king decided that all his guests must see his beautiful queen. So he ordered his seven chamberlains to bring her in, wearing her royal crown.

But the queen said no, and she stayed with the women in her own rooms in the palace.

King Ahasuerus was furious. The queen had dared to disobey the king! What should be done to her?

"My lord, it is worse than that. This thing will be talked about all over the country, and all the women will be thinking they can do as they please." Memucan of the king's court was speaking sternly.

"If it seems wise, let the king make a law and write it with all the laws of the Medes and the Persians that can never be changed.

Make it a law that Vashti is no longer queen and that someone else shall be queen instead. Then all the wives in this great land will listen to their husbands."

So the king made the law that could never be broken. But when he was not so angry, he began to think about Vashti and how there was no one to take her place.

The people of his court made a suggestion: Send the king's officers riding through all the land. Tell them to invite all the beautiful young maidens to come to the palace and stay with Hegai, chamberlain of the queen's court. Then let the king choose one of them to be the new queen.

And so it was done, for the idea pleased the king.

In the country of the Medes and the Persians there were many, many Jewish families. Far from the homeland they had built their houses, tended their farms, or worked at their trades ever since King Nebuchadnezzar's army carried them away as prisoners of war. Proud they were of being Jews, of worshiping and serving God, and they kept themselves a little apart from the others.

Now it happened that in the city of Susa lived Mordecai and his adopted daughter, the beautiful Esther, all who were left of one of the captive Jewish families. When they heard the news, they decided that Esther should go and join the other maidens.

"But tell no one that you are Jewish," Mordecai warned her.

Esther went to Hegai, chamberlain of the queen's court, and so gentle she was, so gracious and charming, that she pleased him greatly. He gave her the best apartment for her own, and gave her seven maids to wait on her. He gave her perfumes and creams with which she made herself even more beautiful while the weeks and months went by.

Each day Mordecai walked past the court of the women to ask about Esther. Each day he and Esther waited to see whether she would be called to go before the king. When each maiden was called, she might ask for anything she wanted—jewels or perfume, anything at all. But when Esther was called she asked for nothing. And so beautiful she was, so charming, that all who saw her loved her.

She went to the king, straight to the royal court, and she stood before his throne. As soon as he saw her he loved her. He placed the royal crown upon her head, and all the court bowed before Queen Esther.

Then the king gave a feast in Esther's honor, and he invited all the princes, all the rulers. He gave out kingly gifts and declared a royal celebration in all the land.

Mordecai went on living quietly in Susa, and every day he would meet the people of the court and do business with them. Of course, it was still a secret that he and Esther were Jews.

One day he discovered that there was a plot to attack the king. He hurried to tell Queen Esther that Bigthan and Teresh, two of the king's chamberlains, were angry and planned to get revenge. So Esther warned the king. There was an investigation. The men were punished. And the whole thing was recorded in the court book of history.

Esther 1; 2

Haman's Plots Against the Jews

In all the king's court Haman was most proud and powerful. And when the king promoted him above all the princes of the land, there was none more haughty. He demanded that everyone should bow before him, all the princes and all the king's servants.

"But Mordecai does not bow before you," they reported to Haman. Those who knew Mordecai best knew why, for Jews would not bow to heathen princes.

Angrily Haman planned his punishment. He would order Mordecai killed. But that was not enough. He would see to it that all Mordecai's people were killed with him. He waited for a day that was supposed to be lucky, and he went to warn the king how dangerous the Jews were.

"There are people scattered all over this land whose laws are different from our laws," he reported. "They do not even keep the king's laws. So the king should have no patience with them.

"If it seems wise to the king, let him make a law that they must all be killed and all their money taken for the king's treasury."

The king nodded, and he took from his finger the king's own ring and placed it on Haman's hand to show that Haman had the king's own power.

"Do with them as you like," he said.

So Haman wrote a letter, signing it with the king's name and sealing it with the mark of the king's own seal:

"To all governors and lieutenants in every province and to all rulers:

"On the thirteenth day of the month Adar destroy and kill all Jews both young and old, men and women and little children, and take from them everything they have."

The king's messengers rode north and south and east and west till the order was published in every city and town. But Haman and the king sat down together to drink. *Esther 3*

How Queen Esther Saved Her People

In all the land wherever a Jewish family heard the news there was mourning and crying. Some dressed in mourning clothes, wearing rough sackcloth and sprinkling ashes on their heads, and they ran out in the streets to cry out the terrible thing that was happening. That was the way Mordecai himself was mourning, but he had to stay outside the palace since no one was allowed to enter the king's house in such a shabby robe.

Someone reported to Queen Esther that he was outside in the

Queen Esther

street in mourning clothes. So she sent a clean robe out to him and begged him to tell her what was wrong.

Mordecai would not come in, for he refused to change his clothes. But he sent the queen a copy of the king's order with this message: "Go to the king. Beg him to save our people."

"I dare not go! I dare not! The king must send for every person who goes into the king's own court. And if anyone should go without being called, it is the king's own law that he must die—unless the king holds out his golden scepter. And I—even I, the queen—have not been called to him this whole month."

They told Mordecai what she said. And he sent back word:

"Do not think you can be safe, even in the king's palace. If you do not speak now, God will find someone else to save his people, but you and your people will die. Who knows? Perhaps you were sent to the kingdom for such a time as this."

Back came Queen Esther's answer:

"Call together all the Jews who live here. For three days ask them to fast, without eating or drinking, and pray, for my sake. My maids and I will be fasting and praying, too.

"Then I will break the law and go to the king. If I am to die, then I must die."

Three days later Queen Esther dressed in her most beautiful gown, and she went to see the king. She stood in the doorway, and she watched him on his throne, watched all the people of the court. She saw him look up. He recognized her, and he seemed pleased. Slowly he held out the royal scepter. So she walked into the room, straight to the throne, and she touched the tip of the golden scepter.

"What is it, my queen? What will you have? It is yours, even if you ask for half my kingdom."

Queen Esther smiled.

"If it seems good to the king, I wish to invite him and my lord Haman to a banquet." That was all she said.

The king smiled, and he ordered Haman to get ready at once. But when they came to the banquet all Queen Esther would say was,

"If the king is pleased, I wish to invite him and my lord Haman to a banquet tomorrow."

Then was Haman proud indeed. At home he told his wife,

"See how the king has honored me, how the queen herself has invited me and no other man, not once but twice."

Suddenly his face grew stern. "But what does it matter? That Mordecai is still out there doing business for the king."

"Why, that is easily settled," said his wife. "Just tell the carpenters to build a gallows for the hanging. Get the king to have Mordecai hanged on it, and go on to your banquet."

Haman smiled grimly, and he ordered the gallows built.

That night the king could not sleep. So he sent for the court book of history.

"Read to me of the affairs of my country," he ordered his servant.

So he read aloud from the history, and he came to the account of the plot of Bigthan and Teresh, and he read how Mordecai had saved the king's life.

"What did we ever do to reward Mordecai?" asked the king.

"Nothing at all, my king."

There was the sound of footsteps outside. Haman was coming in to ask the king to have Mordecai hanged.

"Haman is here, my lord."

"Let him come in."

"Haman, what shall be done for the man whom the king is glad to honor?"

"Let this man wear the king's own robes of blue and white," said Haman. "Let him wear the royal crown of gold. Let him ride out before all the people on the king's own horse. Choose one of the most noble of the princes to take the robe and the crown to him. Let the prince lead him out on horseback through all the streets of the city. And let him tell all the people,

" 'This is the man the king is glad to honor!' "

"Haman, it shall be just that way. Take the robe and the crown to Mordecai."

So proud Haman obeyed the king. All through the streets of the city they went, Mordecai on the king's horse, wearing the king's own crown of gold and the king's own robes of blue and white, and Haman calling out,

"This is the man the king is glad to honor."

Then sadly Haman went home to tell his wife the news. And while they were still talking, the king's messengers came to take him to the queen's banquet.

Queen Esther welcomed the king and Haman, and they feasted together. At last the king said,

"Tell me what it is you wish, Queen Esther. You shall have it, even if you ask the half of my kingdom."

"If it is pleasing to the king, I am asking for my life," Queen Esther said quietly. "I am asking for the lives of my people. For we have been sold, my people and I, to be killed."

"Who dared to do this?" demanded the king.

"Your enemy and mine is this Haman."

Haman stood up to beg for his life. But the king left the table and walked out into the garden. When he came back Haman had fallen on the queen's couch.

"Will he also harm the queen?" Quickly the king called his guard.

"There is that high gallows Haman built for Mordecai," suggested one of the guards.

"Hang him on it," the king ordered.

Then he sent for Mordecai and made him prince of all the land in Haman's place. But Queen Esther knelt before the king.

"If it seems right to the king, and if I have pleased him, give me the lives of my people. Take back Haman's order that on the thirteenth day of the month Adar we are all to be killed."

Then the king gave his orders to Mordecai:

"Write this letter. Sign it with the king's name, and seal it with the royal seal. Write it in all the languages of all the nations from India to Africa. Tell the Jews to rise up and fight against the people who attack them on the thirteenth day of the month Adar."

So out rode the king's messengers, on horseback, on donkeys and camels, to every country from India to Africa to carry the good news. Then there was joyful celebration in every Jewish home. And the day became a day of happiness instead of sorrow, a day for feasting and giving presents. In years to come it was called the Feast of Purim, when Jews around the world would celebrate the memory of the brave young queen who risked her life to save her people.

Esther 4 to 9

CAPTIVES WHO CAME HOME

One Small Altar in the Ruins

"WATCHMAN, what do you see?" the people in the streets called up to the guard in the tower.

"I see two men in a chariot racing this way, traveling fast as the whirlwind across the desert.

"Babylon has fallen! Has fallen! All the gods are toppling! They lie in pieces where they fall.

"Where is Babylon, the queen who sat proudly on her throne? She said, 'A lady I will be all my life; my magicians and my witches will keep me safe.'

"See where she sits barefoot on the ground, no throne left to her. And hatless now she goes to work like any servant to grind the meal between the millstones."

The news was true. The proud empire of Babylon had fallen. The people who had held the Jews captive were now a captive nation. Cyrus the Persian was king.

Soon the Jewish people discovered that this new king was far different from their old enemies. Cyrus was a man who respected people whom he had conquered, and he believed in letting them alone to live in their own lands, in their own way.

So instead of making the Jews work for him, he sent out a proclamation, and his messengers carried it north and south, east and west, to the far lands of his kingdom.

"The Lord God of heaven has given me all the kingdoms of the world, and he has charged me:

" 'Build a house for the Lord God in Jerusalem of Judah.'

"Now, who is there of all my people who will go to build this house? And may the Lord God go with him."

For years and years Jerusalem had been nothing but piles of broken stones and charred wood.

"Our holy, beautiful house where our fathers sang their hymns is burned up with fire, and all the things we loved are rubble in the streets," the homesick captives mourned.

Now the bravest of them volunteered to go back, and from colonies far and near came wise old men and priests and Levites and Temple singers and families with their children and their servants.

King Cyrus gave them gifts from his treasury—the shining golden bowls and silver pitchers the soldiers had stolen from the Temple in Jerusalem. And the people who could not go came bringing gifts, money to help build the Lord's house, and food for the journey, and horses and donkeys and camels to carry the baggage all the hundreds of miles home across the desert.

So the first of the captives came home safely, and they moved into the ruined towns round Jerusalem. Some of them even ventured into the place of the city on Mount Zion, though the walls were broken down and the gates had long ago been burned.

First of all, the men met in Jerusalem with Zerubbabel the governor and Joshua the high priest, and they set to work at once rebuilding the altar to the Lord God.

They cleared the level place where the old Temple court used to be, and they discovered the very spot where the altar had been. This was only a small beginning, but when the men built the altar, even though there was no roof above it, they knew that they had come home.

Proudly the people brought their sacrifice gifts for the morning and the evening services, and the priest led them while the singing people chanted their songs.

The Lord God brought home the prisoners,
And we were like people in a dream.
We began to laugh again,
And we sang as people used to sing in Zion.
The Lord has done great things for us, and we are glad.
Even the heathen were saying,
The Lord has done great things for them.

The next year the people went to work on the foundation of the Temple. They hired stone masons and carpenters, and they ordered lumber from the north country, using some of the oil and food King Cyrus gave them to pay for it.

The day they laid the foundation there was a real celebration. The priests, dressed in their robes, their trumpets in their hands, led the procession. Behind them came the Levites, keeping time with their clashing cymbals. And the people marched along, shouting for joy and chanting a thanksgiving hymn:

Oh, give thanks to the Lord, for he is good,
For his mercy is round us forever.
Oh, give thanks to the Lord, for he is good.
He saved us from enemies when we could not help ourselves.
For his mercy is round us forever.

But the older men were remembering how the Temple used to look with its shining walls and golden columns and all that was fine and splendid, and they wept because they could never hope for anything so beautiful. So some wept for sorrow and some shouted for gladness; and far away, outside the tumble-down city walls, people could hear the sound of shouting.

Isaiah 21:9; 47; 2 Chronicles 36; Ezra 1; 2; Psalms 126; 136

Stone on Stone They Built the Temple

The news spread quickly that men in Jerusalem were busy building a house for the Lord, and neighbors from the north decided they wanted to help. They were the people of Samaria, not true Jews any longer like the Israelites who had lived there before their land was conquered.

The families were grandchildren of some of the poorest and weakest of the Israelites who had been left behind, and people from other lands that the Assyrians had conquered. They had brought their heathen idols with them, and they had also learned in Israel to respect the Lord God of the Hebrews. Now they were worshiping them all.

They sent a delegation to Governor Zerubbabel.

"Let us build with you, for we want to know your God."

But Zerubbabel and Joshua and the wise old men were very sure of this: trouble came when people of other lands, with all their idols and their heathen ways, lived with the Hebrews. Now that they were back home it must never happen again.

"We will build this house ourselves. You have nothing to do with us," they told the people from Samaria.

So, instead of helping, the angry Samaritans began to make all the trouble they could. From that time on, Jews despised Samaritans and Samaritans despised Jews. These unfriendly neighbors complained to the king, pretending they were good citizens who wanted to warn him and asking him to stop the building.

There were other troubles, too. The Jews were beginning to find out how hard their work was going to be. They were working on the Temple without pay, and they had to borrow money to live. Nothing seemed to be going right. They planted their gardens, but there was not enough rain and nothing grew. It was hard to find enough to eat, hard to get enough clothes to keep warm. There was never enough of anything to go around, and it seemed as if all they did was put their money in bags full of holes.

They were discouraged. They spent so much time on their own houses and their own gardens that there was no time for working on the Temple, and they would excuse themselves by saying,

"This is not the right time."

Suddenly something happened to make the Jews brave again and ready to go to work, for a man named Haggai was saying,

"The Lord God is speaking."

It had been a long time since they had heard from God straight from one of his prophets, and they listened—Zerubbabel, and Joshua, and all the rest.

"Is this the time for you to be living in your houses with good roofs while the Lord's house is in ruins?

"Have you given up because you can never build a house as fine as the first? The glory of this house will be even greater, for I will be with you, and I will fill it with my glory."

They all went to work again. But in their worries and their troubles they would forget so easily whose they were and why God had sent them home.

One day the people heard a new preacher named Zechariah, who was preaching in pictures instead of sermons. With his pictures he was answering some of their troublesome questions.

Zechariah was a young man, but he had already discovered something the wise old men were forgetting.

" 'Turn around and come back to me, and I will come to meet you,' says the Lord God."

"How do we know God cares what happens to us?"

Zechariah gave them the picture of the horsemen.

"Down by the myrtle trees in the valley one night, while an angel walked beside me, I saw a rider on a red horse, and behind him I saw more horsemen; their horses were red and sorrel and white.

" 'Who are they?' " I asked the angel.

" 'The Lord God sent us to ride through the lands of the world, and we have gone north and south and east and west, and all the world is at peace.

" 'The Lord God comes back to Jerusalem,' the angel told me. 'His house will be built in his city, and Jerusalem will bring joy to all the world.' "

"How do we know we are safe from our enemies?" the people asked.

"While the angel walked beside me I saw four deadly weapons.

" 'What are they?' I asked.

" 'The power of the nations that drove out the people of Judah, the people of Israel, and the people of Jerusalem, till no one could feel safe.'

"Then I saw four workmen.

" 'What are they doing here?' I wanted to know.

" 'They are the Lord's workmen who came to conquer the enemies of Judah and Israel and Jerusalem.' "

"Will the Lord God really come back to us in Jerusalem?"

"I saw a man going up and down the streets of the city with a tapeline in his hand, measuring the width and the breadth of it.

"An angel came to meet the angel who walked with me, and he said, " 'Run, tell the young man the city will be big and full of people. And the Lord God will be there, protecting his city like a wall of fire, filling it all with his glory.' "

"How do we know the Lord God really wants Joshua for his high priest?"

"Then I saw Joshua, and he was dressed in dusty clothes, standing beside Satan, and Satan seemed to be trying to find something wrong with him. But the angel asked for clean clothes, and he exchanged them for Joshua's filthy clothes, which somehow stood for all the sins of all the people.

" 'Joshua, high priest of the Lord God, if you will keep the laws of God, if you will care for my house and my people when they come to my house, I will honor you above them all.' "

"And will the people be forever sinning and forever forgetting the Lord God?"

"The angel who walked with me told me to watch carefully. I saw them take the wicked old woman whose name was Evil and put her in a barrel and seal the barrel shut. Then I saw two women, and the wind was in their wings. They picked her up and went flying off to the east.

" 'Where?' I wondered.

"To Babylon, to build her a house. Where else?"

So the people looked up from their own homes to the altar and the small beginning they had made on Mount Zion.

"The Temple of the Lord will be finished, 'Not by might or by power but by my Spirit,' says the Lord," Zechariah promised them. "Never doubt the days of small beginnings. With his own hands your governor has begun the work, and with his own hands he will finish it.

"But remember: Speak the truth, every one of you, with your neighbors. 'Quarreling and false tales, these are the things I hate,' says the Lord God.

"For Jerusalem will be called the City of Truth, and Mount Zion will be the Lord's holy mountain. The streets of the city will be wide and safe, safe enough for old people and for boys and girls at play."

So once more the people went to work on the Temple wall, and the governor was right there working with them. The news spread from one village to the next: "They are building in Jerusalem."

When Tattenai, governor of the land west of the Great River, heard what was going on, he sent men to Jerusalem to investigate.

"Who told you to build this house? Give us the name of every workman," the governor's men demanded.

"We have permission from the king," the Jews told them, and they went right on working. Then Governor Tattenai reported to King Darius and asked for his orders.

King Darius sent his secretaries looking in the old record books, and they found the whole story, how King Cyrus had sent the prisoners home, how he gave them gifts and told them to build their Temple.

So this letter came back to Governor Tattenai:

"Let the building project alone and go on about your business. Give them all the help you can. Give them money from the taxes that are paid to you. Whatever the priests need for the Temple services, see that they have it."

So the work went on steadily, month after month. When it was finished the walls stood straight and shining, and the roof was strong against the rain, and the altar waited for the Lord's sacrifice gifts. Though the finished Temple was smaller and plainer than the first Temple, the people were proud.

It was the time for the Passover feast when the Jews celebrated for the first time in the new house of the Lord. Seven days they brought their gifts, and they worshiped together and sang together, for it was a time of glad thanksgiving.

Hallelujah! Sing a new song to the Lord.
Let the children of Zion be glad because of their King.
Praise him with the trumpet, with the harp,
With the loud cymbals, with the high cymbals.
Let every living thing praise the Lord.

*Ezra 4 to 6; Haggai 1; 2;
Zechariah 1 to 5; Psalms 149:1–3; 150:5–6*

Royal Homecoming for Ezra

It was only natural that the young man Ezra would be interested in God's Word. His father, his grandfather, and his great-great-grandfathers all the way back to Aaron, had been priests in the service of the Lord God. So Ezra studied the law of God, and he copied it, and he knew it by heart. The time came when he knew that he wanted more than anything else to go back to Jerusalem and teach his people.

Of course King Artaxerxes must give him permission to travel, and that he gladly did. But Ezra would not have to travel alone, for the king told him,

"All the people of Israel who choose to go with you are free to go. They shall carry with them silver and gold from the king and his seven advisers, and all the silver and gold the people give as a freewill offering. Buy with it all the meat and drink offerings you need for the altar of the house of your God. And use the rest for whatever you need. Take these bowls, these trays, these lampstands for the service of your God. And anything else you need you shall have from the king's treasure house."

Now the road was long across the desert lands, and robber bands would be hiding in the lonely rocky hills. But Ezra was ashamed to ask for a guard. Had he not told the king, "God guards with his own hand all those who serve him"?

So he called his party together, all the priests with their families, all the women and the children and the servants, and they camped together by the Ahava River. They would not stop to eat, and they spent their time praying that God would be with them.

Then Ezra chose twelve of the chief priests, and he divided the treasure among them, all the gold and silver and money and gifts for the house of God.

"Guard them and keep them till you give them to the chief of the priests in Jerusalem," he said.

Then they set out, and God guarded them every step of the way.

But in Jerusalem Ezra heard bad news.

After all the years of punishment for breaking the laws of God, after all their good resolutions to do better in the homeland, the people were breaking the law and marrying women from the heathen lands round about. It was the old, old story. Ezra knew that those heathen wives would bring their heathen idols with them.

"The Lord your God is the only God!" He heard the ancient command as if God had spoken it aloud to him that day.

So, weeping in his grief, he went into the house of God. He prayed before all the people that God would forgive them, and the men of Jerusalem wept with him.

"We have broken the law of God. Yet there is one hope for us," said Shecaniah, the son of one of the priests. "We can promise God that we will send these women home to their families. Let it be done in a kindly and orderly way. You take charge, and whatever you say we will do. Only help us now," he begged Ezra.

So Ezra sent for all the men of the country, and they came together in the early days of winter, standing outdoors by the house of God, waiting for Ezra to speak. They were shivering, partly from fright and partly because cold rain was falling.

Ezra stood before them, and he told them what they must do.

"Give us time, and we will do it," they promised. "Let us go before the elders, each in our own town, and do this thing in an orderly way."

And so it was done, though weeks went by before every heathen woman had been taken home.

Slowly the people of God were learning. Never again were heathen idols worshiped in his Temple.
Ezra 7 to 10

The Leader of the Wall-Builders

The work that began so bravely in Jerusalem had all but stopped. The Temple was finished, and new houses were built. But the ruined walls were no protection against animals or robbers.

One day travelers from Judah came to the palace of the king in Susa. One of them was Hanani, who was looking for his brother, Nehemiah, cupbearer to the king.

"Tell me all the news," Nehemiah begged him.

"It is bad, very bad. The people are in great trouble. The city walls have crumbled away. The gates are charred ruins. No one is safe."

Nehemiah's heart was heavy with worry. He could not eat. He could hardly do his work. But he prayed, prayed for God's forgiveness and his mercy—prayed, too, that the one for whom he worked would help him.

Now a cupbearer's first duty was to be smiling and cheerful. For the first time since he began serving the king, Nehemiah's face was troubled and sad.

The king asked him what was wrong. Frightened though Nehemiah was, he decided to tell the truth.

"May the king live forever! My city lies in ruins. Its gates are burned. That is why I am sorrowful."

"What do you wish?"

With a quick prayer to God for help, Nehemiah answered,

"If it please the king, I want to be sent to Jerusalem. Let me go and see that the building is finished."

© 1960, The Sunday School Board, S.B.C.

Rebuilding the Wall

And the king, sitting there beside the queen, asked agreeably, "When will you return?"

Nehemiah set a time. He said,

"If it please the king, may I have letters to the governors for safe conduct till I come to Judah, and a letter to Asaph, keeper of the king's forest, giving me lumber to make beams for the gates of the city?"

And the king gave Nehemiah all that he asked.

So, riding the king's horse and guarded by the king's soldiers, he set out on the long road back to Judah.

When the news reached Sanballat, chieftain in Samaria, and Tobiah of Ammon, they were angry. They would see about this business down in Judah!

At first Nehemiah tried to keep his visit a secret. For three days he stayed in Jerusalem quietly, just looking the city over. One night when no one was watching, he slipped out with some of his friends and went riding around the city. Out the Valley Gate he went, past the Dragon Well, and he turned and looked back on the tumble-down walls, the charred gates. He went on to the Fountain Gate and the Pool of the King. There the road was blocked by ruins, and his donkey could go no farther. He rode around by the brook, studying the ruined wall as he went. Then he turned back and came into the city again by the Valley Gate.

As soon as his plans were ready, he went to see the priests and the governor and the workmen.

"Let's get to work and build the wall. The king will help, and God himself will stand by us."

So they went to work.

But when Sanballat and Tobiah heard about it they laughed.

"Are you rebelling against the king?" they asked.

"We will build, for God will help us. But there is no place for you here in Jerusalem," Nehemiah told them firmly.

The men of Judah divided by groups and families, each working together. The priests worked on the Sheep Gate, and the men from Jericho worked on the wall beside them. The goldsmiths had their station, and the merchants had theirs.

Sanballat and Tobiah went on laughing.

"Do those poor Jews think they can make a dead city live? Why, even if they do build their wall the first fox that comes along will break it down."

But the people worked on steadily, and half the wall was finished, for they had a mind to work.

By that time Sanballat and Tobiah and the Arabians and the Ammonites and the rest discovered that the people of Judah meant business. So they plotted a sudden attack on the workmen.

But Nehemiah and his people stopped just long enough to ask God for help and protection. Then they hurried back to work. Nehemiah posted guards on the wall to keep a lookout. He stationed the trumpeter beside him ready to give the alarm if they were attacked. He armed everyone, workmen and soldiers and carriers, with swords and spears and bows.

From first morning light until the stars came out the men worked without stopping. At night they stayed together inside the city, but no one undressed, for there was a constant alert.

Then the day came when the wall was finished. High and strong it circled the city. But the gates were not in place.

So Sanballat and Tobiah tried again.

"Come out to the plains and meet us. Let's talk things over."

"I'm too busy with a great work. Why should I leave it?" Nehemiah sent them word.

Four times Sanballat tried that trick. Then he sent a different message.

"We hear you are building the wall so you can be king. It's time to talk this over."

"That tale you are making up," Nehemiah answered quickly. Just the same, the men began to be uneasy.

"O God, make my hands strong," Nehemiah begged.

Tobiah and Sanballat had another trick. They hired Shemaiah to go to Nehemiah.

"Let's meet together in the Temple where we can shut the door. You can be safe there, for no one would kill you in the Temple."

Nehemiah well knew he had no business in the Temple. That was for the priests.

"Am I running away? Shall I try to save my life in the Temple?" he answered.

So they worked till the wall and the gates were finished. Not quite eight weeks it was since the work had begun, and the Jews had worked night and day. Now Sanballat and Tobiah could say no more. This was truly the work of God and not of man.

Nehemiah 1 to 6

Seven Days by the Water Gate

At last it was safe to go to sleep at night in Jerusalem. For at dark the gates were locked and guarded. Not till the sun was warm in the morning were they opened.

Now people began to think of the days when there was time to study, to learn, to listen to the laws of God. They had been busy building and staying on guard for so long. And so they asked to hear the law of God.

It was on the first day of the month, when the people came crowding to the open square by the Water Gate. Round a high wooden pulpit two of the most important men in Jerusalem, Ezra and Nehemiah, with all the priests, came to meet them. Ezra was carrying a scroll, and as soon as he stood in the pulpit, high where everyone could see, he opened the scroll and began to read.

All the Law he read: the law God gave to Moses, the law the teachers had taught the people in Israel, in Judah, in faraway Babylon, and now back again in their own home.

Slowly he read, carefully stopping to explain the meaning so that everyone could understand. And as the people listened to the familiar words, they began to cry because of all their broken promises and their stubborn ways. Ezra and Nehemiah said,

"This is God's holiday, a day for gladness. Go home and celebrate. Feast together, and send a share to the poor."

So they all went home, and there was feasting all day long. But the next day they came back to hear more.

This time they listened while Ezra read about the Feast of Tabernacles, when the people used to make small huts of pine and olive and palm branches in the streets, in their courtyards, even on their flat rooftops. And there for seven days they lived, celebrating the harvest time together.

Not since Joshua led them into the Promised Land had the feast been kept. And this was harvest time—though poor indeed would be the harvest after the summer of hard work.

Out to the hills the people went, and they brought back branches of pine and palm, of myrtle and olive, and they built their huts in the streets of Jerusalem. There they camped for all the seven days of the feast, and every day they listened while Ezra read.

Then on the eighth day there was a solemn worship service. Quietly, soberly, the people confessed their sins, and they listened to the Word of God—all the long, strange, wonderful story of his love for his people ever since he chose Abram and sent him to a far country. Slaves they were in Egypt, and wanderers in the desert, and pioneers in their Promised Land, and proud citizens of their country and sorrowful prisoners in faraway lands, and now, at last, travelers at home again, and never for a minute out of God's protecting love.

With songs and chants and prayers they praised God.

> Blessed is the Lord God who made heaven,
> The moon and all the stars,
> Earth and man, all living things,
> Sea and all beneath its waters.

Then with all their hearts they made a solemn pledge to remember that they belonged to God, to serve and worship him and love him all their lives.

Now, under God's law, the people planned for their new community. They decided that each man would pay a tax for the expenses of the Temple, and they planned the way they would bring their tithes and offerings to the priests and how the priests would use the gifts. They decided that some of the families should move away from Jerusalem and settle in the small towns.

And no matter what happened they would not—*would not*—bring heathen people and their heathen idols back to Jerusalem.

Then came the day when they dedicated the new wall. From all the towns around, the people came—the singers and the trumpeters and the musicians with their cymbals and their psalteries and their harps. Nehemiah lined them up for the procession. He sent half the people round the city one way and half the other, singing, chanting as they went, and they all met by the Temple. So great was their joy, so warm the love in their heart, that, as they all sang together, men and women and children—people in towns across the hills and valleys—stopped to listen.

Still there were lessons God's people seemed to learn so slowly.

Nehemiah had gone back to his work in the palace, but the king was generous, and once more he gave his cupbearer leave to go to Jerusalem.

But this time he had a sad homecoming. How stupid, how stubborn could people be! He found Tobiah, his old enemy, living in a fine apartment in the Temple court. So he threw out Tobiah's furniture and ordered the place be made clean for God's house.

Nehemiah watched farmers and fishermen bringing food to market on the sabbath day, and he watched people buying their food as if it were a day like other days.

"What is this evil thing you do—breaking the law of the sabbath?" he demanded.

Then he ordered the city gates locked at dark, not to be opened till the sabbath day was over, and he sent home the farmers who tried to camp outside all day, ready to dash in to sell their goods the minute the gates were opened.

About that time the prophet Malachi was watching the gifts the people brought to the Temple. He saw moldy bread, blind animals, and lame, scrawny sheep too poor for food. What kind of giving was that?

Once again the people of Jerusalem heard a prophet's voice thundering out:

"The Lord God is speaking!

" 'Will a man rob God? You have robbed me with your tithes and offerings. Bring you all the tithes into the storehouse. Try me, test me, and see if I will not open the windows of heaven to you—pour out blessings until you have no room to hold them.' "

Some who came home were true and held fast their promise to love and honor God. They listened with their hearts, and they talked together, remembering their love for God and God's wondrous love for them.

And they are the ones whose names are written in the Lord's book of remembrance.

"They shall be my own on the day when I make up my jewels."

Nehemiah 8 to 13; Psalm 119:34; Malachi 1:3; 3:17

SONGS AND SAYINGS

Song for the House of God

Sing a joyful song to the Lord, all you nations,
Serve the Lord with gladness,
Come before his presence with singing.

Remember that the Lord is our God:
It is he who made us, not we ourselves;
We are his people, sheep in his pasture.

Come into his gates with thanksgiving,
Into his courts with praise.
Be thankful to him and bless his name.

Come, let us sing to the Lord,
Come to him with thanksgiving,
Sing our songs in gladness.

For our Lord is a great God,
In his hands are the deep places of the earth.
The highest hills are his;
The sea is his, for he made it,
And his hands formed the dry land.

Come, let us worship and bow down,
Let us kneel before the Lord, our Maker,
For he is our God, and we are his people.

Psalms 100; 95

Song of God's Loving Care

Oh, give thanks to the Lord, for he is good,
For his mercy is round us forever.

You whom he saved—from the east, from the west,
From the north and from the south—
Give thanks to the Lord.

His people wandered in the desert,
Hungry and thirsty and ready to die.

Then they cried out to the Lord in their trouble,
And he led them safely
Till they found a city and made them a home.

> Oh, that men would thank the Lord for his goodness,
> For his wonderful works for his people!

Prisoners they were, chained in a dungeon,
And no one would help,
For they rebelled against the words of God
And despised the teaching of the Most High.

Then they cried out to the Lord in their trouble,
And he rescued them.
He led them out of the darkness,
And he broke their chains in two.

> Oh, that men would thank the Lord for his goodness,
> For his wonderful works for his people!

They were feeble and sick when they had broken
   his laws,
They could not eat, they were all but dead.

Then they cried out to the Lord in their trouble,
And he healed them.

   Oh, that men would thank the Lord for his goodness,
   For his wonderful works for his people!

They went to sea in their ships,
And they watched his works,
His wonders out at sea,
For he raised the storm wind that tossed the waves.
They mounted high,
They dropped to the depths.
In their ships they staggered and fell,
Their courage was gone.

Then they cried out to the Lord in their trouble.
He calmed the storm, and the waves were still.
So he rescued them from danger,
And he brought them safe to their harbor.

   Oh, that men would thank the Lord for his goodness,
   For his wonderful works for his people!

He gave them a home in the desert land,
Gave them pools of water and cold, clear springs.
And the grain grew high in the fields.

   Oh, that men would thank the Lord for his goodness,
   For his wonderful works for his people. *Psalm 107*

Song for a Dark Night

He who knows the secret place of the Most High
Shall live unafraid in the shadow of the Almighty.
    The Lord is my refuge, my fortress,
    My God; in him I will trust.
Surely he will rescue you from the trap of the hunter,
And from the deadly sickness.
Cover you with his feathers,
And under his wings you can trust.
His truth is your shield, your armor.
You shall not fear the terror by night,
Nor the arrow that flies by day,
Nor sickness that walks in the darkness,
Nor destruction that wastes at bright noon.

No evil can come to you,
No fever come near your home,
For he gives his angels charge over you,
To keep you in all your ways.
They lift you up in their hands,
Lest you bruise your foot on a stone.

When I am in trouble I will call to God, and he will
    answer me.
When I am afraid I will put my trust in him,
For he will light my candle.
The Lord my God will make my darkness light.
I will lay me down, and I will sleep,
For with the Lord God I am safe.

Psalms 91; 86:7; 56:3; 18:28; 4:8

Song of Spring

He has made everything beautiful in its time.

The hearing ear, and the seeing eye,
The Lord God made them both.

See, now the winter is past,
The rain is over and gone,
The flowers appear on the earth,
The time of the singing of birds is come,
And the voice of the dove is heard in our land.
The fig tree puts out its green figs,
And the vines with the tender grapes give a good smell.
Come, winds from the north, winds from the south,
Blow over my garden, my sweet-smelling garden.

Ecclesiastes 3:11; Proverbs 20:12;
Song of Solomon 2:11–13; 4:16

Song for an Orchestra

Praise the Lord!
Sing praise to the Lord in his temple!
Praise him in the highest heavens!
Praise him for his mighty deeds,
Praise him for his wondrous work!

Praise him with the trumpet sound,
Praise him with the lute and lyre!
Praise him with tambourine and horn,
Praise him with the harps and flutes.
Praise him with the loud cymbals,
Praise him with the clanging cymbals.

Let every living thing praise the Lord!
Praise him, all his angels,
Praise him, sun and moon,
Praise him, all you stars of light.

Praise the Lord from earth,
You sea creatures, dark places of the sea,
Fire and hail, snow and fog,
Stormy wind obeying his word,
You mountains, you hills, fruit trees and cedars,
Beasts and cattle,
Creeping snakes and flying birds.

Praise him with the trumpet sound,
Praise him with the lute and lyre,
Praise him with the harps and flutes,
Praise him with the clanging cymbals.
Praise the Lord!

Psalms 150; 148

Wise Words for Every Day

Unless the Lord God builds the house
The workmen have their trouble for nothing;
Unless the Lord God builds the city
The watchmen might better be sleeping.

Trust the Lord with all your heart,
Depend not on yourself alone.
Never think you know it all,
Give him first place. He is your guide.

The eyes of the Lord see everywhere,
Discovering the good and the evil.
Six things the Lord God hates, yes, seven he despises:
The proud look and the lying tongue,
Hands that kill, a heart that looks for evil,
Feet that race to mischief, talebearers who lie,
And troublemakers among friends.

To have friends a man must be a friend.
    A friend loves forever;
Better is a lunch of dry bread in a friendly home
Than a feast in a house full of quarreling.
    Choose a good reputation rather than riches,
    Friendship rather than silver or gold.

A gentle answer ends a quarrel,
But a cross word stirs up anger.
He who is slow to get angry is stronger than heroes,
    And he who controls his temper does better
    Than one who captures a city.

Pride goes before destruction,
And a proud spirit before a fall.
A merry heart does good like medicine.
    He who gives help to the poor lends to the Lord,
    And the Lord himself will reward him.
Wine is a cheat; strong drink is raging.
Foolish is the man who lets them deceive him.
    Whatever your hand finds to do,
    Do it with all your might.
    Even a child is known by the things he does.

Remember now your Creator while you are young,
Love God, and keep his laws.
Teach me to do your will, for you are my God.
Let the words I am saying, the thoughts I am thinking
Be pleasing to you, Lord God who saves me,
And keeps me strong.

Selections from Psalms 127; 143; 25; 19;
Proverbs 3; 15; 6; 18; 17; 22; 16;
19; 20; Ecclesiastes 9; 12

Song of Small Creatures

    Four tiny things there are, but they are wise:
Small things are ants,
But they store up food in the summer.
Rock-badgers, too, they are feeble folk,
But they build safe homes in the rocks.
No kings have the locusts,
But they travel together in swarms.
Small ways have small lizards,
But they live in kings' palaces.
Four tiny things there are, but they are wise.

Proverbs 30:24–28

Lazybones

Go watch the ant, Lazybones,
Watch her, and be wise.
She has no guide, no watchman,
But all summer she stores up her food.

How long will you sleep, Lazybones?
When will you wake up?
Sleep a little longer, fold your hands,
Poverty comes a-traveling.

I went by the field of Lazybones,
And I saw it was all grown over.
Thorns and thistles, thistles and thorns,
And the stone wall broken down.

Sleep a little longer, fold your hands,
Poverty comes a-traveling.

Proverbs 6:6–11; 24:30–34

STORIES FROM THE NEW TESTAMENT

A CHILD IS BORN

Light of the World

BEFORE THE BEGINNING the Son of God was with the Father,
And every living thing was made by him.
He was the life that was to be the light of men.
That light is still shining in the dark. No darkness ever put it out.

The world was made by him, and he was in the world,
But the world did not know who he was.
He came to his own people, who would not listen to him.
But to all who believed in him he gave the right to become children of God,
Born not in human families, but born in the family of God.

So he became a man and lived awhile with us,
And we saw him in his glory as the only Son of the Father.
No one has ever seen God at any time,
But the Son who lives so near the Father has shown us who he is.

The people who lived in the dark have seen a great light,
For unto us a child is born, unto us a son is given.
In peace he will govern his people, and his name will be
Wonderful Counselor, the Mighty God, the Everlasting Father, the Prince of Peace.

John 1:1–5,9–14,18; Matthew 4:16;
Isaiah 9:2,6–7

A Boy Named John

This is the story of the coming of Jesus Christ, the Son of God who came to earth to live among men.

Zacharias the priest stood by himself before the golden altar in the Temple. (Just once in his life each priest was chosen for this special duty.) He touched fire to the incense on the altar, and a cloud of sweet smoke filled the air. Outside, the people were praying.

Suddenly he knew that someone else was there. As he looked up he saw an angel standing just to the right of the altar.

"Don't be afraid, Zacharias," the angel was saying. "God has heard your prayer, and you and your wife, Elizabeth, are going to have a son. Name him John. You and many, many other people are going to be happy because of him. He will lead people to God, for the Lord is coming. But John is coming first to help them get ready."

"But how do I know that all this is so?" Zacharias wondered. "We are old, Elizabeth and I. Old people do not have children."

"I am Gabriel. I have come to you straight from God whom I serve, to tell you the good news. This is how you can be sure. You are not going to be able to talk until all that I have promised comes true."

Outside, the people were wondering why Zacharias was so late. But when they saw him they knew something had happened. With his hands he showed them that he could not speak.

Six months later, up in her home in Nazareth in the north country, Elizabeth's cousin Mary also had a strange visitor.

"O honored one, the Lord is with you," Gabriel greeted her. She hardly knew what to say. Her angel visitor spoke again.

"Do not be afraid, Mary, for God has chosen you. You are going to have a son, and you are to name him Jesus. He will be called the Son of the Highest. The Lord God will make him a king, and his kingdom will last forever."

"But how?" Mary asked wonderingly. "I am not yet married."

"In the power of God your son will be born, for he is the Son of God.

"And even now your cousin Elizabeth, who thought she was too old to have a child, knows that she, too, is going to have a son. For nothing is impossible with God."

"Let it happen just as you have told me," Mary said thoughtfully. "All I want is to obey the Lord."

Soon afterwards Mary traveled south to the hill country to visit her cousin. No sooner had she called out a greeting than Elizabeth knew her secret.

"Blessed and happy are you of all women. Blessed is the child you are going to have. But how does it happen that the mother of my Lord should come to me?"

Then Mary sang her song of joy:

I praise the Lord
With all my soul I praise the Lord,
And all my heart is glad for God my Saviour,
For he has given honor
To one who serves him humbly.
In all time to come they will call me blessed,
For he who is great has done wonderful things for me,
And his name is holy.
He shows his mercy to those who love him,
To parents and to their children
And to their children's children.
He has brought down the proud and mighty;
He has given the hungry good things to eat.
He has remembered to help our people
As he promised our grandfathers,
Abraham and all his children forever.

For three months Mary visited in Elizabeth's house. Then she went back home to Nazareth.

When Elizabeth's baby was born, the cousins and the neighbors came to admire him, and they were as happy as the parents over the new baby.

"You'll name him Zacharias for his father, of course," they said.

"No. His name is John," Elizabeth told them.

"But no one in your family is named John," they objected, and they looked at Zacharias to see what he would say.

Zacharias made signs that he needed something to write on, and he wrote for them, "His name is John."

The cousins and the neighbors were amazed.

As soon as the words were written, the happy father discovered that he could speak again, and he sang his song of joy and loving praise to God:

> Blessed be the Lord our God
> Who has come to save his people,
> Just as he promised our grandfathers,
> So that when we are safe from our enemies
> We may serve him without being afraid.
> And you, child, will be called
> The Herald of the Highest,
> For you will go ahead before the Lord,
> To make everything ready for him,
> To teach people how he saves them,
> How he forgives their sins
> When his sunrise lights our darkness,
> Takes us out of the shadows of death,
> And guides our feet along the path of peace.

People in all the towns around began to talk about the new baby. "What kind of man will he be?" they were wondering, for God did seem to be caring for him in a special way. Small John grew up sturdy and brave. He ate the simplest foods. As long as he lived he was to drink no alcoholic drinks.

All the time he was growing up he was getting ready for his work.

Matthew 1:1; Luke 1

The Best News Ever Told

Mary and Joseph were engaged to be married. One night Joseph heard an angel speaking to him in a dream.

"Joseph, go on and marry Mary now. She is going to have a son, and you are to name him Jesus, for he will save his people from their sins."

That was the time when the Roman Emperor Augustus ordered a census taken, and everyone had to register in his own family's

© 1960, The Sunday School Board, S.B.C.

Unto Us a Child Is Born

town. So Joseph, who was from David's family, went with Mary to Bethlehem, David's town.

But Bethlehem was so crowded that at first they could find no place to stay, and they had to sleep in a stable. That was where the baby was born, and Mary made a bed for him in a manger.

Out in the fields that night shepherds were watching their sheep. Suddenly God's angel was there beside them, and God's glory was shining all around them. But they were frightened.

The angel began to speak:

> "Fear not. I bring you good news of great joy
> Which is for all people everywhere.
> For today in David's town is born
> A Saviour who is Christ the Lord.
> This is the sign by which you will know him.
> You will find the child wrapped in swaddling clothes
> Lying in a manger."

Suddenly a choir of angels was there and they were praising God:

> Glory to God in the highest,
> On earth peace,
> Good will among men.

After the angels were gone the shepherds began to talk to one another. "Let us go to Bethlehem and see what has happened."

So they hurried to the town, and there in a stable they found Mary and Joseph, and the baby lying in a manger. They told everyone they met what the angels had said, and they went back to the fields thanking God for what they had heard and seen.

When the baby was eight days old, Mary and Joseph gave him his name, Jesus. And when he was forty days old they took him to Jerusalem. For the first boy baby in every Jewish family was carried to the Temple, with a sacrifice gift to God.

There was an old, old man named Simeon who wanted more than anything to see the Saviour God had promised to send to his people. And somehow he knew that God would let him live long enough to see the Saviour with his own eyes.

One day Simeon felt that God wanted him to go to the Temple. So when Mary and Joseph and the baby came in, he was waiting. He saw Jesus, and he reached out his arms to hold him, for he knew this was the Saviour. As he held the baby in his arms he thanked God for answering his prayers.

> Lord, now your servant is ready to go,
> For I have seen your Gift,
> Just as you promised to send him,
> The Gift you have been making ready
> For all the world,
> The Light to guide the people of Israel,
> And the people of all the world.

While Mary and Joseph were wondering about the stranger who recognized their baby, an old, old woman whose name was Anna came out from the quiet place in the Temple where she lived and prayed and worshiped. When she saw the baby she, too, knew who he was, and she thanked God because at last his Son had come to live on earth.

Matthew 1:18–25; Luke 2:1–38

WHEN THE KING CAME

Worshiping Wise Men

WHEN JESUS WAS BORN in Bethlehem some Wise Men traveled westward from the countries of the East to find the King. They went as far as Jerusalem, and there they questioned the people.

"Where is the new king of the Jews? We have seen his star in the East, and we have come here to worship him."

As soon as King Herod heard about another king he was worried. So he sent for the chief priests and teachers of the Jews.

"Where is this king to be born?" he asked.

"In Bethlehem, in Judea," they read from an old book.

" 'Bethlehem, though you are small among the towns of Judah,
   From you will come the king of Israel
   Promised to us since long ago.' "

Secretly Herod sent for the Wise Men. First he asked them when they saw the star. Then he told them the way to Bethlehem.

"Just as soon as you find the king, tell me where he is so I can worship him, too," he told them. But his plan was to have the baby killed.

The Wise Men rode away. Now in the sky overhead they saw the same star, and it went ahead of them until it shone down on the house in Bethlehem where the baby was.

So they went inside. As soon as they saw the baby, with Mary his mother, they knelt down before him. And they worshiped him as they gave him the gifts they brought—the gold, and the incense, and the spicy myrrh.

© 1957, The Sunday School Board, S.B.C.

Jesus Was Growing Up

But they never went back to Jerusalem. God warned them in a dream that they must go home by another road.

After the Wise Men had gone, Joseph had a dream, too. An angel was saying, "Take the child and his mother away to Egypt, for King Herod will try to kill him."

So in the night the three set out on the highway that led south to Egypt. The king's soldiers marched to Bethlehem with the orders, "All small boys not yet two years old are to be killed."

But the baby Jesus was safe in Egypt, and there he lived till Herod died. Then once more Joseph heard an angel's message: It was safe now to travel back to the home in Nazareth.

Matthew 2; Malachi 3:1

His Father's House

Now the boy Jesus was growing up in Nazareth. He grew tall, and he grew wise, learning the ways and the will of his Father in heaven. He learned the words every Jewish boy was taught when the family sat together at home, when they got up in the morning, when they went to bed at night, and when they walked along the road together:

> Hear, O Israel: the Lord our God is one Lord:
> And thou shalt love the Lord thy God
> With all thine heart, and with all thy soul,
> And with all thy might.
> And these words, which I command thee this day,
> Shall be in thine heart.

He was learning the stories of the heroes of his people, Abraham and Isaac and Jacob and Noah and Elijah and the rest. He was learning all that the great prophet teachers had said about God's Son who would some day come to live on earth.

Every year at Passover time in the spring, families and friends used to travel together to Jerusalem to celebrate the holiday. In the beautiful shining Temple high on David's mountain the men would meet with the teachers and the wise men for thanksgiving and prayers. The Passover supper was a family feast. Wherever the travelers were spending the night, they ate their supper of roast lamb, greens, and bread made without yeast, just the way the Jewish people kept the first Passover when they were slaves in Egypt.

When a Jewish boy was twelve years old he came of age. He became a "son of the law," and he was old enough to go with the men when they went inside the Temple. Outside, in the Women's Court, the wives and sisters and mothers and daughters had their service. And from all the altars, smoke would rise from the burning sacrifice gifts.

The year Jesus was twelve he and Mary and Joseph went to Jerusalem at Passover time. It was a happy adventure for all the travelers, and they would sing as they marched along the road:

> I was glad when they said to me,
> "Let us go to the house of the Lord."
> My feet will stand within the gates;
> With all my heart will I praise the Lord.

In Jerusalem for the first time Jesus went into his Father's house to pray and worship with the men. After the celebration was over, crowds of people headed home again. In the Temple the wisest men in the land, who studied and taught all that was known about God, went on with their meetings. A stranger stayed with them, a boy who listened and sometimes asked questions. Whenever he talked, the older men stopped to listen. This boy really understood all that they were talking about.

About ten miles along the road to Nazareth travelers were

stopping to make camp for the night. Mary looked around for Jesus, but he was not with their group. She hunted for him in the camps where kinfolk and friends were resting. He was not there.

So Mary and Joseph went back, all the long way to Jerusalem. And in the Temple they found him talking, asking questions among the great teachers.

"Son, how could you do this to us? Didn't you know that we would worry about you?" Mary asked.

"Didn't you know that I would be in my Father's house?" the boy answered.

And they just wondered what he meant.

The boy left the Temple, and he went back with them to the home in Nazareth, where he obeyed them in every way.

And so he grew up, becoming taller and wiser, and all who knew him loved him. So, too, did God his Father.

Luke 2:39–52; Deuteronomy 6:4–8
Psalm 122:1–2; 145:21

A Preacher with a New Message

The boy who was called John because an angel had told his father that was to be his name, was not like other boys. He liked to be by himself. He liked plain, simple ways of living. When he grew up, he went to the lonely desert country by the Jordan River. There he did a lot of thinking about all the promises God had made to send his Son into the world. He knew that God was telling him that his work was to get the people ready.

So he began to preach, and the people crowded round to listen. They saw a man who wore rough, plain clothes woven from camel's hair, who ate desert food—honey made by wild bees, and locusts roasted and salted. They heard him say,

"Get ready! The kingdom of God will be here, and you aren't fit to be in it. Give up your wicked ways. Be sorry for your sins. Come back and do what is right."

© 1962, The Sunday School Board, S.B.C.

Baptism of Jesus

They watched him baptizing in the Jordan River everyone who truly wanted to do better.

"What must we do?" people wanted to know.

"Prove by the way you live that you mean what you say. If you have two coats, give one away to someone who needs it. Share your food with someone who is hungry.

"You tax collectors, stop taking more tax money than people need to pay. You soldiers, stop making people afraid of you. Stop arresting people who have done no wrong. Be satisfied with the wages you are paid."

No one had preached that way for years and years. Who could this man be? He attracted so much attention that the Jews in Jerusalem sent a committee of priests to find out about him.

"Are you a prophet?" they asked.

"No."

"Could you be the Christ God promised to send?"

"No."

"Then tell us who you are. Back in Jerusalem we are going to have to tell the men who sent us."

"I am a voice calling out in the desert country, as God has said,

> " 'Now I send my messenger ahead
> To make the highway ready,
> For the Lord is coming.
> Straighten out the curves, fill up the low places,
> Level off the steep slopes,
> So that all people everywhere can see him
> When he comes.' "

"Why are you baptizing if you are not the Christ?" they asked.

"I am baptizing in water. But the One who is coming will baptize the hearts of men with the Spirit of God. He is so much greater than I am that I am not important enough to stoop down and untie his shoe."

And John went on preaching about the King who was coming.

Matthew 3:1–12; Mark 1:1–8; Luke 3:2–20; John 1:19–28

Obedient in Baptism

In the north country, in Nazareth where he had grown up, the young man Jesus knew about the wonderful new preacher. He set out to travel the highway to the south, and he came at last to the place by the Jordan River where crowds of people were listening to John.

"Make a road ready for the Lord," John was saying to the people gathered to hear him preach.

"Someone is coming, someone much greater than I."

But when Jesus asked to be baptized, John was surprised.

"You should be baptizing me. Why do you ask that I baptize you?"

"Let it be this way. I must do everything that the Father has planned," Jesus told him. So the two stepped down into the river.

As they were coming up from the water Jesus knew that his Father was very near. The Spirit of God came toward him in the form of a dove, and he could hear a voice from heaven that said,

"This is my Son whom I love, and in him I am well pleased."

From that moment God's Spirit was with Jesus in a special way.

Matthew 3:13–17; Mark 1:9–11; Luke 3:21–22; John 1:29–34

The Fight with Satan

After Jesus was baptized he went off by himself into the lonely wilderness country. Away from other people for a while, he was getting ready to begin his work—thinking, planning, and talking with his Father.

The days went by. He saw no one. He had nothing to eat. That was when Satan found him.

"If you really are God's Son, you can just change some of these round stones into loaves of bread," he suggested.

Jesus must have realized suddenly that he was very hungry. But his answer was in the words he had heard as a small boy, words from Moses' teachings:

"Man does not live on bread alone. He lives by the words God speaks to him."

Satan kept on. They were looking out over the city of Jerusalem from a high place up on a tower of the Temple.

"If you really are God's Son, show the people who you are. Jump down into the Temple court. Nothing will hurt you. Doesn't God's Word say,

" 'He will order his angels to guard you.
    In their hands they will hold you up
    So you will not bruise your foot against a stone' ?"

"Do not tempt the Lord your God," Jesus ordered.

Up on a high mountain they looked out over the world. Satan showed him all the kingdoms of the world, and the glory of them.

"Everything you see can be yours. I will give it to you myself. All you need to do is to worship me," lied Satan.

"Get away from me, Satan!" was Jesus' sharp command. "The Lord God only is to be worshiped. He only is to be served."

So Satan went away for a while. Then angels came to bring Jesus whatever he needed. *Matthew 4:1–11; Mark 1:12–13; Luke 4:1–13*

Choosing His First Friends

In the crowd of people who traveled a long way to hear John the Baptist preach there were two men, Andrew and another John. They were there one day when John pointed out, "Look, there goes the Lamb of God," and they walked over to meet Jesus.

"What are you looking for?" he asked them.

"Teacher, where do you live?"

"Come and see," he invited them.

So they went with him to the place where he was staying, and they spent the day with him. They asked questions. They listened. They made the same discovery John had made.

Andrew hurried off to find his brother Simon.

"We have found Christ. Come, and I'll show you where he is."

So they both went to meet Jesus, and Jesus recognized Simon.

"Jona's son, some day men are going to call you Peter, the Rock," he told the man.

Next day Jesus planned to travel to Galilee. His new friends lived in the same country, and they decided to go together. As they walked along they met Philip, whose home was also in the north, at Bethsaida.

"Come on with me," Jesus invited him.

Philip obeyed without asking why. Soon he was discovering what the others had found out. So he hurried off to tell the good news to his friend Nathanael.

"We have found him. Here is the one our prophets promised—Jesus of Nazareth."

"Now how can anyone famous come from that little town?" Nathanael wanted to know.

"You just come and see."

The minute Jesus saw Nathanael coming he welcomed him.

"Here is one Israelite who does not cheat," he said.

"How did you know about me?" Nathanael wanted to know.

"Before Philip went to find you I saw you standing over there under that fig tree."

"Teacher, you can see what goes on in a person's heart. You really are the Son of God," Nathanael said.

"Do you believe in me because I said I saw you under a tree?

You are going to discover more important things than this," Jesus told him. Then he said a surprising thing:

"You will see for yourself how close the kingdom of heaven is to earth."
John 1:35–51

Guest at a Wedding

Jesus and his mother and his new friends were guests at a wedding in the town of Cana. During the celebration the wine ran out. Jesus' mother discovered the trouble, and she whispered to her son, for it was an embarrassing thing when the host ran out of refreshments.

"It is not yet time for me to show my power," Jesus told his mother gently.

But his mother told the servants,

"Just do whatever he tells you."

Six big water jars were standing on the floor.

"Fill them with water," Jesus told the servants. So they did.

"Now dip out the drink, and take it to the master of the feast."

So they did. And when the man tasted the wine he was astonished. Quickly he sent word for the bridegroom to come.

"Most men serve the best wine first, but you have kept the best till now," he said.

And that was the first sign of his power that Jesus showed in Galilee.
John 2:1–11

Visitor by Night

It was in the spring, the time of the Passover feast, and Jesus was in Jerusalem for the celebration. He had been teaching and preaching, and people were beginning to believe that he really was the Son of God. But some of the strict Jewish teachers hated him. Why, he talked as if he knew more about God than they did, and he was making friends with poor people as if they really mattered.

Many of the people who listened to him did not know quite what to think. One of these was a rich leader named Nicodemus, who was a member of the Jewish Council. One night he came to visit Jesus, and they had a long talk together.

"Teacher, we know that God must have sent you. No one could do the things you are doing if God were not helping him," Nicodemus began.

Jesus did not talk about himself at first. Instead he talked about the kingdom of God and about God's love.

"A man must be born again if he is to live in God's kingdom," he told Nicodemus.

"Now, Teacher, how can that be? Can a man be a baby again after he is grown?"

"A child is born with a body like his parents'. But it is God who gives life to his soul, for God is a Spirit, and it is in your heart that you belong in his kingdom. This is not so strange. You know when the wind is blowing, for you can hear it. But you don't understand how it comes or where it goes. In the same way you know a soul is born, but not how."

Nicodemus could understand about God's being a Spirit. He had learned that from the Jewish prophets. Now he was hearing about God's love.

God loved the world so much that he gave his only Son so that whoever believes in him will never die but will live forever.

For God did not send his Son into the world to judge or punish. He came to show people how to live, to be a light for them in the dark so that he might save everybody in the whole world.

John 2:23; 3:1–21

At Jacob's Well

A Gift of Water

Jesus and his friends were on the way from Jerusalem to the north country. Jesus had chosen to go through Samaria, though Jews never went that way if they could help it.

About noon one day they came to Jacob's well. Jesus was tired, and he sat down by the well to rest while his friends went on to town to buy some food.

A Samaritan woman came out from town to fill her water jar at the well.

"Will you give me a drink?" Jesus asked.

"But you are a Jew. You mean that you would take a drink of water from me? I'm a Samaritan," the woman exclaimed in astonishment.

"If you knew who is speaking to you and what God can give you, you would be asking me for a drink, and I would be giving you living water," Jesus told her.

"But, sir, where did you get any water? This well is deep. You don't even have anything to dip up the water. Do you think you can do more than our great-great-great-great-grandfather Jacob who dug the well for us?"

Jesus went on talking.

"When you drink this water you will be thirsty again. But whoever drinks the water I give will never be thirsty."

"Sir, you sound like a prophet," the woman said politely. "Tell me, you Jews say people ought to go to Jerusalem to worship God. But we Samaritans pray to him right here on our own mountain."

"Are we right—or are you?" was the question in her mind.

"God is a Spirit. Those who worship him must speak to him from their hearts."

"Yes, sir, I know. And I know that when the Messiah comes he is going to tell us all about it."

"I am he," Jesus told her.

His friends were coming back, and so the woman left her water jar and hurried back to town.

"Come quickly! Hurry! Come and see a man who knows everything. Could he be the Christ?" she told everyone she met.

So the people hurried out to the well, and Jesus saw them coming.

"Teacher, you are tired. Stop and eat," his friends urged.

"I am doing what my Father wishes. That is better than eating. Look! You would have said harvest time is four months from now. Look at them coming. I tell you, it is harvest time already."

The Samaritans came running to meet him. They listened while he talked, and many believed that he really was God's Son.

"Stay with us," they begged. So he stopped in their town.

"Now we do believe," they told the woman who went to the well. "Not just because you told us, but because we have seen for ourselves. We know he is the Saviour of the world."

John 4

A Believing Father

Jesus and his friends traveled on to the north, and when they came to Galilee, Jesus began to preach and teach in the synagogues. This is what he was saying:

"The kingdom of God is here. Turn away from your sins, and believe the good news."

Everywhere he went people crowded around to listen, and many of them loved him.

When he came back to Cana, the town where he went to a wedding, one of the king's officers came to meet him.

"My son is sick at our home in Capernaum. I beg you to come home with me and make him well."

"Do you really believe it is possible?" Jesus asked him.

"Oh, sir, come quickly."

"Go on your way. Your son is living."

And the man went back home, for he believed that Jesus knew that his son was safe.

The next day he was almost home when his servants came to meet him.

"Your son is going to be all right," they told him.

"When did he begin to get better?" the father wanted to know.

They told him the time when the fever went down. And the father remembered. That was the very time when Jesus said,

"Your son is living."

Matthew 4:17; Mark 1:14–15; Luke 4:14–15; John 4:46–54

FRIENDS AND ENEMIES

No Welcome in Nazareth

JESUS WENT BACK to Nazareth where he grew up, and on the sabbath day he went to the synagogue, just as he always did. Because he was a visiting teacher he was invited to read from God's Word.

Opening the scroll he read aloud from the writings of Isaiah:

> God's Spirit is within me
> For he has chosen me to preach good news to the poor.
> He has sent me to tell the prisoners they will go free,
> To tell the blind they will see again,
> To free those who are treated unfairly,
> To preach that this is the Lord's year.

He rolled up the book and handed it back to the ruler of the synagogue.

"Today you have seen this all come true," he told the people. And as he went on talking they were much surprised.

"He is a good speaker," they whispered. "But after all, isn't he just Joseph's son?"

"So the old saying is true—a prophet is honored everywhere but in his own home," Jesus said.

He went on to say that God is interested in *all* people. "There were many Jewish widows in the land in the days of Elijah," he stated, "but God sent Elijah to help a Gentile widow. There were many lepers in Israel in the time of Elisha, but through Elisha God showed special mercy to Naaman, a Syrian leper."

Those words made people angry. They forced him to the steepest hill in town. Then they threatened to push him from the edge. Jesus slipped away from them and went safely to Capernaum.

Later he came back home again, and he went to the synagogue just as he did before, and began to teach.

"Where did this man get all his power? How does he know so much? Isn't he just our carpenter's son? Isn't Mary his mother? And aren't his brothers—James and Joseph and Judas and Simon—and all his sisters living here just like the rest of us?"

The people were too busy talking to listen very much. And so Jesus could not help them. He was surprised that so few of them believed him, and all he could do was help a few sick folks.

Matthew 13:54–58; Mark 6:1–6; Luke 4:16–30

Enlisting Special Helpers

One day Jesus was down on the beach talking to a crowd of people. Two little empty fishing boats were drawn up in the shallow water. They belonged to the two brothers, Simon and Andrew, who were nearby washing their fishnets. James and John were not far away.

People came pushing closer and closer all the time, and more people kept coming. So Jesus stepped into one of the boats. Then he called Simon over and asked him to row the boat out a little way from land.

Then he sat down in the boat and went on talking. When he had finished, he told Simon, "Row out there where the water is deep and let down your net."

"But, Teacher, we have been fishing all night, and we never caught one fish," Simon objected. Just the same, he went on and dropped his net. Then came the big surprise. The net was so full that he could not pull it in. He had to call his partners in the other boat to help. There were so many fish that both boats came near sinking.

"Teacher, I shouldn't be here with you. I'm just an ordinary man." Simon was afraid, and he knelt before Jesus in the boat.

"Simon, you have nothing to be afraid of. Come on with me. From now on you are going fishing for men instead."

The four fishermen, Simon and Andrew and James and John, landed their boats. From that time on they gave up their fishing business and went to work with Jesus.

At his office, Matthew the tax collector was busy taking in tax money from the people. As soon as people finished their business with him they hurried away, for the Jews did not speak to tax collectors. Traitors and thieves, they called them.

But Jesus stopped as he passed by Matthew's office.

"Matthew, come along with me," he said.

So Matthew, the man whom nobody but Jesus liked, gave up his job and went to work for Jesus.

The first thing Matthew did was to invite his new friends and his neighbors to come to a feast. Some of the guests were tax collectors, too. Some of them were men who were not very strict about keeping all the rules taught by the priests. None were proper people like the Pharisees and the Jewish teachers who would never have been seen eating in a tax collector's house.

But the Pharisees were watching to see what was going on, and they talked it over. Then they went to the disciples.

"Why does your teacher eat with such people?" they wanted to know.

Jesus heard about it, and this is what he told the faultfinders:

"People who are well do not need a doctor, but sick people do. I did not come to help people who are sure they are good already. I came to be a friend of sinners and bring them to me."

Matthew 4:18–22; 9:9–13; Mark 1:16–20; 2:13–17; Luke 5:1–11,27–32

The Busiest Sabbath Day

In the long ago time when the prophets used to say, "Some day God will send his Son," it was Isaiah who wrote:

> In the land by the sea, beyond the Jordan,
> Galilee of the Gentiles,
> People in the darkness see a great light.

So now Jesus, God's Son, was living in Capernaum, in the land of Galilee.

On the sabbath day he went to the synagogue, and he began to teach the people about God, about his love, and about the way God wanted them to live.

It all sounded so different from the way the priests and teachers talked. Those men were always telling what someone else said. But Jesus' tone and manners showed that he knew what he was talking about.

While they were there in the synagogue, a man suddenly shouted

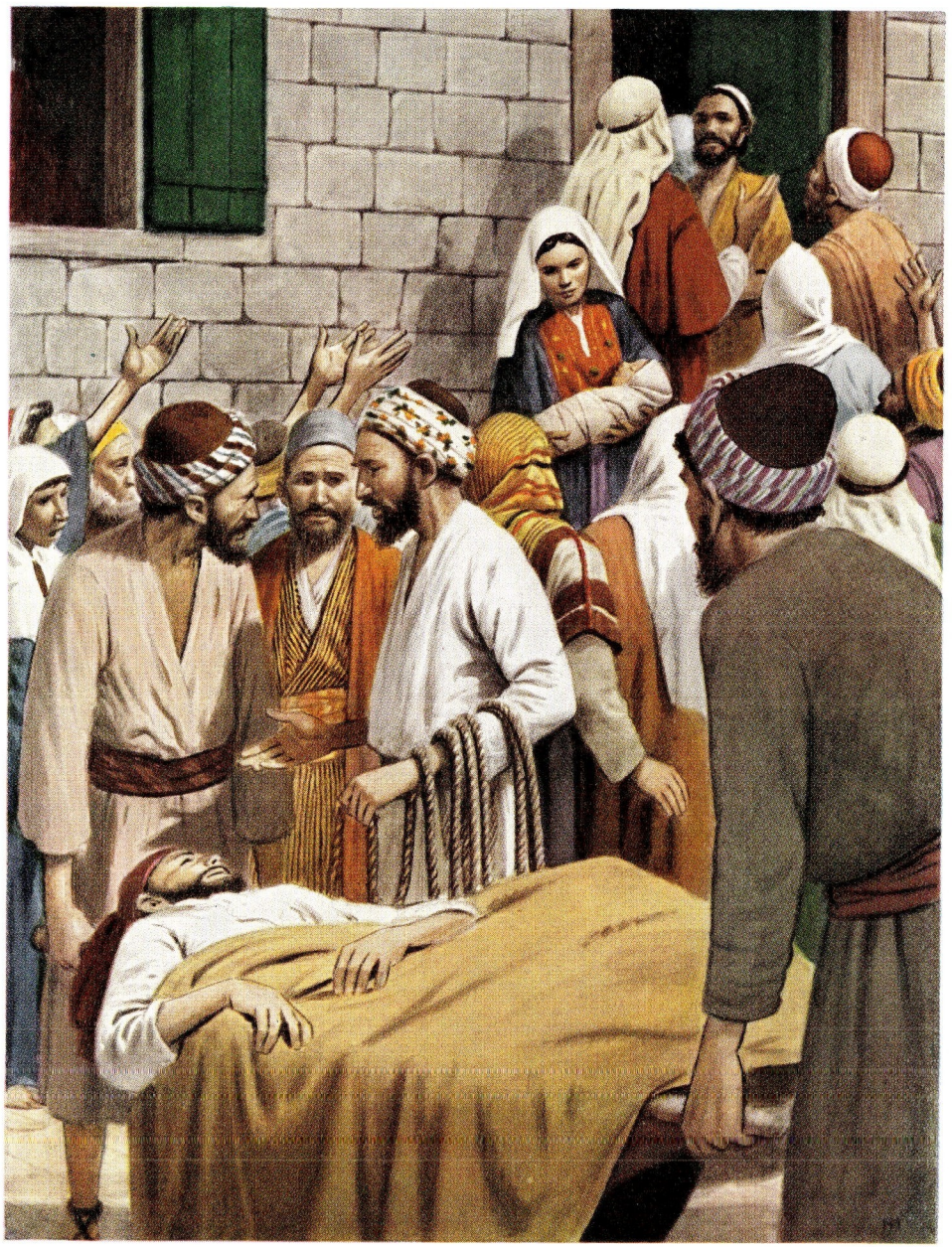

© 1962, The Sunday School Board, S.B.C.

Bringing the Paralyzed Man to Jesus

out, "What are you doing here? I know who you are. You are God's Holy One. Have you come here to destroy us?"

Jesus turned and looked at the man. He understood what was wrong.

"Come out of him, evil spirit from Satan," he ordered.

And from that very minute the man was cured.

"What is happening?" the people wanted to know. "He even has power over the spirits of Satan himself."

And the story spread quickly from one town to the next.

From the synagogue Jesus and James and John and Andrew went home with Simon. When they reached the house they heard bad news. Simon's wife's mother was very, very sick with a high fever.

So Jesus went to her, took her hand in his, and helped her to sit up. Then she was standing. She took a step. The fever was gone, and she felt well again. Soon she was busy helping to get the guests something to eat.

The whole town was talking about the wonderful teacher who was a doctor, too. That evening people came bringing their sick folks to the door of Simon's house. And as Jesus touched the blind and the crippled and all who were hurt or sick, they became well again.

Matthew 4:13–16; 8:14–17; Mark 1:21–34; Luke 4:14–15,31–34

Along the Crowded Roads

Early next morning while it was still dark Jesus left Simon's house and went out of town to a quiet place to talk with his Father. Simon and his friends soon came to get him.

"People are looking for you everywhere," Simon told him.

"We must go to other towns. I must preach the good news of God's kingdom there, too. That is why I was sent," Jesus said.

So Jesus and his friends traveled on together, and everywhere they went crowds of people came to hear what Jesus was saying and to beg for his help.

As they were walking along the road a poor leper came running up to Jesus, and he knelt in the dust beside him.

"Lord, if only you are willing, you can make me well."

"I will," said Jesus gently, touching his ugly body. No one else would have dared to come near a man with leprosy. But as Jesus touched him the scars of his sickness disappeared. He was completely cured.

"Go and report to the priest. You know the law. But don't say anything to the people you meet," Jesus told him.

But the happy man was so excited that he told his story everywhere he went. Then mobs of people came streaming down the road, some to see what was going on, others to ask for help. Jesus could not get into the town. Instead, he went quietly out into the country, where he could meet his Father alone.

Matthew 4:23–25; 8:2–4; Mark 1:35–45
Luke 4:42–44; 5:12–16

Cured—and Forgiven

Several days later Jesus went back to Capernaum. People still crowded round wherever he went in the streets, even in the house where he was staying.

Outside the house there was a man who had to get through the crowd of people. He was paralyzed and could not walk, but he had four good friends who thought of a way to get him to Jesus.

There was no way to push through the crowd, but those four friends carried him, bed and all, up the outside stairs of the house to the flat roof. It was easy to lift a few of the roof tiles to make a space big enough for a man and his bed. Then they lowered him slowly by the four corners of his bed until he lay on the floor where Jesus was standing.

"Son, don't be afraid. Your sins are all forgiven," Jesus told the sick man.

Those words shocked the Pharisees who were watching.

"No one can forgive sins but God. This man is evil," they whispered. Jesus knew what they were thinking.

"Which do you think is easier—to say to this man, 'Your sins are forgiven,' or 'Rise up and walk'? Just so you can be sure I have the right to forgive sins"—he turned to the man on the floor—"Get up. Fold up your bed, and go on home."

So the man stood up and walked out, in front of everybody. The people stared as they made room for him.

"We never saw anything like this before," they said. And they were thanking God because they had been there to see.

But the Pharisees and the rabbis hated him more than ever.

Matthew 9:1–8; Mark 2:1–12; Luke 5:17–26

"Broken Laws"

It was on the sabbath day. "Remember to keep the sabbath day holy, for the Lord blessed the sabbath day and made it his," says one of the Commandments.

"Do no work on the sabbath day, even to help the sick," said the Jewish teachers who taught the Commandments.

Jesus and his friends were in Jerusalem, down by Bethesda Pool in the shade of the porches. Every day sick and crippled and blind people waited there, just waited and hoped. Sometimes the water in the pool gushed up and splashed, and they all believed that the first sick person to step into the water when it happened would be cured.

Jesus came walking by the pool, and he stopped to talk to a crippled man who had not walked for thirty-eight years. Day after day he just lay there watching, waiting.

"Would you like to be able to walk?" Jesus asked him.

"Oh, sir, I have no one to help me into the water at the right time. Someone else always gets there first."

"Get up. Roll up your bed, and walk," Jesus told him.

From that moment the man was cured. Before all the watching people he stood up, rolled up his bed, and walked off with it.

But picking up a bed was called work. The Jewish teachers who were watching stopped him.

"This is the sabbath day. You can't do that."

"The man who cured me told me to," he answered. But when he looked around to point out Jesus, he had gone.

Later on the man met Jesus again in the Temple, and Jesus said to him, "Your sins are forgiven."

Then he knew who Jesus was, and he hurried to tell the Jews.

"This is the sabbath day. You can't do these things," they warned Jesus.

"My Father has always been working, and I am working," he said quietly. I tell you that whoever listens to me and believes in my Father who sent me will never die, but will live on forever."

Then the Jewish leaders were furious.

"He works on the sabbath day!"

"He says God is his Father!"

"He thinks he is as good as God!"

That was what they were saying, but they were thinking, "Kill him!"

One sabbath day, as Jesus was going into the synagogue, he passed a man whose hand was crippled. The Pharisees were watching to see what he would do about it.

"Come on over," Jesus told the man. Then he turned to the spies he knew were watching for him.

"Does the law let you help someone on the sabbath day? Can you save a man's life, or must you let him die?"

No one answered.

"If one of you found that a sheep from your flock had fallen into a ditch on the sabbath day, wouldn't you lift him out? Isn't a man worth more than a sheep? Well, then, it is right to do good on the sabbath day.

"Stretch out your hand," he told the man, and the shriveled fingers were well and strong again.

But the Pharisees who were watching hated Jesus, and they began to plan what they could do to him.

Matthew 12:9–14; Mark 3:1–6; Luke 6:6–11; John 5:1–18

Clean Hands—Dirty Hearts

"Teacher, your disciples have broken the law. We saw them eating without scrubbing their hands up to the wrists. You know they were filthy, and our law orders us to be clean," the Pharisees and the Jewish teachers were complaining again.

"Your rules are more important to you than being honest in your hearts. You wash where it shows, as you would wash the outside of a cup. But inside, your cups are filthy," Jesus told them. "Your own prophet Isaiah said,

> " 'These people honor me with their words,
> But their hearts are far away.
> They teach for commandments the rules they made,
> And when they try to worship me, they fail.'

"Don't you know that God who made the outside of man made the inside as well? But you are full of wickedness inside. You give to God a tenth of all you have, and so you should. But you forget God's justice and his love. Nothing from outside can make a man dirty. But from inside, from a man's heart, come all his evil thoughts, and so he lies and steals and kills. Then he is really filthy."

There was no more talk about unwashed hands. But from that time on the Pharisees and the teachers were waiting to trap Jesus so they could have him arrested.

Matthew 15:1–2,8–20; Mark 7:1–23; Luke 11:37–43,53–54

KINGDOM ADVENTURES

Twelve Helpers Commissioned

AT FIRST THERE WERE four special friends who traveled with Jesus, then five; then more and more joined the group that walked about from town to town. These followers watched their Teacher and learned how he worked. The time had come, Jesus decided, to choose twelve men, train them, teach them, and send them out some day soon to help in his work of bringing people into the kingdom of heaven.

Jesus was spending the night with his friends on the mountain. All night long he talked with his Father. In the morning he was ready to choose the twelve men he wanted for his first disciples.

There were Simon whom he named Peter, and his brother Andrew, James and John the brothers, Philip and Bartholomew, Matthew and Thomas, another James and Thaddeus, Simon the patriot, and Judas who was the traitor.

Matthew 10:2–4; Mark 3:13–19; Luke 6:12–16

Happy Kingdom People

Not far away from the mountain slope where Jesus and his disciples had spent the night, crowds of people were waiting for a chance to hear Jesus speak. He had so much to tell his new disciples now, but as he looked at the people and saw how many of them needed help, he wanted them to listen, too. So Jesus sat down and began to talk. We call his words the Sermon on the Mount. He began by talking about the happy people of the kingdom of heaven:

Happy are you who know how much
   you need God's help—
His kingdom is for you.

Happy are you who are sad—
You will be comforted.

Happy are you who are gentle—
All the earth belongs to you.

Happy are you who are hungry
   and thirsty for goodness—
You shall have all you want.

Happy are you who show mercy—
You will receive mercy.

Happy are you who are pure in heart—
You will see God.

Happy are you peacemakers—
You will be called God's children.

Happy are you who have suffered
  for doing what is right—
God's kingdom is for you.

Happy are you when people blame you and lie
  about you because you have been true to me—
Happy are you, for your reward in heaven is great.

In the Sermon on the Mount, Jesus taught how his followers should treat their friends and their enemies. He talked about right ways to pray. He helped his listeners understand something of God's love and care.

When Jesus finished, people looked at one another in surprise. How different was Jesus' teaching from that of the scribes!

Matthew 5:1–12; Luke 6:20–22

"You Must Choose to Belong"

Traveling along the road to Jerusalem, Jesus would stop in the villages to talk with people who came to meet him, and they would ask many questions about the kingdom of heaven.

"Tell us, Lord, will there be many people in the kingdom?" they wanted to know.

Jesus did not answer that question. Instead, he told them how to get there.

"It is not enough to say, 'Lord, let us in.' You must do the things I am telling you. Or you will hear the Lord say,

" 'I never knew you!'

" 'Oh, but Lord, we used to eat together. You used to teach in our streets,' you will say.

"Then you will be told,

" 'Go away, all of you. Just saying "Lord, Lord" is not enough to get you into the kingdom of heaven. Do what my Father asks you to do. Then you can belong.'

"You must hunt to find the gate, for it is narrow, and the little road is hard to find. But it will take you to the kingdom, while the wide highway where so many people travel will never get you there."

"Let me go with you, Lord," said a man in the crowd. "I will follow you anywhere."

But Jesus warned him that it would not be easy.

"Foxes have holes, and the birds of the air have nests. I have no home."

"Let me go with you, Lord," another man volunteered. "Just let me go home first and tell everyone good-by."

And Jesus warned him,

"The kingdom must come first. A farmer who sets out to plow a straight furrow knows he must plow straight ahead without looking back. That is how it is when you are working for the kingdom."

Jesus gave three tests by which people could check themselves to see whether they really wanted to belong to the kingdom and work for him:

Are you loyal to Jesus first of all? Do you love him more than your friends or your family?

Are you ready to go to work on hard jobs, even to be hurt while you are working for him?

Have you stopped to count how much it will cost you to give up everything that does not really matter and do the kingdom work first of all?

Matthew 7:13–14,21–23; 8:19–20; 10:38–39;
Luke 6:46; 9:57–62; 13:22–27; 14:25–27,33

"Belonging Is Expensive"

"Belonging to God's kingdom is worth everything it could cost a person," said Jesus.

"If a man discovers buried treasure, he will sell everything he has to raise enough money to buy the land where it is buried.

"The kingdom is like buried treasure.

"It is as valuable as a perfect pearl which a jewel merchant discovered when he was looking for fine pearls. So he sold everything he had to raise money enough to buy it.

"When you decide that you want to belong to the kingdom, be sure that you understand how much it is going to cost," Jesus warned.

"Suppose you are going to build a tower. Wouldn't you sit down first of all and count up the cost to be sure you have enough money to finish the job? For if you don't, you may run out of money by the time you finish the foundation, and then the neighbors passing by will laugh and say, 'There's a man who began to build but could not finish.'

"Suppose a king goes out to war, with an army of ten thousand men. He discovers that the enemy is advancing with an army of twenty thousand men. Before he begins to fight, won't he sit down and talk it over with his officers? Or else, while the enemy is still a long way off, he will send messengers to ask for a truce.

"You must be willing to count up the cost and give everything you have to belong to the kingdom."

Matthew 13:44–46; Luke 14:25–35

Locked Out

"Good Teacher!" A young ruler came hurrying to meet Jesus.

"Good Teacher!" Now he was kneeling in the road beside him. "How can I get into the kingdom of heaven? What must I do to have life forever?"

"You know the Commandments," Jesus reminded him. "Do not kill. Do not steal. Honor your father and your mother. You know the others."

"Teacher, I have obeyed them all as long as I can remember."

As Jesus watched the young man he loved him.

"There is something more *you* need to do. Go and sell everything you have. Give all your money away to the poor. Your treasure will be in heaven. Then come back and work with me."

The young man stood up slowly, and he walked away, for he was very, very rich.

"How hard it is to get into the kingdom when money is the most important thing!" Jesus told his disciples. "It is really easier for a camel to get through the eye of a needle."

Was he joking? How could anyone be saved? The disciples looked at one another in astonishment. Jesus knew what they were thinking.

"If it were left to men, no one could. But with God all things are possible," he said.

"Teacher, we left all we had to come with you," Peter began.

Jesus explained, "Whoever willingly and gladly gives away the things he owns to work for the kingdom, or leaves his family and friends to come with me, will be rewarded here on earth and in the kingdom of heaven, too." *Matthew 19:16–30; Mark 10:17–31; Luke 18:18–30*

Some Kingdom Rules

In the Sermon on the Mount, Jesus had talked about the way Christians should live.

"You know the old law: 'You must not kill,'" Jesus said.

"I tell you that whoever is angry with his brother deserves to be punished. If you should be on your way to take your gift to the house of God and remember that your brother is angry with you, go back and make friends with him first. That is more important than the gift. Then go on and take your gift to God.

"You know the old law: 'Pay back anyone who hurts you,'" Jesus said.

"I tell you, do not pay back wrong for wrong.

"If someone should steal your jacket, give him your coat, too.

"If someone makes you walk a mile with him, walk along another mile for good measure.

"Give when people ask you. Lend them whatever they need.

"You know the old law: 'Love your neighbor and hate your enemy.'

"I tell you, love your enemies. Help them and pray for them. Anyone can love a friend. But you are to be like your Father in heaven, who forgives even the ungrateful and the wicked. You must forgive, the way God does."

As Jesus and his disciples were traveling south toward Jerusalem, they had to stop for the night in Samaria. But the Samaritans were especially unfriendly to any Jews on the way to Jerusalem.

So when the disciples went on to a village to find a place to stay, no one would let them in. James and John were furious.

"Teacher," they begged, "let us call down fire from heaven and burn up the people of this village."

"I came to save men, not to destroy their lives." Jesus' voice was stern.

So they just went on to the next village.

"Keep from criticizing other people. While you are busy finding fault with others, you will not be able to see the mistakes you are making.

"How would it be if you should go to your brother and say,

" 'Brother, let me take that speck out of your eye,' when all the time you don't even know there is a big splinter sticking out of your own eye?

"Take care of your own faults first. Then you can see better how to help others."

Along the road to Capernaum the disciples were arguing. They thought Jesus would not find it out, but that evening when they were all together he asked them,

"What were you discussing on the way here?"

No one wanted to tell. The trouble was that each one wanted to be the most important man in the kingdom. But there was a lesson all of them must learn.

"Wanting to be first is a sure way to find yourself last of all. You are to work and serve and wait on other people."

Jesus reached out his arms to a child who was standing near and held him on his lap.

"See. You welcome a child like this, and do it for me, and you are welcoming me. And when you welcome me, you welcome my Father who sent me. You yourselves must be humble and trusting, like little children, before you can get into the kingdom.

"Measure every gift by the Golden Rule. Whatever you wish that people would do for you, go on and do it all for them.

"Give generously," he said, "and gifts will come back to you. Good things will be given to you as grain is poured into a full cup, pressed down, shaken together, until the cup is running over.

"Give without boasting," said Jesus. "When you are giving something away, do it quietly, not showing off where people can watch you and praise you. The only reward that kind of giving deserves is just having people think you are generous. Give so quietly that your gift will be a secret between you and your Father. Then you will have a real reward from him."

One day John reported something he had discovered.

"Teacher, we saw a man curing sick people, and he said he was doing it for you. We made him stop, for he does not belong to us."

"Don't stop him. If he is working for me, he would not be willing to hurt us. If someone should give you just a drink of cold water because you belong to me, he will have his reward," Jesus told him.

All day the Temple had been crowded with people who came to

worship and to bring their gifts. All day the line of people passed by the treasure chest, and golden coins clinked together as rich men brought fine gifts to the house of God.

Jesus was sitting near the treasure chest, and he could watch the people as they passed with their gifts. Some walked noisily and made a great show. One woman came quietly. She stopped.

"Watch!" Jesus whispered to his disciples.

She was by herself. From the clothes she wore, they knew that her husband was dead. Quietly she dropped two small coins into the chest, and then she walked away.

"Hers is the greatest gift of all. The others had plenty of money left over when they had given. But she gave away all she had," Jesus told them.

"Trust the Father for the things he knows you need," Jesus taught. "Living in the kingdom of heaven, you do not need to worry about making a fortune to take care of yourself. Save up the kind of treasure you can keep in heaven, where there are no moths to eat it, no rust to spoil it, and no thieves to steal it.

"Don't worry so much about getting plenty of clothes to wear and food to eat.

"Look at the birds. They do not grow their own food. The Heavenly Father feeds them. Aren't you worth more to him than his birds?

"Look at the lilies in the field. They never make their own clothing, but not even King Solomon could dress so beautifully.

"Aren't you worth more to the Father than flowers that live for just a few days?

"So don't be like the people outside the kingdom who worry so much about getting things. Your Father knows exactly what you need, even before you ask him. First of all, go to work for his kingdom, and he will see that you have every good thing you need.

"You fathers know how to give to your own children. If your

son should ask you for some bread, would you give him a stone? If he asked you for some fish, would you hand him a stinging scorpion?

"If you know how to give good gifts to your children, don't you know how much more your Father in heaven wants to give good gifts to you who are his children?

"Just ask the Father," Jesus told his disciples. "Ask, and he will give to you. Hunt for him, and you will find him. Knock at his door, and he will open it. For everyone who asks will find him giving. Everyone who knocks will find him opening the door.

"The Father loves you, so of course he wants to give you the good things you need," said Jesus.

"You know how it is when you ask your friends for something. Suppose it is late at night. A friend comes to your house. He has been traveling a long way and he is hungry. But there is nothing to eat in your house.

"So you go next door, and you call to your neighbor,

" 'Friend, will you lend me three loaves of bread for my guest?'

"Oh, he may grumble at first and say,

" 'Don't bother me now. The house is locked, and everyone is in bed.'

"But because he is your friend and because you keep on asking, he will get up and give you whatever you need."

If we can get things from men who do not want to give, how much more may we expect to receive what we need from God who wants to give. That was the lesson Jesus was teaching.

"Kingdom people are like salt that makes food taste good and keeps it from spoiling," Jesus said.

"They are like light in the darkness.

"Never hide your light. Let it shine out where everyone can see, and people will know your Father better because they see what you are doing for him.

"Kingdom people are like good trees. You can recognize

them by their fruit. You don't look for grapes on a briar bush or figs growing on thistles. You know that good fruit comes from good vines and trees. When you discover a good deed, you know that it comes from the good treasure of a good man's heart."

Matthew 5 to 7; Mark 9:34–37; 12:41–44; Luke 9:49–56; 11:5–13

How to Talk to the Father

"Don't worry about what you are going to say when you speak to the Father," Jesus told his disciples. "You do not need to repeat many words over and over again. Talk to him this way:

"Our Father, who art in heaven,
  Hallowed be thy name. Thy kingdom come.
  Thy will be done on earth as it is in heaven.
  Give us this day our daily bread.
  And forgive us our debts as we have forgiven our debtors.
  And lead us not into temptation, but save us from evil:
  For thine is the kingdom, and the power,
    and the glory forever."

Two men went up to the Temple to pray. One of them was a Pharisee, very strict about keeping all the religious rules and always careful to let people know he kept them. The other was a tax collector who worked for the Roman governor. Most people never even looked at him if they could help it.

The Pharisee stood where everyone could see, and said,

"God, I want to thank you because I'm not like other people—thieves and cheats and lawbreakers—or even like that man over there who takes the taxes. Why, twice a week I go without eating, and I give away a tenth part of all I get. I keep every rule."

The tax collector stood quietly by himself, and he did not even look up toward heaven. He just bowed his head and said,

"Lord God, help me, for I am a sinner."

When Jesus finished telling the story he added, "That man went home forgiven. For everyone who is proud will be made humble. But everyone who is humble will be honored."

Matthew 6:7–13; Luke 11:2–4; 18:9–14

Who Are Kingdom People?

Were the listeners wondering how people here on earth could be living in the kingdom while around them people kept on disobeying God?

Jesus told two stories to help them understand.

He told The Story of the Weed Crop.

A farmer sowed his field with good seed. One night when everyone was asleep, his enemy sowed weed seeds in the same field.

All the seed sprouted together, good grain and weeds, both.

"Shall we plow up the field?" the farmer's workmen asked him.

"Wait. If you plow it up now you will destroy the good grain, too. Wait until harvest time. Then the reapers can gather the weeds in bundles and burn them. But the grain will be safely stored in my barns."

"Tell us why you told that story," the disciples asked. So Jesus explained.

"The farmer is the Son of man. The field is the world, and the good seed he sowed means the people of the kingdom. The enemy is Satan, and his seeds are the evil people of the world. Harvest time is the end of the world, when all the evil will be forever burned out. But the people of the kingdom, shining like the sunlight, will go into the Father's house."

The Story of the Dragnet was Jesus' second story.

Once some fishermen lowered a great dragnet into the sea, and in it they caught every kind of fish, both good and bad.

They drew the net up on the beach. Then they sat down and separated their catch. The bad fish they threw away, and all the good they saved.

So it will be at the end of time, when God's angels will separate forever the people of the kingdom from the evil of the world.

Matthew 5:13–16; 7:16–20; 13:24–30, 36–43,47–50

Where Is the Kingdom?

"Tell us when this kingdom of heaven will be here," the Pharisees said to Jesus.

"There is no date to mark its coming. You cannot locate it and say, 'There it is.' The kingdom of heaven is here, and you will find it in men's hearts.

"You will find it growing from very small beginnings, small as the tiniest seed of all, the mustard seed. But it grows big and strong as the mustard plant shoots up, and makes so tall a tree that the birds build their nests in its branches.

"It grows the way dough rises when the smallest bit of yeast is worked well into it.

"God takes care of it while it is growing. When a man has planted his seed in the ground, he goes on about his business, getting up every morning to go to work, going to bed at night to sleep.

"All the time the seed goes on growing, but he can't say how.

The plant grows—first the stalk, then the ear, then the full ear of grain. At last the grain is ripe. The farmer has his crop. That is how God takes care of the kingdom as it grows."

Matthew 13:31–33; Mark 4:26–33; Luke 13:18–21; 17:20–21

Rude Guests

Jesus had a story for the people who should have been trying to live in the kingdom of heaven: the priests and the teachers and all the others who insisted their way was better.

Once there was a man who invited many, many guests to come to his house for supper. In those days, just as soon as everything was ready, a servant would go to all the invited guests and say,

"My master wants you to know that it is time for the feast, and he wants all of you to come."

The first guest said, most politely,

"Oh, please excuse me. I have just bought some land, and I must go and look at it. I cannot come to supper."

"Oh, please excuse me," said the next guest. "I have just bought ten oxen, and I really must go and look them over."

"Oh, please excuse me," said the next guest. "I just got married, and I cannot come."

And all the others had excuses, too.

So the servant went back and reported to his master.

"Go out to every street and road. Bring in everyone you can find—the poor, and the hurt, and the sick, and the blind," he was told.

So out he went again, and he found the people, and they all came to supper. But the house was not full. There was room for more.

"Go back to the highways. Look behind the hedges. Tell others to come, for I want my house full," said the master.

So they came, and there was a welcome for everyone. But not one of the rude guests who thought they belonged had a bite of the great supper.

Matthew 22:1–10; Luke 14:15–24

The Great Discovery

Jesus taught that God remembers every service done for love of him.

All the people of all the nations of the earth will stand before the Son of man when he comes with all his angels in his glory. Then he will divide them, the way a shepherd divides his flock, the sheep on the right and the goats on the left.

To the people on his right he will say,

"Welcome, all you whom my Father loves. The home is ready for you, just as he planned it before ever the world was made.

"For I was hungry, and you gave me food.
I was thirsty, and you gave me a drink.
I was a stranger, and you let me come in;
Without clothes, and you clothed me.
I was sick, and you came to help me.
I was in prison, and you came to me."
Then the wondering people will begin to ask,
'Lord, when did we see you hungry and feed you,
Or thirsty and give you a drink?
When did we see you a stranger and take you in,
Or without clothes and clothe you?
When did we see you sick and go to help you,
Or in prison and visit you?'

"Whenever you did these things for one of the least important of my friends, you did it for me," he will tell them.

But he will say to the others,

"There is no room for you here. Go away forever, outside the kingdom of heaven.

"For I was hungry, and you never fed me.
 I was thirsty, but you never gave me a drink.
 I was a stranger, but you would not let me in.
 I had no clothes, and you gave me none.
 I was sick and in prison, but you never came to see me.

" 'But, Lord, when did we ever see you hungry or thirsty or a stranger, or without clothes, or sick or in prison? How could we have helped you?' they will want to know.

"Whenever you failed to help even the least important of my friends, you neglected me," they will hear him say. "Go away from me forever."

These are some of Jesus' teachings about the kingdom, the people who belong there, and the people who never find the gate.

Everywhere he taught, the people began to talk.

"No one ever told us these things before."

"He does not talk like one of our teachers."

"The way he talks makes you believe that he is right."

And whenever they could go with him they followed along to see what would happen next.

Matthew 25:31–45; 7:28–29

HE WENT ABOUT DOING GOOD

Good News Spread Fast

IN THE CITY of Capernaum there lived a Roman captain who liked his Jewish neighbors. To show how much he thought of them, he had given the money to build their fine new synagogue. Now he was in trouble, for one of his favorite servants was very sick, too sick to move and in great pain.

Someone reported that Jesus was on the way back to town, and the captain hurried out to meet him and to ask for his help.

"I will come and heal the man," Jesus told the anxious captain.

"Oh, I wouldn't trouble you to come all the way to my house. I am not worthy. But I know all you need to do is speak, and he will be well. That is the way it is with me. I order one man to go, and he goes. I order another to come, and he comes. So I know that when you give the order for him to be healed, you will be obeyed."

Jesus turned to the friends who were with him.

"Truly, I have not found faith like this among all the Jews," he said.

"Go on home. You believed it will happen, and so it will," he told the captain.

At home the captain found that while he was still talking to Jesus, his servant had been healed.

Not long afterward a sad little funeral procession was walking slowly toward the gate of the town called Nain. Jesus and his disciples met the people on the road. There was a group of sorrowing friends who carried the body of a young man to the cemetery.

There was his mother, who was alone now, for her husband was dead, and there was no one left to take care of her.

Jesus stopped because he was so sorry.

"You need not cry any more," he told the mother.

He stepped over and stopped the bearers.

"Young man, get up," he said.

And the young man sat up and began to speak to them. Jesus had given him back to his mother.

The news of what was happening spread far and wide.

"God has really come to visit his people," they were saying everywhere.

Matthew 8:5–13; Luke 7:1–17

Jesus' Crowded Day

Jesus and his friends had just come back from a trip across the lake, and they found people already waiting. Before Jesus left the beach a man came running to him and knelt at his feet. The rest of the people drew back to make room for him, for this was Jairus, the ruler of the synagogue, a most important man.

"My little girl is dying. Come! Just touch her so she will get well," he begged.

They moved slowly through the crowd. No one noticed that a woman was pushing closer and closer to Jesus.

"If I can just get through. If I can just touch his robe, I'll be well again after all these years," she was thinking.

But Jesus noticed her, for he felt that something had happened.

"Who touched me?" he wanted to know.

"Why, everyone's crowding around. What do you mean—who touched you?" Peter wanted to know.

The woman was so frightened that she was shaking.

"I did it." She was kneeling beside Jesus.

"Daughter, trusting me has made you well. You have nothing

to be afraid of. Go on home, and don't worry any more," Jesus told her.

While they were still hurrying on, messengers came from Jairus' house with sad news.

"Your little girl is dead. Don't bother the Teacher any more."

"Don't be afraid. Just keep on believing," Jesus told Jairus quickly.

They pushed on through the crowd, past the friends who were mourning for the little girl, past the musicians who were playing funeral music at the house.

"She is not dead. She is sleeping," Jesus told the people at the door, but they just laughed at him.

So he sent them out of the house, and he took her father and mother and three of his friends into the little girl's room and closed the door.

He walked over to the bed, and he took the little girl's hand in his.

"Little one, it's time to get up," he called gently.

She opened her eyes. She sat up, and then she walked across the room.

"Now she will need something to eat," Jesus told her father and mother.

Another wonderful thing happened that day. Two blind men groped their way toward Jesus and followed him all the way home.

"Help us, too," they begged.

"Do you believe that I can?" Jesus wanted to know.

"Yes," was all they needed to say.

He just touched their eyes.

"Because you believe, it will happen," he told them. And then they knew. They could see.

Matthew 9:18–34; Mark 5:21–43; Luke 8:40–56

He Loved the Children

It was hard to find Jesus in the crowd of people. So many grownups were always talking or listening or pushing to come closer. Hardly anyone noticed the children.

But the disciples saw them. They saw the mothers with babies in their arms, and very small children walking beside them, holding to their skirts for fear of getting lost.

"Don't come any closer. Don't bother the Teacher. Can't you see that he is busy? He has no time for you now," they told the mothers.

Jesus stopped talking to listen to them, and he did not like what he was hearing.

"Let the children come to me. Don't ever keep them away."

People drew back to let the small ones through. He must have reached out his arms for the first child, then another and another.

"Remember this, and never forget it. The kingdom of God belongs to them. And you yourselves must be like children before you can come into it."

So he took them up in his arms, and while he held them close and loved them he gave them all his blessing.

Matthew 19:13–15; Mark 10:13–16; Luke 18:15–17

Jesus with a Mother and Child

Traveling Two by Two

Jesus was busy traveling from one town to the next, wherever people needed him. The twelve disciples and other friends traveled with him and helped him when they could. There were women in the group, too, who gave their money to pay for food and for places to sleep along the way. One of them was Mary from Magdala. Another was Joanna, whose husband was an important man in King Herod's palace, and a third woman was named Susanna.

Wherever they stopped, Jesus would teach and tell the good news about God's love and the kingdom, and he would heal those who were sick.

There was so much to do. So many people needed him, and he was so sorry for them. They needed someone to help them the way a flock of lost, frightened sheep needs a shepherd to bring them together and keep them safe.

"The harvest is so big," he told his disciples, "and the workers are so few. Pray that God will send out more workmen to bring in his crops."

Now the time had come for which he had been planning. He would send out his helpers to share in his work, to teach and heal the sick just as he was teaching and healing.

Then he called the twelve to him: Simon (called Peter) and Andrew his brother, James and John the brothers, Philip and Bartholomew, Thomas and Matthew, James (who was Alpheus' son) and Thaddeus, Simon the patriot, and Judas.

"You are ready now to go out and preach as I have taught you," he told them. "Tell the Jews everywhere that God's kingdom is here for them to live in and enjoy.

"Take care of people who are sick, and make them well.

"You have been learning so much. God has given so much to you. Now go and share with others.

"Do not worry about carrying a lot of money or extra clothes. You will earn your food as you go along.

"If you come to a town where the people will not listen to you, hurry on to the next town.

"Be careful. You may be arrested. But don't worry about what you will say when they bring you before the judge. Your Father will be there to tell you what to do.

"Don't even be afraid of men who have the power to kill you. Two sparrows may be sold in the market for just one small coin, but your Father knows when one of them falls to the ground. You are more valuable to him than flocks of sparrows.

"Remember when you are standing up in front of people, telling them that you are my friends, that some day in front of my Father I will be glad to claim you for my friends.

"Whoever welcomes you will be welcoming me. And whoever welcomes me welcomes my Father who sent me. Whoever gives just a drink of cold water because you have taught them kindness will be rewarded."

So the disciples went out to work, traveling two by two through the country. Jesus kept on teaching and helping all who were sick or who needed him in any way.

Matthew 9:35–38; 10; Mark 6:6–13; Luke 8:1–3; 9:1–6; 12:4–12

Picnic Supper by the Lake

The disciples came home from their first missionary tour, and it seemed as if they could never finish telling Jesus all that had happened along the way. Besides, people were crowding around again, and there was no chance for them to talk quietly together.

"Come away to a quiet place where you can rest awhile," Jesus suggested.

So they all got into a boat to cross the lake. But the people were watching to see which way they went, and they hurried around by the shore. When Jesus and the disciples landed, there were all the people again, jostling and milling around.

Jesus looked at them. He was so sorry for them that he stopped to help. All day he taught and he healed.

Toward evening the disciples began to think about supper.

"Teacher, hadn't we better send these people back to the village where they can buy food?"

"You don't need to send them away. Give them something to eat," Jesus told them.

"Teacher, should we go and buy some bread?"

"See how much you have."

"Here is a boy who has five loaves of bread and two fish," Andrew told him. "But that isn't anything for a crowd like this."

"Make the people sit down," said Jesus. So they sat down on the green grass by the sea in rows and by groups. Then Jesus took the food in his hands, and he looked up toward heaven and gave thanks for it.

He began to break the bread and divide the fish, and he kept on breaking and dividing. As he handed the food to the disciples, they passed it to the hungry people. There was more—and more—and more, until everyone had plenty to eat.

"Be sure to save what is left so that nothing will be wasted," Jesus reminded the disciples.

And when they had picked up all that was left, they had twelve baskets of food left over.

"Now we know that this really is the prophet we have been waiting for," said all the people. They began to plan how they would make Jesus their king. But he slipped away from them to a quiet place in the hills to talk with his Father.

Matthew 14:13–21; Mark 6:30–44; Luke 9:10–17; John 6:1–15

Friend to the Rescue

The evening after the picnic supper by the lake the disciples started back across the lake by themselves. By the time it was dark the wind began to blow. The waves were running high, and no matter how hard the men tried to row, it seemed as if they were helpless on the stormy water.

About that time Jesus went out to meet them, walking across the water. But when they saw him coming they began to scream for fear.

"Don't be afraid. It is I."

Peter burst out, "Lord, if it is really you, let me walk out to meet you."

"Come on," said Jesus.

So Peter stepped out of the boat. But he was terrified when he looked at the wind-tossed whitecaps, and he began to go under the water.

"Help! Lord, save me!"

Jesus just reached out his hand and caught him by the arm.

"You didn't have much faith, did you? Why couldn't you trust me?"

They both climbed into the boat. It was all very still now. The wind had died down, and the water was calm.

"You really *are* the Son of God," the men said wonderingly.

Matthew 14:22–33; Mark 6:45–52; John 6:16–21

A Mother's Trust

In the north country Jesus tried to get away from the crowds. He needed quiet and rest. He found a house where no one was apt to find him.

But there were so many who needed help, and desperate people hunted for him until they discovered where he was.

One of these searchers was a Gentile mother who had a great problem. Her little daughter was sick. She knew the feeling of Jews toward her race, yet she dared to ask Jesus for help.

"Help me, O Lord," she begged, and she knelt beside him. "My daughter is so sick."

"Tell her to go away. She makes too much noise," the disciples whispered.

"I was sent here to be the shepherd of the lost sheep of Israel," Jesus told her.

She just came a little closer and kept on begging for help.

"But it would not be proper to take the children's bread from them and throw it away for dogs to eat," Jesus said.

"Yes, but even the puppies are allowed to eat the crumbs that fall from the table," she answered.

"Your faith is very great. Your prayer will be answered."

When the woman went home, she found that her daughter was well.

Matthew 15:21–28; Mark 7:24–30

"If You Believe"

Jesus had been away in the mountains with Peter and James and John. As they walked back together they saw a crowd of excited people in the valley. The Jewish teachers were trying to find out what was wrong. When the people caught sight of Jesus, a man came running toward him.

"Teacher, help my son. He has been an epileptic since he was a baby. No one has been able to help him. Often when he has a spasm he falls into the fire or into the water and hurts himself.

"I took him to your disciples, but they could not help him. If you can do anything, please help us."

" 'If I can,' " Jesus repeated. "Anything is possible when you believe."

"Oh, I do. I do believe. But help me even if I don't believe very well," the father begged.

Just then the boy had a bad spasm, twisting and beating his body on the ground. When it was over he lay limp and helpless.

With his quiet words and a touch of his hand, Jesus cured the boy. He lifted him to his feet, and he gave him back to his father, completely well again.

Later when they were together indoors and no one else was listening, the disciples asked,

"Why couldn't we cure him? We tried."

"You have not enough faith yet. With just a little real faith—small as a tiny mustard seed—you will find that nothing is impossible for you."

Matthew 17:14–20; Mark 9:14–29; Luke 9:37–43

Her Second Chance

A crowd of people came to the Temple, for Jesus was teaching, and they did not want to miss a word he said.

Suddenly they turned to look toward the entrance. Some of the Pharisees were pulling a woman into the crowd. They dragged her across the floor until she stood right in front of Jesus.

"Teacher, we caught this woman breaking the law. You know the law Moses taught us. She deserves to be stoned to death. What do you say?"

The Temple was very quiet. The men were waiting. Jesus leaned over and wrote on the ground with his finger as though he did not hear them.

The men spoke again.

"Teacher, didn't you hear? What do you say?"

Jesus stood up.

"Whichever one of you has never done wrong—let him throw the first stone," he said. He stooped down and wrote on the ground again.

One man slipped out, then another, and another. Jesus and the woman were left.

He stood up again.

"Where are they? Is there no one left to accuse you?" he asked.

"No, Lord."

"I do not accuse you either. You are free. Go, and sin no more."

John 8:1–11

At Martha and Mary's House

Jesus never had a home of his own after he grew up, but there was a home in Bethany where he liked to visit, and it must have been almost like his own home. It belonged to Mary and Martha and their brother Lazarus, all of them Jesus' good friends.

One day when Jesus came to visit, Martha hurried off to cook a company supper. Mary just sat with their guest and listened to everything he said. Martha was working so hard. Where was Mary? Wouldn't she ever come to do her share? At last Martha was so cross that she ran in and interrupted the two as they talked.

"Lord, don't you even care that my sister has left me to do all the work? Tell her to come and help me," she said crossly.

"Martha, Martha, you are anxious and worried about getting so much to eat. We need only a little. Mary is really the wiser one, for she has been discovering something no one can take from her."

There came a time when Lazarus was sick, so sick that no doctor could cure him. Someone sent word to Jesus, who was far away in another part of the country.

"Our friend is asleep. I am going to him and wake him," Jesus told the disciples.

"But he'll be all right if he is just sleeping."

"Lazarus is dead," he told them plainly. "And I am glad that I was not there when it happened. Now when you see what is going to happen, you will really believe me."

In Bethany the sisters heard that Jesus was on the way. Martha hurried out to meet him. Mary stayed quietly at home.

"If you had been here, it would not have happened," Martha said. "Just the same, whatever you ask of God he will give you."

"Your brother will live again."

"Yes, I know he will live again some day, in the time of the resurrection."

"I am the resurrection and the life. He who believes in me, though he should die, will live. Whoever believes in me will never die. Do you believe this, Martha?"

"Lord, I do believe. You are the Christ, the Son of God."

She ran back to the house to find Mary.

"The Teacher is here, and he is asking for you," she said.

Mary hurried out, and when she met Jesus she was crying.

"Lord, if only you had been here, my brother would not have died."

"Where is he?" Jesus asked, and he was crying, too.

"Look how much he loved Lazarus," said the neighbors. "Wouldn't you think that, if he could make blind people see, he could have kept his friend alive?"

They walked out together to the grave, which was in a cave, with a big stone covering the opening.

"Martha, I told you that if you believed, you would see the glory of God. Have the stone taken away."

He looked toward heaven, and all the people at the grave heard him praying.

"Father, I thank you because you have been listening to me. I know that you always do, but I wanted all these people to believe that you sent me.

"Lazarus!" he called. "Come out."

Then Lazarus, who had been dead, came walking out because he heard Jesus calling to him. *Luke 10:38–42; John 11*

One Said Thank You

The sick, miserable men huddled together, watching from far off. They did not dare go closer. As long as they were sick with leprosy they must stay away from people for fear they would spread the disease.

They could see Jesus and his friends as they came toward the town, and they called at the top of their voices,

"Jesus! Master!"

Was it possible? He heard them! He was looking their way. He came toward them.

"Go to the priests, and let them examine you," he told them.

That was not what they expected. A man went to the priest for a checkup after he was cured. But they went, all ten of them, and they heard the priest tell them they were well, completely well, and free to go back to their homes.

Nine men hurried away. One man—and he was a Samaritan—looked at his arms, his hands. The sores were healed.

"Thank you, God. Thank you, oh, thank you!" he shouted. And he ran every step of the way back to Jesus to kneel before him and to thank him.

"Weren't there ten of you?" asked Jesus. "Where are the other nine? Is a foreigner the only one who came back to say thank you to God?"

"Come, get up," he said gently to the man who was kneeling beside him. "You may go anywhere now. Your faith has made you well."

Luke 17:11–37

Blind Beggarman

Beside the road to Jericho a beggar sat with his hand stretched out for money. But no one in all the hurrying crowd would stop.

"What's happening? Where is everyone going? Who's there?" he shouted at the people passing by.

"It's Jesus from Nazareth," someone turned and called over his shoulder.

"Jesus, Son of David, help me."

The noisy crowd hurried on.

"Jesus, Son of David, help me!" he shouted louder.

"Hush! Don't make so much noise!" someone told him.

But Jesus had heard the cry for help, and he stopped.

"Tell him to come here," he said.

"It's all right. Get up. He is calling for you."

Someone gave him a push in the right direction. Blind Bartimaeus jumped up, threw off his coat that would only get in his way, and ran toward the voice.

"What do you want me to do for you?" he heard Jesus ask.

"Teacher, let me see."

"You shall. Your faith has given you your sight."

Bartimaeus looked straight at Jesus, and he saw him.

Then he joined the crowd that was walking along with Jesus.

"Thanks be to God. Thanks be to God," he was singing in his heart.

Matthew 20:29–34; Mark 10:46–52; Luke 18:35–43

"Zacchaeus, Come Down"

Short Man in a Tree

Up in a tree a short man perched carefully and watched down the road. Zacchaeus was an important man. He was chief tax collector, and he made a great deal of money. But any tall beggar had something Zacchaeus could not buy. A tall man could see what was happening when there was a crowd.

Zacchaeus watched the crowd of people coming nearer and nearer. Now he could see which one was Jesus. He was coming closer. He was under the tree. He was stopping. Now he was looking up.

"Zacchaeus, hurry and come down. I need to stay at your house today," Jesus said, and everyone was listening.

Down came Zacchaeus as fast as he could, so glad and honored to receive his guest.

People began to talk.

"He has gone with that man."

"He is staying in a sinner's house."

Zacchaeus stood as tall as he could, and he said,

"Lord, I am going to give half of everything I have to the poor. And if I have cheated anyone, I'm going to give him back four times as much as I took."

"Today you have found your way to God's kingdom," Jesus told him. "This is the reason why I came—to hunt and to save those who were lost."

Luke 19:1–10

WHO IS HE?

Winds and Waves Obey

ONE EVENING Jesus said to his friends,

"Let's take a boat and cross over to the other side of the lake."

So they set sail, and Jesus went to sleep on a cushion in the stern of the boat.

Suddenly out on the deep water a storm blew up. The wind whipped the waves high, and the boat pitched so badly it began to fill with water.

"Teacher! Teacher! Wake up!" Jesus' friends were all so frightened.

"Teacher, don't you care? We're all going to be drowned!"

Jesus opened his eyes.

"Peace! Be still!" he told the wind.

Then there was a great calm, and the water was smooth again. The whitecaps had disappeared.

"Why were you afraid? Don't you trust me yet?" Jesus asked them.

They just whispered to one another,

"Who is this person whom even the wind and the waves obey?"

Matthew 8:18–27; Mark 4:35–41; Luke 8:22–25

John's Question

It had been a long time since John the Baptist had seen Jesus. He had been busy preaching, baptizing his followers, and warning sinners. There was not a man in all the land of whom he was afraid. So when he heard how King Herod was breaking laws like any common criminal he began to preach against him, too. It was not long before the king's guards came to arrest John, and that was the end of his preaching.

In jail it must have seemed to John a long, long time since he had been so sure that Jesus was the Son of God. What was Jesus doing? What was he saying? What did people think? At last John asked two of his disciples to find Jesus and ask him one question.

"Are you really the Christ we have been watching for? Or must we still wait for someone else?"

This was Jesus' answer:

"You go back and tell John what you have heard and seen. The blind can see. The crippled can walk. The lepers are well. The deaf can hear. Those who were dead are alive. And the poor have the good news preached to them."

While John had been in prison, many of his friends had forgotten about him. But Jesus never forgot.

"When you went out to the country to hear John, what did you expect to find?" he asked the people round him. "Did you look for a weak reed blown this way and that by the wind? Or did you look for a man wearing fine clothes? You find them in kings' palaces. Were you looking for a prophet?

"I tell you he is much more than a prophet. He is the one about whom a prophet said,

" 'I am sending my messenger before you come, and he will make the road ready for you.'

"Of all the men who ever lived there has been none greater than John."

But the people would argue.

"John is no prophet. He is too strict. He would never eat or drink with us."

And there were others who said,

"Jesus is not strict enough. He is no prophet—he goes around eating and drinking with sinners and keeping all kinds of bad company."

"You are just like children playing in the square who cannot be satisfied," Jesus told them. "Their friends call out to them, 'We played gay music for you, but you would not dance. We played sad music, but you would not play funeral with us!'

"How wise you are!" said Jesus, and the people could not say a word.

And John was never free to preach again. King Herod was persuaded that he should be killed, and so he gave orders for John to be beheaded. *Matthew 11:2–19; Luke 3:19–20; 7:18–35; 9:9*

Peter's Answer

All along the roads they traveled together the disciples watched Jesus as he went about his work of healing. They saw him cure a deaf man who could not even speak plainly. They watched him cure a blind man.

"Can you see anything?" Jesus asked.

"I can see men walking around—they look like trees."

"What do you see now?"

"I can see—clearly!"

Jesus and the disciples went away by themselves to Caesarea Philippi near the foot of Mount Hermon. In this beautiful spot Jesus gave his disciples a test.

"What are people saying about me?"

"Some of them say you are John the Baptist come back to life."

"Some say you are Elijah."

"Some believe that you are one of the prophets—Jeremiah or one of the others."

Then Jesus asked the important question.

"Who do you say I am?"

Peter knew the answer.

"You are Christ, Son of the living God."

"Blessed are you, Peter, son of Jona. No one could have told you. My Father taught you who I am. Strong as a rock is your faith. Upon this rock I am going to build my church."

But he warned his disciples that it was not yet time to go around telling everyone that he was the Christ.

On the disciples and Jesus traveled together.

Matthew 16:13–18; Mark 7:32–36; 8:23–30; Luke 9:18–20; John 6:69

Arguments and Complaints

In Jerusalem the people were celebrating the Feast of Tabernacles. There were hundreds of visitors—Jesus with his disciples, and others who could leave their homes to go to the city for the feast.

Everywhere people were talking about Jesus.

"He is a good man," some of them were saying.

"He is not good. He pretends to be the Son of God," others would say.

The Pharisees and the teachers had been watching Jesus cure sick people and listening to him teach. They had begged Jesus to give them some sign to prove that he had the right to teach as he did.

"Can't you read the signs you see?" he had asked them. "When the sky is red in the evening you say, 'Tomorrow will be clear.' When the sky is red in the morning you say, 'It is going to be stormy today.'

"When you see a cloud in the west you say, 'A shower is coming.' When the south wind blows, you say, 'It will be hot.'

"If you can read the weather signs, why do you not read the signs I have been showing you?"

But they would not listen.

When Jesus went to the great Temple at the time of the feast and began to teach, some people were curious about him and wanted to know,

"How is it this man can read? He never went to our schools."

"Is this the man everyone is talking about?" someone asked. "Do they really think that he is the Christ? Why, we know the very town he came from. When Christ comes no one will know where he comes from."

Jesus' teaching was the answer to that.

"You know me. You know where I come from. I did not send

myself here. The true God sent me. But you do not know him. I know him because I came from him and he sent me."

Many people did believe him.

"After all, when Christ comes, how could he do more than this man has done?" they were saying.

But the leaders of the council sent officers to arrest Jesus in the Temple.

"I will be with you a little while," the men heard him say. "Then I am going back to the Father who sent me. You will look for me, but you will not find me. I am going where you cannot come."

"Where is he going? Will he travel to other countries and teach the Greeks instead of the Jews? Where can he go that we cannot follow him?"

"If any man is thirsty, let him come to me and drink the water I give," they heard him say.

"Truly, this man must be the Prophet."

"He is the Christ."

"What? Would Christ come from up there in Galilee? Everyone knows the prophet Micah said he would be coming from Bethlehem."

So the arguments went on and on.

The officers who were sent to arrest him went back and reported that they had failed.

"What have you to say for yourselves?" the council asked.

"No man ever talked the way he does."

"Has he led you astray, too? None of us take him very seriously."

One of the council members was an old friend of Jesus, Nicodemus who came to Jesus one night to learn more about him and the things he taught. He listened to all the discussion, and finally he said, "Wait. Our law says that a man has a right to speak for himself before he is judged."

"Are you one of those Galileans, too?" they answered him angrily. "Just remember that no prophet ever came from Galilee."

Jesus went right on teaching.

"I am the light of the world. Whoever follows me will never walk in the dark."

"That is not true," said the Pharisees.

"If you live by my teachings, you are truly my disciples. You will know for yourselves what is true, and you will be free."

"We are descendants of Abraham. We have always been free," said the Pharisees.

"Everyone who sins is the servant and slave of sin," Jesus told them. "If I make you free you can never be slaves. I am telling you the things I learned from my Father."

"God is our Father," the Pharisees insisted.

"If God were your Father, you would love me, for I am from God."

"You're nothing but a Samaritan, and you are evil!" the Pharisees shouted, and they picked up stones to throw at him. But he hid from them, and then he slipped out of the Temple.

Matthew 12:38; 16:1–4; Luke 12:54–57; John 7:11–52; 8:12–59

"I Do Believe!"

On the sabbath day Jesus walked along the streets in Jerusalem with his friends.

"Teacher, do you see that blind beggar over there? Is his blindness a punishment for something he did? Or is the blind son his parents' punishment for doing wrong?"

"His blindness is not a punishment. But this is a time to show what God can do to help a man, and I must go to work while there is still time," Jesus told them.

He made a paste of saliva and dust, and he smoothed it over the blind man's eyes.

"Now go and wash it off in Siloam Pool," Jesus said to him.

The man groped his way to the pool. He came back, his eyes wide open. He could see!

The neighbors began to talk.

"What happened? Are you the same man who sat there begging?"

"The man named Jesus made a paste and put it on my eyes. He told me to go to Siloam Pool and wash. I did, and now I can see."

The people took him off to the Pharisees. This business concerned them, because it all happened on the sabbath day.

"How did it happen?" they wanted to know.

The man told his story again. "Now I can see," he said.

"This man never came from God or he would not break the sabbath laws."

"But how could an evil man cure blindness?"

The Pharisees argued back and forth.

"Maybe the man never was blind at all," one of them suggested.

So they sent for his father and mother.

"Is this really your son? Was he really blind? How does it happen that he can see?"

"We know that he is our son, and he was born blind. But how he sees, we do not know. He is of age. Ask him."

So they called the man back.

"Come on, now. Give God the glory. We know this man could do no good. He is a sinner."

"I don't know about his being a sinner. One thing I do know. I used to be blind. Now I can see."

"But how did he do it?"

"I told you how. Why, do you want to be his disciples?"

"We are disciples of Moses. We know God spoke to him. But this man—we don't even know where he came from."

"I know. That's the wonderful tning. Since the beginning of time no one has been able to heal the eyes of one born blind. If this man did not come from God, he would not be able to do his work."

That was too much for the Pharisees.

"You! You're nothing but a sinner yourself! Do you think you can teach us?"

For punishment they took away his membership in the synagogue.

When Jesus heard all that had happened he hunted until he found the man.

"Do you believe in the Son of God?" he asked gently.

"Tell me who he is so I can believe."

"You have seen him. He is speaking to you."

"Lord—I do believe." The man knelt to worship at Jesus' feet.

John 9

The Mountaintop Discovery

Once Jesus went up into a high mountain in Galilee, and he took Peter and the brothers, James and John. He began to talk with his Father, and the three grew sleepy. But they were wide awake when they noticed that the look on Jesus' face had changed. It was shining with a glory like the sun. His robe was dazzling white.

Then the disciples saw that two men were with Jesus. They heard them talking with Jesus about his coming death in Jerusalem. They knew as they listened that the men were Moses and Elijah.

"Master—it's wonderful that we're here!" Peter burst out before he thought.

While he was still speaking, a cloud swept round them.

"This is my beloved Son in whom I am well pleased. Hear what he has to say," a voice was saying from the cloud.

The three were so frightened that they fell on the ground and hid their faces. They felt Jesus' hand touching them, heard him say,

"Get up. Don't be afraid." When they looked, they were alone with him. Together they walked down the mountain.

"Tell no one what you saw, not until I live again," Jesus warned.

They wanted to ask what he meant. Instead they asked:

"Why did the scribes say Elijah must come before the Christ?"

" 'Elijah'—the prophet—has come, but men did not know him. They did what they wanted with him. So will they treat the Son of Man."

The three understood that he meant John the Baptist, the prophet who had come to make the world ready for the Son of God. But they said nothing, not till long afterward. Though they did not understand, the disciples knew they had seen Jesus the Christ, the Son of God.

Jesus traveled through the towns and cities bringing the good news of the kingdom of God, healing the sick, teaching the people to love one another the way he loved them.

"Who are you?" the wondering people asked. "If you are the Christ for whom we have been looking, tell us plainly," said the Jews. "I have told you, but you would not listen," Jesus answered. But those who were willing to trust him, and to learn his way began to understand. Some of them made the great discovery, "Jesus is the Son of God."

Matthew 17:1–13; Mark 9:2–13; Luke 8:1; 9:28–36; John 10:24

STORIES JESUS TOLD

MANY WERE THE stories Jesus told while he was teaching. Sometimes he would be sitting on the beach with crowds of people round him, or out in a boat a little way from shore. Or he would be walking with his friends as they traveled through the country. Or he would be high on a hill where people on the sloping land below could watch and listen.

The people of his stories were people his listeners all knew: shepherds and priests, farmers and fishermen, and guests at a wedding. Usually the careful listeners who wanted to understand knew what he meant by a story. Sometimes he would give a special explanation to his disciples when they were alone together.

A Tale of Two Houses

"Whoever listens to my teaching and does what I teach is like a man who built his house on rock," said Jesus. He told this story.

Once there was a wise man who built a house, and he dug deep so that he could build the foundations on rock. When the storms came, the rain poured down and the wind blew. The river burst out over its banks, and flood waters dashed against the house. But the walls were strong, for they were built on strong foundations.

"Whoever listens to me and does not do what I tell him is like a foolish man," said Jesus.

The foolish man did not wait to dig foundations. He built his house on the sandy ground.

When the storms came, the rain poured down and the wind blew. The high flood waters poured over the ground and beat against the house. Down fell the walls, and the house was a ruin.

That was the end of the story. The people said, "What a wonderful teacher! He *knows* what he is talking about."

Matthew 7:24–29; Luke 6:46–49

The Farmer and His Seed

A farmer went out to plant his seed. As he sowed it, some dropped along the pathway where the birds found it, and they ate it all up. Some of the seed fell on hard, stony ground where it sprouted quickly. But as fast as it grew it withered away in the hot sunshine, for the roots could not find soil deep enough.

Some of the seed fell into ground that was already full of weed seeds. As fast as it grew, the weeds grew, too, and choked the small plants.

But the seeds that fell into good soil—not hard or thin or weedy, but plowed and ready—those seeds sprouted and grew. The crop brought a hundred times more grain than the seed that was planted.

A little later when the disciples were alone with Jesus they asked, "Why did you tell that story?"

"Couldn't you guess?" Jesus asked them. "The seed means God's teaching. People who hear but never listen are like the pathway. As quickly as they hear they forget, for Satan snatches away their thoughts of God the way the birds steal the seed the farmer sows.

"Some people listen and intend to remember. But afterward they give up too easily when it is hard to live God's way. They are like the ground where the plants with no roots wilt away in the hot sun.

"Some people listen, but they listen to everything else they hear, and they are too busy with too many things to do any work for God. They are like the soil where the weeds grow as fast as the grain.

"But listeners whose hearts are honest and good will listen and remember and then do as they have been taught. Patiently they keep working until they have finished. And their deeds are like the farmer's good crops."

Matthew 13:3–9,18–23; Mark 4:2–20; Luke 8:5–15

Forgiving Is Forever

Peter was asking a question about forgiving.

"Lord, how many times must I forgive my friend? Would seventy times be enough?"

"Forgive from your heart seventy times seven, and just go on forgiving," said Jesus. And then he told a story.

A king decided to pay all his bills and collect all the money people owed him. He discovered that someone owed him ten million dollars. But the man could not raise enough money to pay his debt.

"Sell the man, with his wife and children, to be slaves," the king ordered. "Sell everything he owns, and bring me the money."

"Oh, my king, be patient with me. Give me time, and I know I can pay all I owe you," the man begged.

The king felt sorry for him, and so he changed the order. He decided to forgive the man's debt.

As the man was going home he met one of his friends who owed him about twenty dollars.

"It's time for you to pay me every cent you owe me," he said.

"Oh, my friend, be patient with me. Give me time, and I know I can pay back all that I owe you," begged the poor fellow.

"Lock this man up in jail till he pays back every cent," the man ordered.

That was more than the rest of the people could stand, and so they reported what had happened to the king.

"Bring the fellow back to me," was his order.

"You wicked man! I forgave you all of that debt you owed me. You ought to have done as much for your friend. Now you will be punished until you pay back the last penny."

To Peter and the others, Jesus added, "You have been forgiven so much by my Father. Now be willing to be friends without counting the times that you forgive.

"For if you forgive others for their sins against you, then my Father will forgive your sins. But if you do not, then neither will he forgive you."

Matthew 18:15–35; 6:14–15

Stories of Lost Treasure

Wherever Jesus went he found some people who were good, but a great many more who were not so good. And when he would stop to talk with them or have supper with them, the respectable people like the Pharisees would grumble, "Why, this man makes friends with people who are not respectable."

So Jesus told The Story of the Lost Sheep.

Suppose you owned a hundred sheep. One of them strays away. You still have ninety-nine that are safe. But one is lost. Wouldn't you leave all ninety-nine that are safe, to hunt the stray? Wouldn't you keep on hunting till you found it?

At last you discover it, lonesome and needing help. You pick it up and lay it carefully across your shoulders. And you are glad—all the way back you are happy, because you found the lost one.

You take all the flock back home, and you tell your friends the good news.

"You will be as glad as I am," you say. "I found my lost sheep."

"That is the way it is in heaven," Jesus said. "There is more celebration when one lost sinner changes his evil ways than there is because of ninety-nine good folks who do not need to be forgiven."

And Jesus told The Story of the Lost Coin.

Once there was a woman who had ten silver coins. But she lost one of them. Then she began to hunt. She lighted her lamp to shine in all the dark corners. She hunted everywhere. She swept the whole house. And then at last she found the coin.

She hurried to tell the neighbors, for she knew they would be as excited as she was. The lost coin was found!

"And that is the way the angels in heaven celebrate when one sinner asks to be forgiven," said Jesus.

And Jesus told The Story of the Lost Boy.

There was a man who had two sons. One brother liked to live at home, working with his father on the farm. But the other brother wanted to travel far away to find adventures in other lands.

And so he asked his father,

"Will you let me have my share of the family property now?"

The father divided all that he had and gave the boy his share. A few days later the son began his travels.

In a strange country, far, far from home, he spent his money and wasted it on good times, fine clothes, and gay parties.

One day he discovered that his money was quite, quite gone. It was during famine times when food was hard to find and expensive to buy. So he had to go to work, and he hired out as a farm worker. His job was to feed the pigs, and he was so hungry he wanted to eat the food he gave those pigs.

He began to remember all the good food at home, where even

the servants had more than they could eat. And so, when he was almost starving, he made up his mind.

"I will go to my father and tell him,

"'Father, I have hurt you, and I have broken God's laws. I don't deserve to be your son any more. Just let me come back and be one of your servants.'"

So he traveled the long, long way home.

His father saw him coming when he was still far down the road, and he hurried out to meet him, and he threw his arms about his thin, dirty, tired son.

"Father, I have done wrong. I don't deserve to be your son—" the boy began. But his father was not listening.

"My son is here! The lost is found," he called to the servants. "Go and get him clean clothes, the best there are. Bring him shoes—a ring for his finger. Get ready for a feast. Go kill that fat calf in the pen and have it roasted. Now we can celebrate, for my son has come home."

Out in the fields the other son heard strange sounds coming from the house. Music! Dancing! What was going on? One of the servants told him the news.

"Your brother has come home, and your father is celebrating because he is safe and sound."

Angrily, the brother turned back to his work.

"I won't go home," he said to himself.

Finally his father had to go out to get him.

"Look, all these years I have worked for you. I never did anything wrong. Did you ever kill one little kid for me to celebrate with my friends? Now this one comes home with all his money wasted, and you kill a calf!"

"Son, you are always here with me. Everything I have is yours. Don't you understand? This is the time to be glad and celebrate. Your brother was lost. Now he is found. He was dead. Now he is alive and with us here at home again."

Luke 15

© 1963, Broadman Press

The Lost Son

The Stupid Rich Man

People crowded around to ask Jesus questions. One man said,

"Teacher, tell my brother he ought to give me my share of the money our father left us when he died."

"The things you own never make you rich," Jesus warned. Then he told a story.

Once there was a farmer who was very, very rich. His crops were so big that there was not room in his barns to store all his grain.

"What shall I do?" he wondered. "I know. I'll tear down my barns and build bigger ones. Then when I have stored away all my grain, I'll have no worries.

"I can stop working so hard. I'll just eat, drink, and have a good time."

But that very night God said to him,

"Foolish one! Tonight your life is over. And what will happen to all your things?"

"That is how it is," said Jesus, "when people spend all their time getting things for themselves instead of doing things in love for others."

Luke 12:13–21

The Bridesmaids

On the night of a wedding ten bridesmaids took their lamps and went to meet the bridegroom. Five of them were wise and took time to get ready. Their lamps were full of oil, ready to burn and give light for a long time. The other five bridesmaids did not get enough oil.

But the bridegroom was late, and they all fell asleep while they were waiting. At midnight someone called,

"Here comes the bridegroom! Come on out to meet him."

Up jumped the bridesmaids.

"Oh, our lamps are going out. We have no more oil. Give us some of yours," begged five of them.

"No, indeed. We have just enough for our own lamps. Go to the market and buy your own oil," the wise ones said.

But while the foolish girls were gone, the bridegroom came, and all the wedding party and the guests went in the house to the wedding supper. At last the other five girls came back, and they knocked on the door. "Let us in," they called.

"I don't know who you are," came the answer. No one opened the door.

"Watch, and be ready," Jesus ended his story.

Matthew 25:1–13

The Talents

A man was going on a trip to a faraway country. Before he went away he told his servants what to do while he was gone. He gave each of them some talents. (In those days a talent was a large sum of money.) To one he gave five talents, to another he gave two talents, and to the third man he gave one talent. Each man received as much as he was able to work with.

The first man went to work, and he worked and he worked

until he had made a profit of five more talents for his master.

The second man went to work, too, and he made a profit of two talents.

But the third man just dug a hole in the ground, and there he hid his master's money and did nothing at all.

A long time later the master came home, and he asked for a report on the work his men had done.

The first man came bringing ten talents, and he said,

"Sir, here is your money. I used it to make as much as you gave me."

"Well done! You have been a faithful workman on a small job, and I will give you more important work to do. Now we can celebrate together."

The second man came bringing his talents, and he said,

"Sir, here is your money. I used it to earn as much as you gave me."

"Well done! You have been a faithful workman on a small job, and I will give you more important work to do. Now we can celebrate together."

The third man dug up his talent and came bringing it back to the master.

"Sir, I was afraid, for I know you are a stern man who always wants a profit. I went and hid your money in the ground. See? Here it is. You have your own money back again."

"Lazy workman! You knew I want my work done well. So you should have taken my money and gone to work with it. Now it will be taken away from you and given to the man with ten talents.

"Turn this man out of the house. He does not work for me," the master ordered.

"Whoever works in the kingdom deserves to have more. But he who does not work deserves to lose what he has," Jesus said.

Matthew 25:14–30; Luke 19:11–27

The Good Shepherd

A shepherd was an important person among the people Jesus knew, and raising sheep was important business.

Early each morning the shepherd would go to the sheep pen close to the village to take his flock outside. The gatekeeper would recognize his call and open the only door so the sheep could go out. One by one they would leave their safe shelter and run to their friend the shepherd.

He knew each of them by name, and he called to them as he led them out to grass and water far from the crowded village. The path might lead through dark valleys between high rocks, but he was there to guide them. A wolf might prowl around trying to steal one of them, but he was there to fight it off with his club. A lamb might stray away, but he was there to draw it safely back with the curved crook of his long staff. A shepherd was on guard day and night.

When Jesus was a boy he must have learned the shepherd song of his great-great-many-times-great-grandfather David:

> The Lord is my shepherd; I shall not want.
> He maketh me to lie down in green pastures:
> He leadeth me beside the still waters. . . .
> I will fear no evil; for thou art with me;
> Thy rod and thy staff they comfort me. . . .
> Surely goodness and mercy shall follow me
>   all the days of my life.

And he must have learned the words the prophet Isaiah wrote about the Saviour God promised to send:

> He shall feed his flock like a shepherd:
> He shall gather the lambs to himself,

And carry them in his arms,
And gently lead the mother sheep.

"My sheep hear my voice, and I know them, and they know me," said Jesus. "For I have come to help them find life and to enjoy it, and I give to them eternal life. They will not be destroyed, nor will anyone be able to take them away from me.

"I am the Good Shepherd. The Good Shepherd gives up his life to protect his sheep. A hired shepherd would run away if he saw a wolf, and leave the frightened sheep to scatter and be lost. He runs away because he is not the owner, and cares nothing about the sheep.

"I have other sheep besides the sheep in this flock. I must bring them, too, so that they can hear my voice.

"I am the Good Shepherd. I know my sheep and they know me.

"I will give up my life for my sheep. No one takes it away. I give it up myself, and I know I have the Father's love because I give it up."

John 10; Psalm 23; Isaiah 40:11

The Friendly Foreigner

"Love my neighbor? Who is my neighbor?" a man wanted to know.

So Jesus told the story of The Good Neighbor.

A man was traveling down the road from Jerusalem to Jericho. On the way robbers jumped out and attacked him. They stole his clothes, beat him, and left him lying in the road half dead.

Now it happened that a priest was traveling that way, too. He discovered the man lying there. But he just crossed the road and went on his way.

Then there came a man who belonged to the tribe of Levi, the tribe of the priest teachers. He discovered the man lying there, so he hurried across the road and went on his way.

A foreigner from Samaria came riding down the road, and when he saw the man he dismounted from his donkey. Kneeling there in the road beside the man, he poured medicine on his wounds and bandaged them.

Then he lifted him up on his donkey. And so the two came to the nearest inn. The man from Samaria took care of the stranger. Next day he went to the keeper of the inn and paid their bill.

"Take care of him, and if he owes you more than this I will pay you when I come back this way," he said.

"Now which of the three was the neighbor of the man who was attacked by robbers?" Jesus asked.

"The man who took care of him."

"Then you go on and be a neighbor, too."

Luke 10:29–37

JESUS, SON OF GOD

The King Is Coming

IT WOULD SOON BE the time of the Passover celebration. Jesus and his twelve disciples were going straight to Jerusalem to keep the feast as they always did, though the priests of the Temple had given orders that anyone knowing where Jesus was should report to them at once.

It would be safer to stay every night with friends in Bethany, not far from Jerusalem. Jesus planned to work in the city during each day. When the travelers came to Bethany they stopped, and Jesus said to two of the disciples,

"Go on to the next village. There you will find a colt tied up in a doorway where two streets come together. No man has ever ridden it. Bring it to me. If anyone should ask what you are doing, just say, 'The Lord needs it.'"

Just inside the village they found the colt standing, tied in a doorway, as Jesus had said.

"What are you doing?" someone standing by asked the disciples as they untied the animal.

"The Lord needs this colt," they said, and they untied the little animal and led him back to the house where Jesus was waiting. It was long, long ago that a wise man had said,

> "Tell the news in Jerusalem,
> Tell the news, the King is coming,
> Riding to Jerusalem.
> Gentle, kind, and humble,
> The King comes riding on a colt."

Now Jesus mounted the little beast and rode away, straight up the hill to Jerusalem.

"Tell the news! The King is coming!" people shouted along the road.

"Blessed is his kingdom. Blessed is the King who comes to us from God!" the people chanted as he came in sight.

They tore branches from the palm trees and spread them in the road before him. They threw their coats on the road for a carpet for the King. And there was shouting and singing for joy that the King was coming.

Up the last hill he rode, up to the gates of the Temple. And the Pharisees were watching.

"Cannot you do something about all this?" each one was asking the other. "The whole world is running after him."

Into the Temple they went, and the children began to sing, "Glory to David's son!"

"Did you hear that?" scolded the priests.

"Yes," Jesus answered them. "Have you never read,

" 'From the words of children
God hears perfect praise'?"

And the priests did not dare to keep him out. When evening came he went back to stay with his friends in Bethany.

Matthew 21; Mark 11; Luke 19:29–39; John 11:55–57; 12:1,12–19; Zechariah 9:9

"My Father's House"

The next day Jesus and the disciples went back to Jerusalem, back into the beautiful Temple built for worship and praise and honor to God. But now it was noisy and dusty and crowded, and there was no place for quiet worship.

The people who came to the Temple were to bring their animal

© 1963, Broadman Press

The King Is Coming

gifts for the priests to offer to God as sacrifices. And if they had no animals of their own, they could buy some from the traders inside the Temple. But everyday business money was not supposed to be used to buy a gift for God. So before they could buy anything, the people who came to worship first had to change their money into Temple money.

All the place was full of men buying and selling and making change, full of birds to be sold, full of traders trying to make all the money they could at the business.

In his Father's house Jesus stopped in anger at all the commotion and the noise.

"My house shall be a house of prayer for all people. But you have turned it into a robber's den," he said sternly. And he drove them out—moneychangers, hucksters, and all. Tables were overturned, benches were upset, and the noisy men ran, taking their birds and their money with them.

"You are not to make my Father's house a market house." Jesus' voice was severe.

"What right have you to do this?" demanded the Jews. "Show us some proof."

This is what Jesus told them:

"You can destroy this Temple, and in three days I will raise it up again."

"But remember, it took forty-six years to build this Temple of ours. Do you think you could build it back in three days?" asked the Jews.

Of course, Jesus was talking about the temple of his body. Later when he really did rise again his disciples remembered what he had said. But that day no one understood.

"Who sent you to teach?" the priests demanded.

Jesus told them the story of The Son Who Was Not Wanted.

Once a man planted a vineyard. Round it he set a hedge to keep out thieves and animals. Inside he built a high watchtower and a deep press for the grapes. He rented it to some farmers, and then he went traveling to another country.

When the grapes were ripe he sent messengers to the farmers to collect his share of the profits. But they beat one messenger, killed another, and stoned another.

So the owner sent more messengers, but the farmers treated them worse than ever.

"I will send my son. They will respect him," the owner said.

"This is our chance," the farmers plotted. "Let's kill him, and then we can have the vineyard for ourselves."

So they caught the owner's son, threw him out of the vineyard, and killed him.

Jesus looked at the priests.

"Now what do you think the owner will do when he comes?"

"Punish the farmers and rent the vineyard to others who will work it for him," they answered quickly.

Did they understand?

Jesus was still looking straight at them.

"Did you ever read in the Scriptures:

" 'The stone which the builders threw away has been made the cornerstone of the building'?"

The son the farmers did not want! The stone the builders did not want! The priests and the Pharisees knew what he meant. They were the farmers. They were the builders. He was the Son, the cornerstone.

And they plotted to arrest him, but they knew they must be careful because of the people who were sure he was a prophet.

Matthew 21:12–13,33–46; Mark 11:15–18; 12;
Luke 19:45–48; 20:9–19; John 2:16–22

"I Have Chosen You"

"Look, Teacher, what wonderful stones! What beautiful buildings!"

The great Temple in Jerusalem with marble floors and stairs, great stone arches and doorways, golden ornaments and lamps was a beautiful place. The disciples were admiring it.

"Look around you," Jesus told them. "Of all these great buildings there is not going to be one stone left on top of another."

Quietly they walked out of the city to rest on the Mount of Olives. As soon as Peter and James and John and Andrew had a chance to speak to Jesus privately, they wanted to know all about the Temple's being destroyed.

"When will it happen? How will we know?"

"When you see armies ready to attack Jerusalem you will know the city is going to be destroyed. Try to escape to the mountains if you can.

"But you are going to have other problems. Men will arrest you and drag you before the council and beat you in the synagogues. You will be ordered to come before kings and governors to explain why you have been teaching about me. For the good news must be preached around the world.

"This will be your chance. Make up your minds now not to worry about your speeches. You will be taught the right thing to say. Really it will not be you speaking, but the Holy Spirit will be speaking through you.

"You are going to be betrayed by members of your own families, by your parents or your own brothers or perhaps by your friends. But remember, if people hate you because you have been with me, they hated me first. They will put you out of the synagogue. And because they do not know the Father they are going to think they are obeying God by killing you.

"If you were like them they would be friendly. But you do not belong with them, for I have chosen you out of all the world.

"Remember, I told you that a workman is never more important than the one for whom he works. If they attacked me, they will attack you. If they listened to me, they will listen to you, too."

Matthew 24:1–3; Mark 13:1–13; Luke 21:5–19

Plotting Priests

If only they could find a way to trick Jesus into saying something the people would not like, or something that would really get him in trouble with the law or the priests! The priests puzzled, and they plotted, and they planned.

"Tell us who gave you the right to heal people on the sabbath day," they asked him one day in the Temple. "Tell us who gave you the right to go around telling the people you know more about God than we do."

"First I will ask you one question," Jesus told them.

"Who gave John the right to baptize people? Was it God, or was John speaking for himself?"

The priests just looked at one another and answered not one

word. If they said, "He was speaking for himself," they were afraid of the people who believed that John was a great teacher. If they said, "It was God," Jesus would say, "Then why did you not believe John?"

"We do not know," was all they could say.

"And I will not tell you who sent me," said Jesus.

Jesus' enemies tried again. This time the Pharisees were sure they could catch him.

Someone stopped him when a great many people were listening.

"Teacher, we know that you are a good teacher, and you teach the truth about the way of God, no matter what people may think. Tell us, do you think we Jews ought to pay taxes to the Roman Caesar?"

"Why are you trying to trick me?" Jesus asked him. "Bring me a coin."

He held it up before them.

"Whose picture is this?" He pointed to the head on the coin.

"Caesar's."

"Then pay to Caesar what belongs to him. Return to God what belongs to him."

Jesus kept right on preaching in the Temple.

"I have come into the world as a light. No one who trusts me needs to live in the darkness. Whoever believes in me believes in my Father who sent me. When you see me you have seen my Father.

"I am not teaching you my own ideas. The Father who sent me gave me a commission to teach. So what I am telling you is just what he told me."

There was nothing more that anyone could say.

A lawyer came to him to ask,

"Teacher, what is the most important law?"

"Listen, O Israel. There is one God. Love the Lord your God with all your heart, with all your soul, with all your mind, with all your strength. That is the most important. The rest is much like it. Love your neighbor the way you love yourself. No other law is more important."

"You are right," the man agreed. "There is one God. And loving him with all your heart and understanding and strength, and loving your neighbor as much as you love yourself is more important than all the gifts you can make to God."

"You are not far away from the kingdom of heaven," Jesus told him.

But for fear of the Pharisees there were many people who did not dare to talk to Jesus. Even the important people who believed in him were afraid because the Pharisees had the right to turn them out of the synagogue. Having the approval of others was more important to them than earning God's approval.

Matthew 21:23–27; 22:15–22,34–40;
Mark 11:27–33; 12:13–34; Luke 20:1–8,20–26;
John 12:42–44

Judas' Fearful Bargain

"Watch out," Jesus told the people in the Temple. "You are wise when you listen to these teachers of yours, for they teach the same laws Moses taught. But you cannot trust the things they do. They like to parade up and down in fine robes. They want to be first and have the best places. They pray loudly, and their prayers are long, for they want everyone to hear. But when no one is looking they steal from the poor. They insist on your keeping a great many rules, and they make more rules.

"Remember that the most important person is not the leader in the highest place but the one who serves and helps others."

Far below the Temple Jesus could see the flat roofs of little houses. He could see narrow, crowded streets. Hungry people, tired and unhappy people, sick, worried, and troubled people who needed him lived in the little houses along the crowded streets.

"Oh, Jerusalem, Jerusalem, city that kills the prophets who are sent to you! How often I have wanted to bring your people together the way a hen nestles her chicks under her wings! But you would not let me," he said.

In two more days it would be the time of the Passover celebration. At the home of Caiaphas, the high priest, the chief priests and the teachers held a meeting to decide how to arrest Jesus and have him killed.

And then someone came to them with plans that suited them exactly.

Judas had slipped away from the other disciples. Now he stood before the men who wanted Jesus out of their way.

"How much will you pay me to help you capture him?" he asked.

So they made a bargain. Some time when Jesus was away from the crowds of people Judas would tell them where he was. And gladly they bargained to pay him thirty silver coins.

Matthew 23:1–14,37; 26:14–16; Mark 12:38–40; 14:1–11; Luke 20:45–47; 22:3–6

Mary's Memorial Gift

Jesus and all the disciples were dinner guests in the home of Simon who used to be a leper but now was well again. Martha was helping to serve the dinner. Lazarus was one of the guests, and Mary was there, too. She had brought with her a rare and wonderful gift, a bottle of the finest sweet-smelling ointment. As they were eating, Mary broke the jar and poured the ointment on Jesus' hair. The whole house smelled of the sweet, rich perfume.

Judas, the treasurer of the disciples, sat watching.

"What good is all that waste?" he grumbled. "She ought to have sold that perfume, and she could have given the money to the poor."

"Do not scold her. She has done a beautiful thing," Jesus told him. "You will always have the poor with you, and you will always be able to help them. But you will not always have me with you.

"Because of her love she has given me a gift ahead of time for my burying. And I tell you that wherever the good news is told in all the world people will tell the story of what she has done."

Matthew 26:6–13; Mark 14:3–9; John 12:2–8

The Last Supper Together

It was Thursday and that evening would be the time for the Passover supper.

"Where shall we go to keep the Passover?" the disciples wanted to know.

"Go into the city, and you will meet a man who will be carrying a pitcher of water," Jesus told Peter and John. "Follow him home, and tell the owner of the house,

" 'The Teacher would like to know where the guest room is, for he is coming to eat the Passover supper.'

"He will show you an upstairs room that will be ready, and you can get everything we need for the Passover."

It all happened just that way. In the evening Jesus and his disciples met in the upstairs guest room.

"I have wanted so much to be able to eat this supper with you," Jesus told them.

But the disciples were arguing about which one was the most important and who ought to have the first place in Jesus' kingdom.

"I have lived with you to serve you," Jesus reminded them. "You know how it is with the Gentiles. They expect to have rulers to give them orders. And those rulers have rulers over them. But it should not be that way with you. Whoever is to be great among you is to be a servant, and the greatest of all will be the one who does the most for others. For I came to live with you as one who serves you."

He poured some water into a basin, picked up a towel, and began to wash the dusty feet of the disciples as if he really were a servant.

"Oh, but, Lord, you aren't going to wash my feet," Peter objected.

"If I do not make you clean you can never be with me," Jesus warned him.

"Then, Lord, don't wash just my feet. See—my hands, and my head, too," Peter insisted.

"You are clean—but not all of you." Jesus knew that Satan had already entered into the heart of Judas.

Then he sat down with them again.

"Do you understand what I have done for you? You say that I am your Teacher, and I am. If I, your Teacher, your Lord, have done this for you, you must be ready to wait on one another. You know these things. Blessed will you be when you remember to do them."

They went on with the supper.

"From now on I am going to tell you what will happen," Jesus told them. "One of you here tonight is going to betray me."

They all looked sadly at one another.

"Who is it?" "Tell us who it is."

"Is it I, Teacher?" Judas asked loudly as he reached for the bread Jesus dipped in the sauce for him.

"You have said it. Now, whatever you are going to do, do it quickly."

Judas slipped away from the table and out into the darkness.

Jesus went on talking with his friends.

"I will be with you only a little while longer. You will look for me, but I am going where you cannot come.

"Now I am going to give you a new rule.

"Love one another the way I have loved you. The people will discover by your love that you are my disciples."

"Lord, where are you going?" Peter wanted to know.

"Where I am going you cannot follow me now. But later you shall come, too."

"But why can't I come now? I am ready to do anything for you. Why, I'll go to prison with you. If you have to die, then I will die, too."

"Will you, Peter? Before the cock crows you will have said three times that you do not know me."

"Oh, no! Even if they kill me, I will never do that."

Peter was very, very sure.

Matthew 26:17–25,31–35; Mark 14:12–21,28–31; Luke 22:7–15,21–38; John 13

The First Lord's Supper

As the disciples and Jesus went on eating together at the supper table, Jesus took some bread in his hands. He blessed it. Then he broke it in pieces, and passed it to the disciples.

"This bread is my body which is given for you. Take it, and eat, remembering me."

Next he picked up the cup, and he gave thanks to the Father.

"This means the new promise between God and his people. It is my blood which is shed for the forgiving of sins. Take it, all of you."

So ever afterward Jesus' followers would know that when they ate the bread and drank the cup, they would be telling about the Lord's death until he came back.

Matthew 26:26–29; Mark 14:22–25; Luke 22:17–20; 1 Corinthians 11:23–25

Jesus' Good-by Message

"Do not let your hearts be troubled. You believe in God. Believe in me, too. In my Father's house are many rooms. I would have told you if it were not so. I am going to make a place ready for you, and I will come back for you so that you can be with me there. You know where I am going, and you know the way."

"But, Lord, we don't even know where you are going. How can we know the way?"

"I am the way, and the truth, and the life.

"I am the way to the Father. If you had recognized me, you would have known my Father, too. From now on you do know him. You have even seen him."

"If you will just show us the Father, we will be satisfied," said Philip.

"Have I been here with you all this time and you still do not recognize me, Philip? Whoever has seen me has seen the Father, too. Don't you believe that I am like the Father and the Father is like me?

"I use his words when I speak. He works through me.

"Believe that it is so. Truly I tell you, whoever believes in me will do greater things than I have done, because I am going to my Father. And whatever you ask in my name I will do it.

"I am not going to leave you alone. In a little while people will not be seeing me any more. But you see me. And because I shall be living, you will be living, too.

"I will ask the Father to send you another Helper, the Holy Spirit, who will stay with you forever. Others will not know him, but you will, for he will come to live with you. He will teach you and help you to remember all the things I have taught you while I was with you.

"If you love me, remember to live by my teaching. Whoever knows my commandments and keeps them loves me, and whoever loves me will be loved by my Father.

"This is my commandment: Love one another as I have loved you. Greater love has no man than this, that a man lay down his life for his friends.

"You are my friends if you do the things I command you. I have told you the things I have heard from my Father.

"I have so much more to tell you, but you could not understand it all now. When the Helper, the Spirit of Truth, comes to you, he will teach you.

"Remember that I came from the Father. I lived in the world awhile. Now I am going back to my Father. If you loved me you would be glad I am going away because I am going to be with my Father."

"Now you are telling us what we can understand," said the disciples. "We know that you came from God."

"Are you very sure? In just a little while you will all desert me, and you will go back to your own homes. But I will not be alone, for the Father is with me.

"I have told you all this so that you will not worry. As long as you live, you will have trouble and sorrow in the world. But keep your courage. I have overcome the world.

"Peace I leave with you. My peace I give to you."

John 14 to 16

Prayer for All He Loved

As Jesus finished talking with his friends, he began to talk to his Father:

"Father, the time has come. I have honored you on earth. I have finished the work you gave me to do. I have given eternal life to all whom you gave me. And this is eternal life—knowing the only true God and Jesus Christ whom you sent.

"I have taught these men whom you gave me. I have told them about you, and they know that I came from you. I am praying for them, for all the people whom you have given me, for they are yours.

"Now I will not be in the world any longer. But they will stay here while I come to you. Father, take care of them and keep them together, working together. I am not asking that you take them out of the world. Just keep them away from evil.

"And I am not praying just for these men, but for everyone who is going to believe in me because of the work these men are going to do. I am asking, Father, that all whom you gave me may come to be with me so that they can see the glory which you gave me, for you were loving me before the world was made.

"And I am asking that you give them the same love you gave me and that they may know that I am near them."

John 17

How Jesus Was Captured

It was late Thursday night. Jesus and his friends sang a hymn together, and then they left the guest room. They walked together down the street, across the Kidron Valley, toward the Mount of Olives to the Garden of Gethsemane, a place where they had often gone together when Judas was with them.

Jesus was saying to them,

"Tonight you are all going to be confused because of me. You will all be separated like sheep when something happens to their shepherd. But when I am alive again I will go on ahead of you to Galilee."

"Oh, no! Everyone else may be confused. But not I," Peter interrupted.

Jesus and the disciples went into the garden, and Jesus said, "Sit here while I go yonder and pray." But he asked Peter and James and John to go with him. He was greatly troubled—very, very sorrowful.

"Stay here and watch," he told the three, and then, just a little way from them, he began to talk with his Father.

"Anything is possible for you to do. If you are willing, take all this suffering away from me. But, Father, I am not asking to have my way. I pray that your will may be done."

He went back to find the others. But they were asleep.

"Peter, could you not keep watch for just an hour? Stay awake now and pray, so that you will be strong when temptation comes. Your spirit wants to do the right thing, but your body gives up so easily."

He went away again to pray. When he came back the disciples were asleep. One more time he left them to talk with his Father. They were still sleeping when he came back to them.

"Now you can rest. The time for watching is past, and the traitor is nearby," he told them.

He was still talking when Judas came hurrying out to the dark olive grove, leading a band of Temple police. They all carried lanterns and torches, and they were armed with swords and clubs.

"The man you want is the man I will kiss. Arrest him, and keep him under guard," Judas had told them.

He slipped ahead of the shadowy figures and went to meet Jesus.

"I greet you, Teacher," he said as he kissed him.

"Friend, why are you here?" Jesus asked him.

The soldiers rushed forward. Instantly Peter drew the sword to defend Jesus, and he struck a man named Malchus, a servant of the high priest Caiaphas, cutting off his ear.

"Peter, put up your sword. Those who fight with swords are killed by swords," Jesus said quietly. Then, touching Malchus, he healed the wound.

To the men who came to arrest him he said,

"Did you come out to get me the way you would arrest a thief, with swords and clubs? Every day I have been with you, teaching in the Temple, and you did not arrest me. But this is your hour, and it had to be this way."

The disciples had nothing to say. Every one had run away.

Matthew 26:30–56; Mark 14:43–52;
Luke 22:47–53; John 18:1–12

On Trial

The soldiers bound their prisoner with strong ropes and took him to the house of the high priest, Caiaphas. All the council members and the chief priests and the teachers were quickly called together. They must find some evidence that Jesus was guilty of breaking laws for which the penalty was death.

© 1963, Broadman Press

Judas, the Traitor

Now by Jewish law two people must agree on the same charge before a prisoner could be tried. But no two people could agree on the same stories about Jesus, for none of their stories were true.

Caiaphas turned to Jesus.

"What have you to say? What do all these people have against you"

Jesus stood quietly, saying nothing.

"I order you to answer. Tell us if you are the Christ, the Son of God."

"I am," Jesus said.

"You don't need any more witnesses to prove that he is guilty. He just said it himself. He is guilty of disrespect for God."

"He deserves to die!"

They blindfolded him, and they made fun of him, and they slapped him.

"Now, prophet, tell us who struck you. Tell us—if you really are a prophet."

Peter had followed the crowd to Caiaphas' house, but he stayed a long way off. When they took Jesus upstairs he came as far as the courtyard door. Inside he could see soldiers standing around a fire. It was a chilly night, so Peter came over to the fire to get warm.

One of the maids came by, and she looked hard at Peter in the firelight.

"Why, you were with that man from Nazareth," she exclaimed.

"I don't know what you're talking about," Peter said quickly. He turned away and walked out to the porch.

There another maid saw him, and she pointed him out to the people who were standing around.

"That man was with Jesus."

"I swear I don't even know the man," Peter shouted.

A few minutes later someone said,

"You really must be one of them. You talk like a man from Galilee, and that's where he came from."

"Man, I don't know what you're talking about. Why, I never even knew him."

Far off, Peter heard a rooster crow. Now he remembered.

"Before the cock crows you will have said three times that you never knew me."

Peter walked away alone, sobbing miserably.

Early in the morning the Jewish council had a meeting in the council hall, and they brought Jesus over from Caiaphas' house.

"If you really are the Christ, tell us now," they ordered him.

"If I tell you, you will not believe. And if I ask you questions, you will not answer. But from now on the Son of man will be with God."

"Are you really the Son of God?"

"You say that I am."

"That is all we need. By his own words we have proof. Guilty!"

Now by law the council could not order Jesus to be killed. But the Roman governor could. So they took Jesus to Pilate.

"We heard this man teaching that it is wrong to pay taxes to Caesar. He says himself he is a king. He is stirring up the people, and they will make trouble," they told the governor.

"Are you the king of the Jews?" Pilate asked.

"My kingdom does not belong to this world. If it did, my army would fight for me," Jesus answered.

"The priests keep accusing you of doing wrong. What have you to say?"

Jesus said nothing at all.

"I can't see that he has done anything to deserve punishment," Pilate told the priests.

"He has. He has made trouble all over our country ever since he started out up in Galilee."

That gave Pilate an idea. If the man came from Galilee, King

Herod of Galilee would have to decide what should be done, and Herod happened to be in town for the Passover.

So he sent Jesus to Herod.

For a long time King Herod had been hoping for a chance to meet the man everyone was talking about. Perhaps he might even watch him do something wonderful. But Jesus did not answer his questions, and he stood quietly while the priests accused him.

Finally Herod gave up. He could find nothing wrong. He and the soldiers made fun of the prisoner by having him dressed up in a king's royal robe, and then he sent Jesus back to Pilate.

Matthew 26:57–75; 27:2–14; Mark 14:53–72; 15:1–5; Luke 22:54–71; 23:1–12; John 18:15–38

"Crucify Him!"

Every year at Passover time the governor let one prisoner go free, anyone the people chose. Pilate knew very well that the priests were accusing Jesus because they were jealous of him, but he began to hope he could get them to set him free after all. So he called the council back.

"I have examined this man you accuse. I cannot find that he has done anything to deserve punishment. Neither has Herod. I will have him beaten. Then I can release him for the Passover."

"No! No!" they shouted. "Not this man. Let Barabbas go free."

Now Barabbas was in jail for murder. Quietly the priests walked among the people and told them what to say. They began to shout:

"Give us Barabbas! We want Barabbas!"

Pilate brought Jesus out before the people.

"Look! Here is the man," he announced.

"Crucify him! Crucify him!" they all shouted.

"Take him away and crucify him yourselves. I find no evil in him."

"He claimed to be the Son of God. Our law says he must be punished by death. He wanted to make himself a king, and everyone knows a man like that is no friend of Caesar's. If you let him go, you are no friend of Caesar either."

"Take your king. I will have nothing to do with him," said Pilate. And he let Barabbas go free.

Matthew 27:15–23; Mark 15:6–15; Luke 23:13–25; John 18:39–40; 19:1–16

End of the Story of Judas

Jesus was sentenced to die. Now that it was too late, Judas wished it had never happened. He wished he had never been a traitor, wished he had never taken those thirty silver coins. He could not undo his evil deed, but he could get rid of the money.

He went straight to the chief priests in the Temple.

"I have betrayed an innocent man," he told them.

"What does that matter? It's your affair," they said.

He hurled the silver coins on the floor. Then he disappeared.

Out in a lonely place Judas hanged himself.

Matthew 27:3–5

To the Hill of the Skull

In the great hall the soldiers had been pretending that Jesus was their king. Thorns were his crown. A dry stalk in his hand was his scepter. They bowed before him, and they mocked him and shouted,

"Hail to you, King of the Jews!"

And they laughed, and they struck at him with their hands. Then they led him away to the Hill of the Skull, there to crucify him on a cross.

A criminal had to carry his own cross. Jesus was so weary that he fell beneath the weight of it. When a man named Simon, on his way into town from the country, passed that way, the soldiers ordered him to pick up Jesus' cross and carry it out to the hill.

Jesus' friends followed as closely as they dared—all the people he had loved and who loved him—and they were crying as they walked behind the procession. So at last they came to the Hill of the Skull.

Matthew 27:27–33; Mark 15:20–23; Luke 23:26–33; John 19:16–17

When God's Son Gave His Life

Just outside the city three men, their bodies nailed on three crosses until they died, were to be given the worst punishment under the Roman law. Two of them were thieves. Over the cross in the center was a sign that read,

"This is Jesus, the King of the Jews."

"Father, forgive them, for they do not know what they are doing," Jesus prayed.

At the foot of the cross the soldiers divided Jesus' clothing among them. They gambled to see which of them could have his beautiful coat which was made in one piece without a single seam.

The priests stood watching.

"He could save others. Why doesn't he save himself?" they mocked, and they wagged their heads.

One of the thieves was talking.

"Are you really the Christ? Why don't you save yourself and us, too?"

"Hush!" said the other thief. "Don't you have any respect for God? We are all in this together. You and I deserve our punishment. But this man never did anything wrong." He looked toward the cross in the center.

"Jesus, remember me when you are king."

"Today you will be with me in heaven," Jesus told him.

Some women were standing near the cross. There was Mary, Jesus' mother, and his mother's sister, and Mary Magdalene. Jesus was watching them, and then he saw John whom he loved.

"Woman—your son," he said lovingly to his mother. "Son—your mother," he told John. That day Mary went to live in John's home.

A strange darkness began to cover the earth.

People standing near heard Jesus cry out to his Father,

"God, oh, my God, why have you left me all alone?" Then they heard,

"Father, into your hands I give my spirit."

"It is finished," he said at last, and then he died.

The Roman captain in charge said thoughtfully, "This man really was the Son of God."

In the Temple before the great altar, where no one but the high priest ever went to meet God, a great thick curtain was hanging.

At the moment Jesus died, the curtain split from top to bottom. Now the way to God was forever open for all people.

Matthew 27:33–54; Mark 15:22–41; Luke 23:33–49; John 19:17–30

New Tomb in a Garden

Joseph from Arimathea was a member of the Jewish council. All the time the council was voting for the death of Jesus he voted no. But he was not able to stop them. Now there was something he could do. He was afraid of letting the other council members know his plan; so he went secretly to the governor and asked if he might take Jesus' body and bury him in his own tomb. Another old friend, Nicodemus, the council member who had talked with Jesus at night, asked if he might help.

So the men laid Jesus' body in Joseph's new tomb in a rocky cave in a garden. Across the opening of the cave they rolled a heavy stone.

Back in the governor's palace some of the Jews had a conference with Pilate.

"Sir, we just remembered this deceiver used to say that after three days he would be alive again. If his disciples should steal his body and say he is alive, things would be worse than ever."

"You may have a guard," Pilate told them. "Go on and make everything secure."

So they sealed up the stone door of the cave, and the Roman guard watched to see that it was done right.

Matthew 27:61–66; Luke 23:50–56

© 1963, Broadman Press

He Is Risen

Resurrection Day

Early Sunday morning three women hurried out to the tomb in the garden, taking gifts of spices for Jesus' body, for that was the custom in those days. On Friday Jesus was buried. The next day was the sabbath. Jewish laws would not allow people to go to a burial place on that day.

"Who will roll away the big stone door of the tomb for us?" the women worried.

It was growing light now, and they could see more clearly.

"Look! The stone is gone! Now we can go inside."

It was still shadowy inside the rock tomb. But someone was sitting there, someone they could see clearly, for his robe was shining.

"Don't be afraid," he said to them. "You are looking for Jesus who was crucified. He is not here, for he is alive again, just as he said. Look, you can see the place where they laid him.

"Now hurry and tell his disciples and Peter, too, that he is going on ahead to Galilee, and he wants them to meet him there."

So they ran to tell the angel's good news. But the disciples would not believe them. Just the same, Peter and John went running to the tomb. John stooped and looked inside, but Peter rushed in. All they could see was the pile of white clothes in which Jesus had been buried. They went back then, wondering what this was all about.

But Mary Magdalene stayed just outside, and she was crying. She stooped and looked inside the tomb, and she saw two shining angels, one at the head, one at the foot, where Jesus' body had been lying.

"Why do you weep?" someone asked her.

"They have taken my Lord away, and I do not know what they have done with him." She turned away.

Someone was standing beside her. She looked up at him, but she did not recognize him.

"Why are you crying? For whom are you looking?"

He must be the gardener, she thought.

"Sir, if you carried him away, tell me where you took him."

"Mary!"

She knew that voice.

"Teacher!"

"Go on and tell my disciples, and tell them that I am going to my Father and your Father."

Mary ran off to tell the good news.

"I saw him! I saw him! I saw the Teacher, and he is living."

Two of Jesus' disciples walked slowly down the road to Emmaus, about seven miles from Jerusalem. As they walked along, talking about all the things that had been happening in Jerusalem, a third person joined them. He listened to them awhile, and then he asked, "What have you been talking about?"

"Are you the only traveler to Jerusalem who doesn't know what has been going on?"

"What?" the stranger asked.

"Why, this Jesus from Nazareth was truly a wonderful person, sent to us by God. But our priests and rulers sentenced him to die. And we did hope so much that he was the one who would make our nation free again.

"Now it has been three days since it all happened. Some women went to the tomb early this morning. They could not find his body, but they said something about angels telling them he is alive. But when some of us went to see, we could not find him."

"Oh, you are so slow to believe," the stranger said. "Didn't you understand that Christ had to die this way so that he could live again?"

As they walked along he explained the writings of the prophets who had said that God would send his Son.

The travelers came to Emmaus. The stranger started to go on.

"It is late. Why don't you stay with us?" they invited him.

So he went with them to the house where they would spend the night. When they sat down to supper, he picked up the bread and gave thanks for it. Then he broke it and handed it to them.

Then they knew. But before they could speak Jesus slipped away. They talked it all over.

"Didn't we know? Couldn't we tell, when our hearts were so glad all the time he was talking to us?"

Late as it was, they hurried back to Jerusalem to find the other disciples, all but Thomas, meeting together in a room that was locked, because the disciples were afraid.

"The Lord really is living. Peter has seen him," the disciples heard the news from their friends. Then the two from Emmaus told what had happened to them.

"It was when he was at the table with us. He broke the bread and passed it to us. Then we knew who he was."

While they were talking they knew that someone else was there. They looked, and they were so frightened they were shaking.

"Peace be to you. What is worrying you? Why are you still doubting? It really is I. See the marks on my hands and my feet."

No one could think of anything to say. They were all too surprised to believe.

"Have you anything to eat?" Jesus asked.

They brought him a piece of broiled fish, and they watched while he ate it. Now their doubts were gone. This really was their beloved Jesus.

"Peace be to you," he was saying again. "Now I am going to send you out to work just as the Father sent me."

Of course they went to find Thomas and tell him the news.

"I don't believe it. I've got to see him myself. I've got to touch his hands myself before I believe," said Thomas.

Matthew 28:5–8; Mark 16; Luke 24; John 20

"Love as I Have Loved You"

A week later they were all together. This time Thomas was there, too. And this time they carefully locked the door, just as they did before.

And then there was Jesus with them.

"Thomas, reach out your hands and touch my side and my hands. See for yourself and believe," he was saying.

Thomas the twin walked slowly toward his Master. Now he could not help believing.

"It is—my Lord—my God!"

"Did you believe me because you saw me with your own eyes, Thomas? Blessed are all the people who are going to believe in me, though they never saw me," Jesus told him.

Peter and Thomas, the twin, Nathanael and James and John and two other disciples went back to the north country by Lake Galilee. It was hard to get back to work. They missed their Friend who had been with them for three years.

"I'm going fishing," Peter decided, and he went to his boat.

"We'll go, too," the others said quickly.

But they fished all night long without catching a single fish.

In the early morning light they could see someone standing on the beach, but they could not tell who he was.

"Friends, have you anything to eat out there?" he called.

"No," they shouted across the water.

"Then drop your nets on the right side of the boat. That is where the fish are."

So they did, and the net was so heavy with fish that they could hardly drag it in.

Something about the stranger reminded the disciples of old times.

"Peter! That's the Teacher!" John exclaimed.

Without stopping to think, Peter jumped into the water and waded ashore. The others brought the heavy boat in as fast as they could.

There on the shore they found fish cooking over a fire, and a loaf of bread.

"Bring some of your fish. It is time you had some breakfast," said Jesus, and he gave food to all of them.

When they all had had plenty to eat, they sat together awhile on the beach.

"Peter, do you love me more than these others do?" Jesus asked.

"Of course, Teacher. You know that I love you."

"Then feed my little lambs."

A little later Jesus asked,

"Peter, do you love me?"

"Of course, Teacher. You know that I love you."

"Then take care of my sheep."

One more time Jesus asked him,

"Peter, do you truly love me?"

By this time Peter's feelings were hurt.

"Teacher, you know everything. You can tell that I do love you."

"Feed my sheep," said Jesus.

John 20:26–31; 21; Matthew 28:16–20; Mark 16:15–20; Luke 24:50–53

Marching Orders

Where should they go? What should they do? How would they do it? Jesus gave his disciples their marching orders.

"Go to all the countries of the world. Tell the good news to everyone. Go and make disciples everywhere. Baptize them in the name of the Father, of the Son, and of the Holy Spirit. And remember, I am always with you, to the very end of the world."

The last time the disciples heard Jesus give their marching orders they were on a mountain near Jerusalem.

"You are to go to Jerusalem and wait there. When the Father sends the Holy Spirit to you, you will be ready to teach the love of God for his people, teach his forgiveness of their sins for Christ's sake, teach how Christ died and is alive again.

"Begin in Jerusalem. Then go throughout Judea, and Samaria, then to all the countries of the world."

Then a cloud swirled over the hill, and Jesus was gone.

The disciples could not believe it. They just stood there looking toward the sky.

"Men from Galilee!"

They turned around. Two men in white robes were there.

"Why do you keep on looking toward heaven? He has gone back, but he will come again."

"Wait in Jerusalem." They remembered his words.

So they walked back down the mountain and on into the city to wait and to pray while they were waiting, all together, in an upstairs room.

Matthew 28:16–20; Luke 24:50–53; John 21:25; Acts 1:1–12

BEGINNING IN JERUSALEM

The Day That Changed the World

SOMEWHERE in Jerusalem, in a safe upstairs room, the men and women who had known Jesus best were waiting, just waiting. And while they waited they were praying together. Mary, Jesus' mother, was there, and the other women who loved Jesus and who worked with the disciples.

There were twelve disciples now. Peter had reminded the eleven that it was time to choose a man to take the place of Judas who turned traitor. He must be someone who had known Jesus ever since his baptism, someone who had been there at the resurrection. Two men had been nominated. Then the disciples asked God to help them decide, and they elected Matthias.

Now the twelve were: Peter, James, and John, Andrew, Philip, and Thomas, Bartholomew and Matthew, James who was Alpheus' son, Simon the patriot, Thaddeus and Matthias.

"Wait in Jerusalem," Jesus had told them. "Wait until the Father sends the Holy Spirit to be with you forever. He will teach you and guide you. He will help you to tell what you have been learning here with me.

"Go on and tell the good news. Tell it first in Jerusalem and Judea. Then go on to Samaria. Then go to the whole world."

So the disciples were waiting, and the days went by. Then it was the day of the Feast of Pentecost, celebrating the end of the summer harvest.

Jesus' followers were gathered together, one hundred and twenty of them, when it happened. First they heard a sound like wind filling all the house. They saw brightness like fire, and it divided into flames and glowed above each disciple's head.

Suddenly the disciples discovered that they were talking in strange languages they had never spoken before, languages of far-off lands and places.

Now the Feast of Pentecost was so important that Jews traveled from far away—from Rome and Egypt and Africa and Asia and Crete and Arabia—to bring their gifts and to worship in the Temple at Jerusalem. Passing by a house that morning, a crowd of pilgrims stopped in surprise, for they could hear excited voices, and they crowded to listen.

"These people can speak *any* language!"

The news spread fast. People could hardly believe it.

"Why, these men are from Galilee. How can we be hearing them talk in our own language?" they wondered.

But some just laughed. "Just drunks making a noise!"

Peter was the first to speak for the disciples. And he talked with strange new power since God's Spirit had come into his heart. The fisherman who had run away when he was afraid had become Christ's Rock Man. Clearly he spoke, loudly, and the last man at the back of the crowd could hear.

"You men of Jerusalem, listen! It's only nine o'clock in the morning. These men could not be drunk." For they all knew that Jews would neither eat nor drink before the morning service on Pentecost.

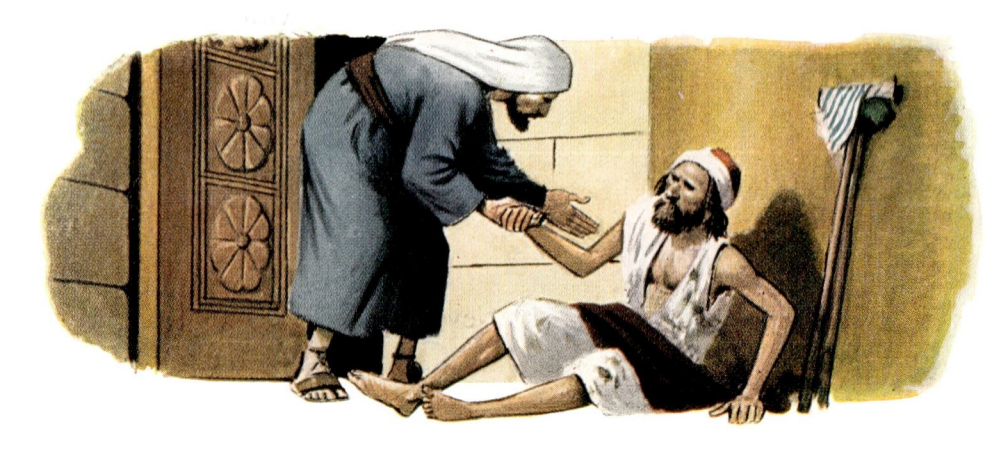

"You have just seen a miracle happen," Peter went on. "Listen to me, men of Israel! You yourselves knew Jesus who came from Nazareth. You watched him. You listened to him. Then you murdered him. But God would not let death keep him. Jesus is alive forever. We know he is, for we have seen him—many times. Now he has gone to be with his Father, and God has made him our Lord and Christ. But before he went away he promised us that God would send us his Spirit. Just now God kept the promise. Straight from the Father the Spirit has come to be with us forever."

Something was happening. No one laughed now. Men were remembering things it hurt to remember.

"What shall we do?" someone asked.

"Repent! Be baptized, every one of you, in Jesus' name. Then the Holy Spirit will come to you, too. This is God's promise to you and to your children and your grandchildren, to people here and to people far away."

He went on talking to them, and gladly, eagerly the people crowded about him. Gladly they were baptized, and gladly they became a part of the first group of believers, about three thousand of them that first day. And every day more of them came into the new fellowship.

They went to one another's homes to eat together. They shared everything they had so that no one would go hungry. And every day they went to the Temple, thankfully, gladly, for the joy of being together and knowing God's Spirit was with them all.

John 15:26–27; 16:13; Acts 1:8–26; 2

To Work!—for Jesus' Sake

Day after day a crippled beggar sat by the Beautiful Gate where people walked into the Temple to pray, and he reached up his hand for money as they passed. Never in all his life had he been able to walk, only to sit wherever his friends brought him.

It was three o'clock, time for afternoon prayers, when Peter and John came that way.

"Give! Give!" called the beggar, and he reached out his hand.

The men stopped.

"Look at us!" said Peter.

The beggar reached up for his gift.

"I have neither silver nor gold, but I'll give you what I do have," Peter told him. "In the name of Jesus of Nazareth, get up and walk."

He took the beggar by the hand and helped him up. Suddenly the man was standing with feet and ankles strong and straight. He jumped for the joy of it. Then he walked on into the Temple with Peter and John, and as he was walking and leaping he was thanking God.

The three of them had gone as far as Solomon's Porch when people began to notice the man who used to be lame. They all came crowding to see what had happened.

Now Peter began to preach again, and he made it very plain that God had cured the man. He told the people about Jesus, the Son of God, how he had died and had risen from the dead.

"We were there when those things happened," he said.

While he was talking, up came the priests and the captain of the guards and some of the Sadducees, who allowed no one to teach that a man could live after he was dead. They arrested both Peter and John, and they held them until morning. Just the same, the people in the Temple believed what they had seen and heard. Five thousand more of them joined the new group.

In the morning Peter and John were called before the council and all the priests.

"What right did you have to cure this man? Who told you to do it?" they demanded.

Peter could hardly wait to speak.

"Rulers of the people, you ask how this man was cured. It was in the name of Jesus Christ of Nazareth. You remember—you crucified him, and God brought him back to life. He is the only one who can save us. There is no other."

The men of the council could not hide their surprise. Peter and John had never gone to the Temple school. Yet here they were speaking before the wise ones. They were remembering how those two had been with Jesus, and they watched them carefully, but they could find nothing wrong. Just the same, they sent Peter and John outside while they talked together.

"Everyone in town knows that a miracle has happened. We can't hide it. But this kind of thing cannot go on," they were saying.

The priests called Peter and John back.

"There will be no more teaching in the name of Jesus," they warned.

Quietly the men who had been with Jesus told them,

"Whether it is right in the sight of God to listen to you rather than to God, you judge. As for us, we have to tell what we have seen and heard."

So many people were crowding around, and there was so much excitement that the priests did not want to punish Peter and John. So they just warned them and let them go.

Peter and John and the rest of the twelve went on teaching and healing the sick. From all Jerusalem people came to meet them. From the towns nearby they crowded into the narrow streets, carrying their sick on mats and cots. Some of them were hoping that at least Peter's shadow might fall on them, for they were sure that just being near him would help.

One day, without warning, all the twelve were arrested and locked up in prison. That night God's angel opened the prison doors.

"Go back to the Temple, and keep on preaching," he told them.

In the morning the high priest was meeting with the council.

"Call the prisoners!" he told the guards.

In a few minutes the men came running back.

"The prison was safely locked. The guards were on duty outside the door. But the prisoners are gone!"

Where was this thing going to end? While the council members were still trying to puzzle it out, someone burst into the room with the news that the prisoners were back again, teaching in the Temple. So, very quietly, for fear of what people might do, the captain of the Temple took his guards out to arrest the disciples.

Quietly the twelve walked back into the council room.

"Weren't you ordered not to teach in the name of that man Jesus? Are you trying to stir up trouble by saying we killed him?" the high priest demanded angrily.

Peter looked him in the eye. He said calmly,

"We have to obey God—not men. We have to talk about Jesus—whom you killed—for God has honored him as our Saviour. We have to talk about him because we were with him, and we know that he came to forgive us and save us."

At that the council members became so angry they began to plot how to have all twelve killed. But one member of the council, whose name was Gamaliel, stood up and began to speak to them.

"Men of Israel, be careful what you do. If these men are just working for themselves, the excitement will all die down. But if God did commission them, you will be fighting God if you keep on interfering."

The Jewish leaders realized that he spoke the truth. They decided to let the twelve go, with a whipping and another warning to stop talking about Jesus.

The twelve walked away, proud that they deserved to be punished for Jesus' sake.

And every day they went on teaching and preaching in their homes and in the Temple.

Acts 3 to 5

"They Laid Their Hands Upon Them"

A New Idea of Sharing

The people of the new church liked to be together, to do things together, and they shared whatever they had. No one must go hungry if a brother had food or money to share. Soon the members were selling land and houses and bringing the money to the twelve to be divided among the poor in the church.

A man named Ananias and his wife, Sapphira, saw what was going on. They heard the others being praised for bringing their gifts. So they sold some land, too, but they agreed to keep part of the money for themselves.

Ananias laid his gift before the twelve as if he said,

"Here it is, all of it."

But Peter knew.

"Ananias, why do you lie? Wasn't the land your own? When you sold it, wasn't the money yours? You have lied—not just to us; you have lied to God."

And Ananias, who thought he could cheat God, fell dead in front of them all.

Several hours later Sapphira came in. Peter asked,

"Tell me, did you sell your land for that money over there?"

"Yes, that's right."

"How could you plot to cheat God?" Peter accused her.

As suddenly as Ananias had died, Sapphira was gone.

Cold fear came on the members of the new church. It was no little thing to serve the Lord God in Jesus' name.

Acts 4:32–37; 5:1–11

Choosing the First Church Helpers

The twelve were busy men when the church was new. Teaching, preaching, healing the sick, taking care of the poor, they had more than they could do. And every day more people were coming into the church, more and more.

There came a small trouble over giving food to the poor. Greek-speaking Christians complained that Jewish widows were getting more than their share, while the others were hungry. The twelve called the church together to talk over the problem.

"Brothers, it does not seem reasonable for us to stop teaching and spend our time serving food. So you choose seven men whom you can trust, men who are wise and honest, who love God, whose hearts are full of his Spirit, and appoint them for the work of feeding the poor."

Everyone liked the idea, and so seven men were chosen: Stephen and Philip and Prochorus and Nicanor and Timon and Parmenas and Nicolaus. As the twelve laid their hands on the men's heads, they dedicated them to become servers and workers in the church. So the first helpers went to work.

And all the time the church was growing, growing.

Acts 6:1–7

Stephen, First to Die for Jesus' Sake

Stephen, whose faith was strong and whose heart was brave, was preaching to crowds of people every day. Some of the Jews, especially some men from Egypt and Syria and Asia, tried to get the best of him by arguing with him in public. But so wise he was, so strong because of the power of the Spirit, that he won every argument. So then his enemies hired men to say that he was saying evil things about Moses and about God.

Up until now most of the people had been friendly to the new church. But they began to get excited when they heard the rumors about Stephen, and they took sides with the wise old men and the scribes of the Jews, and they all helped to capture him and take him before the council.

The hired witnesses began to tell their lies again.

"This man keeps talking against our Temple and our law. We

ourselves heard him say that Jesus of Nazareth is going to destroy the Temple and change all the laws of Moses."

Everyone was watching Stephen, but all they could see was a man with the face of an angel.

"Is this true?" the high priest asked.

"Men—my brothers—my fathers—listen," Stephen began. Step by step he reminded them how the God of glory came first to talk to Abraham, then to each of their leaders and their prophets, to keep his people close to him. He told them how, ever since God had chosen the Hebrew people for his own, they disobeyed him and forgot him and insisted on having their own way.

"You killed the prophets! You killed Jesus himself, you murderers! Straight from the angels you had God's law to keep, to live by. But you would not have it. You fought against God's own Spirit."

The angry voices were louder now. The mob was shoving furiously, closer and closer.

Stephen stood quite still.

"I can see heaven opening, and there stands Christ himself, beside God," he said calmly.

At that they clapped their hands over their ears, and they shouted, and they ran him outside the city, beyond the high walls. There they stoned him, stone after stone hurtling down on him until he could not stand.

Kneeling, he prayed,

"Lord Jesus, take my spirit into your care." Then he cried out, "Lord, do not blame them for their crime."

Lovingly his friends buried his body, and sadly they mourned for him.

Now in the maddened crowd that killed Stephen was a young man from Tarsus, who had been a student of the teacher Gamaliel in Jerusalem. This young Saul hated everyone who criticized the teachings of the priests, hated the new teachers, hated the twelve, hated the people who crowded to join the new church. So when Stephen was dragged out to be killed, Saul just stood by, holding the coats of the men who hurled the stones and watching Stephen die.

Stephen's death was like an explosion. Now there was out-and-out war against the new church. Saul was busy going from house to house arresting believers and taking them off to jail.

As quickly as they could, the people of the church escaped, finding new homes outside Jerusalem, in Judea and Samaria. And everywhere they went they kept telling the good news about Jesus the Son of God. Only the twelve stayed on in Jerusalem.

Acts 6:8–15; 7; 8:1–4; 22:3

ADVENTURES IN JUDEA AND SAMARIA

The Greedy Magician

ALL THE TOWN was talking. Probably there had not been that much excitement since Jesus himself had met a woman by a well, and all the people of her village had learned to love him. Philip from Jerusalem was preaching good news. He was healing sick people. Lame folks were walking again.

Even Simon the magician was impressed. People were always most respectful when they spoke to Simon, for he was important. He said so himself, and they believed what he said, with all his tricks.

Simon and all the rest listened to everything Philip said about the kingdom of God and about being baptized. Gladly they believed him. Gladly they were baptized—even Simon, who kept watching Philip.

The news quickly traveled to Jerusalem, to those of the twelve who were still there. They sent Peter and John to help Philip. Now the very new believers in Samaria did not yet know the Holy Spirit in their hearts. But when Peter and John came, laying their hands on the heads of the believers, they felt the new, strange power that had come first to the believers in Jerusalem.

Simon wanted to be able to give people this power.

"Let me have the secret," he begged Peter. "See, I'll pay you well."

"You and your money! Do you think you can buy God's gift? You will have no share in it!" Peter exploded.

Simon the magician was a very important person. He said so himself. But now Simon the man was saying very quietly to Peter, "You pray to the Lord for me."

Acts 8:5–25

One Man from Africa

Philip went traveling on, for an angel messenger sent him down the road that led south to the desert country. Now it happened that an important man from Africa, treasurer at the court of the queen of Ethiopia, was on his way home from Jerusalem. And as he rode along in his chariot, he was reading from the book of the prophet Isaiah.

"Go on and speak to him," the angel urged Philip. So he went up to the chariot.

"Do you understand what you are reading?" he called.

"How can I, with no one to explain? Come on and ride with me," the stranger invited.

Philip did, and he glanced at the words the man had been reading:

> He was led like a sheep to be killed,
> Like a lamb at sheep-shearing time.
> He had no fair trial.
> And what of his family, his sons?
> He was never to have them, for he was taken
>   away from the earth.

"Who is he writing about—himself or some other man?" the stranger wanted to know.

So Philip began the story of the good news, of Jesus who went about doing good and who was killed without a fair trial. He told of the new believers who were being baptized for love of Jesus and in obedience to him.

© 1949, The Sunday School Board, S.B.C.   *Philip and the Traveler from Africa*

The stranger pointed to the side of the road.

"Why can't I be baptized in that water over there?"

"If you believe with all your heart, you may."

"I do believe! Christ is the Son of God."

One man from Africa. But he would take the good news home with him, on its way to the far countries of the world.

Acts 8:26–40

Murdering Saul—Brother Saul

Saul, proudest of the Jews, who was named for Israel's first king, had just one idea. Run them out! Kill them! Wipe out believers in Jesus, and destroy everything this Jesus of Nazareth ever said or did!

For in his heart he firmly believed that the only way to worship God was the old way; that the only teachings a man could believe were the teachings of the priests. And these who talked of a new way—the Way, they called it, remembering how Jesus had said, "I am the way"—must be hunted down and punished, all of them. Who could do that better than Saul, proudest of the Jews?

Saul asked the high priest for letters to all the synagogues in Damascus, with permission to arrest any refugees and bring them back for trial in Jerusalem. Then he headed north on the Damascus road.

Suddenly, just at noon, he was stopped by a light that was brighter than any light on earth. He heard a voice calling,

"Saul! Saul!"

Blinded by the light and shaking for fear, Saul stumbled to the ground.

"Why are you fighting me, Saul?"

"Who—who are you, Lord?"

"I am Jesus whom you are fighting. Saul, you can't fight against God."

"Lord, what must I do?"

"Get up. Go on into town. Someone will tell you what to do."

Slowly Saul stood up. He reached out groping hands in the dark. The men who were with him had seen no light, but they had heard a strange voice. Wondering and puzzled, they took him by the hand, and they led him to the home of a man named Judas.

For three days Saul stayed there. He could not see. He could not eat or drink. But in the darkness he prayed.

Not far away there lived a loyal follower of the Way, a man named Ananias. In a vision Ananias heard the Lord send him on a strange mission.

"Go to Straight Street, to Judas' house, and ask for Saul."

But Ananias objected.

"Lord, I've heard all about that man, all the harm he has done to your people in Jerusalem. Right now he has papers giving him the right to arrest anyone who even talks about Jesus."

"Go on, Ananias. Saul is praying now. He is the man I have chosen to go to the Gentiles for me, to the kings of the earth, and to the children of Israel. I am going to teach him what it will cost to work for me. Go on, so that he may get back his sight."

In his dark, lonely room Saul felt friendly hands touch him and heard a friendly voice say,

"Brother Saul! Our Lord Jesus has sent me to you."

The darkness was gone. Saul looked into the face of his new friend. And in his heart the dark and bitter hatred was gone. Instead there was joy and great peace and a new, fierce readiness to work for his Lord.

First he was baptized. Then he had something to eat. Gradually his strength came back, and he began to get ready for his work. Soon he was in the synagogue preaching.

"Jesus of Nazareth is the Christ, the Son of God."

People who heard him could hardly believe that Saul the persecutor had become Saul the preacher.

Saul just went on preaching. He knew that Jesus was the Christ, God's own Son, and he could prove it. Angrily the Jews turned against him, and they talked of killing him. The governor himself gave orders for his arrest, and guards watched the city gates day and night.

Someone reported to Saul that he was in real danger, and his new friends helped him to escape. One night they lowered him in a basket down the outside of the city wall. In the shadows he slipped away. For several years he stayed out of the country, living quietly somewhere in Arabia. When he came home he went to Jerusalem to join the believers and work with them. Just at first they were afraid of him. But Barnabas introduced him to the disciples, and he told them how Saul had met Jesus on the way to Damascus and now was preaching for Jesus instead of fighting the people of the Way as he had planned.

So Saul went to work, and everywhere he went people listened.

But he made enemies as well as friends. Soon he was preaching to a group of Greeks who became so angry they were ready to kill him. So friends helped him to escape, and he went home to Tarsus.

And now for a while the new churches had no more trouble. In Judea and Samaria and Galilee they were growing strong, and many were the new members who were learning the peace and the comfort and the splendor of the Way.   *Acts 9; 2 Corinthians 11:32–33; Galatians 1:11–18*

Healing in Jesus' Name

Peter traveled round the country visiting the people of the Way. One day when he was in Lydda he met a man who had not walked for eight years. Peter stood looking at the man's sick, shaking body, and he told him,

"Aeneas, Jesus Christ is curing you. Get up, and fold up your mat."

Right away Aeneas stood up, completely well.

The news spread quickly, and everywhere people were believing that all they heard about Jesus was true. He really was the Christ, the promised Son of God!

Over in Joppa by the sea the friends of good, kind Dorcas were meeting sorrowfully in her home.

"She spent her life helping other people," they were saying.

"She must have made coats for all the poor folks in town."

"She was always giving to someone else."

"Send for Peter!" one of the friends suggested. So the two men hurried to Lydda. Before long they were back, and Peter was with them.

The sorrowing friends took him upstairs to the room where Dorcas' body lay, and they showed him all the clothing she had been making.

Quietly Peter sent them outside. Then he knelt down beside Dorcas, and he prayed.

"Dorcas, get up," he said.

She opened her eyes. Then she recognized Peter, and she sat up. Gently Peter took her hand and helped her to stand. Then he called the friends back to welcome her. Afterwards, for a time, Peter stayed in Joppa by the sea with Simon. *Acts 9:32–43*

Peter's Discovery

Captain Cornelius was stationed in Caesarea. He was a Gentile soldier, with a regiment of Roman soldiers in his charge, but he and all his family worshiped the Lord God of the Jews. Generous he was with his gifts to the poor, and true to God in every way that he knew.

One afternoon he saw quite clearly the Lord's angel standing by him, and quite clearly he heard,

"Cornelius, the Lord God has been listening to your prayers, and he is remembering all your gifts. Now send your men over to Joppa to get Peter. They will find him in Simon's house by the sea. Peter is going to tell you what you should do."

So Cornelius chose two of his faithful household servants and one of his guards, who worshiped God, too, and sent them off to Joppa.

About noon the next day Peter was alone on the rooftop terrace, praying. He began to feel hungry, but before dinner was ready a strange thing happened. He seemed to see a great sheet lowered by four corners from the clouds to earth. In it he could see all kinds of creatures—four-footed beasts and crawling things and flying birds. He heard a voice saying,

"Peter! Get up! Kill something for your food, and eat."

Peter drew back in horror.

"Oh, no, Lord! Never in my life have I touched anything that is common or unclean."

Then he heard the voice saying, "What God hath cleansed, do not call common."

Peter had the same vision three times. Then, while he watched, the sheet disappeared in the clouds.

He was still wondering what it all could mean when he heard someone knocking at the door. The Voice that speaks to a man's heart was saying,

"Peter, three men are downstairs looking for you. Go on down and meet them. I have sent them myself, so don't hesitate to go with them."

So Peter welcomed the men, invited them to spend the night, and the next day he and six of the brothers accepted their invitation to go to Caesarea with them.

Cornelius' house was full of people, for he had invited all his family and his friends to meet his guest. And when Peter really stood in the doorway Captain Cornelius knelt before him.

"Stand up! I'm just a man." Peter stopped him at once. They walked in together to meet the guests, and Peter said to him,

"I came just as soon as I could, though by the laws of our priests I should not be here at all. But I knew God was sending me to you. Now tell me what you wanted."

Quickly Cornelius told him about the angel visitor.

"I see it now," Peter said. "It's all clear. God has no favorites among the people of the world. No matter who they are, if they are true to him and obey him, they belong to him.

"You have heard the story—people are telling it all over the country—how God sent the good news of his love by his own Son. You have heard how Jesus went from town to town teaching and helping people and healing the sick.

"I saw it all myself. I saw him when he was killed, and I saw him afterwards when he was alive again. I heard him tell us to teach and preach and tell the people how God planned it all long ago so that we might have a chance to be forgiven for our sins."

While he was talking it happened: The Holy Spirit came to be with all who were at Cornelius' house, and they felt the strength and love of Jesus in their hearts.

The Jews in the house could hardly believe what was happening. These Gentiles belonged to God, too!

Peter turned to his friends.

"Would any of you forbid these men to be baptized? The Holy Spirit has already come to them."

The news traveled fast to Jerusalem, and the rest of the twelve and the brothers began to worry. So when Peter came home they wanted to know what he meant by eating with Gentiles.

Peter told them the whole story. He ended with the discovery he had made.

"When the Spirit came to us there in Cornelius' house I remembered something Jesus told us:

"'John baptized with water. You shall be baptized with the Holy Spirit!' That was it—a baptism in the Holy Spirit. If God gives the Gentiles the same gift he gave us, who are we to hold back?"

It was true, then. God wanted Gentiles, too. For wonder at such love, they worshiped God, and they thanked him, all together.

Acts 10; 11:1–18

Nothing Could Stop Them

For several years neither the Roman government nor the Jews made trouble for the followers of the Way. Then King Herod began the persecution all over again. He killed James, who was John's brother, and when he saw how much that pleased the Jews, he plotted against Peter, too.

During the Passover celebration Peter was arrested. In a prison cell he was chained to two guards while fourteen other soldiers stood watch. That night he went to sleep. But in John Mark's home Peter's friends were awake, praying for him straight through the night.

Suddenly Peter was wide awake. Startled by a bright light, he could see an angel beside him. He felt a friendly tap on his side. He heard the angel say, "Get up quickly. Dress, and follow me."

Peter did as he was told, and the chains fell off his hands; but it all seemed like a dream. Out they went, past the first guards, then past the next. They came to the iron gate that opened into the city, and it swung wide open before them. They walked on down the street, and then Peter realized that the angel was gone.

Now he knew it was no dream. He was free! He headed straight for John Mark's house, and he knocked loudly at the gate. Rhoda the maid came running out to see who was there. But when she saw Peter she just stood there, too surprised to let him in. Suddenly she turned and raced back to tell the others.

"You're dreaming!" they laughed.

Peter kept on knocking. Finally they all went out to see the visitor. It could not be—but it was! There stood Peter, still knocking.

Quickly he told them what had happened. "Be sure to tell the brothers," he said. Then he slipped out of town. *Acts 12:1–19*

INTO ALL THE WORLD

The Church at Antioch

> If the trumpeter sounds afraid
> How will the army know to attack?
> This charge I give you:
> Fight the good fight as a soldier of Christ.

THE REFUGEES from Jerusalem were traveling. Some of them found homes in towns in Phoenicia. Some went to the island of Cyprus, and some went as far as Antioch, the capital of Syria. Wherever they went they were preaching and teaching the Way of Jesus the Son of God. They no longer preached just to the Jews. Now they were talking to Greeks and Romans, too, and everywhere they went they found people interested in the Way, asking whether they could belong, too.

Back in Jerusalem the church heard the news. The leaders were careful men. Just to make sure the traveling preachers were not making any mistakes, they decided to send Barnabas out to see.

Now Barnabas was a good man, brave in the Spirit of the Lord, and a faithful worker. Whatever he reported they would believe. As soon as Barnabas met the new friends in Antioch he knew that something wonderful was going on, and he decided to stay and help. But first he went to Tarsus to bring Saul back to help him.

For a whole year the two men worked together in the new mission in Antioch. And there in Antioch the followers of the Way were given a new name. Christians, they were called. Whether they were Jewish or Gentile, Greek or Roman, it made no difference. All were alike in the church of Antioch.

It was not long before the people of that church were doing something to show their love for other Christians. They decided to take up a missionary offering for the Jerusalem church.

Visitors had come to the Antioch church, and one of them was Agabus who could tell things that were going to happen. Hard times were coming, he reported. People all over the world would be hungry.

The people of the Antioch church thought first of all of their friends in Jerusalem who had already had so much trouble. So they brought their gifts, every man of them, as much as they could give. And when the relief fund was raised they sent it by Barnabas and Saul to the elders of the church in Jerusalem.

Acts 11:19-30; 1 Corinthians 14:8; 1 Timothy 6:12

Paul's First Missionary Journey

Praying, teaching, studying all the time to find out God's plans for them, the members of the Antioch church were the first to send out foreign missionaries. Plainly they had been hearing the Holy Spirit telling them,

"Send Barnabas and Saul away to do the work for which I have called them."

So they commissioned the men. After they prayed together they laid their hands on the heads of the two new missionaries and sent them on their way.

It was just a few miles down the valley to Seleucia where Paul and Barnabas and John Mark, who was chosen to be their assistant, found a boat ready to sail to the island of Cyprus, the home of Barnabas.

At first the missionaries preached just to the Jews in the synagogues, from Salamis where they landed, and on across the island till they came to Paphos on the western coast. There the governor himself, Sergius Paulus, asked to see them, for he was an understanding man who honestly wanted to know more about God.

But on the governor's staff there was a magician named Elymas who did his best to make Sergius Paulus get rid of the missionaries. Saul (who by now was known as Paul) stood his interference as long as he could. Then he burst out angrily,

"You child of the devil himself, how long will you try to get in the Lord's way! Blind you are, and blind you shall stay for a time."

That minute Elymas reached out gropingly for someone's hand, for all about him dark mist was swirling.

Nothing could stop the work of the men whom the Spirit of God was leading.

Next, Paul and the others sailed north to the mainland, then up the river to Perga on the coast of Asia Minor. About that time something happened to make John Mark decide to give up and go home. It looked to Paul like plain desertion. He and Barnabas kept on, going north to another Antioch.

On the sabbath day the missionaries went to the Jewish synagogue, and they listened to the reading from the Law and the Prophets. Then, because they were guests, they were invited to speak. This was the chance Paul had waited for.

He began by telling about the adventures of the Hebrew people in Egypt. He talked about the years they lived in Canaan, about the splendid kings of Israel, and about the prophets who used to tell of God's promise to send his Son into the world.

"Men of Israel, my message is for you! I am here to tell you the good news. The promise came true. But men murdered Jesus, the Son of God, in Jerusalem.

"He died for us. He took the punishment for all our sins, so that God can forgive everyone who believes. And God brought him back to us. The Lord Jesus is alive!"

The service ended, and the Jews went home. But the Gentiles could not wait a whole week to learn more, and they stayed to talk.

The next sabbath day nearly the whole city turned out to hear the missionaries. The Jews were furious. Gentiles and outsiders coming to the synagogue to hear about their God! As soon as Paul began to speak they shouted him down, arguing, contradicting whatever he said.

Paul and Barnabas stood there calmly, and they were not afraid. Something about the way they spoke hushed the shouting crowd.

"We had to come to you Jews first. But you yourselves have decided you don't deserve to be children of God. Now we are going to the Gentiles," Paul told them.

Light for the Gentiles! Salvation for the far corners of the earth! The Gentiles began to celebrate, thanking God for the good news that was coming to them. But the Jews stirred up their leaders, men and women both, and they drove Paul and Barnabas out of town.

So the missionaries headed eastward to Iconium in the mountains, about ninety miles away, and there things were not much better. But before the two pioneer missionaries had to leave town, there were always a few who listened and believed and went on teaching others what they had learned.

Quietly the two men slipped away from Iconium and went to Lystra. One day as they walked down the street they passed a lame man who had never walked in all his life. Something made Paul stop. He knew that this man had faith, faith enough to be cured.

"Stand up!" Paul called to him.

The man jumped to his feet. He took a step, and then another.

The people could hardly believe their eyes. They decided that their gods had come down to earth, walking just like ordinary people. They were sure that Barnabas was Jupiter, king of the gods, and that Paul was Mercury, his messenger. There must be a parade in their honor. They must prepare a sacrifice. They must worship their gods in the proper way.

"No! No!" Paul tried to stop them. "We are just men like you. We came here to teach you to throw away your idols. We came to tell you about the Lord God who made heaven and earth and sea and every living creature."

No matter what he said, the people of Lystra would not listen, and it was all Paul could do to keep them from praying to him and Barnabas.

Suddenly everything changed, for trouble-making men had followed the missionaries all the way from Antioch and Iconium. The first thing Paul knew the crowd turned on him, and stoned him till he fell to the ground. Thinking he was dead, the mob dragged him out of town.

But while his worried friends stood around him he slowly stood up. Then they all walked back to town together.

Lystra might not have seemed important. For all that is known, there was not even a synagogue in town. Paul and Barnabas probably taught in someone's home or out in the streets. But somewhere listening to the missionaries were people who were to be important to Paul and his work later on. Perhaps young Timothy's Greek father, or Lois, his Jewish grandmother, or Eunice, his Jewish mother, were listening. Perhaps young Timothy himself decided even then, "I am going to be a teacher, too."

For the next time Paul came that way Timothy was ready.

Now Paul and Barnabas headed back through all the towns they had visited, back to Attalia by the sea, to find a ship sailing for Antioch.

© 1957, The Sunday School Board, S.B.C.

Young Timothy

They had exciting news to tell when they got there, and the brothers crowded around to listen. Such wonderful things God was doing! So many people there were to help! So many new churches working for love of Jesus! And the Gentiles loved him, too.

Acts 13; 14

What About the Gentiles?

In Judea some people were saying that believing in Jesus was not enough to make a person a Christian. It was necessary to become a Jew, they said, and keep all the old Jewish laws as every good Jew was taught to keep them. Only then could a person become a Christian. It was as if you could earn your way into the family of God.

Now Paul and Barnabas and Peter and some of the other Christians had already discovered that God invites even Gentile people to come straight to him. The only requirement was belief that Jesus loved them enough to die for them and to trust him as their Lord and Saviour.

There were so many arguments, and the question was so important that the Antioch church sent Paul and Barnabas with several friends to talk it over with the Christians in the Jerusalem church. Then in Jerusalem the arguments began all over again. So the brothers and the elders of the church called a meeting.

First there was a long discussion, and some insisted that the old ways must be kept. Then Peter stood up and asked to speak.

"Brothers, you yourselves know that God told me to preach to the Gentiles. Now why should we try to make it harder for them? He himself sent them the Holy Spirit, just as he sent him to us. To God we are all alike.

"None of us could keep all the old laws ourselves. But we do believe that we were saved in spite of our sins by the love of Jesus we do not even deserve. So are they."

Quietly the men listened while Paul and Barnabas told about their adventures with the Gentiles. Then James said,

"Brothers, the Lord God intends to bring all the people of all the world into his church. We have no right to make it hard for them. I suggest that we ask them to follow Moses' teaching about the meat they eat and about keeping their bodies pure. That much of the Jewish law everyone should obey."

So the men wrote a letter and they sent it back by Paul and Barnabas, with Barsabbas and Silas from Jerusalem.

"Greetings to the Gentile brothers in Antioch and Syria and Cilicia:

"We have heard how you have been worried by teachers insisting you must be Jews first and then Christians. Our beloved Barnabas and Paul, who have often risked their lives to work for our Lord Jesus Christ, will tell you themselves that this is all we ask you to do: Eat no food that has first been offered to heathen idols. And keep your bodies pure and clean. Remember this, and all will be well."

Great was the joy in Antioch when the letter was read aloud. Now it was official: Gentiles, too, could become Christians by trusting Jesus as their Saviour. Nothing else was necessary.

Acts 15:1–35

The First Trip to Europe

All along the roads that Paul and Barnabas had traveled there were new churches now, some large and strong, some small and having a hard time. Paul was homesick to see again the members of these little churches. Barnabas wanted to go.

But there was trouble. Barnabas wanted to take John Mark

along. Paul could not agree to this. He could not forget that Mark had left them on their first trip. So the two friends decided to go on separate missions. Barnabas and Mark sailed for Cyprus. Paul chose Silas for his partner, and these two traveled north along the road to Derbe, then on to Lystra.

At Lystra the young man Timothy welcomed Paul. He had been working in the new church, studying, getting ready, and the brothers in Lystra and Iconium spoke well of him. When Paul needed another man for the team, Timothy was ready to go. Gladly he set out with Paul and Silas.

The mission began well. North the three missionaries would travel, on and on, farther and farther "into all the world." But something they did not understand was stopping them.

They would plan to go into a certain province, and then, clearly and plainly, God would let them know that they were not to go.

As long as the missionary team traveled west, Paul was sure that they were moving in the right direction. That was all he could be certain about.

Slowly, then, the three missionaries traveled west until they came to Troas, a town on the Aegean Sea. Just across the sea lay Macedonia in Europe.

While he was in Troas, Paul had a vision in the night. A man of Macedonia was calling to him, "Come over into Macedonia and help us."

So Paul, Silas, Timothy, and Dr. Luke, who had joined them, took a boat to Macedonia. The gospel was on its way to Europe.

Acts 15:36–41

The Friendly Jailer at Philippi

The first place the missionaries stopped in Europe was Philippi, the biggest city in Macedonia, where there was a Roman colony. Probably only a few Jews lived there, for Paul found no synagogue.

But he learned that there was a place of prayer outside the city wall, by the river.

So on the sabbath day the missionaries went out to the river bank. There they found a group of women meeting for prayer. And that was where Paul preached the first Christian sermon in Europe. Listening to every word he said was Lydia, whose business was selling purple cloth. Already she worshiped God. And as she listened she believed all that Paul was saying about the Son of God. So she asked to be baptized, with all her family.

"Now come and stay in our home," she invited the missionaries.

One day when Paul and the others were on their way to a prayer meeting, they heard shouting in the street behind them. People were hurrying from all around to see what was going on.

A poor half-crazy slave girl who made money for her masters by telling fortunes came running after Paul, and she was shouting,

"There go those men of the Most High God! They know the Way! They know the Way!"

Paul and the others just walked on faster. But the next day the same thing happened again. Every time Paul went out, there she was. At last he stopped beside her, and he looked straight into her eyes.

"Come out," he said sternly to the crazed spirit within her. "I command you in the name of Jesus."

From that moment she was quiet, sane as anyone else. And she no longer talked in the wild, queer way that her owners called fortune-telling. They would make no more money out of her. Then the trouble began.

They dragged Paul and Silas to court and turned them over to the magistrates.

"These Jews are making trouble. They are going around teaching Romans to do things they have no business doing," they charged. And all the people crowding round began to shout angrily.

© 1963, Broadman Press

Paul Talking with Lydia

"Have them whipped and lock them up," the magistrates ordered.

So the two were beaten, then dragged into the inside prison and locked up, with their feet held fast in the stocks. There all alone, their backs bruised and aching from the beating, they began to pray. By midnight they were singing their love for God, and in the outer cells the prisoners were listening.

Suddenly there was an earthquake. The ground began to rock and sway. Prison walls cracked. Locked doors were sprung open. Chains fell from every prisoner. Stocks lay broken and loose beneath their feet.

The jailer woke up from a sound sleep, and he was terrified. The earthquake did not worry him half so much as the open prison door. He knew the prisoners must have escaped, and he had failed in his duty. There was nothing to do but kill himself, and so he drew his sword.

"Don't!" Paul called out. "We are all here. Everything is all right."

"Get me a light," the jailer called. He was shaking with fear when he caught sight of Paul and Silas. Humbly he knelt on the floor.

"Gentlemen, tell me what to do. What must I do to be saved?" he begged.

"Believe in the Lord Jesus Christ, you and all your family. You will be saved," they began, and once more they told their story of the good news.

The jailer invited them into his own apartment so that his family could hear, too, and he washed their bruises himself and brought them supper. Then he and all his family asked to be baptized.

In the morning the magistrates sent the sergeants to free the prisoners. But Paul's face was stern.

"They beat us publicly, without a trial, and we are Roman citizens. They locked us up in jail, and now they want us to go away quietly. Tell them to come themselves and set us free."

This was a different matter. As soon as the magistrates heard that they had put Roman citizens in prison without a trial they came hurrying to the jail to apologize. Just the same, they begged the men to leave town for their own safety.

So Paul and Silas walked out of jail and went back to Lydia's house where they talked awhile with their Christian friends. And then they traveled on.

Acts 16

"The World Upside Down"

Now Paul and the others set out on their travels again, walking down the wide highway the Romans had built through Greece. A hundred miles from Philippi they came to the big city of Thessalonica, and there they went to stay with a man named Jason.

Paul began his teaching in the synagogue, and every sabbath for three weeks he taught that Jesus was the Saviour who lived and died and was alive again.

Quickly a group of Jews and Greeks and some of the important women of the town organized a new church. The missionary work was going well. Then Paul's enemies began to make trouble. They hired some of the tramps who were always hanging around the streets to start shouting and calling names, and soon an excited mob was milling around Jason's house, looking for Paul and Silas. When they could not find the missionaries, they dragged Jason and some of the new Christians before the magistrates.

"Here are these men who are turning the world upside down. They're going around saying that Jesus is king. Everyone knows what Caesar will say to that," was their charge.

The magistrates were worried about the riot, but they just made Jason and the others put up bond money to keep the peace and let them all go. That night Paul and Silas went quietly out of town. But they had left the beginning of a brave new church.

The missionaries hurried on to Berea, high in the hills, looking out over a beautiful valley. There they went straight to the synagogue, and they found the people friendly from the beginning. They wanted to learn, and every day they would meet to study all the Scriptures to see whether Paul was telling the truth. Many people, both Jews and Greeks, both men and women, believed him. Their new church began to grow.

But news traveled fast back to Thessalonica, and Paul's enemies came hurrying over to Berea to make trouble again. Quickly the brothers helped Paul to escape, and they went with him as far as Athens. Silas and Timothy were to come soon.   *Acts 17*

World Travelers and Letter Writers

While Paul waited for Silas and Timothy, he went sight-seeing, for Athens was the most beautiful city in Greece. Up and down the streets he walked, past temple after temple. He looked in horror at the statues of the gods—hundreds of them, at the doors of the temples and along the streets, statues and altars to every god man's mind could imagine. Athens was supposed to have more statues of gods than any other city in Greece.

© 1963, Broadman Press

Paul, Priscilla, and Aquila

Paul came to the market place, and there he stopped to listen to the talk. For there the teachers and the students met to teach and discuss, and the wise ones would argue with one another for hours at a time.

He went to the synagogue, as he always did, to talk to the Jews. Soon he, too, began to teach in the market place. People stopped to listen curiously.

"What's that fellow talking about?"

"Some new teaching—some new god. He keeps talking about Jesus."

Now the people of Athens were always interested in new ideas. So they invited Paul to come up to Mars Hill, up there where the highest court in all the land would meet, and tell them more.

Up on the hill Paul stood looking all about him. There were temples, large and small, statues of gods beyond counting. Before him, waiting, were the wisest men in the land.

"Men of Athens," he began, "I can see that you are very religious. You have altars and temples everywhere. I noticed one altar inscribed with these words, 'To the God No One Knows.'

"Men of Athens, I have come to tell you about him."

So Paul talked on, and he told the people how God, who is Spirit, made the world, created all the people of all the nations of the world, made them for his own, to be forever lonely until they discovered him.

The men of Athens listened politely. But when Paul declared that Jesus had risen from the dead, some burst out laughing.

"Foolishness! Foolishness!" They nodded their heads wisely.

Others said politely,

"Some other time you must tell us more." And they turned away from him to talk of other things.

Paul left no new church in Athens. But a few people believed him. There was the judge, Dionysius, there was the lady Damaris, and some others. Only a few. Because of the good they did and their love for Christ, Paul had not wasted his time in Athens.

Next, Paul hurried on to Corinth, the beautiful city between the seas, the city whose ships sailed to all the world. Corinth was bigger even than Athens. Paul found the city crowded with people —Greeks and Romans and Jews.

One family became Paul's good friends. Aquila and his wife, Priscilla, were tentmakers. Since that was the trade Paul had learned when he was growing up, they invited him to be a partner in their business.

At first Paul preached in the synagogue. Tired he was, and sick and lonely, too, in spite of having new friends. Then Silas and Timothy came to Corinth and they brought a gift of money from members of Paul's first European church for their beloved pastor. They brought good news, too. The new churches were working hard. The new Christians were true to their faith.

Now Paul went back to preaching every day. But his enemies shouted him down, and they cursed him, for hatred was in their hearts. It was enough for Paul.

"I have done my duty. From now on I am going to the Gentiles," he told them sternly, and he marched out of the synagogue.

He set up his headquarters in a house next door that belonged to Titius Justus, and there he went on preaching. But he knew what mobs of angry men could do, and he was worried.

One night something happened to give him courage to keep on.

He heard the Lord say to him,

"Stop being afraid, Paul. I am right beside you, and no one is going to harm you here. Go on with your work. There are many people in this city who belong to me."

Nothing could stop Paul now.

One day his enemies attacked Paul and brought him to the governor.

"We caught this fellow teaching people to worship God in ways our law forbids," they accused Paul.

"They are your own Jewish laws, not the laws of Rome. Take care of the matter yourselves," said the governor. And he dismissed the case.

Acts 17:16–34; 18:1–17

Letters to the Thessalonians

Nearly two years Paul stayed there in Corinth, teaching, preaching, writing letters to the friends he had made in the new churches along the way. He could not visit them now, and he missed them. But he could go on teaching them in his letters.

Paul dictated his letters, and one of his friends, usually Timothy, wrote them down. Sometimes he signed his name himself. Often Timothy would sign the letter, "From all of us," and Timothy or another friend would carry the letter all the long miles to the Christians in distant places.

While he was in Corinth, Paul wrote letters to the Thessalonian church.

May grace and peace be yours, from God our Father and from Jesus Christ.

I am always thinking of you, remembering how faithfully and lovingly you have been working. You set an example to the whole country, and the news of what you are doing traveled faster than I could tell about you.

You welcomed me, brothers, and you gave me courage to tell you of God's good news, though I had just had such a hard time in Philippi. I tried never to be any trouble or expense to you. I worked at my trade from early morning till late at night, for I believe whoever will not work does not deserve to eat.

You remember I warned you that I would have trouble wherever I went, and trouble I have had. But now that Timothy tells me you want to see me as much as I want to see you, all I need to know is that you are faithful and true. I had to leave you before I was ready to go, and I have often wanted to go back and visit you. For I love you the way a father loves his children.

Keep living as I taught you. I don't need to remind you to love one another. You do that already. Just keep on loving more and more.

Children of light you are, not confused in the dark any more. So keep busy working all the day. Tend to your own affairs so that outsiders can find no fault with you. Listen well to your teachers. Live peacefully together. Help all who are not as strong in their faith as you are. If men treat you badly, pay them back by helping them. Keep on giving thanks to God for everything.

Ask questions. Find out for yourselves what is true. Don't believe everything you hear.

Remember that the Lord keeps his promises, and he will keep you strong, keep you safe from evil.

Read my letter to all the brothers, for I send you all my love. Remember to pray for us.

Now I pray that God will send me back to you. May he give you love in your hearts for all men, as much as I have for you. May he keep you holy in your love for him.

      Paul—I have signed my name myself—
      and Silas and Timothy

From 1 and 2 Thessalonians

Magicians and Mobs

From Corinth Paul headed back to Jerusalem. His friends, Aquila and Priscilla, went with him as far as Ephesus. There the Jews begged him to stay with them, but he hurried on, for he wanted to be at the Jerusalem church in time for the Feast of Pentecost and report on the work he had done.

"I will come back if the Lord lets me," he promised.

And so he did, and for about three years he worked there in Ephesus.

"The City of the Goddess Diana," people called Ephesus. Here a temple had been built for the worship of the goddess. Inside the temple there was a huge statue of Diana. After the people had bowed in worship before the statue, they would buy small silver statues to take home with them.

At first Paul had no trouble in Ephesus, but it was not long before enemies made him stop teaching in the synagogues. So he moved to a school run by a man named Tyrannus, and there he taught for two years.

Crowds came from far and near, from the country towns, from all the streets of Ephesus to hear Paul preach and watch him heal the sick "in Jesus' name."

Some of the Jewish magicians decided he must know a good trick, and they thought they would try it. One day they visited a man whose crazed evil spirit made him sick in mind and body.

"In the name of Jesus whom Paul is preaching about—come out of him," the magicians ordered.

Madness flamed in the poor man's eyes, and a voice that was not his own shouted,

"Jesus I know, and Paul I know. But who are you?" And with a crazed man's strength he attacked the magicians and ran them out of the house.

The story spread quickly. Something about Jesus was stronger than any charms in the magicians' books. First the men were frightened. Then they came hurrying to learn. After they listened to Paul they gathered up all their books of magic, and out where everyone could see, they made a huge bonfire of them. The old ways were going. Men were choosing the new Christian Way instead.

Paul's work was going well, but he could not rest.

"I must travel on, back to Macedonia, to Greece. And then I must see Rome," he would say. How were the friends in Macedonia? Were the churches growing? Were the people generous with their gifts for the poor folks back in Judea? He could not leave Ephesus to find out. So he sent young Timothy with Erastus to see how things were going.

Paul preached day after day, "Gods made by men's hands are not gods." So people who listened and believed were throwing away their little silver images of Diana.

Demetrius, whose business was making the little Dianas, was worried, and he called a meeting of the other silversmiths. Business was very bad, they agreed. Why, this fellow Paul would stop at nothing. People were not buying. They would be deserting Diana's beautiful temple next.

Angrily the men dashed out of the house.

"Diana! Diana! Great is Diana of the Ephesians!" they shouted, up one street and down the next. People came running from every direction. No one was quite sure what it was all about, but soon the people were shouting, running this way and that. Someone discovered two friends of Paul's who had been traveling with him, and they dragged them into the big outdoor theater. Paul tried to rescue them, but his friends begged him not to risk his life.

No one knew just what the riot was about. They were all shouting all kinds of things, and everyone was confused.

Someone in the crowd saw Alexander, a Jew, who was the town

clerk. Alexander was just the person to settle all this trouble.

"Go on. They will listen to you." Someone pushed him forward.

Alexander stood quietly, one hand raised, to get the crowd's attention.

"He's a Jew!"

"Diana! Diana! Diana!"

Alexander waited. Now they were quieter.

"Men of Ephesus, everyone knows your city guards the temple of Diana. No one argues about that. Now if Demetrius or any of these craftsmen has a case against any man, the law courts are open. Let them make their charge in the usual way. We are in danger of getting into serious trouble with Rome over this affair today, and we will not be able to give any reason for what is going on."

The mob began to quiet down. Slowly people went home.

Acts 18:18–22; 19; 20:1

Letters to the Corinthians

After the riot in Ephesus Paul decided to go back to Europe to visit his friends in the churches. Quickly he said good-by, and with several friends he slipped out of the city. The missionaries stopped on the way to preach at Troas. Then on they went across the sea to Philippi. There Timothy and Titus met them with good news. The people of the church in Corinth were working hard. They were growing up as Christians instead of acting like children.

Paul smiled, remembering them. There had been some trouble there in Corinth. Paul was thinking of the letter he would write them—a long postscript to a first rather stern letter he had written probably months before from Ephesus. Titus and Luke and Trophimus would deliver the letter for him.

Paul sent these words in the two letters to his friends in the church at Corinth.

My Body—God's Temple

Don't you know that the Spirit of God lives in you? You belong to him, not to yourselves. You are the temples of the living God. "I will live with you and walk with you," says the Lord God. "I will be your God, and you will be my people. I will be your Father, and you shall be my sons and daughters."

You know how an athlete keeps training, obeying the rules so he can win the race. He does it to win the prize—a crown of leaves that will dry up and crumble. The prize we must win lasts forever. This is why I keep training myself, temperate in everything I do. I would not teach others the way to race, and break the training rules myself.

Be careful! Just when you are sure you could not do anything wrong is the very time you are likely to stumble. Just remember that you are not the only ones who ever had trouble. Everyone is tempted to do wrong. But God will not let you be tempted without showing you a way to escape. You can fight any temptation that comes to you, for God is your faithful helper. Be on your guard! Keep your faith strong! Be courageous. Act like men!

I Corinthians 6:19–20; 9:24–27; 10:12–13; 16:13

Love Is the Best Gift

We work together with God. We work in different ways. For God has given us different skills. Some of us are wise and understanding. Some of us study and learn easily. Some of us have great faith. Some of us are good doctors. Some of us are missionaries. Some are teachers. Whatever our special gifts are, we work together for Christ's church the way our hands and feet and eyes all work together in our bodies. Of course we all would choose the best talents for ourselves. But there is something more important we all can have.

I may be able to speak in every language or talk like the angels themselves. But if I have no love in my heart, I sound like a noisy trumpet or tinkling cymbals.

I may be able to understand all the secrets of earth and heaven. I may have faith enough to do anything. But if I have no love in my heart, I amount to nothing at all.

I may give everything I have to feed the poor, but unless I give with love in my heart, giving does no good.

Love is very patient, very kind. Love never says, "Give me what you have." Love is not proud. Love is very quiet, very kind. Love never tries to get its share, does not get angry over little things. Love does more than its share—believes and hopes and keeps on loving. Love never gives up.

Love lasts forever. When I was a child I used to talk and think and understand like a child. But I am a man now, and I am through with the ways of a child. We have so many things to discover. Now we see things as if we were looking in a mirror, dimly. Some day we shall see clearly, face to face, and we shall be putting away some of the things we think are important now, as a man puts away childish things.

But faith and hope and love will last forever. And greatest of them all is love.

So put love first when you pray for gifts from the Spirit of God.
1 Corinthians 3:9; 12:4–11,28; 13; 14:1

Paul's Story of the Lord's Supper

This is how the Lord's Supper began. I tell you the story as I learned it from the Lord Jesus himself.

The night he was arrested he was having supper with his disciples. When they had finished he picked up the bread. First he gave thanks to God, and then he broke it and divided it among the disciples.

"Take this and eat it, remembering how my body was broken for you," he said.

Next he took up the cup.

"This is the new covenant promise between God and man, made for you by my death," he said. He passed the cup to the disciples and said, "Drink this, remembering me." For whenever you eat this bread and drink this cup you are telling about the Lord's death until he comes again.

1 Corinthians 11:23–26

I Know That Jesus Is the Christ

First of all I told you what I learned, how Christ died because of our sins, how he was buried, and how he lived again, just the way the prophets said it would happen. Peter saw him first, then the other disciples, and then more than five hundred people saw him at once. Some of them are still alive. James saw him. So did all the apostles. And then I saw him, too, least of all the apostles though I am. Not that I deserve to be called an apostle after fighting him as I did.

But by God's love I have become what I am today.

1 Corinthians 15:1–10

The Gift for the Jerusalem Church

Let me tell you about the gift for the poor people of the Jerusalem church. I have already told the churches in Galatia about it.

You do so many things well. Your faith is strong. You know how to talk about your trust in Christ. You work hard. You have shown your love for me. Now be ready to give as generously as God has given to you.

The first day of every week each of you put away some money. Then when I come you will have the fund ready. Be thinking whom you want to send to Jerusalem with your gift. Perhaps we can travel together.

Let your hearts tell you how much to give. Don't give unwillingly or just because you think you should. God loves a joyous giver. For your gifts do more than help people who need help. They are a way to show your thanksgiving to God.

>Farewell, brothers.
>I pray to God that you do no wrong.
>Live in peace.
>May God's love and peace be with you.

2 Corinthians 9; 13:11–14

No Rules Against Love

It was hard for many of the strict Jews to give up the old ways of thinking. They would not listen when Paul came telling of God's love, and after Paul traveled on they would insist that the new people of the Way must keep all the rules of the old law if they would please God.

To his friends in the towns of Galatia Paul wrote a letter. First he told them why he had a better right than their leaders had to teach them Christ's way. Then he taught them over again how the Christian is forever free.

Here are some of the messages Paul wrote in his letter to the Galatians.

>Children must obey rules, because they must be taught what to do.
>You must not pray to idols.
>You must not hate.
>You must not quarrel.
>You must not kill.

You must not, you must not, said the Law. How else can you please God?

Try as hard as we would, we could never keep every law, every "you must not." For something in us was forever liking to do the things that were forbidden.

When the time came, as God had planned it, and we were ready to learn more, God sent his Son to live in the world, to show us how to live. Believing him and wanting to live like sons of our Father, our sins forgiven and forgotten, we are forever free because now we are different. This is God's gift.

We are free to be patient and gentle, faithful, good, self-controlled, happy, free to love one another. There are no "you must not's" against this way of living—the way of love we learn by believing, trusting the Son of God.

We are free to love a neighbor, warning him as a friend when he does wrong, remembering we could be tempted, too. Free to give him all the help he needs. Free to help carry a neighbor's burden, but keeping on carrying our own load, too, for being tired is no excuse for giving up.

Before God gave us his Gift to bring us close to him, we were like children going to school. Laws were our teacher. But now we are free to live the way Christ gave us, all of us, Jews and Gentiles, men and women, in every land throughout the world.

From the Letter to the Galatians

Paul's Letter to the Romans

For months the missionaries traveled on. Sometimes they stopped in towns where there were no churches. When they came back to Corinth, Paul was thinking more and more about Rome. The work was going well, but he wanted to push on, farther and farther west, to preach at last in the biggest city in the world.

So he wrote a letter to the people of Rome, a message we call the Letter to the Romans. He gave it to his good friend Phoebe, who was traveling that way herself.

> To all of you in Rome whom God has chosen for his own:
>
> I am thanking God for you because wherever I go I hear about your faith. For a long time now I have been trying to come to you, for I have always been wanting to be a pioneer in places where there are no churches. So when I set out for Spain I plan to come to Rome.
>
> First I must go back to Jerusalem with the gifts from Macedonia and Greece for the poor. There may be danger, for I have many enemies in Judea. You be praying that God will protect me.
>
> I used to preach just to the Jews. But I have so much to tell all the world, Jews and Gentiles both. So I must come to you in Rome.
>
> For whoever calls to the Lord, believing, having faith, will be saved. You see, faith comes with hearing, and hearing comes with preaching the Word of God. But how can people call to him if they have never believed? How can they believe if they have never heard? How can they hear without a preacher?
>
> We are all alike. We have all sinned. None of us has measured up to God's glory. I know how it is myself. I try to do right, but I fail. I find myself doing the evil things I hate. How can I get rid of this sin in my heart? I know that no matter how much sin there is, there is always much more of the forgiving love of God that we could never deserve.
>
> While we were still doing wrong, God showed how much he loves us, for he gave us his Son to take the punishment for our sin in our place. For the punishment for sin is death. But God's gift is life to everyone who believes in Jesus.
>
> Here we are, then, adopted children of the Father's family, and if God is on our side, who can be against us? For we know

that all things work together for good for us who love God and trust his will for us.

Who could ever hurt us? Could anything keep us away from Christ—troubles or disgrace or hunger or cold or danger or war? No, I am sure that no matter what happens we are safe with him. For I know that nothing can separate us from God's love—not death, not life, not angels, nor the law, nothing that is happening now or is going to happen, not the highest mountains or the deepest oceans, not anything in all the world can come between us and God's love.

Now, my brothers, don't try to live like everyone else, but keep your minds on living his way. Keep your bodies clean and strong. You will be using them in his service. Live together lovingly, without cheating, without pretending. Be glad when you can give someone else the first place. Keep busy. Share generously with the others of the Way. Be quick to share your friends' happiness. Sympathize with them when they are in trouble.

Never pay back evil for evil. Never try to get even. Revenge is God's affair, not yours. Don't let evil beat you, but get the best of evil with love. And if you possibly can, live peacefully with everyone. Respect your government. Pay your bills, for all that you should ever owe anyone is love.

Our friend Phoebe is bringing this letter. Many a time she has helped me. So give her any help she needs while she is with you.

Give my greetings to my friends, Aquila and Priscilla. They have often risked their lives for me, and I am grateful. My greetings, too, to the members of the church that is meeting in their house and to all my other friends in Rome.

May the grace of our Lord Jesus Christ be with you.

Paul, Christ's servant

From the Letter to the Romans

On to Jerusalem

Paul wanted very much to stay near Ephesus to see his friends again. But there was not much time, for he felt he must be in Jerusalem with the love offering from the churches before the Pentecost feast began. So he sent word to the leaders in the church at Ephesus asking them to meet him when the ship docked at Miletus.

Gladly they hurried down to see him, though Miletus was thirty miles away. Paul had much to tell them, for somehow he knew that he would not be seeing them again. Soberly they listened while he said a last good-by.

"You know how I have worked for you with all my heart, humbly and patiently in spite of all the Jews tried to do. You remember how I taught you in your homes and in meetings, Jews and Greeks. Believe in our Lord Jesus Christ, I told you.

"Now I am going to Jerusalem. I do not know what is going to happen, but God warns me there will be trouble. My own life does not matter to me. The one thing I must do is to keep on telling about God's love—as I heard it myself from the Lord Jesus.

"I know that after I am gone you will be having trouble. Bad teachers will come after your people like wolves hunting sheep. Guard these sheep well, for the Lord Jesus died for them, and the Holy Spirit put them in your care.

"All the time I have been with you I have been working to earn my own living instead of taking money from you, for I remember how the Lord Jesus said, 'It is more blessed to give than to receive.' I have tried to teach you that the strong must take care of the weak."

Then he told his friends good-by, and they all walked with him to his ship.

Acts 20:13–38

THE PREACHING PRISONER

Arrested in the City of Peace

"Don't go to Jerusalem!" Everywhere Paul went, his friends were warning him. In Tyre they tried to stop him. When he was staying in Philip's house in Caesarea a visitor from Judea tried to tell him he was sure to be captured if he went on to Jerusalem. Then Luke and all the rest begged him not to go.

But on to Jerusalem Paul went, and his friends just shook their heads and said, "The Lord's will be done."

Friends and enemies both were waiting in Jerusalem for Paul and the other missionaries. There was much excitement in James' house the day all the Christians listened while the travelers told of their adventures in the lands across the seas.

"The Jews are saying you are teaching that no one needs to keep the old ways or obey the laws of Moses," James warned.

So just to prove he was still a loyal Jew, Paul decided he would go at once to the Temple, along with four other Jews who were going for a special ceremony. The Jews who hated Paul were waiting.

"We saw him with that man from Ephesus right here in Jerusalem," they whispered.

"Paul's with a man from Ephesus," the rumor spread.

"Paul's going around with a foreigner."

"Paul brought a foreigner into the Temple!"

"Foreigners in the Temple!" someone shouted. "Men of Israel! Help!"

People came running from every direction. Rough hands grabbed Paul and dragged him outside. The Temple doors slammed behind them. The mob would have beaten Paul to death on the spot if the Roman captain had not heard the noise. He hurried to the Temple with his guard, and he ordered Paul's arrest.

"Who is this man? What has he done?" he demanded.

They all began to shout at once. So the captain ordered his men to take Paul quickly into the castle where he would be safe.

"Take him away! Away!" the mob in the street was shouting.

Halfway up the stairs Paul stopped.

"May I speak to you?" he asked the guard, using the Greek language.

"Do you know Greek? I thought you were that troublemaker from Egypt."

"I am a Jew and a citizen of Tarsus. I ask your permission to speak to these people."

The captain nodded. Quietly Paul raised his hand. The noisy mob was still. Now Paul was speaking in Hebrew.

"I am a Jew, born in Tarsus, but I went to school here in Jerusalem. Gamaliel was my teacher. I learned the strict law of our fathers, and I fought for it as you are fighting now. I fought the people of the Way, and I arrested them and turned them over to the high priest."

They listened while he told them what happened on the Damascus road, how he heard a voice he had to obey, and how, ever since, he had been following God's directions, even the order, "I send you to the Gentiles."

Then the shouting began all over again.

"Take him away! He's not fit to live. Take him away!"

What had the fellow really done? The captain had to know. So he gave orders for Paul to be whipped till he confessed.

They tied him up.

"Can you whip a Roman citizen who has not had a fair trial?" Someone whispered,

"Captain, be careful. The man really is a citizen."

And then the captain was afraid. But he had to find out what his prisoner had done. So he decided to ask the council of the Jews to examine him.

The next day Paul stood before the council. But, before the wise men of the Jews could question him, they fell to arguing among themselves, and so angry they grew that the captain sent his guard to rescue Paul and escort him back to the castle.

That night Paul could feel the Lord close beside him.

"Don't be afraid, Paul. You have been my witness in Jerusalem, and you will go on to teach in Rome." *Acts 21:1 to 23:11*

The Governor's Prisoner

In the morning Paul's enemies made their plot. They would ask the captain to bring Paul back for questioning, and then before ever he reached the council they would kill him. They swore they would not eat nor drink till that was done.

But Paul's nephew discovered the plot, and he hurried to warn his uncle. Paul sent his nephew to the captain with the news and quickly the captain gave his orders. So that night two hundred soldiers, seventy horsemen, and two hundred armed guards were to escort Paul as far as Antipatris on the way to Governor Felix's headquarters at Caesarea. In the morning the horsemen would take him the rest of the way.

So Paul became a prisoner of the governor.

"I will try you when your accusers come," said the governor.

Five days later Ananias, the high priest, appeared before the governor with some of the councilmen and a lawyer.

"The man's dangerous," they told Felix. "He travels around the world stirring up revolutions. He's a ringleader among those Nazarenes. He tried to bring foreigners into the Temple. You question him and you'll see, Governor."

Governor Felix asked Paul to speak.

"I did not quarrel with any man," he said. "Nor did I try to stir up trouble. They cannot prove their charge. But I do confess I follow the Way, and I serve the God of our fathers."

Felix was interested, for he knew something of the Way. But he wanted to keep the friendship of the Jews. So he decided that he would hold Paul as his prisoner and make up his mind later what to do about him. Besides, he was thinking, Paul might offer him a bribe in return for his freedom.

Days went by. Then Felix sent for Paul. He and his wife Drusilla wanted to hear more about the Lord Jesus.

So Paul began. The Way meant giving up lying and cheating and stealing. The Way meant no more drunkenness. The Way meant justice for all—no more taking bribes from the rich and punishing the poor who had no bribe money.

Governor Felix, who had a way of doing just those things, looked uncomfortable. The great governor was actually afraid.

"Enough! Stop! I'll hear you some other time when it is more convenient."

Two years went by. A new governor was sent by the Roman emperor to take the place of Felix. Paul was still in prison.

The first time the new governor, Festus, went to Jerusalem, the chief priest lost no time telling him all about Paul.

"Have the man sent back here for a trial," he suggested, knowing well that the Jews would kill him on the way.

"The trial will be held in Caesarea. You will go there and accuse him," said the governor.

The day came at last for Paul's hearing. Enemies from Jerusalem were ready to make all kinds of false charges against him. This was Paul's defense:

"I have not broken the laws of the Jews, nor of the Temple, nor of Caesar."

Governor Festus thought he saw a good chance to make the Jews his friends.

"Are you willing to go back to Jerusalem and let the Jews try you?" he asked Paul.

Paul had thought it all over. If he went to Jerusalem the Jews would surely kill him. But as a Roman citizen he had the right to ask for a trial in Rome before the emperor Augustus Caesar. Besides, Rome was the very place he wanted to go. He longed to preach about Jesus in the largest city in the world.

"I appeal to Caesar," he said.

"Then to Caesar you shall go."

Acts 23:12 to 25:12

Preacher to the King

Not long after Paul made his appeal to be tried before Caesar, King Agrippa came with the Lady Bernice to visit the governor. Festus reported to the king about his strange prisoner, for Paul's case was puzzling him.

"The men who accuse him talk only about their religion, about someone named Jesus. Paul insists this Jesus is still living, though everyone knows he was condemned to die on the cross. I cannot find out what Paul is supposed to have done, and I hardly know how to report to Caesar."

"I would like to hear him myself," said the king.

So the next day, with much ceremony, Agrippa and Bernice came into the governor's hall, where the captains of the guard and the leaders of the city were waiting with the prisoner.

"You are permitted to speak for yourself," Agrippa told Paul.

Paul stood quietly for a moment. Then, reaching out his hand toward the king as if he had something special to tell him, he began,

"I am happy to defend myself before you, King Agrippa. You know the ways and the customs of the Jews so well yourself. Listen to my story."

He talked about growing up in a strict Jewish family, going to school and studying as a Jewish lad should. He told how he had been sure that he must fight one called Jesus of Nazareth until the day he met him in a blinding light on the Damascus road, and he heard his marching orders,

"Stand up, Paul. Go and teach where I shall send you."

"So, King Agrippa, I was not disobedient. In Damascus, in Jerusalem, and in all Judea I would go first to the Jews and then to the Gentiles. I told them just what Moses and the prophets had been saying—how God's Son, the Christ, must suffer for his people and die, and how, when he lived again, he would bring light to Jews and Gentiles both."

There it was again, that talk of a man being alive after he had died.

"Paul, you're mad. You have studied so much that your mind is gone," the governor broke in.

"Your excellency, I am not mad. I speak the truth as I believe it. The king knows what I am talking about. King Agrippa, you do believe the prophets, don't you?"

Slowly the king answered him,

"Paul, you almost persuade me to be a Christian."

"I wish that you and everyone listening here could be just like me—except for these chains."

Quickly the king and Bernice and the governor all stood up and walked out of the room.

"That man is not guilty," said one.

"He might have gone free if he had not appealed to Caesar," said the king.

Acts 25:13 to 26:32

Shipwrecked in a Northeaster

Captain Julius was in charge of the prisoners bound for Rome. North they sailed in a small ship, along the coast to Sidon, and while they stopped, Julius allowed Paul to go ashore to visit his friends.

Next, the ship sailed for Myra, where the passengers changed to a ship from Egypt loaded with a cargo of grain. There was time to reach Italy before the winter storms made sailing dangerous, and all the ships would anchor in the nearest port. But day after day went by, and there was scarcely enough wind to fill the sails. Time was running out. Finally the ship managed to reach Crete and dock at Fair Havens.

Paul was worried, and he begged Julius to persuade the ship's owner and her captain to stop here for the winter. But the harbor was very small. Besides, everybody was in a hurry to get to Rome. At least they could try to make Phoenix, at the eastern end of the island of Crete. And when the wind began to blow gently from the south they were sure they were right. So the captain gave orders to weigh anchor and sail close to shore.

They had hardly left Fair Havens when the northeaster swept down on them, driving them westward until they came to the shelter of a small island. They stopped just long enough to lower the small boat and run heavy ropes beneath the ship, trying to hold the timbers in its storm-beaten hull tight against the sea.

They could not stay where they were, for the wind would drive them straight on the quicksands of Africa. Overboard went the sacks of grain, to lighten the ship. Overboard went baggage and tackle. No sun shone, and no stars by which a seaman could guide his ship. Day and night and day and night the little ship tossed and pitched. The hungry crew and the prisoner passengers gave up hope. Then one morning one of the prisoners took charge.

"Gentlemen, if you had listened to me and stayed in Crete, all this would not have happened," he could not resist saying. "But everything will be all right," he said quickly. "We cannot escape being shipwrecked. But we shall be safe. I know it now. This very night I saw the angel of God, whose I am and whom I serve, and he told me I am to appear before Caesar and that God has granted me the lives of every one of you."

Day and night, day and night for two weeks the ship floundered on, and then one night the sailors picked up the sound of booming breakers on a beach. Land was near. They dropped four anchors from the stern to try to hold the ship from crashing on the rocks along shore. It was all they could do till daylight came.

But the sailors would not wait for morning, and they tried to lower the small boat from the bow, pretending they were going to drop more anchors. Paul discovered them just in time and reported to Julius and the guards.

"Unless we all stay on the ship we don't have a chance," he warned.

The guards cut the ropes, and the empty boat dropped into the water. Now it was beginning to grow light.

"You need some food. Come on. Not one of you will be harmed." Paul picked up a piece of bread, and he gave thanks to God for it. One by one they reached for some bread, and now they were more cheerful. When they had finished their breakfast, they threw overboard all the wheat they could spare. The ship must be as light as they could make it if she was to ride the breakers and get to land safely.

When daylight came, they could see a bay and a beach. Was it the time to run the ship aground?

They cast off the anchors. They hoisted the foresail, and they headed toward the beach. But the cross currents of the seas caught the ship and hurled her ashore. The bow held fast in the sand, and the waves began to pound the stern.

"The prisoners! They'll swim ashore and escape! Kill them quickly!" shouted the guard. But Paul's captain friend would not have it.

"All of you who can swim—overboard! The rest of you find planks and float ashore."

And so they landed on the island of Malta.

A cold rain was falling. People of the island came running to the beach to help the shivering men build a fire. Now it happened that Paul had picked up a bundle of sticks to throw on the fire, when a small snake crawled up on his hand.

"Look! He must be a murderer. He may have escaped from the sea, but he'll be punished now," people were whispering.

Paul quietly shook the snake off in the fire. The people stared. His hand should be swelling. He should be falling down—dying.

"He is a god!" they whispered.

Now Publius, who was an important man on the island, invited the shipwrecked travelers to his home, and for three days they ate and slept and rested. Paul discovered that Publius' father was very sick with a high fever. Praying for God's healing and laying his hands on the sick man, Paul cured him. News spread fast on the island. Soon others were bringing their sick to him to be healed.

Three months later it was safe to go to sea again. Honored by the islanders, laden with gifts and supplies, Paul and Dr. Luke and their guards boarded a ship bound from Egypt for Rome. The south wind sped them north, and they landed at Puteoli on the Bay of Naples. There the brothers of the Way were waiting to welcome Paul, and the news traveled fast to Rome,

"Paul is coming."

Acts 27:1 to 28:14

In Rome at Last

Out the Appian Way friends hurried to meet Paul. And so he came at last to Rome. Knowing that he had friends there in the great city, he thanked God. What was there to fear?

Three days later he was settled in his quarters, in a house he was allowed to rent. With his soldier-guards on duty night and day, he invited the Jewish leaders to visit him.

"I am a prisoner because of enemies at home," he told them. "I have done nothing wrong. I have broken no laws of our people. But the Jews accused me. The Romans would have set me free, but the Jews would not allow that. So I had to appeal to Caesar."

"We have received no letters. None of our brothers have reported you to us," they said. "Tell us what you are teaching. Everyone is talking against the people of the Way."

So they set a day, and a crowd of people came to Paul's house to hear him. Some of them believed him, and some would not. They could not agree, and when they went home Paul said,

"How wise Isaiah was when he said:

> 'Go to those people and say,
> You will hear, but you will not understand.
> You will see, but you will not discover.
> Your hearts are dull, your ears are deaf,
> Your eyes are closed. For if you should see,
> If you should hear, if you should understand,
> And turn around and come home to me,
> I would heal you.'

"This message is for the Gentiles. They will hear!"

Acts 28:15–31

Letters from a Prisoner

Two years Paul lived there in Rome. He preached and he taught and he welcomed everyone who came to see him. Never for a minute was he afraid. Though he was not allowed to go out where he could preach to crowds of people, he could have visitors in his house. And, though he was guarded by soldiers, no one objected to his teaching.

Friends came to see Paul with messages from faraway churches. He could write letters to the people he could no longer visit, and Timothy and Mark and Luke helped him. Some Christian on his way to far lands would deliver Paul's letters.

One day Tychicus, who was one of Paul's best friends, left

Letter to Philemon

Paul's home on an important mission. In his traveling bag he carried letters. Across the sea he would go, back to the old friends of the Way.

One of the letters was addressed to the people of the Colossian church, one of the places Paul had never visited. But Colossian people had traveled far to hear Paul preach, and then they had gone home to build their own church in a city where people worshiped many, many gods.

> Though I am far away from you, I am close to you in my love, and I am grateful to God that you belong to the Lord Jesus Christ who came to show us what God is like.
>
> Now that you know Jesus, live like him. You have put away your angry ways and your lying speech. Be patient, loving, forgiving. Whatever you do, in your words or your actions, do everything for the Lord with all your hearts.
>
> Don't let anyone teach you to trust in other gods. Christ alone will give you all you will ever need, for God has given him the power and the glory.
>
> Dr. Luke and Mark and the others all send you their greetings.

The second letter was addressed to Philemon, who lived in Colossae. The church used to meet in his house, and he and Paul were old friends. The letter to Philemon was about a runaway slave whom Paul had met in Rome.

> My partner, because you love an old man who is a prisoner now in Rome, I have a favor to ask of you.
>
> Onesimus, the useless one, your slave who ran away from you, is with me here in Rome. But he is not the useless one any more. In fact, he has become most useful to me, and he will be to you. I wish I might keep him here to help me, but I would not keep him without your permission.

He knows that he did wrong in running away, and he is ready now to go back to you. Perhaps he left you for a while so that you could have him back forever, not as a servant but as a beloved brother of mine and yours.

I am sending him back to you. Welcome him home. If he stole anything from you, I myself will pay you all he owes. Welcome him as you would welcome me. My partner, my brother, do this for me.

And find a place for me to stay, for I am hoping that I may be able to come to you soon myself.

Epaphras, who is in prison here with me, and Mark and Aristarchus, and Demas and Luke all send you their greetings.

A third letter from Rome Paul wrote to his friends the Ephesians and to the churches in nearby towns.

You Gentiles used to hear that you could not belong to the family of God. Now you know that is not true. For Christ has broken down the wall that kept us apart, and because we love him we can both believe in the Father, Gentiles and Jews. So now you are not strangers or foreigners. We are all members of the family of God, all of us together, building a temple for him. The apostles and the prophets are the foundation. Jesus Christ is the cornerstone, and we are the building.

Don't worry because I am held prisoner. For though I am least important of those who love God, he gave me the gift of preaching to you the wonder of the love of God for us. For you I am praying, that he will live in your hearts through your faith and that you will know for yourselves the love of Christ, how wide and long and deep and high it is, beyond anything that we can imagine.

Here I am, a prisoner, begging you to act like Christians. Be gentle and patient. You are not the same now as you were before you became Christians. Put away your lying and tell the truth. Don't steal. Work for your living. Put away your angry, noisy ways. Be kind with one another, gentle, forgiving one another, just as God has forgiven you for Jesus' sake.

As Paul was writing he could watch his guard. Shield and sword, helmet, breastplate, armor for the legs, shoes and belt—these made up the uniform of a Roman soldier.

> You will be fighting enemies you cannot see, not human soldiers but evil in every form. Put on God's armor to protect yourselves from evil. Stand up and fight his enemies.
> Stand up! Your belt is truth. Your breastplate, goodness. On your feet wear the good news of the peace of God. Pick up your shield of faith to protect you from the burning arrows of the wicked one. Your helmet is God's salvation. Your sword is the word of God.
> Stand up and fight. And when you have done everything you can do, keep on fighting.
> Pray, and keep on praying. Pray for all who love Christ, especially for me, that I may go on speaking without fear, though I am a prisoner in chains.
> Peace to you, and love.
> Paul, a missionary for Christ, commissioned by God.

Friends far and near did their best to help Paul. Dr. Luke was with him. Timothy visited him often. Epaphroditus came from Philippi, Paul's first mission station in Europe, to bring loving greetings from the church and to stay with Paul and help him.

Gladly Paul welcomed his old friend. They had worked together and fought together as soldiers of God. It was good to be able to work together again. But Epaphroditus became sick, so sick he nearly died. The bad news went back to Philippi, and now the sick man was worse than ever, worrying because they knew at home that he had failed on his job.

Lovingly, Paul sent him home with a letter. We call this message the letter to the Philippians.

Welcome our friend back and honor him. For the work of Christ he came near to dying, not thinking about himself, just of me and your wish to help me.

I am so thankful for you. After I left you, you were the only ones who thought about sending gifts to me. I am not really worried about getting the things I need, for I have learned to be satisfied whatever happens. I can be happy when I have plenty, but I can be just as happy when I must do without. I can do anything through Christ who gives me strength.

Now I have so much—your gifts you sent me by Epaphroditus. And my God will give you all you need from the riches of his glory through his Son Jesus Christ.

So be glad you belong to him. Learn not to worry, but ask him in your prayers for whatever you need, thanking him as you pray. And you will have God's comfort beyond our understanding.

Remember, whatever is true, whatever is honest and just and pure and lovely, put your minds on these things. Keep on as I have taught you, and do the things you have seen me do.

Not that I take the credit for anything I am. Whatever I do that is good I do with the help of Christ whom I trust and love. I am not perfect by any means, but I keep on following him. My mistakes I have left behind and forgotten. This one thing I do: I press on to reach my goal, God's goal for me, and the way is by trusting in Jesus Christ.

The brothers here with me send you their greetings.

After a time Paul was released from prison in Rome. Back he

went to his work in the churches. From Macedonia in Europe Paul wrote a letter to the young man Timothy whom he had won to Christ in Lystra.

This young man was now Pastor Timothy, working with Paul for the new churches he had established.

Later, when Paul was arrested and sent to Rome a second time, he sent another letter to Timothy.

Here are some of the words Paul wrote in those letters to his young friend:

> My beloved son,
> Be a good soldier of Jesus Christ even when the way is hard. Remember always what you believe. Remember the people who kept the faith and handed it down to you. Keep on fighting your good fight. Hold fast to the things you believe.
> Keep working to meet God's approval, studying God's Word, and you will be a workman who will never be ashamed.
> Timothy, I am thanking God in my prayers for you night and day. How I wish I could see you! Remember always your gift for teaching in God's spirit of power and love.
> Don't ever be ashamed of me because I am in jail. I am not ashamed. For I know him whom I believe, and I know that he will keep me and all I have trusted to him forever.
> Timothy, try to come to see me soon, before winter, and bring the coat I left in Troas. And the books—bring the books. Do come soon. Luke is the only one here with me now. Demas left me. And I sent Tychicus to Ephesus. Come, and bring Mark with you. Do your best to come soon.
> I am not afraid. I know that I shall not live long, and I am ready to go. I have fought a good fight. I have finished my work. I have kept the faith. The Lord, who is a fair judge, has his reward ready for me, and for all of us who love him.
> But, Timothy, hurry.

Did Timothy get to Paul in time to see his friend before his death? We do not know. The words of his second letter to Timothy are the last we have from Paul or about him.

But those words make a good ending to the life story of Paul—Jesus' greatest follower, greatest missionary, greatest preacher.

From Letters to Colossians, Philemon, Ephesians, Philippians, 1 and 2 Timothy

MORE NEW TESTAMENT LETTERS

The Letter to the Jews

"HOLD FAST to your faith—this is the better way." That is the message of the Letter to Hebrew Christians whose enemies were at work to make them give up their new belief in Jesus the Son of God.

Faith means believing with our minds the things we never saw with our eyes. Faith means believing that God made the world and the stars, the sun and moon, and all the worlds we cannot see.

For Abel, faith meant understanding how to offer a gift to God lovingly and thankfully.

For Enoch, faith meant living so close to God that he walked straight from this world to the next with his hand in God's.

For Noah, faith meant believing God's warning and building a ship on dry land to rescue all his family.

For Abraham, faith meant obeying God's orders to go to some far place he did not know and build a home for his family, where all their days they could live close to God.

For Sarah, faith meant believing God's promise that she and Abraham would have a son.

Faith made Moses' father and mother brave and wise to hide their baby. Faith made Moses suffer with his own people instead of living as a prince of Egypt. Faith made him lead his people away from Egypt to freedom, and he was not afraid, for by faith he knew that God was always near.

For Joshua, faith meant marching round Jericho till the walls tumbled down and he captured the city.

And there were Rahab and Gideon and Barak and Samson and David—all the rest of the host of witnesses who trusted God and were obedient.

But God had something better planned for us. For us he sent his Son—who lived on earth, learning obedience to his Father, giving up his life for our sakes—so that we, when we believed, might be sons of the Father.

Near to us he is, for he calls us brothers, all who love and trust him. Understanding, he is; for he was tempted to do wrong as we are, and he offers his help when we are tempted.

Ahead of us by faith we can see him, and where he is he would have us, too.

So let us throw away everything that holds us back, all the heavy sins that slow us down, and run the race ahead of us without giving up, without getting tired.

Keep on loving one another as you love your own brothers.

Remember to welcome strangers, for sometimes strangers turn out to be angels in disguise.

Be content with whatever you have, and do not worry about getting the things that belong to others.

Remember that the Lord has told you, "I will never leave

you alone." And you can say, "The Lord is my helper. I am not afraid of anything anyone can do to me."

Now may the God of peace who brought again from the dead our Lord Jesus, that great Shepherd of the sheep, make you perfect in every good work to do his will, working in you all that is well-pleasing in his sight, through Jesus Christ. To him be glory forever and ever. *From Hebrews 11 to 13*

The Letter from Pastor James

For Jewish Christians far from the homeland Pastor James wrote a letter. He wanted to write words that would give them courage for living in dangerous times, and good rules for living with all kinds of people, whether or not they were friendly.

> From James, who is God's servant, to the Jews who are living far from home:
>
> Brothers, be glad for the trials and sufferings that are coming to you, for your faith grows as you learn how to be strong in spite of them.
>
> If any of you need more understanding, ask God for help, for he gives generously, without finding fault. But you must ask believing, not changing your mind the next minute.
>
> Never think it is God who is sending your troubles. He does not tempt you to do wrong. Every good gift and every perfect gift comes to us straight from the Father.
>
> Every one of you must be quick to hear, slow to speak, slow to get angry.
>
> Remember how much harm chattering tongues can do, like a small flame starting a great fire no one can tame. We have managed to tame all kinds of animals, but no one has succeeded in taming the tongue. One minute we are praying

lovingly to God, and the next we are cursing men whom God created. Be careful what you say, and tell no evil thing about your brother.

You have been listening to the Word. But listening is not enough. You are to be doers of the Word you hear, not just listeners, for you prove your faith by your deeds.

Would you tell a hungry, freezing person who needs your help, "Good-by. I hope you will find some warm place to eat" and give him nothing?

This is what the Father asks of us who love him:

"Help the widows and the orphans in their trouble. Keep yourselves clean from the evil in the world." This is faith in action.

Love your neighbors as you love yourselves. This is the royal law. Suppose two men come to church, one well dressed, the other ragged and poor. Would you tell the rich man, "Welcome! Come and sit in the front seat"?

Would you tell the poor man, "Go on back and sit down there in the corner"?

You believe there is one God. Fine! The evil spirits do, too, and they are afraid of him, but they still are wicked spirits. You must prove you believe in God by the way you live.

Say no to the devil—he runs away.
Move closer to God—he comes to you.

From James 1 to 4

Letters from Peter

"Fiery trials" Peter called the troubles new Christians were suffering for being true to Christ. His letters were written to help them to be strong in every test and to remind them how much they could count on God's loving care.

To the new Christians living among the heathen:

Be glad you are called on to suffer for your belief in the Lord Jesus Christ, whom you love though you never saw him. Be proud that he chose you for his own people.

The heathen will accuse you for your faith. Be careful. Be careful to keep every law. Honor all men. Love the brothers. Obey God. Honor the emperor.

Who can harm you if you are true to what is good? Men may make you suffer, but you will not be afraid. Always be ready to give a good answer when people ask you why you are a Christian, but answer gently and without anger.

Never think that it is strange when you are called on to suffer, to share in Christ's sufferings. One day you will share his glory. Let none of you have to be punished for being a thief or a murderer; but be proud to be punished for being a Christian.

Be sympathetic with the brothers, gentle, good-mannered. Don't pay back evil for evil, but bless the one who hurts you.

> To be happy all your days
> Say no words that are evil,
> No words that are untrue.
> Give up evil and choose the good.
> Seek to find the ways of peace.

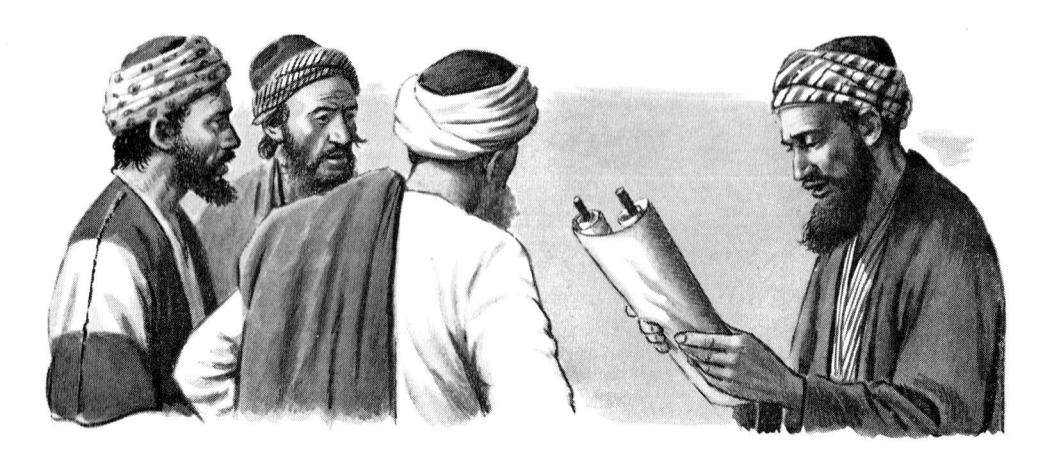

Give God your cares and worries, for he cares about you.

Be on your guard all the time, for your enemy, the devil, stalks around like a lion roaring for his prey. Remember the same thing is happening to other Christians wherever they are. Be strong in your faith.

You believe in God, for you trust his Son.

> To your faith add goodness;
> To goodness add knowledge;
> To knowledge add self-control;
> To self-control add patience;
> To patience add loyalty to the Father;
> To your loyalty add neighborly kindness; and
> To all this add Love.
>
> *From 1 and 2 Peter*

Letters from John

To the new Christians John wrote letters telling of love and light and life. Loving God, he said, we will not be confused in the dark, for his clear light shows us the way to go. Loving him, we show love for his children, for God is love.

> I saw him with my own eyes, heard him talk, touched him with my own hands. I know that he was Jesus Christ who was with the Father from the beginning.
>
> I am writing to you, little children, because your sins are forgiven for Jesus' sake. I am writing to you, young men, because you have beaten Satan and you are strong. I am writing to you, fathers, because you know the Lord Jesus.
>
> God is all light, and where he is there is no darkness. Walk in his light, loving your brothers. For when you hate them you are stumbling in the dark. You may make your brother

stumble. Show your love, not just in words but truly in your deeds.

If we say, "I never sin," we are lying. But if we are honest and say, "I have sinned," God who is faithful and just will forgive us for Jesus' sake.

God is love, and he showed us what love is like when he sent his only Son into the world to pay the penalty for our sins. We love him because he loved us first. If God loved us that much, we should be loving one another.

None of us ever saw God, but when we love one another God is in our hearts. We can know that it is so because he has given his Spirit to us who love him.

And we can be sure he hears us when we ask for the things he wants us to have. We know that when he hears he will answer, and he will give us all we ask and need.

To the lady whom we all love, and to her children: I beg you to keep the commandment we all know, that we love one another, obeying God in all we do.

To Gaius, good friend of the missionaries who travel to the churches: You are doing a good thing when you welcome these guests, especially the strangers.

All the friends send their greetings to you. I hope to see you soon.

From 1 John, 2 John, 3 John

NEW HEAVEN AND EARTH

~~~~~~~~~~~~~~~~~~~~~~~~~~~~

> Blessing and honor and glory and power
> To the king upon his throne
> Forever and ever and ever.

A LONELY OLD MAN looked out across the sea from the island called Patmos. Exiled there for his preaching, John was far from his old friends. And they were in danger now, for the Roman emperor had declared war on all Christians everywhere.

On the island John heard his beloved Master speaking, heard promises and saw bright visions of angels and golden lampstands, shining stars, and beasts and horsemen. Each picture had a message. There were special messages for seven churches. And there were pictures of times to come. Jesus would return to earth. Satan with all his wicked ways would be destroyed. And in all heaven and earth God's people would love him and serve him as Lord of lords and King of kings. There would be no more crying in that time, no more sadness, no more dying.

Knowing what he had heard and seen, John would probably have liked to write to his friends in the churches:

"Be strong! Keep faith! Never give up! The Lord Jesus is more powerful than all the Roman emperors who ever lived or ever will live."

But such plain writing would be too dangerous. Instead, John wrote to his friends about his strange and beautiful visions, and so he could share with them what he learned to make them strong in times of trouble.

Letters for Seven Churches

On the Lord's Day I heard a voice behind me like a trumpet. I turned to look, and I saw One standing there in the midst of seven golden lampstands. His face was shining like the sun.

"I am he who lived and died. See, I am alive forevermore. Write down the things you see, things that were, things that are, and things that are to be.

"Write to the Church in Ephesus this message from One who walks among the golden lampstands: I know how hard you work without giving up, I know your patience. I know how much you hate all that is evil. But I have something against you. You no longer love people as you did when first you knew me.

"Have you ears to hear? Listen well. To him who fights and wins I will give life with God forever.

"Write to the Church in Smyrna this message from One who was dead and is alive: I know you are faithful. Though you are poor and troubled, you are rich in many things. Fear nothing. Keep on being faithful, even to death, and I will give you life with God forever.

"Write to the Church in Pergamum this message from One who has a two-edged sword: Though you live where Satan has his house, I know that you are true to me. But I have a few things against you, for you have allowed bad teachers to go among your people. Send them away quickly. Have you ears to hear? To him who fights and wins, I will give life with God forever.

"Write to the Church in Thyatira this message from One whose eyes glow with the warm light of fire: I know how hard you work. I know your love and your faith, stronger now than when first you knew me. But I have a few things against you, for you let that evil woman teach her wicked ways. Hold fast to your faith until I come, and I will give you life with God forever. Have you ears to hear? Listen well.

"Write to the Church in Sardis this message from One who knows the spirits of the churches: Wake up! You call yourself a church, but you are forgetting who you are, and your work is failing. A few of you are faithful, and they are worthy of life forever. Have you ears to hear? Listen well.

"Write to the Church in Philadelphia this message from One who is holy: I know you are not great or powerful, but you have been true to me. I have opened wide the door for you, and no man shall shut you in. Because you have been true I will guard you in the days of greatest trouble. Hold fast to your faith, and you will be people of God. Have you ears to hear? Listen well.

"To the Church in Laodicea write this message from One who is forever with God: I know your works! Neither hot nor cold—just lukewarm and worthless. You say that you have everything you need. You do not know how blind and miserable and poor you are. All those I love I warn and punish when they do wrong. So go to work!

"See, I stand at the door and knock. If any man hears my voice and opens the door, I will come in and stay with him. Have you ears to hear? Listen well."
Revelation 1 to 3

The City of Light

I saw the King upon his throne. All around him were crowds of people from all the lands of all the world. And they wore fair white robes, and they were singing the glory of the King, and the angels sang with them,

> Blessing and honor and glory and power
> To the King upon his throne
> Forever and ever and ever.

Someone asked me,

"Who are these people in white robes? Where did they come from?"

"Sir, *you* know," I answered. And he told me,

"These have come here after the greatest troubles on earth. They are worthy now to wear their white robes, because he has made them clean. So now they serve God day and night. Never hungry any more, never thirsty, never hot or tired. For God himself takes care of them. He will wipe every tear from their eyes."

And I heard the trumpets blow. And I saw the new heaven and earth, for the first were gone.

I saw the golden city with its walls of shining jewels, emeralds and topaz, amethysts and sapphires. Straight through the city flowed the broad, clear river of life, and along its bank grew the trees of life. Twelve kinds of fruit were growing there, ripening every month of the year. And the leaves of them were medicine for the healing of the people of the world.

The gates were made of pearls, and the streets were golden. I saw no temple within the city, for no temple was needed. God himself was living there. I saw no sun, no moon, no stars. The shining glory of God made the light, and there was no darkness anywhere.

I heard a voice from heaven, "See, God lives with men. There is no death, no sadness or crying or pain. For all the old ways are gone. I have made everything new. God himself is living with his people, and they will be his own forever."

The wicked ones, the liars and the cheats, the murderers, all those with hate in their hearts can never go through those gates of pearl. No one can bring trouble within the walls. But all the nations, all whom God saved, are free to walk there in the light. No need to lock the gates, for danger never enters there. No darkness and no evil can be found in the city of light.

Happy are they all, all who lived in obedience to the King, for they have the right to walk through the wide gates of pearl, and they can see him face to face.

"Come," he says to them. "The water of life is for you."

That was the voice like a trumpet.

And the chanting went on:

>Blessing and honor and glory and power
>To the King upon his throne
>Forever and ever and ever.
>Blessing and honor and glory and power
>Forever and ever. Forever and ever.

Revelation 4 to 22

SUPPLEMENT

LET'S GO EXPLORING
In the Bible

Open thou mine eyes, that I may behold wondrous things out of thy law.

Psalm 119:18

THE BOOKS OF THE BIBLE

The Old Testament—39 Books

The Five Books of the Beginnings and the Law

Genesis   Exodus   Leviticus   Numbers   Deuteronomy

The Twelve Books of History

Joshua	1 Samuel	2 Kings	Ezra
Judges	2 Samuel	1 Chronicles	Nehemiah
Ruth	1 Kings	2 Chronicles	Esther

The Five Books of Poems and Writings of the Wise Ones

Job   Psalms   Proverbs   Ecclesiastes   Song of Solomon

The Five Books of the Major Prophets

Isaiah   Jeremiah   Lamentations   Ezekiel   Daniel

The Twelve Books of the Minor Prophets

Hosea	Obadiah	Nahum	Haggai
Joel	Jonah	Habakkuk	Zechariah
Amos	Micah	Zephaniah	Malachi

THE BOOKS OF THE BIBLE

The New Testament—27 Books

The Four Books of the Good News of Jesus Christ

Matthew   Mark   Luke   John

The Book About Early Churches and the First Missionaries

The Acts

The Nine Letters from Paul to New Churches

Romans	Galatians	Colossians
1 Corinthians	Ephesians	1 Thessalonians
2 Corinthians	Philippians	2 Thessalonians

The Four Letters from Paul to Friends

1 Timothy	Titus
2 Timothy	Philemon

The Eight Letters to New Churches and Their Members

Hebrews	1 John
James	2 John
1 Peter	3 John
2 Peter	Jude

John's Book About the Defeat of Satan and the Glory of Heaven

The Revelation

HOW THE BIBLE CAME TO US

Writing Materials of Long-Ago

LONG BEFORE the first book was printed, before pens and ink and paper were invented, men were learning different ways of keeping written records.

At first they had scratched and painted pictures and letters on rocks and stones. Then they learned how to chisel out the letters so that the writing would last. In Abraham's time, small bricks made of soft clay were used for writing. After the soft bricks were baked hard, the writing was plain to read.

The Egyptians learned to make a kind of paper from the inside of the stalk of a water plant called papyrus. The three-sided stalks sometimes grew as high as fifteen feet, and they were about five inches thick. The Egyptians cut the stalks in sections and sliced the pith inside the stalks into thin strips. They laid the strips side by side to make a layer. Then they placed another layer on top, with strips going crosswise. This made one sheet of papyrus. Probably they pounded the strips while they were still wet to make them stick together. Perhaps they used a kind of glue to make the sheets strong.

The finished sheet was polished with a piece of ivory or shell until it was smooth and strong and ready for writing. Then sheets could be joined together side by side, making a long roll of strong writing material. In Rome, merchants graded papyrus according to its quality and size.

Writing on papyrus was the slow, careful work of scribes who used pens made from hollow canes or reeds, and ink made from soot or from the liquid made by cuttlefish.

The Romans and the Greeks liked wax tablets better than papyrus for keeping records. A piece of wood or ivory, about the size of one of our books, was hollowed out in the middle, leaving a flat space inside the frame. Into this hollow space melted wax was poured. When the wax cooled, it was solid but soft enough to be marked with an ivory or bronze pen called a stylus. One end of the stylus was pointed for writing. The other end was round for smoothing out mistakes. Holes could be punched along one side of the frames of the tablets so that several could be fastened together by rings, like the pages of a book. The Romans called such a bound tablet a codex.

Men also learned to make parchment for writing from the skin of sheep or goats or calves. Stretched and scraped and dyed, parchment was a smooth, sturdy writing surface. It was stronger than papyrus, lasted longer, and it could be used for writing on both sides.

The Romans discovered that they could fasten parchment sheets together just as they fastened the wax tablets. People liked the bound sheets better than scrolls, for they were easier to carry around.

Parchment and papyrus and wax tablets were the materials used for writing for business, for the libraries, and for important records. School children often used broken pieces of clay pots for their scratch pads.

In the second century, while the early church missionaries were still copying parts of the Bible on papyrus and parchment, the Chinese invented paper. The Arabs learned from the Chinese how to make paper, and they taught the art to people in Europe. But it was to be hundreds of years before paper would become so plentiful that it could be used for the making of books in such large numbers that nearly everyone could own one.

The Bible's Name

At first the Greek name for the bark of the papyrus plant was *"biblos."* Later the Greeks gave that name to the pith from which they made papyrus. Still later they called the writing on a roll of papyrus *"biblos,"* meaning book. Many books in Greek were *biblia*.

The word *Biblia,* or Books, became the name for the books of the Bible, and when the Greek word traveled into the Latin language, then into English, the collection of the books of God's Word was called "Bible"—many books in one.

The Old Testament

The Bible was written long ago, in languages people living today can learn to read by hard study. The wonder is that in the United States, in Europe, India, Africa, wherever man is free to worship God, he can hold in his own hands and learn to read in his own language the Bible, which is God's Word for him.

Hebrew was the language of the Old Testament, except for parts of Daniel and Ezra and some words in Jeremiah. These were written in Aramaic, a language much like Hebrew, which became the language of the Jews after the exile in Babylon.

The time came when many of the Jews who had traveled far from the homeland could not remember how to read Hebrew. After Alexander and his Greek army had conquered the lands around the Great Sea, people everywhere began to speak Greek. More than a hundred years before Jesus was born, the Jews who were living in Alexandria, Egypt, asked for the Scriptures in the language they could understand. So the first translation into another language was made. The story is told that seventy-two of the wisest Jewish teachers, who knew both Hebrew and Greek well, traveled from Jerusalem to Alexandria to do the work of translating the Scriptures from Hebrew into Greek. Their translation is called the *Septuagint,* from a word meaning seventy.

The New Testament

The first missionaries set out to tell the good news "in all the world" as Jesus directed them. Wherever they traveled, they were busy teaching, preaching, and healing. But they could not travel everywhere. People who had not heard them began to ask, "What was Jesus like? What did he say? What did he do?"

Mark knew, for he had heard the story of Jesus' life from Peter. He was the first to write of Jesus' life, of his love for all people, and of the wonderful things he did. Then Matthew wrote his account, thinking especially of the Jews, and writing in a way that would prove to them that Jesus was the Messiah whom God had promised to send. Luke wrote his history of Jesus' birth, life, death, and resurrection. A few years later he wrote another history, the Acts of the Apostles, which told of the adventures of some of the first missionaries. John's book which tells of Jesus is the fourth of the books called "Gospels"—books of the Good News.

The new churches which the missionaries organized were having small problems and big troubles. They needed answers to their questions about Christian ways of living. Even before the writers of the four Gospels finished their accounts of Jesus' life, Paul was writing to his new Christian friends. In the collection of letters in the New Testament there are also many other letters, some by John, some by Peter, one by James, one by Jude, and a letter addressed to the Hebrews.

In the new churches Christians began to read from the letters and the Gospels, as well as from the writings of the prophets, during the worship service. By the time John finished Revelation, with its special message to all Christians everywhere that God will save his people and Satan will be defeated, the Good News and the letters had traveled far. Gradually, as the Holy Spirit led those first Christians in writing and sharing what they had written, all the books of the New Testament were complete.

The Latin Bible

Years went by. Rome had been the ruler of all the world so long that in many lands people were speaking and reading Latin, the language of the Romans.

"Give us the Bible in our own language," they begged the scholars.

Here and there someone would try to translate parts of the Bible into Latin. But a man must know both Latin and Greek well to make all the meaning in one language clear in another. Few men were wise enough to do the work.

About four hundred years after Jesus was born, there lived in Rome a man named Jerome who had spent most of his life studying his Greek Bible. He was chosen for the great work of translation. He left his home to study in the land of the Bible, and he worked in Bethlehem for fifteen years. Then he gave to the people, in their own language, the version of the Bible called the "Vulgate," from a Latin word meaning common or usual.

Copies of the Bible were made slowly, carefully, by hand, and each copy was expensive. Only a few people could buy Bibles of their own. But the Good News was to travel into all the countries of the world.

In years to come the adventures of the Bible as it traveled were to be stories of high courage and great hardship, of prison and death, and of brave men who took up the task when others failed.

The Bible in English

The Roman army invaded Britain and conquered the British tribes who lived on that island. Later, Roman missionaries traveled to Britain to teach the Christian faith. It would be hard to know how much the Britons understood at first. They could not read, even words of their own language, and the Latin Bible was the only Bible in the land.

But in small ways the beginning was made.

Caedmon, the shepherd, used to slip away after supper when the men took their turns at singing and storytelling round the fire in the great hall, for he knew no song, no story to tell.

One night he dreamed a strange dream. He thought he heard the Lord saying to him,

"Sing."

"I cannot. What should I sing?" he answered.

"Sing of the beginnings."

Caedmon could not read Latin. But he had friends who could, and they translated the words of the Bible into his language. He listened while they read of the beginning of the world, of the life of Jesus, and of the love of God for all people.

One evening he stayed with the others by the fire, and when his turn came he picked up his harp, and he began to sing his song about the beginnings.

The men liked his singing. He sang again and again, telling stories from the Bible. And people listened, for they were hearing something from the Bible in their own language.

A boy named Bede was seven years old when Caedmon died. For years Bede studied Greek and Latin. He studied the Testaments, Old and New. Then he translated into the people's language the Gospel of John and parts of some other books of the

Bible. He wrote a history of his times, and he wrote the songs of Caedmon just as the shepherd used to sing them by the fire.

Years went by. The language people were speaking was changing. It changed so much that there were few who could understand the words of Bede's translation. King Alfred the Great worried because his young people had no way of hearing the Bible in words they could understand. For them he translated the Ten Commandments and parts of the Psalms. "Every free-born boy should be able to read the Bible," said Alfred.

But the Bible for everyone, for each in his own language, would not be possible for many years. For a long time kings and priests said that ordinary folk should not read the Bible.

Five hundred years later a man named John Wycliffe—his enemies called him John Wicked-Believe—determined to give the Bible to his people. He used the old Latin translations which few but kings and priests could read, and he translated the entire Bible for the people. He was arrested, then set free. But the King of England made a law that whoever read a copy of Master Wycliffe's Bible must lose his lands, his cattle, his house, and his life.

In Germany an invention by a man named Johann Gutenberg was to change the ways of making books, so that thousands could be printed in the time a scribe had been able to make one copy.

Gutenberg knew that pictures and words could be carved on wooden blocks. When the blocks were dipped in ink and pressed on paper, pictures and words were printed. But a block once carved could not be changed easily. To print another message a new block must be carved.

"Why not mold each letter of the alphabet on the end of a small metal bar?" Gutenberg wondered. The bars could be arranged so that their letters spelled words. Then the bars could be fastened together, inked, and pressed on paper. With this movable type the letters could be used over and over again in printing presses that quickly printed page after page. Gutenberg experimented until he had a workable printing press. Never again would it be necessary to copy books by hand, the slow, expensive way.

The first book printed on the new press was a Latin Bible. The next translation, a part of the Bible in English, was made by William Tyndale. Wycliffe had used Jerome's Latin translation. William Tyndale decided to go all the way back to the Greek and the Hebrew of the first Bible to be sure of the meanings of the words.

So he began to study. He knew Latin. He had to learn Greek and Hebrew. And all the time he must be on guard. If his enemies discovered what he was doing and had him arrested, he would not be able to work. Nothing must stop him.

He traveled from England to Germany to finish his work on the New Testament. There it was printed on the new press. Hundreds of copies were shipped back to England. Tyndale's enemies did their best to destroy them, but the books kept coming. Now even poor people could pay for Testaments of their own.

The King of England tried to stop the new translation. He sentenced Tyndale to death. The great translator's last prayer was, "Lord, open the King of England's eyes."

Miles Coverdale carried on Tyndale's work of translation. In 1535 the entire Bible was ready for the English people in their own language.

Then Tyndale's prayer was answered. The king ordered "one book of the whole Bible, in the largest volume, to be set up in some convenient place within the church" for people to read. Because they were so scarce, Bibles had to be chained to the tables on which they lay!

Years went by. The English language had changed, and the words of Tyndale's translation were hard to understand. King James of England commissioned, or authorized, the wisest scholars of the time to make the best translation possible from the original writings into English which people of the time were speaking. That Bible, published in 1611, is called by his name, the King James Version.

Today people no longer speak in the language of 1611. Ancient papyrus and parchment manuscripts have been discovered which explain and make clearer some of the words of the earliest manuscripts. So other versions have been made since the King James: the Revised, the American Standard, the Revised Standard, and many others, which use language more like that which we speak today.

The Bible Travels On

The work of translation into other languages goes on around the world. The first Bible printed in America was in another language. It was for the Indians in New England. Through the work of the American Bible Society and the British and Foreign Bible Society and other groups, the Bible goes into all the world, so that each may read God's Word in his own language. For the blind there are Bibles in Braille and talking books on records.

The Bible has been translated into more than a thousand languages and dialects. And still the work must go on, for there are those who have not heard, who have not yet read God's Word in their own languages. "Go into all the world. Tell the good news to all people." Those were the marching orders of the Great Commission. So, wherever Christians obey that commission, the Bible travels on.

AT HOME WITH THE FAMILY

"I HEAR there is a new baby in Reuben's home. It's a boy!" That was just about the best news a neighbor could tell. For Hebrew families wanted many children, especially boys.

The new baby was probably lying in a cradle-swing made of wool. When his mother carried him outside, she might strap this woolen cradle to her back.

The "swaddling clothes," which all babies wore, were wrapped carefully around his body. His mother laid him on a square cloth, one corner under his head and the opposite corner under his feet, and she folded the cloth carefully around him. Then she placed his hands at his sides, and wrapped his body snugly with long, narrow bands of cloth. Whenever she changed the bands she rubbed his body gently with olive oil, and perhaps she dusted him with powder made from myrtle leaves. Mothers believed that tight swaddling clothes would help small arms and legs and backs grow straight.

The Houses Where They Lived

If the family was poor—and there were many poor people in Palestine—they lived in a square house with just one room. There was no chimney, and no fireplace. The mother would do her cooking and baking over a fire in the yard, or court, outside the house.

Before the Hebrews came into the Promised Land they had been tent people, pitching their tents where grass was green for goats and sheep. Goats' hair made fine tent material, keeping out both rain and the heat of the noonday sun. The simplest tent houses had two rooms, the front room for the men of the family and for guests, and the inner room for women and children.

When the family became too large to live in one tent they just made another tent. This was the women's work. They made new tents or they patched the old ones when they wore out. At moving time they took the tents down, packed them, and stowed them for traveling. Wherever the new home was to be, they unpacked, pitched their tents, and set up housekeeping.

Probably the first houses were built of bricks molded of clay-mud and baked dry in the sun. Later, houses were built of stone. Outside the door there would be a courtyard fenced in with stone. In the courtyard lived the family's animals: a donkey, a goat or two, a few sheep, perhaps a cow or an ox. When the weather was stormy, the animals went indoors with the family. In some houses a raised platform was built across the back of the house, above the dirt floor.

The little houses were dark inside. Windows were small. Some houses had no windows at all. So a lamp burned all night long, and in the daytime, too, if work was being done indoors. The little lamps were homemade dishes, like small saucers with a spout on one side, and they were made of clay. The mother filled her lamp with olive oil or oily butter, laid a wick made of hemp or linen in the oil, with one end at the tip of the spout. This she lighted. Then she set the lamp high so that its tiny light would shine as far as possible in the dark little house.

The roof of the house was flat. Wooden poles made the rafters. These were covered with branches of trees and thick clay which had to be rolled firm and smooth with a big roller every time it rained.

A stairway up the outside wall of the house led to the roof, which was the family's favorite place in the whole house. On hot summer days the roof was just right for drying grain and figs and raisins. In the evenings it was much more comfortable than the hot little house. Even the small children were safe up there, for every house must be built with a wall or railing around the roof. That was one of the laws which Moses had taught the people.

The houses were built so close together that the neighbors could talk easily across the rooftops. Everyone knew that the best way to tell the news was to go upstairs and shout it from the housetops.

Many of the larger houses were built with a room on the roof. This was often a guest room, like the room which was made ready for Elisha and furnished with a bed, a table, a chair, and a lamp. The finest homes were built with many rooms around a courtyard where flowers might be blooming and a fountain splashing gaily.

In the poorer homes there was little furniture. Families slept together at night on the floor, on a mat and some quilts. The mother might have a fine top quilt for her family. But most people just took off their outer coats or robes, which they wore all day, and used them for blankets. No one undressed, and usually it was easy to keep warm.

An old, old law said that if a poor man needed to borrow money, and he offered his coat to the moneylender for proof that he would pay his debt, the coat must be returned to him at sunset. A man needed his cover at night.

When the family woke up in the morning, quilts and mats were rolled up and stored along the wall, or in a chest.

Food to Eat

Meals were very simple in the homes of the poorer people. The mother cooked the food over a clay stove or in a small oven, or over burning charcoal in a hole in the ground, just outside the door. She gave her family milk, usually goats' milk and sometimes milk from sheep. She gave them cheese. She made butter from sour milk. First she had poured the milk into a leather bag hung from poles; then she pushed the bag back and forth until the milk turned to butter.

Every day but the sabbath the mother would bake bread for her family. First she would grind her grain in a stone mill. Two people were needed for this, so two neighbors would share the work. Or when the girls in the family grew big enough, they would take turns at grinding.

Poor folk made their bread of barley flour. Finer bread was made from wheat. First the mother mixed flour with water. Often she added olive oil. Then she kneaded the dough with her hands. She divided it into flat, round cakes which she baked quickly in her hot oven made of stone or metal. If she had time to let the dough rise, she would add a little leftover sour dough or leaven, and make light bread. But one time in the year, during the Feast of Unleavened Bread, she must be careful to use no leaven, to have not even one crust of bread made with leaven in the house.

Sometimes the family had a little boiled or roast lamb or veal, seasoned with herbs which grew in the garden. More often they had fish. But meat and fish both were special treats. Usually people ate only fruit and vegetables with their bread and milk. Apricots, melons, pomegranates, figs, grapes, or raisins were their favorite fruits. They liked thick soup made with lentils or beans, and they liked leeks and onions, cucumbers and garlic. Honey was often served, and, like the figs which grew everywhere, it was so plentiful that everyone could enjoy it.

Nuts, roasted or dried grain, and roasted locusts were favorite nibble food. Any hungry person who happened to be walking through a field of ripe grain might pick a few stalks and eat the grain as he walked. And people who were going through a vineyard where the grapes were ripe might eat all they wanted. But they were forbidden by law to carry any away with them in a jar.

The best meal of the day was supper, when the father was home from work, and all the family were together. They sat in a circle on the floor around a bowl of good soup or meat cooked with vegetables. Crisp crusts of bread were their spoons, and they all served themselves from the bowl.

When Jesus visited in homes of wealthy friends, he probably ate with them in the style which the Greeks and Romans had made fashionable. Food was served on a table. Along three sides of the table were long couches on which guests sat or reclined, leaning on one arm as they ate.

Water to Drink

The thirsty Hebrew travelers on the way to the Promised Land had dreamed of a country "flowing with milk and honey." And so it was. When they had settled in their new homes and begun to raise goats, they had plenty of milk. They soon discovered that bees made their homes in hollow trees, in crevices in the rocks. Honeycombs were easy to find, and honey was plentiful.

The travelers had heard that their land was a good land, a land of brooks of water, of fountains and springs flowing out into the valleys and the hills. And so it was. But when the dry months came between the rains, and the small streams dried up and the earth baked hard, the people learned to guard their water carefully.

There were some springs and fountains which never went dry. But all their water, and the water of the rivers, too, was not enough for all the herds and the gardens and the fields and the people. The families learned to dig cisterns deep in the ground close to their houses. A gutter round the roof would catch the rain that fell during the rainy months and drain it safely down into the cistern.

People learned to dig wells. Sometimes a well supplied water for one family and its animals; sometimes for a whole village.

In the evening, when it was cool, the women and the girls would carry their empty water jars to the village well. Such talking as went on then! All the news of the day, all the stories the men had brought home from the market place the women shared as they talked and listened while they took turns lowering a leather bucket on the end of a rope into the cold, clear water. Then, when the last bucket was emptied, each one balanced her brimming pitcher atop her head, and they all walked slowly home.

Sometimes in long spells of hot, dry weather, wells and springs and brooks in a neighborhood went dry. Then the families had real trouble, for they must find a way to bring water to their homes. Men and women both would travel to the nearest well or stream with all the empty leather bottles they could find, fill the bottles, and carry the precious water home, either on their animals' backs or on their own.

Cities where many people lived needed much more water than the villages, and the water supply must be safe at all times. A city might be protected from enemy soldiers by a high, strong wall with gates that could be locked. But if the city's water came from wells or streams outside the wall, enemies could easily attack the people when they came out for water. And if there was no water in the city, the people would surrender without even fighting.

Long, long ago, people found out how to bring water in underground tunnels flowing under the city walls and into the city itself. Jerusalem was one of the cities which had a fine, safe water supply brought inside the city in this way.

Clothes to Wear

Men and women dressed very much alike, except that on her head a woman wore a long veil, while a man's head was covered with a turban. The undergarment was made of linen or wool, and was something like a very long shirt. Over this went a heavier coat, full and loose and long, and made to open down the front. A girdle or belt held the coat close to the body. When there was work to be done, and the long coat was in the way, it was just tucked up under the girdle. For outdoors, there were a long cloak and shoes.

The mother made most of the clothing for her family. She spun the wool which the father had sheared from their sheep, and she wove the woolen thread into cloth. She made warm garments for all the family, perhaps scarlet coats for the children to wear in the snow, or fine, soft clothing made of camels' hair. She knew how to make sturdy mantles of brown or black goats' hair.

Linen cloth made from flax was used for towels and lampwicks, nets and sails. Turbans and veils and underclothes were made of linen. But usually only the priests and the wealthy people had fine linen garments. Cotton and silk were brought from other lands. These, too, were expensive, and were used by wealthy folk.

People did not wear shoes indoors, for that would have been impolite. Sandals laced over feet and ankles might be worn outdoors, but these were always left outside at the door. So were the finer shoes of cloth or fur or other materials. A thoughtful host would always offer water to a guest so that he could bathe his dusty feet before walking into the house.

At School at Home

School, for the younger children, was their home. The boys learned how to bow, kneeling on one knee and bending forward until their heads touched the ground. The girls learned how to help with the grinding of the meal, how to bake the thin, flat cakes in the oven, how to carry brimming water jars home from the village well without spilling a drop.

At home the father told stories of his people, stories of Abraham and Isaac and Jacob, about Moses and the beginning of the nation. He taught them what to do and say at the Passover supper.

The father taught the children in the home, "The Lord our God is one Lord, and you shall love the Lord your God with all your heart, and with all your soul, and with all your might." While they were sitting together at home, while they were walking outdoors, when they went to bed, and when they got up in the morning, Hebrew families talked together about God and his loving care of his people.

As the boys grew older, their father taught them the Law as he had learned it from his father. He taught them the meaning of the words which were written on the small parchment scroll in the "mezuzah," the little box fastened to the right-hand post of the door of every Hebrew house. "Hear, O Israel: the Lord our God is one Lord," the words began. The little mezuzah was a reminder that God lived with them in their house, and that they were his people.

WORKMEN ALL

As soon as a boy of Palestine grew old enough, he would begin to learn a trade. Every Jewish man was expected to be able to earn his living with his hands.

Jesus learned from Joseph to be a carpenter. Paul, though he was trained to be a teacher, knew how to make tents. And he was proud of being able to earn money as a tentmaker even when he was busy as a missionary. Usually a boy learned his father's trade. If there were many sons they might have several choices of ways to make a living.

In the early days, when the Hebrews were settling in the Promised Land, most of the boys chose to be farmers or shepherds, for food and clothing were among the first needs of the people. The people had found food trees growing in their land—olive trees and date palms, fig and nut trees. They learned to plant grain and grapes, fruit trees and herbs.

The Work of the Farmers

As soon as the first fall rains fell, the farmer went to work plowing the land. Then he scattered grain over his fields. He tossed the seed out with his hands instead of dropping it into long, straight lines. Then, before the birds could steal his seed, he spaded or plowed it into the soil.

When harvest time came, all the family and the neighbors went to work together. The reaper would take a handful of grain in one hand, swing his sickle, and cut the stalks off near the tops. The workmen must always be careful to leave a little grain as they worked, and to leave all that grew in the corners of a field. For after they had finished, the poor people would come to glean their share.

After the grain was cut, it was tied into bunches, or sheaves, and loaded on oxcarts, or carried to the level threshing floor.

Then came the work of threshing. Sometimes the grain was beaten. Or oxen would be driven back and forth across the threshing floor to break the grain loose from the stalks.

Next came winnowing. Wind and farmer were partners now, for the wind blew steadily at harvest time. When the workers tossed piles of straw and grain high into the air with big winnowing pitchforks, the wind picked up the light chaff and the straw. Straw blew away. The chaff floated off like dust. The grain fell back on the smooth, hard dirt floor.

There was one more task to be done before the grain could be stored away in jars or in underground pits carefully lined with stone. It must be sifted clean of trash and dirt. Then it was ready for the women to grind it into flour.

In the warm Jordan Valley the farmer might add flax to his crops. Then his wife could make fine linen clothes for her family, or to sell in the market place.

Harvesting flax was quite different from cutting ripe grain. The flax stalks were pulled up, roots and all. Then they were beaten with sticks to shake off the seeds, and dried in the sun, probably on rooftops. The dry stalks were soaked in water for a week so that the woody part of the stalk would rot and the strong fibers could be pulled loose. Then came another trip to the rooftops for drying, and another beating. At last the strands could be carefully separated and made into strong thread for linen cloth.

Farmers liked to have olive orchards and vineyards as well as grain fields. Grapes grew everywhere, even in the hills and on rocky ground where wheat and barley would not grow. A fine vineyard was a family treasure. Around it was a stone wall to keep out foxes and other prowlers. The owner was always watching to see that all the stones were in place, and the wall strong and safe. Somewhere along the wall he built a watchtower where his workers could guard against human prowlers when the grapes were ripe.

Grape-picking time called out all the family to help. Parents and children worked from dawn till dark. At night they stayed on guard, sleeping in small huts which they made out of boughs of trees. There was singing and merrymaking as the families carried their fruit to the winepress or laid it out on their roofs to be dried.

In Palestine, olive trees were almost as plentiful as grapevines. They grew everywhere except in the higher mountains. Olives were one of the most important crops of the country. Olive oil was food. It was used in cooking and in baking bread. It was used for rubbing the body and the hair, and for healing wounds. It was fuel for lamps. It was used in sacrifice and worship services and for anointing kings.

Olive trees grew best in warm, sunny places. They grew slowly, but they lived a long, long time. Their gnarled, twisted trunks and gray-green leaves were sturdy even in wind and storm. But the farmer could have trouble before he could be sure of his crop. Locusts might swarm down and eat the leaves. Or, if the wind blew just at blossom time, the white blossoms might fall before ever the small green fruit began to grow.

Harvest time came in the fall. The women and the boys did the work of harvesting the ripe olives. They would pick the fruit by hand, or they would shake the limbs carefully with a stick. The old law of the olive harvest was that after a tree was once shaken, the rest of the olives must be left. These were for the poor people who would come after the harvesters to glean the leftovers for their food.

Some of the olives would be eaten fresh. Some would be preserved in salt water. But most of the crop was crushed or beaten to make olive oil.

The oil was made by pounding the olives in a mortar, or by crushing them in a big stone press, or by grinding them in a mill, or by treading on them with bare feet.

Farming was hard work, and year-round work. Perhaps the Hebrew boy who learned to write this jingle about the farmer's calendar long ago had spent all his playtime helping on the farm:

> "Two months for harvest,
> Two months for grain planting,
> Two months for late planting,
> And a month for pulling up the flax.
> One month for barley harvest,
> One month to harvest and celebrate,
> Two months for working the vines,
> And a month for fruits of the summer."
>
> *From the Gezer Calendar discovered by R. A. S. Macalister in 1908. The calendar was written on a stone plaque about 950–918 B.C.*

The Work of the Shepherds

The farmer might turn his cattle out to graze by themselves in the hills. But sheep need a shepherd. They depend on him for their food, their water, and their protection from danger. Sheep know their own shepherd. They come to him when he calls their names, but when someone else calls, they do not answer.

In Palestine the shepherd would take his sheep out to pasture during the day and bring them home each night to the sheepfold or pen. In cold weather the sheep spent the night in a big square building covered with a sturdy roof made of tree branches, straw, and earth. When the shepherd brought them in at the end of the day, he shut the door, and they were safe from prowling bears or wolves.

The summer shelter had no roof. There were walls, and there was an entrance, but no door. Once the sheep were inside, the shepherd slept at the entrance to guard them from danger.

Early in the morning he called the sheep out into the sunshine. He would walk on ahead, leading them to the best place to graze in some green meadow, and then to rest beside a quiet pool. When he stopped with them at noon in the cool shade he brought out his own lunch of bread and cheese, olives and dried fruit.

All day he watched. If one sheep snagged a foot on a sharp stone, or if a small lamb strayed recklessly away and a snake nipped its nose, the shepherd was ready with healing oil or butter to rub on the wounds. And if the small lamb was too badly hurt to walk, the shepherd carried it in his arms back to the sheepfold.

"Butcher, Baker, Candlestick Maker"

At first, farmers raised the food for their own families. Gradually other workers took over part of the great business of feeding the people. There were butchers and bakers. There were fishermen, who caught their fish in different ways. Some fishermen used a hook and line. Some had small weighted nets which they whirled around over their heads and then tossed into the water. Many used large dragnets which they drew through the water, bringing in the fish to their boat or to the shore.

There were fruit growers. There were milkmen who led their goats up to the door and delivered fresh milk straight from the goat to families who had no goats of their own.

A man might choose to be a smith, or metal worker, learning to make beautiful things of gold or silver or copper. Or he might learn to work in the copper mines.

There were potters who made clay dishes and jars. There were leather workers and shoemakers, weavers and tapestry makers.

There were dry cleaners who cleaned the heavy woolen coats which could not be washed in water. The cleaners, who were called fullers, had their field outside Jerusalem where they worked on the soiled clothes, then spread them out to dry in the sun.

There were brickmakers and bricklayers. There were carpenters and stone masons. There were shipbuilders.

There were barbers. There were apothecaries, who were men who worked with drugs and spices, making perfumes and incense and ointments and medicine.

"Doctor, Lawyer"

In the laws for living which were given to the Hebrews during the years when they lived in the wilderness there were rules for good health and rules for treating many kinds of sicknesses. There were rules for quarantine, and rules for checkups after being ill.

The priests, who were the men of the tribe of Levi, were put in charge of all the keeping of the law, the laws for worship, for living with people, even the laws for treating sickness.

Some of the great prophets had healing skills. But it was many, many years before men began to study the human body, to study how to heal sickness, and how to keep people well. The Greeks made many discoveries about the body. Their medical schools were famous. Dr. Luke may have been a student in one of those schools before he met Paul and became a missionary.

Hebrew priests were teachers of health rules. They were also teachers of the law. For the law by which the people lived was the law of the Old Testament, the law which directed every act of their living.

While the Jewish people were captives in Babylon they began to treasure more than ever before the law of their people. Men called "scribes" (the word means writers) studied the law. They copied it. They added explanations. And they began to add their own ideas about stricter keeping of the law.

After the Jews came home to Jerusalem, scribes became much more important. They were teachers. They were the experts who taught the meaning of the laws. They became the most important people in Jewish communities.

The scribes, or lawyers, were the men who attacked Jesus for his teaching, "Give help to anyone who needs help, even though this means doing work on the sabbath day." The lawyers taught, "Do no work on the sabbath day. That is the law." For most of them insisted that living by the words of the law was more important than loving God with heart and mind and soul.

Not all the lawyers turned against Jesus. Some became his friends and loyal followers. But most of them failed to understand the meaning of his teaching.

"Merchant Chief"

Travelers on the Highways.—When a boy was twelve he was old enough to go to the great Temple festival services. If he lived outside Jerusalem he and his family would join a party of friends and neighbors and they would all set out together for the city. Robbers might be hiding along the way, waiting to jump out on people who were foolish enough to travel alone. So groups went together; and when evening came, they stopped together along the road to eat supper and make camp for the night.

For the pilgrims, walking along the dusty road was slow traveling. But there was time to watch the other travelers on the highway. Riders on fast little donkeys would catch up with the pilgrims, gallop ahead, and disappear in a cloud of dust. Chariots drawn by prancing horses, faster than anything on the road, rumbled toward them, and the pilgrims scurried out of the narrow road to watch them go by. Two people rode, standing up, in a chariot. Sometimes there was a third person to hold an umbrella over their heads when the sun was hot. The fast little chariots had two wheels. They were built high in front and on the sides, and they were open at the back.

Rich merchants and poor peddlers traveled the highways from many lands to the towns and cities of Palestine. Camel caravans would come from far away, bringing shipments of grain or fine cloth or silver and gold to sell in the market place of a town along the way, or to unload in a port city for shipment across the sea.

Half a mile away the music of the tinkling camel bells could be heard as the caravan came near. Five, six, seven, or eight camels, their backs piled high with bundles, would be fastened in the camel train, one behind the other. Their leader rode a small brown donkey.

Where had they been? Where did they go? From far lands to other lands far away.

At the city gate or inside the city walls the merchants would unpack their wares, set up shop in the open square inside the gate, and then move on to the next market.

The most exciting market in all the land was in Tyre, far to the north, on the shore of the Mediterranean Sea. This was the only good harbor south of Sidon. Ships came from far countries to anchor in the blue water, unload their cargoes, and take on new supplies to sell in other ports.

On the Seas.—A ship that sailed far seas must be well built and sturdy. Planks from strong fir trees made the hull. Its mast was cut from a tall cedar of Lebanon. Wood for the decks was pine from trees on the island of Cypress. A wealthy merchant might have inlaid designs of fine ivory on his decks.

The sails were made from fine Egyptian linen, and so were the awnings, dyed bright blue and purple, which shaded the decks. When there was no wind to fill the sails, strong men must row the ship. They used stout oars which usually were made of oak.

Deep in the hold might be a cargo of silver and iron, tin and lead. In the busy market the owner would sell his wares, and he might take on a shipment of fine bowls made of bronze.

One ship brought war horses and mules. Another had ivory tusks and ebony from far away. A merchant unloaded his chests of emeralds, coral and agates, and purple embroidered wool and fine linen; and he bought wheat, olives, figs, honey, oil, and balm to sell in other ports.

Wine and white wool came from one ship; and wrought iron, with cassia and calamus to be used in making anointing oil, were unloaded from another. Huge bundles of saddlecloths for riding were piled high along the roadway where a shipload of lambs and rams and goats trotted noisily toward the market place.

Spices, precious stones, and gold were in the small chests which sunburned sailors carried from another ship. And, last to anchor in the busy harbor, one small ship unloaded bale after bale of blue and embroidered cloth and gay-colored rugs.

In a few days the ships, laden with new treasures, would be off to other lands. But the blue waters of the harbor would be gay again with colored sails. For as fast as one ship spread her sails and disappeared over the horizon, another wanderer, heavy with food or gold or clothing or livestock, would anchor in the harbor.

The Soldier and His Armor

When young David volunteered to fight Goliath for the honor of God and the Hebrew people, King Saul sent for a soldier's armor. The lad should not go out to fight a giant with no more protection than a slingshot and his courage!

So over David's head went a bronze helmet. Over his shoulders, protecting his body, went a coat of mail, a heavy coat on which small metal pieces were fastened, overlapping, so that the soldier could move, but strong enough to turn aside the blade of ax or javelin.

David strapped the sword belt round his waist. And he could hardly move, for the strange, heavy weight of the armor on his body. "I cannot wear these things. I am not used to them!" he said.

So with his slingshot he went out to fight a giant armed head to foot, with his shield-bearer before him. And with one well-aimed stone from his slingshot he brought the giant low.

Slings were dangerous weapons in the hands of skilful marksmen. The tribe of Benjamin had seven hundred left-handed soldiers who could "sling a stone at a hair, and not miss."

Bows, and arrows made with iron tips, were common weapons. An archer needed both hands to hold the bow and draw the arrow. So he had beside him a shield-bearer who held a stout shield to protect him while he took aim.

A soldier who fought with sword or spear or battle-ax or lance could wear his own smaller shield or buckler on his left arm when he heard the trumpet call to battle:

> Polish your spears! Put on your coats of mail!
> Sharpen your arrows! Take up the shields!
> Take your stations with your helmets.
> Harness the horses! Mount, you horsemen!
> Make ready buckler and shield. Advance to the battle!
>
> *From Jeremiah 46;51*

Chariots drawn by swift horses raced against the enemy. They could be safe places from which to fight. And they could be dangerous. When the Egyptian army was pursuing the Hebrews, their chariot wheels stuck fast in the mud as the waters of the Red Sea closed over the dry land. When King Ahab, disguised as a common soldier, rode into battle in a chariot, a stray arrow struck him between his coat of mail and his breastplate. "Carry me back," he ordered. But so fierce was the battle that his driver could not escape. So the king died, propped up in his chariot, and his men brought him to Samaria to be buried.

In the beginning of the Hebrew nation, all the able-bodied men twenty years old and older were expected to serve in the army when they were needed. The priests of the tribe of Levi were not regularly enlisted as soldiers, but in times of special danger they, too, joined the army.

In the early days there were rules for being excused from service. A man who had built a new house must have time to dedicate it as the home of a family that would worship God. A man with a new vineyard should have time to harvest his first crop. A man who had just married was excused. And so was a man who was afraid to fight.

In New Testament times there was no longer a Jewish army, and the Roman Government which ruled the land did not require that Jews serve in the Roman army. But every Jew knew well what soldiers looked like, for Roman soldiers were stationed throughout the empire to keep peace.

Probably Paul was looking at the soldier who was guarding him in prison when he wrote about Christians putting on the armor of God.

"Wear truth for a sturdy belt," he wrote to his friends in Ephesus. "Put on righteousness for a breastplate. Wear the Good News of peace for shoes, faith for a shield to keep off all the flaming arrows of the evil one. Put on salvation for your helmet, and take the Word of God for your fighting sword. Pray always."

Helmet on his head, strong belt and breastplate to protect his body, sword by his side, shield on his arm, and sturdy shoes on his feet, the soldier stands ready for action.

With Trumpet, Lute, and Harp

Music was an important part of everyday living, and most important on special occasions. Musicians played for feasts, for weddings, and for funerals. They welcomed soldiers home from war. When David brought the ark to Jerusalem, musicians in the procession were "making merry . . . with all their might with songs and lyres and harps and tambourines and castanets and cymbals."

In the Temple services there were four thousand musicians of the tribe of Levi. Twenty-four choirs were trained to chant the psalms of praise.

There were stringed instruments, wind instruments, and percussion instruments, the three families of a modern orchestra. But orchestral music, as we hear it, was not written until many, many hundreds of years later.

Of course, musicians in David's procession could never have used the tall harp which we know. Their harp was much smaller, more like a lyre, and it could be easily carried in a procession. Among the stringed instruments there were the sackbut, or trigon, which had four strings, a psaltery, which was a small harp, and a lute, which was something like a guitar.

Loudest of the wind instruments was the shophar, or ram's horn trumpet. This was used more often for calling signals in battle than for making music. It sounded the beginning of the new year, and of the Day of Atonement. Silver trumpets called the people to worship on feast days, on the first day of the month, and whenever sacrifices were offered. During the traveling days in the wilderness, when the people heard two trumpets sound, they hurried to meet Moses at the entrance of the tent of meeting. If they heard one trumpet only, the leaders came alone.

On moving day the trumpet would sound, and all the families

on the east side of the camp would begin to travel. On the second trumpet call the south side would move. And so the procession would set out in an orderly way.

Other wind instruments included the pipe, which may have been something like the modern oboe, and the flute, first made from reeds and later from wood, bone, or ivory.

There were many kinds of percussion instruments. There were metal cymbals, both "loud" and "high sounding." Loud cymbals were struck together, one on top of the other, and the result was noise, sharp and loud. "High sounding" cymbals were struck like modern cymbals and made a clear, clanging musical sound. The timbrel, or tabret, was a hand drum made of two skins stretched over a wooden hoop frame. Castanets rattled much as our castanets do. And there were tambourines and bells, some of them so tiny that they could be sewed around the hem of the priests' robes.

THE EARTH IS FULL OF HIS CREATURES

Animals of the Bible

IF THE ANIMALS in the Bible were collected in a zoo, lions would roar, lizards would glide under rocks, sheep would follow-the-leader over low rock walls, oxen would plod slowly down the field, and bats would flip out of their caves into the evening sky. Animals, strange and familiar, would growl or snarl, or try to make friends, or go quietly about their business.

There were sheep in Palestine, many flocks of sheep with broad, fat tails. Children liked to keep a pet lamb of their own at home where they could pull grass for it to eat, and feed it from their own cups.

There were long-eared goats. They were black, and the males had curving horns. Nearly every family had at least one goat, for goats' milk, and cheese made from the milk, were favorite foods. Goat meat was good to eat. The skin could be made into useful water bags or bottles. And coats, curtains, pillows, and tents were made of goats' hair.

There were cows. There were oxen, gentle beasts with horns. Oxen were trained to work in teams, yoked together with big wooden yokes across their shoulders.

There were mules, and there were gentle little donkeys, patient, surefooted, dependable for riding, even on long journeys.

A family might have a dog—a puppy that snatched the crumbs the children dropped on the floor, or a watchdog that guarded the door. Sometimes shepherds had dogs to help them guard their sheep. Every town had its snarling, half-wild dogs. They were no one's pets, and they were always hungry. At night, when all the doors were locked, they roamed the streets, hunting every scrap of food that had been thrown out of the houses during the day. They fought. They growled. They snapped at anyone who might walk down the dark streets.

There were no pigs on Hebrew farms. For the old, old law declared that pigs were not clean animals. No Jew who obeyed the Law ate ham or pork, or even touched a live pig.

Horses were for soldiers, not for farmers. Horses drew chariots, and they carried armed men into battle. This is a Bible picture of a war horse:

> Snorting, he leaps like a locust,
> Paws at the ground, and laughs at fear.
> Though far be the battle, he hears the shouting.
> The trumpet sounds, and he charges forth.
> Swords, javelins, spears rattle round him;
> No sword turns him back.
> Fiercely he snorts in his rage.

From Job 39:19–25

In the gardens, small snails inched their way round pebbles and green stalks. Frogs croaked their deep-voiced song along the edge of the streams, while young ones sang their quick, high, peeping calls.

In the caves or in the clefts in rocky hillsides, coneys made their homes. Little gray or brown creatures they were, with long hair, short tails, round ears, and soft white undersides.

Out on the hills lived deer and small, graceful antelopes called gazelles, and mountain sheep, and ibex, or wild goats. Bears liked to live high up in the Lebanon Mountains in sunny days of summer. But when winter came and snow covered the lower slopes as well as the mountaintops, the bears would go down to the villages to raid the gardens and make much trouble for the farmers.

Jackals and foxes and leopards, wolves and wild boars stole food when they were hungry. Often farmers set up whitewashed jackal-scares made of stone to keep the jackals away from their vineyards. The owners of vineyards were always on guard against the foxes that might jump over the stone wall and ruin the vines. This is a song the farmers might have sung as they worked in their vineyards:

> Catch us the foxes, the little foxes
> That spoil our vineyards.
> Catch us the foxes, the small foxes,
> For our vineyards are blooming.
>
> *Song of Solomon 2:15*

Out in the hills there were weasels and hares, rock badgers and porcupines. Mice might be anywhere, stealing whatever they could find.

Two strange creatures of other lands had strange names. There was Leviathan. No fisherman could catch him with a hook.

> Lay hands on him—you'd not do it again.
> His back is covered with scales like shields
> Too close to be pierced with a spear.
> Red are his eyes. Sparks fly from his mouth,
> And smoke from his nostrils. His breath is hot.
> He crawls over iron, and it crackles like straw,
> Over bronze, and it crumbles like powdery wood.
> Arrows and slingstones, javelins and clubs—
> He laughs at them all. He crawls over mud.
> He dives in the river. The water boils round him.
> Behind him he leaves a foaming wake.
> On earth there is not his like.
>
> *See Job 41*

This is a picture of Leviathan, a splendid crocodile thrashing and snorting on the riverbank and plunging out of sight.

There was Behemoth. He ate grass like an ox. But his muscles and his bones had the strength of cedar wood, of bronze, or iron. Where the wild beasts played, he hunted his food. Under the lotus plants by the brook he snoozed in the reeds, in the shade of the willows. He was afraid of nothing, not floodwaters, not hunters' hooks nor snares.

That was Behemoth. In a zoo today the sign over his cage might read: Hippopotamus.

In far lands there were big apes and small monkeys. There were elephants. Ivory from elephants' tusks was a treasure brought into Palestine by camel caravans long before the Romans brought elephants for their armies.

From far away came camels, sturdy one-humped animals that could travel long distances across the desert, living on little food and less water. Their strange bodies stored water in their paunches and food in their humps. A young camel could run fast. But he was valued as a strong pack animal, more than he was for his speed.

Wild beasts had their lairs, and friendly beasts lived with men as they do today. Isaiah said that when all the world knows God there will be no more fighting. Even wild animals will live peacefully with man and with animals of the farm.

> No lion prowls the land, nor any harmful beast.
> The wolf and lamb live together; leopards and
>   small goats sleep side by side,
> Calf with lion cub, cow and bear;
> And a small child leads them.
> For none shall hurt or destroy on all God's holy
>   mountain.

Isaiah 11:6–9

Birds of the Air

Roosters crowed in the dark of the night, and mother hens clucked to their baby chicks in Bible times just as they do now. Doves and pigeons cooed, and sparrows chirped. Owls called out their lonesome hoots, and swallows dipped and darted across the sky.

Hunters set their traps or spread nets and snares for quail and partridges and pheasants.

Kings had peacocks in their palace gardens. Job must have watched an ostrich bury her egg in the sand and then race away so fast that no man on horseback could catch her.

Eagles and vultures, kites and falcons had their homes in the lonely hills. There were hawks of many kinds, and big black ravens.

There were seagulls near the coast. Herons and water hens, pelicans and cormorants were among the birds that liked the marshes by the lakes.

It would be hard to find a list of all the birds that nested in the lands where the Hebrew people lived. We do know that Palestine is in the lane of the great migration flights of birds traveling south before the winter and northward again in the spring. Once when the prophet Jeremiah was begging his people to remember who they were and what they owed to God, he said, "Even the storks and the swallows and the cranes know their schedules for migrating, but God's own people do not even know his law."

Storks were always welcome when they came flying in on their great white wings. The Hebrew name for the gentle birds that took such good care of their families was *chasidah*, which means kindness.

Ants and Beetles, Flies and Fleas

Insects had their place in everyday living in Bible times just as they do today. And some of them made even more trouble.

Ants are mentioned in Proverbs as being small but very wise, busy storing up food in the summer for the winter months.

Bees were everywhere. Their honey was a favorite food of the Hebrew people, easy to find, for the bees liked to swarm in hollow trees, in cracks in the rocks.

The pest of the land was the locust. He was something like a grasshopper, brown, and about three inches long. Sometimes the hot wind from the desert blew swarms of locusts across the land. They flew into the houses. They ate the woodwork. They ate every blade of grass. Clouds of locusts flew across the sky and darkened the sun, and the noise they made was like rain. Joel described in these words the terrible damage they did:

What the cutting locust left, the swarming locust has eaten,
What the swarming locust has left, the hopping locust has eaten,
What the hopping locust left, the destroying locust has eaten.
Joel 1:4

There were moths and crickets and caterpillars and grasshoppers, too, but the locust was blamed for the greatest damage.

Fleas and flies there surely were. The flea is famous because David teased King Saul. David had escaped into the hills when Saul was trying to have him killed. The king and his soldiers were close by. Twice David slipped close to Saul, but the king did not suspect that he was near.

From a safe distance David laughed at the king. "Whom were you hunting? Did you come out here after a flea?" he called.

Swarms of hungry flies were among the plagues in Egypt before

Pharaoh allowed the Hebrews to leave his country. Hornets must have swarmed, too. Larger than wasps, they were fighters, and their stings were dangerous.

Spider webs are mentioned twice in the Bible. Isaiah scolded the people for not being true to God, and he told them they had been spinning spider webs instead of good cloth. Job's friend Bildad talked about the man who forgets God and has nothing to keep him strong. He is trusting a spider web to hold him up, said Bildad.

GIFTS OF EARTH

Trees of Field and Forest

DATE PALM TREES were a familiar sight to the Hebrews when they lived in Egypt. Traveling through the wilderness the people must have been happy to stop and make camp at Elim by the twelve wells of cold water in the shade of seventy tall palm trees.

When the Hebrews reached the Promised Land they found palm trees growing in the warm lowlands. Jericho, in the hot Jordan Valley, was called the City of Palms.

The people learned to use palm leaves for covering the sides of houses, for making mats and baskets. The fruit was good to eat. Even the hard stones in the dates could be ground up to make food for camels.

Traveling through the wilderness the Hebrews had learned to know the sturdy acacia tree. From wood of that thorny tree, shittim wood it was called, they cut fine timber for building the tabernacle and for making the ark and the altar.

The Hebrews found that the green woods in the Promised Land were a treasure far greater than they had dreamed. Trees gave them food, gave them wood for building, gave them cool shade on hot summer days.

As the pioneers found their homes in their new country, they were taught to plant new trees for food. And they were taught conservation of fruit and nut trees. Moses had said, "When you besiege a city for a long time, you shall not cut down the trees. Are you fighting trees or men? Only the trees which you know are not good for food may you cut down to build your ladders and platforms and all that you need to break through the city wall."

Fig trees grew everywhere, even in cracks in the walls. They grew along the roadside, in the fields. Any traveler could help himself to ripe figs when he was passing by a tree. Every house could have its own fig tree for food and shade.

Two and sometimes three crops of figs ripened during the year. The first figs were ripe in June, and the late crop was ready in August or September. Figs were good to eat fresh from the tree, and they could be dried and pressed into cakes which would last a long time without spoiling.

A different kind of fig grew on the sycamore, which was a tall evergreen tree with sweet-smelling leaves. The fruit was small and spotted, not fit to eat until it had been punctured to let out the tiny insects which lived inside. It was never really good to eat, but it could be food for hungry people.

Almonds and pistachio nuts were favorite food. Jacob told his sons to take gifts of food to "the man" down in Egypt, who was really his own son Joseph, and the gifts included pistachio nuts. First of all the trees to blossom in the springtime was the almond tree. Its name in Hebrew meant the wakener.

"No pomegranates!" the Hebrews mourned out in the wilderness country. They remembered the juicy red fruit that grew in Egypt, and they were homesick. But when they reached the Promised Land they had their pomegranates again, plenty of them, to eat as fruit, and to make into a cool drink in the summertime.

Carved figures of pomegranates decorated the tops of the pillars of Solomon's Temple. Round the hem of the high priest's robe were small embroidered pomegranates, blue and purple and scarlet, with small golden bells tinkling between them. The Hebrews liked pomegranates!

Sweet-smelling wood, something like sandalwood and very beautiful, came from the algum, or almug, tree which grew in Ophir. This wood was imported to use in building Solomon's Temple and his house. It was also used in musical instruments.

Another sweet-smelling wood, very expensive, came from the aloes, a tree which grew in India sometimes as high as 120 feet. This wood was imported into Palestine.

Pines and cedars grew in Palestine. But nothing matched the wood from the tall cedars of the Lebanon Mountains and the cypresses which King Solomon ordered from King Hiram of Tyre for the building of the Temple. Great trees were cut down, and the logs were floated by sea, as many as Solomon needed, and he paid the bills with shipments of wheat and olive oil.

The myrtle was an evergreen tree whose white blossoms and sweet-smelling fruit were used in seasoning food and in making perfume. Branches of myrtle were torn down every year to build booths for the celebration of the Feast of Tabernacles.

There was a small tree called styrax, or storax, a beautiful little tree with flowers like orange blossoms. From this tree probably came the gum, stacte, which was used in making Temple incense.

There were great forests of oak trees in the land long ago. There were terebinths, which looked something like oaks. There were plane trees and poplars. There was a tree called the wild carob which had long pods men fed to the pigs. When the prodigal son was hungry he found that people could eat them, too.

Along the streams grew willow trees. In drier places the juniper or broom tree was hardy. This was not a tree with a trunk and branches, but a tall, thick, scrubby growth of many slender branches. Travelers in the desert found that it gave shade from the hot sun and protection from storms.

Herbs and Spices

In the herb garden or along the roadside grew plants that were used for seasoning food and for medicine. Some were used in making ointments, some for incense.

There was anise, which we call dill, used in making pickles. There was cane, which may have been calamus, of the iris family. Or it may have been cane like our sugar cane.

Coriander seeds came from a small plant which was found growing almost everywhere. The seeds were used for seasoning pickles and soup and in medicines.

Cummin looked like our caraway, but it had a bad taste. It was used in seasoning.

Hyssop may have been our marjoram. It was used as an antiseptic. It was used for cleansing lepers.

Mint and rue were used in food and medicine.

Saffron, which came from the crocus flower, was seasoning for food, and it was also a yellow dye.

In the book of Exodus there is a recipe for making incense:

> Take the same weight of sweet spices, stacte, and onycha and galbanum, sweet spices with pure frankincense. Season with pure salt, and beat very fine. *See Exodus 30:34-36*

Stacte may have been gum resin from the storax tree. Galbanum was a brownish resin from a plant.

An ancient recipe for making oil says:

> Take one part (250 shekel weight) sweet-smelling cinnamon, one part aromatic cane, two parts (500 shekel weight) liquid myrrh, and two parts cassia. Add one and one-third gallons (one hin) finest olive oil. *See Exodus 30:23-24*

Myrrh was made from the resin of a shrub which grew in the desert country in Arabia, and from rock roses which grew in Palestine. Sweet-smelling cinnamon was the finest kind of cinnamon from the bark of a tree at least four years old. Cassia was something like the stick cinnamon we use today.

Flowers of Palestine

Spring comes suddenly to the land of Palestine. November and December bring the rain. The sunbaked hills and fields grow moist again. In February and March come sunshine and showers, and growing things burst into bloom.

> Winter is past, and rain is over and gone;
> The time of singing birds has come.
> And the voice of the dove is heard in our land.
> Ripe figs on the trees, and the vines are in bloom.
>
> *From Song of Solomon 2:11–13*

There are fields of anemones, or windflowers, all colors, some red and purple and gayer than King Solomon's robes. Some are blue, and pink, white and cream-colored.

Grape hyacinths grow thick in fields and rocky places in the hills. In the shallow water by the edge of ponds, yellow iris turns the green banks to gold.

Yellow crocuses and red tulips, yellow and white narcissus, and oleander blossom in the springtime garden. Star-of-Bethlehem's white flowers dot the green fields where baby lambs and goats frolic in the warm spring sunshine. Sweet white henna blossoms and mandrake's fragrant purple blooms perfume the air.

Beds of sweet herbs and spices are thick with strange-smelling leaves and blooms for medicines, for perfume, and for seasoning food.

For a little while the land is a magic-colored carpet, all thick with green grass and sparkling bloom. Then the summer sun grows hot. There is no more rain until fall. The flowers fade. But spring will come again.

IN THE YEARS BETWEEN THE TESTAMENTS

THE STORY OF the Jews in the Old Testament ends with their homecoming to Jerusalem after the captivity in Babylon. The New Testament begins with the birth of Jesus. In the four hundred years that passed between those two events, great changes were taking place in Palestine and in other countries of the world. The Bible does not tell us about those years between the Testaments, but history-writers left records of the times.

Greek Ways and Words

Persia had been the strongest nation of the world. But when Alexander the Great led his Greek and Macedonian army eastward against Persia, he was able to conquer Persia and all the lands under Persia's rule. These lands extended as far east as India, as far south as Persia.

Alexander died. His four generals could not agree on a new leader. So they divided his great empire among themselves. Small Judea, which was between Egypt and Syria, belonged at first to Egypt and later on to Syria.

Wherever Alexander's army of Greek and Macedonian soldiers had traveled, Greek ways and words traveled, too. Everywhere, people began to speak the Greek language. Greek games and sports became their sports. Towns and cities built gymnasiums where boys and young men trained and exercised. It became fashionable to wear Greek clothes and to act like Greeks.

The most important difference between the Jews and the Greeks was in their worship. The Greeks prayed to many gods and goddesses whom they believed to be fairy-tale supermen and women ruled by Zeus, all-powerful king of the gods.

People were traveling more than they ever had before. Jews were moving away from their homeland to settle in cities north and south. Many of them had remained in the land where they had been taken as captives. Thousands of them moved to Alexandria, the beautiful new city Alexander had built in Egypt. Jewish merchants could do business in many lands, for there was no longer a problem of working with people who spoke strange languages.

For a time life in Judea was untroubled, although the wise old men shook their heads sadly because the young men were dressing like Greeks and spending all their time in the gymnasium playing games as Greeks did.

Everything changed under the Syrian king Antiochus, called "the Splendid." He broke into the Temple and stole its treasures. He set out to force the Greek way on everyone. He made it against the law for the Jews to keep the sabbath, to own a copy of the Law and the Prophets, to sacrifice to God on the Temple altars. For men who disobeyed, the punishment was death. Disobedient mothers and children were sold to be slaves.

The Maccabees

The people disobeyed quietly. It was not the time to fight for freedom, for they had no strong army. Antiochus grew impatient. The Jews were too slow in taking up Greek ways. He wanted no troublemakers. So he marched his soldiers into the Temple, and he took away all the treasures used for sacrifice and worship, all the bowls, and the golden lampstand. On the altar which was always kept according to the Jewish law, he burned a pig, because Jewish laws called pigs unclean. Then he set up a statue of Zeus inside the Temple, and he dedicated the building as a place of prayer to Greek gods. He ordered the Hebrews to sacrifice pigs to God as a part of their worship.

The time to fight had come. Mattathias, an old man who was the priest in Modein, was the first rebel. With his five sons he had been quietly disobeying the new laws. But the day he watched another Jew praying to Zeus at the order of a Syrian soldier, he drew his sword and killed them both.

The six patriots fled for their lives, to hide in caves in the hills. Other loyal Jews joined them. Mattathias died, and his son Judas became the leader. They defeated Syrian soldiers sent against them.

Although the patriots had no army, they could fight in surprise night raids. Their attacks were like the quick, smashing blows of a hammer. Judas was nicknamed "the Hammerer," or Maccabaeus, and all his family were called Maccabees.

The raids continued for years until the Maccabees drove the Syrians out of Judea, all of them except the soldiers in the fortress built into the wall of Jerusalem.

At last the loyal Jews could clean up their Temple, smash the statue of Zeus, and rebuild their own altar. How they celebrated as they dedicated that altar to God! The first Feast of the Dedication was the beginning of a new Jewish holiday, one of the happiest of all the year. It is also called the Hanukkah, or Feast of the Maccabees.

Judas could not rest from fighting until all the land was free. After he died, his brothers carried on the battle. Then John Hyrcanus, son of Simon, one of the brothers, led the Jews out into neighbor lands. From the Syrians they took Samaria, then Galilee, then Idumea. For the last time, the land of the Jews was free and independent.

Under Roman Rule

A new nation in the west had set out to rule the world. The army of Rome, with elephants, and troops mounted on swift horses, could invade the best-defended cities.

General Pompey of Rome led his troops into Judea. His great battering rams began to pound against the walls of Jerusalem. The Jews were able to hold out for three months. Then they had to surrender. Many people were killed. Many were taken prisoner and sent away to Rome.

From that time on, the Roman Government appointed the rulers in Palestine. The Jewish Sanhedrin, or court of seventy men, was allowed to be in charge of all matters of Jewish life and law, and Jews were free to worship in their Temple and in their synagogues.

At first, men of the Maccabee family were chosen as governors. But these men were not brave leaders like Judas and the first Maccabees. So Rome made a man from Idumea governor. His son, Herod, became king of Judea, then of all the lands along the Great Sea from Egypt north to Syria. Herod the Great, King of the Jews, he was called.

Herod built fine cities. In Jerusalem he rebuilt the Temple, and he made it far larger, far more splendid than Solomon's Temple had been.

And so the years between the Testaments came to an end, for in the time of Herod the Great, Jesus was born in Bethlehem in Judea.

HOLY DAYS
FEASTS AND FESTIVALS

THE HEBREW WORD *sabbath* means day of rest. God gave to his people one day out of seven to spend in rest and worship. "Six days shalt thou labor and do all thy work; but the seventh day is the sabbath." That was the fourth of the Ten Commandments given by God through Moses.

The Hebrew sabbath began at sunset on Friday and lasted until sunset on Saturday.

Sabbath eve was a happy time in Hebrew homes. At the sound of a ram's horn blown by a priest from the roof of the house of worship, the mother would light the sabbath candle, and parents and children would sit down to the evening meal. This was a special meal, the best of the week. Fathers, mothers, and children showed their respect for the day by dressing in their best clothes. The father said a blessing, and the family talked about the holy beginnings of this day—the time of the beginnings of all things when God created the world and everything that is in it in six days and rested on the seventh.

The *day of the new moon,* which was the first day of each month, was a holy day for the Hebrews. It was much like the sabbath. The Temple was open for worship, and all business stopped, as it did on the sabbath. Sacrifices were offered in the Temple, and the people enjoyed a special meal in their homes.

Passover, Pentecost, and the Feast of Booths (also called Tabernacles) were the three most important festivals of the Hebrew year. The Hebrews celebrated these holy days in their homes and at their places of worship. They were special times for giving to God, for worshipping him at home and in the Temple, and for enjoying happy times as families in the homes.

The *Feast of the Passover* came first in the year. It was the most important. Every Hebrew male over twelve years of age was required to observe this feast.

In observing the Passover feast, the Hebrews were remembering the night when God had delivered them from slavery in Egypt. That night, when the firstborn of all the Egyptian families had died, the death angel had passed over the homes of the Hebrews and had spared their children. So the Hebrews named their festival "Passover."

Because of the people's haste to escape from Egypt, there had been no time to cook the usual kinds of food. They had eaten bread made without yeast (called unleavened bread), bitter herbs, and lamb. So, through the years the Hebrews ate those same foods when they celebrated the Passover.

Every house was cleaned before the Passover festival. All yeast or leavened bread had to be burned. Children and parents would search everywhere, using lamps in the dark corners, to be sure no crumb was left.

After the father of the family asked the blessing, the family ate the herbs; next, they ate the unleavened bread, which was like dry crackers; and last of all, the roasted lamb. But before the meat was eaten, the oldest son would ask, "What do these services mean?" His father would tell the story of the first Passover and the escape from Egypt. During the supper the family would recite Psalms 113 and 114, then 115 to 118; sometimes, too, Psalms 120 to 138.

At first the Passover was a family festival, celebrated in the homes. Later, all the families who could travel would make the journey to Jerusalem to worship in the Temple. Families from the country would visit their friends in the city, and when there was no more room in the crowded houses, the visitors would camp in tents outside the city wall.

On the day after the Passover supper, the Feast of Unleavened Bread began. For seven days the people ate unleavened bread and no other kind. On the second day of the feast they offered sheaves of new wheat to God in thanksgiving for the gift of grain.

On the sixth day of the third month, seven weeks (or fifty days) after Passover, the Hebrews celebrated the *Feast of Pentecost.* That word means "fiftieth day." Sometimes the Hebrews called the festival the Feast of Weeks. This was a day of thanksgiving for God's gift of grain, and it was celebrated at the end of the harvest of barley and wheat. As a thank offering, two loaves of bread were made from the finest of the new flour and offered to God. Only after the gift of the new loaves could the people enjoy the good food made from grain of the new harvest.

Passover and Pentecost were both times of thanksgiving, but the special thanksgiving feast of the year came in the fall. On the fifteenth day of the seventh month began the seven-day celebration called the *Feast of Booths* (also called the Feast of Tabernacles). All the crops were harvested—the grapes, the olives, and the fruit as well as the grain. Food was ready for the winter. "The Lord your God blesses you in all your produce and in all the works of your hands so that you can be altogether joyful," read the Law.

In the land of Canaan, where fields were green after refreshing rain, the people would remember gratefully how God had helped their ancestors to find food in the dry wilderness country after their escape from Egypt. In their good, safe houses, the Hebrews remembered the homes their ancestors had made in the wilderness. Those houses had been huts or shelters made from the branches of bushes and trees. So during the fall thanksgiving festival they left their houses, and for seven days they lived in huts or shelters made from branches of olive and palm, myrtle and pine trees. In the streets, on the flat rooftops, in the courtyards, outside the walls of the garlanded cities, the little booths were set up, gay and green, and the people were happy as they celebrated.

There was a special offering to be made each day, and on the last day a solemn worship service was held. In the Temple in Jerusalem the trumpets sounded, and the priest came through the Water Gate carrying water from the pool of Siloam in a golden pitcher. And every evening in the Court of the Women, when eight great lamps were lighted, the families celebrated together. The Feast of Tabernacles was one of the happiest times of the year.

Passover, Pentecost, and the Feast of Tabernacles became times of pilgrimage when Hebrew families from all over the Roman world who could travel went to Jerusalem to celebrate.

The seventh month, when the Feast of Tabernacles was celebrated, became a special month in the Hebrew calendar. The month began, as all months did, with a day of worship when the trumpets called the people to pray and worship. But the first day of the seventh month was a *Day of Blowing of Trumpets,* the new year's day of the business and official year.

> "Blow the trumpet at the new moon,
> At the full moon, on our feast day,
> For it is a law for Israel, a law for Judah.
> Hear, my people, while I warn you.
> O Israel, if you would listen!
> I am the Lord your God."
>
> *Psalm 81*

In the same month the tenth day was the *Day of Atonement,* a day of solemn prayer, a day of fasting, not of feasting. This was a day for remembering all the broken promises, all the disobedient ways, all the unfaithfulness that kept God's people from being close to him. In the Temple, the high priest, dressed in special white linen robes, went into the holy of holies to pray that God would forgive the people's sins. Outside, the people were praying, too. And there were special offerings, special animal sacrifices.

All these feasts and holy days were a part of the Jewish calendar from the days when they first became free people. Two other festivals are mentioned in the Bible, both times of celebration.

The *Feast of Lights,* or the *Feast of Dedication,* began on the twenty-fifth day of the ninth month and lasted eight days. The story of the celebration goes back to the time of the Maccabees. Great danger had come to the Jews in Jerusalem when Antiochus, their Syrian ruler, forbade them to worship in their way.

Judas Maccabaeus led a band of loyal men straight into the Temple where Antiochus had set up heathen idols. With a trumpet call and a prayer for God's help, the loyal Jews went to work. They tore down the heathen altar, and they built a fine new altar of clean stones. On the twenty-fifth day of the ninth month they dedicated the Temple to God. Perhaps they remembered stories of Solomon and the great day of dedication. Perhaps they remembered Ezra and the dedication of the second Temple where they worshiped now. This, too, was a dedication to remember, and so Judas and all the congregation decreed that the festival should be celebrated every year.

Purim was celebrated on the fourteenth and fifteenth days of the twelfth month, about one month before the Passover. Like the Feast of Lights it had not been planned when the Hebrews first became free people. It celebrated the story of a later event.

Purim was the celebration of Queen Esther's bravery in saving her people when Haman would have had all the Jewish exiles in Persia killed. The day before the festival was a solemn day of fasting. On the evening of the fourteenth day, the book of Esther was read in the synagogues. When Haman's name was mentioned in the reading the people would call out, "Let his name be blotted out!" and the young people would rattle noisemakers.

The next morning there was another service in the synagogue. Then the fun began. There was feasting. Friends and kinfolk gave gifts to one another. Special gifts and food were provided for the poor. It was a day of happiness and celebration for all.

PLACES FOR WORSHIP

AT JACOB'S WELL a Samaritan woman asked Jesus, "Where should we go to worship God? Here on the mountain in my country? Or must we go to the Temple in Jerusalem?"

"God is spirit," Jesus told her. "And true worship of God comes from the hearts of those who love him."

For many, many years the Jewish people had been learning how to worship God. They discovered that a special place set aside for worship helped them to think of God. At first they built outdoor altars. Then they built the tent house of meeting, or tabernacle. In Jerusalem they built the Temple. Later they built synagogues in towns and cities, where they met to worship and to study God's Word.

The Outdoor Altars

The first altars were made of earth and stone. Sometimes they were built to hold sacrifice offerings for God. Sometimes they were memorial markers to show where some important event had happened. Always the altars were placed where men had met God and had learned something important from that meeting—his will for them or the answer to their prayer.

The first altar described in the Bible was built by Noah in thanksgiving to God after he and all his family landed safely from the ark. When Abram reached Shechem in Canaan on his long journey to an unknown land, he heard God say, "To your descendants I will give this land." And so Abram built an altar there under an oak tree. At the foot of Sinai, the mountain where Moses met God and received the Law from him, Moses built an altar with twelve stone pillars, one for each of the twelve tribes.

Those first altars were more than places for gift offerings. They were a sign of man's need to meet with God. For God had given man this need when he made the first people.

"An altar of earth you shall make for me and sacrifice on it your burnt offerings . . . in every place where I cause my name to be remembered I will come to you and bless you," God promised his people when they were on their way to the Promised Land.

The Tabernacle

When the Hebrews were wandering in the wilderness and living in tents, there was a special tent of meeting set up. Here Moses would go to meet and talk with God. On Mount Sinai, after God had given Moses the laws for living for all the people, he gave plans and directions for a tent house for worship, to be set up in the center of the camp. The directions, in the book of Exodus, are so complete that today careful workmen can follow them and make a model of that tabernacle.

With gifts of cloth and metal and other treasures which the people gladly gave, and with wood of the acacia trees that grew in the wilderness country, the Hebrews worked to build their first place of worship. Materials were rich and beautiful. Gold and silver and brass were used freely. Blue, purple, scarlet, and white linen, woven goats' hair and leather and wood were collected for curtains and tent coverings. Fine spices and incense and olive oil were given to be used in the worship services. Jewels and gold and brass and fine cloth were used to make the robes and the decorations which the priests wore.

The tabernacle was to be much more than an altar. Outside the tent there was a courtyard, with walls made of curtains hung from poles. There the people brought their offerings of meat and grain and bread and salt and oil to the priests. On the great bronze altar between the entrance to the court and the door of the tent the priests burned the sacrifice offerings. There in the courtyard people and priests worshiped God.

The people could go no farther. The priests, wearing their beautiful robes, would enter the first room in the tent, the holy place. First they washed hands and feet in water from the huge bronze bowl that stood between the altar and the door of the tent.

Inside the tent they burned special incense on the golden altar. They refilled the seven lamps of the golden lampstand with purest olive oil. And once a week on the sabbath they placed twelve loaves of fresh-baked bread on the table as a thank offering to God for his gift of food.

Beyond the holy place was a quiet room, the holy of holies. Between the two rooms a beautiful curtain hung from four pillars. It was blue and purple and scarlet, and it was embroidered with figures of cherubim. Only the high priest could go beyond that curtain, and he could go on only one day in the year, the Day of Atonement, when he prayed that God would forgive the sins of the people.

In the holy of holies was the people's greatest treasure, the ark of God's promise, which was a wooden chest covered inside and out with gold. Over the chest was a golden cover with the figures of two golden cherubim. God had promised that he would be with his people, there in the holy of holies, beneath the wings of the cherubim, and that once every year he would meet there with the high priest.

Inside the ark were the stone slabs on which God had written the Ten Commandments. Two more treasures were added later during the years of wandering. One was a golden bowl of manna. The other was Aaron's rod which budded the night after there had been an argument among some of the men who wanted to take Aaron's place. The buds on Aaron's rod were a sign to the people that Aaron was God's choice for the position of high priest.

When the Hebrews crossed the Jordan River to enter the Promised Land, the priests carried the ark safely to the edge of the river. When the water stopped flowing, they waited with the ark until all the people had crossed over safely on dry land.

The ark was taken to Shiloh, and there it stayed until the sad day when Hebrew soldiers carried it with them into battle, thinking that surely they would win if they had the ark there beside them. Instead, the ark was captured by the enemy and kept for a long time.

Years later, King David had the ark carried up to his new capital city, Jerusalem, and there he placed it carefully in a tent. King Solomon built the Temple where his father had hoped to build it. In the Temple, once again the ark was placed in the holy of holies, placed reverently and with all honor. Though the splendid new Temple was far finer than the tabernacle, the two places of worship were alike in having the quiet inside room where the Hebrews kept their greatest treasure.

Somewhere, somehow, in all the adventures of travel and battle, the bowl of manna and the rod that budded disappeared. The stone slabs with the Ten Commandments were still safe in the golden chest beneath the golden cherubim.

Solomon's Temple

Three temples, one after another, were built in Jerusalem. The first, Solomon's Temple, was exactly twice as large as the tabernacle. It was built on the plan of the tabernacle, with a porch instead of a courtyard, a holy place, and a holy of holies. Built of shining gold and marble and fine cedar wood from Lebanon, it was as beautiful as man could build a house for God.

When the Babylonians besieged Jerusalem and starved the people into surrendering, they burned the Temple along with the palaces and the houses and the gates in the city wall. Was the ark carried off to Babylon with the Hebrew people? Did those who were left behind and who decided later to go away to Egypt take it with them? Or was it burned in the fire that ruined the Temple? Whatever happened is a mystery.

Seventy years went by. Persia conquered the Babylonians. The Persian leaders did not treat conquered people as the Babylonians had done. They allowed them to remain in their own country if they would live there peaceably. Those who had been carried away into captivity were allowed to return to their homes in the land of Judah.

At last the promise made by so many of the prophets had come true. When the people had served their time of punishment for all their wicked ways, God brought them home.

Zerubbabel's Temple

In Jerusalem, Zerubbabel the governor and Joshua the high priest led the work of rebuilding the Temple. Compared to the wondrous Temple of Solomon, the new building was plain, for the Jews who came back home had no royal treasury. But some of them had gold and silver of their own. They carried gifts from the king of Persia and gifts from the Jews who had decided to stay in the land of Persia. Gladly these people gave their money to buy cedar wood from Lebanon and gold for the Temple walls and doors.

Workmen followed the plan of the first Temple. Outdoors there were courts for sacrifice and worship. Indoors there was the holy place and the holy of holies. An altar for incense, a lampstand, and a table for twelve loaves of offering bread were in the holy place. Some of the gold and silver treasures from the first Temple, stolen by the Babylonians, were returned by the Persian king. The holy of holies was empty. The ark had disappeared.

Herod's Temple

The third Temple was larger and far more splendid and more beautiful. People used to say that it was the most beautiful building anywhere in the world outside of Rome.

This Temple was the gift of Herod the Great, whom Julius Caesar had appointed to be king of the Jews. When Herod first told the Jews of his plans to rebuild their Temple some of the men objected. They were afraid that he might tear down their Temple and never finish the work of rebuilding. So he promised to collect all the materials for the new Temple before work would begin. For two years the work of collecting went on. During that time some of the priests and Levites were being trained to work as carpenters and stone masons so that they would help in building.

Around the courts and buildings and the long covered porches outside the new Temple there was a high, strong wall. On the northwest corner of the wall there were stairs leading to the Castle of Antonia, a Roman fortress. Paul stood on those stairs when he tried to quiet an angry mob of Jews who wanted him arrested.

Handsome gates in the high wall were the entrance to the paved grounds around the Temple, called the Court of the Gentiles. Through those gates Gentiles were allowed to go with the Jews, and there the Gentiles who came to worship gave their offerings to the priests. But a sign which read "Let no Gentiles enter" warned them that they must stay in the Court.

An inner wall enclosed the Temple and its courts. From the outer Court of the Gentiles, gates in the wall opened into the Court of Israel and into the Court of the Women. There were four gates on the northern side, four in the southern wall, and on the east wall was the splendid entrance which was probably the Beautiful Gate where Peter cured the lame man. The doors of the eastern gate were seventy-five feet high and decorated with silver and gold.

Just inside the gate was the Court of the Women. Jewish women were allowed to go that far, but there they must wait while the men went on up the stairs to the Court of Israel. Just beyond was the Court of the Priests. There was the altar where every evening and every morning the priests burned the sacrifice offerings. Beyond and high above all the courts and the porches was the white marble Temple. There in the holy place were the incense altar, the golden lampstand, and the table for twelve loaves of bread. A beautifully embroidered curtain hid the holy of holies, where one day in the year the high priest placed a golden censor in which incense was burning.

As long as the Jews lived peaceably as subjects of Rome, they were free to worship in the Temple and free to observe all their Jewish ceremonies. But there came a time when men talked of freedom from Rome, and they plotted rebellion and revolution.

A band of men called Zealots worked for years to stir the Jews up to fight for their freedom. Battles were fought, and a few were won. At last Roman Emperor Titus sent four legions of Roman soldiers against the people of Jerusalem. After five months of terrible fighting, the people had to surrender. Titus gave orders that Jerusalem was to be destroyed. With the city went the Temple of marble and gold. Only smoke-blackened ruins were left.

The Synagogues

From the time King Solomon dedicated the first Temple, Jewish worshipers thought of Jerusalem as the place where they must go to keep the great feasts and holy days. The Temple was the most beautiful and most important place of worship in all the land.

But when the Hebrew people discovered that God is everywhere, that he was with them even in Babylon, far away from the ruins of their Temple, men began to meet together to study and to pray wherever they were. More and more often they met in groups, or assemblies. The Hebrew word for the meeting was synagogue, or assembly.

Back home again in Judea, the men built synagogues in their towns and villages. The rules were simple. Ten men could organize a synagogue. Women were never members, but they went to the services, where they sat by themselves on one side of the house. The members elected elders to keep order and to see that the people obeyed the laws of God. A ruler, or chairman, was in charge of the service. He guarded the scrolls on which the Word of God was written. He saw to it that the building was clean and repaired when necessary. Scribes or rabbis taught the Law.

The synagogue service opened with a prayer by one of the members, a prayer which always began:

> Hear, O Israel:
> The Lord our God is one Lord;
> And you shall love the Lord your God
> With all your heart,
> And with all your soul,
> And with all your might. *Deuteronomy 6:4–5*

Then all the people stood, and at the end of the prayer they said amen. Someone read from the books of the Law. The man who opened the service read from one of the prophets. Then there was a sermon, either by the same speaker or by another man. If a priest was present he pronounced the benediction.

At first the men met for the service on the sabbath day. They liked to go to Jerusalem for the feast days. But not all the men could make the trip. So they began to have feast-day services in the synagogues. By the time Jesus came to live on earth the Jews were having services on the sabbath, and on Mondays and Thursdays, too, so that country folk who brought their grain and fruits and livestock to market might be able to attend the services.

As the Jews began to travel away from their homeland and make their homes in Egypt and in the northern lands, they built their synagogues wherever there were as many as ten men in a town. When the first missionaries set out to tell the story of Jesus, they looked for the synagogues first of all, and when they found friends among the Jews, there in the synagogues they told the good news of the coming of Jesus.

THE MONTHS OF THE YEAR

THERE WERE TWELVE MONTHS in the year by the Jewish calendar. Each month began on the day of the new moon. Now, months measured by the moon have 28 days. Twelve moon months add up to 354 days and a few hours. Today we use a calendar of twelve months of 365 days, marking the time the earth turns round the sun. Since that time is really a little more than 365 days we add an extra day in leap year. The Jews used to add an extra month in their leap years to keep their calendar and the journey of the earth around the sun agreeing.

In the Bible we find the months of the year called "first month," "second month," and so on. There are also names given to the months, names in part borrowed from neighbor nations.

The year began in the spring with the month Abib, or Nisan as it was called later. It was in this month that God led his people out of Egypt to freedom. With Abib the year of religious feasts and celebrations began. The year of business and law began with the seventh month, about our late September or early October.

Because the Jewish months followed the moon pattern they cannot be compared exactly to the months of our calendar.

First month: Abib, or Nisan, was about like our April. The winter rain was almost over. The Jordan River was overflowing its banks and flooding the valley. Near the sea, barley was ripe, and in the hot Jordan Valley the farmers were harvesting the first wheat. Fields were green, and flowers were blooming everywhere.

Second month: Ziv was about like May. Warm, dry weather began. Probably there would be no more rain until Elul, our

September. Barley was ripe in the hills, wheat in the lowlands.

Third month: Sivan was about like June. Days were hotter. Near the sea, apples were ripe. Figs and almonds were ready to eat.

Fourth month: Tammuz, about like July. Skies were clear, and days were hot. Early grapes were ripe, and in the high, cooler fields the last of the wheat was being harvested.

Fifth month: Ab, hottest month of all, was about like August. Some clouds were in the sky, and dew was beginning to appear. Olives were ripe.

Sixth month: Elul, about like September. There were flashes of lightning and a very little rain. Grapes were ready for picking. Dates and summer figs were ripe.

Seventh month: Ethanim or Tishri, was about like October. This was the beginning of the rainy season, a time of thunderstorms and of heavy dew. Pomegranates and pistachio nuts were ripe. Farmers were busy plowing and planting barley and wheat.

Eighth month: Bul, about like November. Heavy rain was falling. Olives were ripe in North Galilee.

Ninth month: Chislev, about like December. There were hailstorms and heavy rain. Winter figs were ripe.

Tenth month: Tebeth, about like January. There was heavy rain, snow in the mountains, and sometimes in Jerusalem. But in the warmer lowlands, pastures were turning green, and early spring wild flowers were in bloom.

Eleventh month: Shebat, about like February. Rain continued, and there was some snow, but in the lowlands almond trees and figs were blossoming.

Twelfth month: Adar, about like March. There was heavy rain. Oranges and lemons were ripe in the warmer lowlands. Near Jericho the first barley of the season was ripe. Pomegranates were blossoming.

Thirteenth month: Ve-adar (the *additional* Adar) added in leap years.

"THE LAND" OF THE BIBLE

"The Land" has had many names. It was Canaan, home of the Canaanites. It was the Promised Land to the Hebrews who traveled from Egypt to a homeland of their own. After King Solomon died, and the kingdom was divided, the northern part of the country was called Israel, the southern part, Judah. Then the Assyrians conquered Israel and carried the people far away. The kingdom of Israel came to an end. The land which had belonged to Israel came to be called Samaria.

Many years later, after Judah was conquered, and after the Jews came home again, Judah was called Judea. The Romans who conquered The Land called all the country Palestine, naming it for the Philistines who had been living along the seacoast before the Hebrews came into the land.

Names of the country have changed, but to the Jews their homeland was always The Land, a special gift to them from God. And for nearly two thousand years, to Christians around the world the land where Jesus lived has been the Holy Land.

When Jesus lived in The Land, the southern division was called Judea. To the Jews who loved their country, Judea was the most important part, because Jerusalem was in Judea, and the Temple was in Jerusalem.

North of Judea was Samaria, home of the Samaritans who boasted that Abraham was their ancestor. They worshiped God in their own temple on Mount Gerizim.

North of Samaria was Galilee, home of many, many Gentiles as well as Jews. Nazareth was in this part of the Holy Land.

Geography of The Land

Palestine is a small country. The coastline is about 180 miles long. The distance from the foot of Mt. Hermon to the southern end of the Dead Sea is about 150 miles. From the center of the Dead Sea to the Mediterranean is only sixty miles. Though Palestine is so small, it has sandy beaches and snow-capped mountains, low plains and hill country, rivers and lakes, and the Dead Sea, which is the lowest lake in all the world.

The map shows the smooth coastline on the west, broken only where the ridge of Mount Carmel juts out into the sea. The land along the coast is flat, except for Mount Carmel. Gradually, eastward from the sea, the land becomes hillier. Then the hills rise to mountains. On the eastern side of the mountain ridge the land slopes steeply to the valley of the Jordan River.

The Jordan comes from springs far in the north, where Mount Hermon's three peaks are more than 9,000 feet above sea level. The water flows into tiny Lake Huleh, then out into a narrow stream that splashes downhill to the Sea of Galilee. From the Sea of Galilee to the Dead Sea, the Jordan River twists and turns, flowing always downhill. And when it empties into the Dead Sea, there the water stays. There is no way out.

The strange lake which was called in the Bible the Salt Sea is about 1300 feet below sea level. The water is so full of chemicals that no fish can live in it. It feels greasy, and the hot breeze that blows across it smells of sulphur.

East of the Jordan Valley steep mountains rise, and beyond the mountains are desert lands.

These eastern mountains are higher and steeper than those on the west. From their tops a plain stretches away to the desert. The plain is mostly fertile and provides pasture lands for cattle.

The Climate

With so many changes, from mountaintops to low valleys in such short distances, there are many changes from cold to heat. Most of the time the temperature in Jerusalem is comfortably cool. Down the steep mountainside in Jericho, only fifteen miles away, it is so much warmer that tropical plants are growing, and summers are too hot to be comfortable.

Instead of four seasons in the year, Palestine has two, the rainy season and the dry. In October the wind begins to blow from the sea, bringing rain clouds, and the rains continue until April. This is the season when the farmers work hard, for after April there will be almost no rain until October.

In the summer the wind shifts, and cool breezes blow from the northwest. Sometimes in the early fall a cool wind blows from the north. The fearful east wind, the whirlwind out of the hot eastern desert, is the wind the people fear. It can whip down, scorching grapes and figs and olives, making people hot and uncomfortable (and angry at one another) and The Land unbearable until it has blown itself out.

The Roads

The roads of Palestine were old, old roads. They were not wide, as roads are built today. Probably they were not paved until the Romans had conquered the land. But they were wide enough for camel caravans and riders on slow-stepping donkeys and galloping horses, as well as for people who walked, as Jesus and his disciples walked so many times from one town to another.

The most crowded road was the Way of the Sea, from Damascus

across the Jordan River, between Lake Huleh and the Sea of Galilee, past Capernaum and Nazareth, across the plain to Ptolemais on the sea. This was a Roman road in New Testament times. The Romans collected taxes on all goods carried along the Way of the Sea. Somewhere along that road Matthew was collecting taxes for the Romans the day when Jesus met him.

The shortest road from Jerusalem to Capernaum went north on the mountain ridge through Shechem. That was the way Jesus was traveling when he stopped at Jacob's Well and asked a Samaritan woman to give him a drink of water. Few Jews chose to travel that road. Most of them despised Samaritans too much to go through their land.

The longer road from Jerusalem to Capernaum went from Jerusalem to Bethany and Jericho and on across the Jordan River. Then it turned north. South of the Sea of Galilee the road forked. The right-hand road went all the way to Damascus. The left-hand road turned toward the west and led to Capernaum.

The fourth of the most important roads of Palestine ran along the coast, from Gaza far to the south. A few miles north of Gaza a road branched off to the east to Hebron and went on north to Bethlehem, then to Jerusalem. The road by the sea went straight up the plain to Joppa, then on to Tyre and Sidon far in the north.

INDEX OF STORIES

The Old Testament

IN THE BEGINNING 13
How God Made the World 13
The First People 15
The Beginning of Trouble 16

THE TRAVELING PEOPLE 19
The First Two Brothers 19
People Good and Bad 20
The Ship That God Designed 21
The Rainbow Promise 24
A Song of Thanksgiving 25
The Tower of Pride 27

GOD'S FAMILY 28
Pioneer Abram 28
The Story of a Choice 29
The Battle of the Kings 31
New Names 33
Guests at Abraham's House 35
A City in Flames 36
Two Boys in Abraham's House ... 37
Abraham's Great Discovery 39
A Bride for Isaac 40
The Twins Who Made a Bargain .. 43
The Man Who Hated Quarreling .. 44
Jacob, the Cheat 46
The Runaway's Discovery 49
A Bride for Jacob 52
When the Runaway Went Home .. 53
How the Quarrel Ended 55

THE STORY OF JOSEPH 59
How a Brother Was Sold 59
Honor and Shame in the Palace ... 61
Governor Joseph 62
The Hungry Brothers 67
"I Am Joseph" 70
A New Home in Egypt 74
The Grandfather Blessing 77

THE LEADER GOD CHOSE ... 81
The Adopted Baby 81
Runaway from the Palace 83
How God Called His Leader 84
The Fight for Freedom 87

A New Holiday 90
Across the Sea to Freedom 93
Thirsty Travelers 95
Nothing to Eat 96
A Tired Leader 98
God's Ten Laws 99
Forgotten Promises 101
Rules for Living 103
A House for God 105
When It Was Time to Travel 108
Giants and Grasshoppers 110
Troubles in the Desert 113
Victory March 115
The Talking Donkey 116
It Happened on the Mountain 118

WARS OF GENERAL JOSHUA .121
Adventure of the Spies 121
Dry Path Through the River 123
When the Trumpets Sounded 124
Stolen Treasure 127
A Roadside Dedication 128
Tricky Travelers from Gibeon 130
The Battle of the Longest Day 131
Homesteaders in a New Land 132
The General's Good-by 133

THE HERO JUDGES 135
Judge Ehud's Victory 135
Captain Lightning's Muddy Battle .136
How Gideon Was Drafted 139
How the Captain Chose His Army .141
The Battle of Lights and Noise ...142
Story of the Talking Trees 144
"Say the Password" 145
Strong Fighter for Israel 146
Stolen Silver, Stolen Priest 151

THE STORY OF RUTH 153

THE MAN WHO ASKED WHY .159
Testing Time for Job 159
The Friends Who Came to Help ..161
Job's Discoveries 163
"I Want to Understand" 164

When Job Stopped to Listen 166
And So Job Passed the Test 167

JUDGE SAMUEL 168
God Sent a Baby 168
God Spoke to a Boy 169
No Magic in the Ark 172
How the Ark Came Home 173
They Wanted a King 175

ISRAEL'S FIRST KING 177
How Samuel Chose the King 177
The King's First Victory 179
How Saul Lost His Kingdom 181

ISRAEL'S GREATEST KING ..184
Youngest Son, the Shepherd 184
Music-Maker in the King's House .186
The Boy Who Fought a Giant 187
When David Joined the Outlaws ..189
Four Hundred Mighty Men 193
A Shepherd Named "Foolish" 195
How David Rescued His Family ..197
David's Royal Prisoner 198
When the King Died 200
How David Became King 202
A New Capital for the New King .203
Music and Marching Feet 204
The Little Lost Prince 208
Trouble at David's House 209
Traitor Absalom 211
Temple Plans and Treasures 216
A Commission for Solomon 217
"God Save the King!" 220

SOLOMON, THE SPLENDID ..222
The Young King's Prayer 222
A House for God's Honor 224
Rich and Wise Was Solomon 228
When the King Lost His Kingdom .231

A KINGDOM DIVIDED 233
How the Kingdom Was Divided ..233
Two Kingdoms and Two Capitals .234
In the Days of Good King Asa ...236
Elijah, the Fighting Prophet 238
The Battle with the Baal Priests ..242
God's Quiet Voice 244
The Royal Thief 246
Two Kings Who Went to War ...248
Victory Before the Battle 251
The Prophet Who Took Elijah's
    Place 252

Water Safe to Drink 254
Soup Fit to Eat 254
Money for a Mother's Debts 255
The Most Welcome Guest 257
Help for the Great Captain 258
"Tomorrow About This Time" ...261
Choosing the New King 263
The Baby King in the Secret Room .265
A Chest Full of Gifts 267
Uzziah, Who Wanted His Own
    Way 268

GOD'S WATCHMEN 270
They Spoke for God 270
Amos, the Shepherd Preacher 271
Hosea's Discovery 275
Jonah, the Unwilling Missionary ..277
Isaiah, Messenger to Kings 280
Farmer Micah 285

PROUD ISRAEL'S END 286

LONELY JUDAH 289
Housecleaning in the Temple 289
Dangerous Neighbors 291
The Army That Disappeared 294
The King Who Had a Second
    Chance 296
Message from Isaiah 297
Idols in the Temple 298
Jeremiah's Call 299
An Old Book in a Dusty Corner ..300
No One Was Listening 301
Dangers Far and Near 304
Prophet on a Watchtower 306
The Prophet No One Liked 307
The Teacher in the Street 308
The Lesson of the Broken Pot 309
The Family That Kept Its Promise .310
The Message in the Book 311
Then It All Came True 313
Prisoner in the Slime Pit 316
Captured King, Ruined City 317

EZEKIEL'S PICTURE
    SERMONS 321
God's Shining Glory 321
The Horrors in the Temple 323
The Toy War 324
The Bad Shepherds 326
The Dead and Dusty Valley 327
The Picture of the New World ...328

667

STORIES OF DANIEL 329
Four Young Men in Training 329
The Image in the Dream 331
Four Who Walked in Fire 333
A Dream About a Tall Tree 336
Mysterious Message on the Wall .. 338
Into the Lions' Den 340
The Dream of the Shining
    Kingdom 342

QUEEN ESTHER 344
A Jewish Girl Chosen Queen 344
Haman's Plots Against the Jews .. 346
How Queen Esther Saved Her
    People 347

CAPTIVES WHO CAME HOME . 353

One Small Altar in the Ruins 353
Stone on Stone They Built the
    Temple 356
Royal Homecoming for Ezra 361
The Leader of the Wall-Builders .. 363
Seven Days by the Water Gate ... 367

SONGS AND SAYINGS 372
Song for the House of God 372
Song of God's Loving Care 373
Song for a Dark Night 375
Song of Spring 376
Song for an Orchestra 377
Wise Words for Every Day 378
Song of Small Creatures 379
Lazybones 380

The New Testament

A CHILD IS BORN 382
Light of the World 382
A Boy Named John 383
The Best News Ever Told 386

WHEN THE KING CAME 390
Worshiping Wise Men 390
His Father's House 392
A Preacher with a New Message .. 394
Obedient in Baptism 397
The Fight with Satan 397
Choosing His First Friends 399
Guest at a Wedding 401
Visitor by Night 401
A Gift of Water 404
A Believing Father 405

FRIENDS AND ENEMIES 407
No Welcome in Nazareth 407
Enlisting Special Helpers 408
The Busiest Sabbath Day 410
Along the Crowded Roads 412
Cured—and Forgiven 413
"Broken Laws" 414
Clean Hands—Dirty Hearts 416

KINGDOM ADVENTURES 418
Twelve Helpers Commissioned ... 418
Happy Kingdom People 418
"You Must Choose to Belong" ... 420
"Belonging Is Expensive" 422
Locked Out 423

Some Kingdom Rules 424
How to Talk to the Father 429
Who Are Kingdom People? 430
Where Is the Kingdom? 431
Rude Guests 432
The Great Discovery 433

HE WENT ABOUT DOING
    GOOD 435
Good News Spread Fast 435
Jesus' Crowded Day 436
He Loved the Children 438
Traveling Two by Two 440
Picnic Supper by the Lake 441
Friend to the Rescue 443
A Mother's Trust 444
"If You Believe" 445
Her Second Chance 446
At Martha and Mary's House ... 447
One Said Thank You 449
Blind Beggarman 450
Short Man in a Tree 452

WHO IS HE? 453
Winds and Waves Obey 453
John's Question 453
Peter's Answer 455
Arguments and Complaints 457
"I Do Believe!" 459
The Mountaintop Discovery 461

STORIES JESUS TOLD 464
A Tale of Two Houses 464
The Farmer and His Seed 465
Forgiving Is Forever 466
Stories of Lost Treasure 467
The Stupid Rich Man 471
The Bridesmaids 471
The Talents 472
The Good Shepherd 474
The Friendly Foreigner 475

JESUS, SON OF GOD 477
The King Is Coming 477
"My Father's House" 478
"I Have Chosen You" 482
Plotting Priests 483
Judas' Fearful Bargain 485
Mary's Memorial Gift 486
The Last Supper Together 488
The First Lord's Supper 490
Jesus' Good-by Message 491
Prayer for All He Loved 493
How Jesus Was Captured 493
On Trial 495
"Crucify Him!" 499
End of the Story of Judas 500
To the Hill of the Skull 501
When God's Son Gave His Life .. 501
New Tomb in a Garden 503
Resurrection Day 505
"Love as I Have Loved You" 508
Marching Orders 510

BEGINNING IN JERUSALEM . 511
The Day That Changed the World . 511
To Work!—for Jesus' Sake 513
A New Idea of Sharing 518
Choosing the First Church Helpers . 518
Stephen, First to Die for Jesus'
  Sake 519

ADVENTURES IN JUDEA AND
  SAMARIA 522
The Greedy Magician 522
One Man from Africa 523
Murdering Saul—Brother Saul ... 525
Healing in Jesus' Name 528
Peter's Discovery 529
Nothing Could Stop Them 532

INTO ALL THE WORLD 533
The Church at Antioch 533
Paul's First Missionary Journey .. 534
What About the Gentiles? 539
The First Trip to Europe 540
The Friendly Jailer at Philippi 541
"The World Upside Down" 545
World Travelers and Letter Writers 546
Letters to the Thessalonians 550
Magicians and Mobs 552
Letters to the Corinthians 554
No Rules Against Love 558
Paul's Letter to the Romans 559
On to Jerusalem 562

THE PREACHING PRISONER .564
Arrested in the City of Peace 564
The Governor's Prisoner 566
Preacher to the King 568
Shipwrecked in a Northeaster 570
In Rome at Last 573
Letters from a Prisoner 574

MORE NEW TESTAMENT
  LETTERS 582
The Letter to the Jews 582
The Letter from Pastor James ... 584
Letters from Peter 585
Letters from John 587

NEW HEAVEN AND EARTH .. 589
Letters for Seven Churches 590
The City of Light 592

INDEX OF CHARACTERS

Aaron, 82, 86–115, 361
Abdon, 145
Abednego, 329f, 334ff
Abel, 19ff, 582
Abigail, 196f
Abijah, 235
Abimelech, 144f
Abinadab, 174
Abinadab (son of Jesse), 185, 204f
Abishai, 199
Abner, 189, 192, 199, 202f
Abraham (or Abram), 28–45, 50f, 79f, 369, 582
Absalom, 211–215
Achan, 127f
Adam, 16ff
Aeneas, 528
Agabus, 534
Agrippa, 568ff
Ahab, 238, 241f, 244, 246ff
Ahasuerus, 344
Ahaz, 283f, 286–289
Ahaziah, 263ff
Ahijah, 232
Ahikam, 308
Aholiab, 106
Alexander, 553
Amnon, 211
Amos, 270f, 275f
Amram, 82
Ananias, 518ff
Ananias (of Damascus), 526
Ananias (high priest), 566
Andrew, 399, 408, 412, 418, 440
Anna, 389
Aquila, 549, 552, 562
Araunah, 217, 225
Arioch, 332
Aristarchus, 577
Artaxerxes, 361

Asa, 236ff
Asaph, 365
Asher, 54, 132
Athaliah, 263, 265ff
Augustus (see Caesar)
Azariah, 237, 269, 329

Balaam, 116ff
Balak, 116ff
Barabbas, 499
Barak, 137f
Barnabas, 527, 533ff
Barsabbas, 540
Bartholomew, 418, 440, 511
Bartimaeus, 450
Baruch, 312, 318
Bathsheba, 209
Belshazzar, 338, 340
Belteshazzar, 329, 336
Benhadad, 238
Benjamin, 58f, 69ff, 132
Bernice, 568ff
Bethuel, 41ff
Bezaleel, 106
Bigthan, 346, 350
Bildad, 162ff
Boaz, 154–158

Caesar, 386, 484, 498, 568, 574
Caiaphas, 486, 495ff
Cain, 19ff
Caleb, 110, 112, 115, 133
Chilion, 153
Christ (see Jesus), 399
Cornelius, 529
Cyrus, 342, 353ff, 360

Damaris, 549
Dan, 53, 132
Daniel, 329–342
Darius, 340ff, 360
David, 184–235, 266
Deborah, 137f
Delilah, 148f
Demas, 577, 581

Demetrius, 553
Dinah, 54
Dionysius, 549
Dorcas, 528
Drusilla, 567

Ebed-melech, 316
Eglon, 135f
Ehud, 135f
Eleazar, 115
Eleazar (son of Abinadab), 174
Eli, 168ff
Eliab, 185
Eliakim, 294f
Eliezer, 41ff
Elihu, 165
Elijah, 238–253, 461
Elimelech, 153
Eliphaz, 161ff, 167
Elisha, 246, 252–263
Elizabeth, 383
Elkanah, 168f
Elymas, 535
Enoch, 21, 582
Epaphras, 577
Epaphroditus, 579
Ephraim, 67, 78f
Erastus, 553
Esau, 44, 46ff, 55
Esther, 345–351
Eve, 16ff
Ezekiel, 270, 321–328
Ezra, 361f, 367ff

Felix, 566ff
Festus, 568

Gabriel, 383
Gad, 54, 132
Gaius, 588
Gamaliel, 516, 520, 565
Gedaliah, 318
Gehazi, 254, 257ff
Gideon, 139–144
Goliath, 188f

Habakkuk, 306
Hadad, 232
Hagar, 38f
Haggai, 357
Ham, 22
Haman, 346f, 350ff
Hanani, 238, 363
Hananiah, 314, 399
Hannah, 168f
Haran, 28
Hazael, 246
Hegai, 345
Herod, 390, 392, 453, 455, 499, 532
Hezekiah, 289–296, 307, 329
Hilkiah, 300, 303
Hiram (artist), 225
Hiram (of Tyre), 204, 224
Hosea, 270, 276
Hoshea, 287
Hur, 98

Ibzan, 145
Imlah, 248
Isaac, 37, 39–58, 79f
Isaiah, 270, 280ff, 292ff, 329
Ishbosheth, 202f
Ishmael, 38f
Israel, 56
Issachar, 54, 132

Jabin, 136ff
Jacob, 44, 46ff, 59ff, 69–80
Jael, 138
Jairus, 436
James (disciple), 408, 412, 418, 440, 461, 494
James (Jesus' brother), 408, 564, 584
James (son of Alpheus), 418, 440, 511
Japheth, 22
Jason, 545
Jehoahaz, 305
Jehoiachin, 313f
Jehoiada, 265ff
Jehoiakim, 305, 312, 329

Jehoram, 263
Jehoshaphat, 248, 250f, 263
Jehu, 246, 263ff
Jehudi, 312
Jephthah, 145f
Jeremiah, 298–319
Jeroboam, 232ff, 271
Jesse, 185f
Jesus, 386, 388–510, 536
Jethro, 84, 87, 98f
Jezebel, 238, 240, 244, 247, 263f
Joab, 202, 211, 214f
Joah, 294f
Joanna, 440
Joash (Gideon's father), 140
Joash (the king), 265ff
Job, 159–167
Jochebed, 82f
Joel, 289
John (apostle), 399, 408, 412, 418, 440, 461, 488, 494, 502, 505, 508, 511, 587, 589ff
John (the Baptist), 383, 394ff, 453, 483, 514
John Mark, 532, 534, 541
Jonah, 277ff
Jonathan, 181, 189, 191f, 194, 200, 202, 208
Joram, 263f
Joseph (of Arimathea), 503
Joseph (husband of Mary), 386, 391, 392ff
Joseph (Jesus' brother), 408
Joseph (son of Jacob), 54, 59–80, 93
Joshua, 98, 102, 112, 115, 121–134, 354, 583
Joshua (high priest), 354, 356f, 359, 368
Josiah, 298, 300, 305, 311
Jotham, 144f, 269
Judah, 53, 61, 70, 72f, 76, 132
Judas (of Damascus), 526
Judas (Iscariot), 418, 440, 485, 487, 495, 500
Judas (Jesus' brother), 408
Julius, 570

Laban, 42, 52ff
Lamech, 21
Lazarus, 447ff, 486
Leah, 53
Levi, 53, 108, 132
Lot, 28–31
Luke, 541, 554, 564, 573ff, 577, 579, 581
Lydia, 542

Maher-shalal-hashbaz, 284
Mahlon, 153
Malachi, 370
Malchus, 495
Manasseh (Joseph's son), 67, 78f
Manasseh (prince), 296f
Mary (of Bethany), 447, 486
Mary (Jesus' mother), 383, 386ff, 392ff, 401, 502
Mary Magdalene, 440, 502, 505
Martha, 447, 486
Matthew, 409, 418, 440, 511
Matthias, 511
Melchizedek, 32
Memucan, 344
Menahem, 275, 283
Mephibosheth, 208f, 212, 215
Meshach, 329f, 334ff
Messiah, 404
Methuselah, 21
Mica, 209
Micah, 151f
Micah (prophet), 270–285, 307
Micaiah, 248ff, 312
Miriam, 82f, 95, 115
Mishael, 329
Mordecai, 345–352
Moses, 83–121, 133, 461, 519, 569, 582

Naaman, 258ff
Nabal, 195ff
Naboth, 246f, 264
Nahor, 28, 41
Nahum, 304
Naomi, 153–158
Naphtali, 53, 132
Nathan, 209f, 216, 220f
Nathanael, 400, 508
Nebuchadnezzar, 313ff, 329–345
Neco, 304f
Nehemiah, 363–370
Nicodemus, 402, 458, 503
Nicolaus, 519
Nicanor, 519
Nimrod, 27
Noah, 21–27, 582

Obadiah, 241
Oded, 286
Og, 116
Onesimus, 576
Orpah, 153

Parmenas, 519
Paul, 535–581
Pekah, 283
Peter, 399, 418, 443, 461, 488, 494, 497, 505, 508, 511ff, 528ff, 539
Pharaoh, 62ff, 74, 76ff, 81, 84–94
Philemon, 576
Philip, 399ff, 418, 491, 511, 522, 564
Phoebe, 560, 562
Pilate, 498ff
Potiphar, 61ff
Priscilla, 549, 552, 562
Prochorus, 519
Publius, 573

Rabshakeh, 294f

Rachel, 52ff, 58
Rahab, 122, 126
Rebekah, 42f, 46
Rechab, 310f
Rehoboam, 233ff
Reuben, 53, 60f, 69, 132
Rezon, 232
Rhoda, 532
Ruth, 153–158

Samson, 146–150
Samuel, 169ff, 177, 185, 200, 308
Sanballat, 365f
Sapphira, 518ff
Sarah (Sarai), 28–43, 582
Satan, 153ff, 359, 398
Saul, 177, 186–202
Saul (see Paul), 520ff, 525
Sergius Paulus, 534
Seth, 20
Shadrach, 329f, 334ff
Shalmaneser, 287
Shaphan, 300
Shaphat, 246
Shear-jashub, 284
Sheba, 230f
Shebnah, 294f
Shecaniah, 362
Shem, 22
Shimei, 213
Shishak, 236
Sihon, 115
Silas, 540–546, 549
Simeon (son of Jacob), 53, 69, 71, 132
Simeon (in Temple), 389
Simon (Jesus' brother), 408
Simon (the leper), 486
Simon (the magician), 522
Simon (the patriot), 418, 440, 511

Simon (Peter), 399, 408, 412, 418, 440
Simon of Cyrene, 501
Sisera, 136ff
Solomon, 216–236
Stephen, 519ff
Susanna, 440

Tattenai, 360
Terah, 28
Teresh, 346, 350
Thaddeus, 418, 440, 511
Thomas, 418, 440, 507, 511
Tiglath-pileser, 283
Timon, 519
Timothy, 537, 541–546, 549ff
Titius Justus, 549
Titus, 554
Tobiah, 365ff
Trophimus, 554
Tychicus, 574, 581
Tyrannus, 552

Uriah, 209f
Urijah, 308
Uzziah, 268f, 280

Vashti, 344f

Zacchaeus, 452
Zacharias, 383
Zadok, 212, 220f
Zebulon, 54, 132
Zechariah, 275, 358f
Zedekiah, 249f, 314, 317
Zephaniah, 299
Zerah, 237
Zerubbabel, 354ff
Ziba, 208f, 212ff
Zophar, 163ff

Gaza
Joppa
Emmaus
Bethlehem Jerusalem
Bethany
DEAD SEA